Narratives of Peace in Religious Discourses

Religions and Peace Studies

Series Editor: Alessandro Saggioro, Sapienza University, Rome

Peace and religion intertwine and, since they are crucial to all human cultures, they require a more and comprehensive analysis to be understood beyond all the clichés that portray religions either as warmongering or peace-promoting factors.

Dealing with peace and religion means navigating the concepts of border and boundary, identity, alterity, and diversity, questioning the role of historical narratives in conflicts and their resolutions.

This book series explores the nexus between peace and religion, providing a reference tool for interdisciplinary, diachronic, and comparative research approaches. Furthermore, it aims to collect and develop scientific analyses dealing with all types of sources, such as sacred texts, literature and art, symbols and musealized objects, official documents about peace issued by governmental and nongovernmental institutions, historical records, and many others. Also, a variety of sub-topics are included, all revolving around the peace-religion axis and ranging from ecology to sustainability, from migration to gender issues, and from economy to literature and art.

The interdisciplinary dimension of the book series is grounded in a discursive approach to conflict and (re)conciliation through the languages of history, philosophy, anthropology, sociology, law, literature, and arts. The time span covered is broad and encompasses past civilizations and empires and their legacy, up to the dislocation and crisis of their memory in the present.

Finally, one of the most significant challenges of this book series is to make room for a consistent reflection on the history of the study of religions and peace and the methodological approaches scholars have adopted over the centuries to shape the discipline.

Narratives of Peace in Religious Discourses

Perspectives from Europe and the Mediterranean in the Early Modern Era

Edited by
Ludovico Battista, Maria Fallica and Beatrice Tramontano

SHEFFIELD UK   BRISTOL CT

Published by Equinox Publishing Ltd.

UK: Office 415, The Workstation, 15 Paternoster Row, Sheffield, South Yorkshire, S1 2BX
USA: ISD, 70 Enterprise Drive, Bristol, CT 06010

www.equinoxpub.com

First published 2024

© Ludovico Battista, Maria Fallica, Beatrice Tramontano and contributors 2024

All rights reserved. No part of this publication may be reproduced or transmitted in any form or by any means, electronic or mechanical, including photocopying, recording or any information storage or retrieval system, without prior permission in writing from the publishers.

British Library Cataloguing-in-Publication Data
A catalogue record for this book is available from the British Library.

ISBN-13 978 1 80050 387 8 (hardback)
         978 1 80050 388 5 (paperback)
         978 1 80050 389 2 (ePDF)
         978 1 80050 466 0 (ePub)

Library of Congress Cataloging-in-Publication Data

Names: Battista, Ludovico, editor. | Fallica, Maria, editor. | Tramontano, Beatrice, editor.
Title: Narratives of peace in religious discourses : perspectives from Europe and the Mediterranean in the early modern era / edited by Ludovico Battista, Maria Fallica, and Beatrice Tramontano.
Description: Sheffield, South Yorkshire ; Bristol, CT : Equinox Publishing Ltd, 2024. | Series: Religions and peace studies | Includes bibliographical references and index. | Summary: "This volume explores the role of religious discourse in the construction of the concept of peace from the Renaissance to the Enlightenment, analyzing the narratives which in Europe gave extrahuman value to peace, with a focus on the processes of idealization of peace and the relationship with the concept of toleration"-- Provided by publisher.
Identifiers: LCCN 2023030994 (print) | LCCN 2023030995 (ebook) | ISBN 9781800503878 (hardback) | ISBN 9781800503885 (paperback) | ISBN 9781800503892 (pdf) | ISBN 9781800504660 (epub)
Subjects: LCSH: Peace--Religious aspects--Christianity. | Religion and politics--Europe--History. | Religion and politics--Mediterranean Region--History. | Nicholas, of Cusa, Cardinal, 1401-1464.
Classification: LCC BT736.4 .N337 2024 (print) | LCC BT736.4 (ebook) | DDC 261.8/73--dc23/eng/20231018
LC record available at https://lccn.loc.gov/2023030994
LC ebook record available at https://lccn.loc.gov/2023030995

Typeset by S.J.I. Services, New Delhi, India

Contents

Foreword   vii
Alessandro Saggioro

The Crux of Peace: An Introduction   1
Maria Fallica

1. Theological and Philosophical Bases for Dialogue between Religions in Cusanus's *De pace fidei*   12
   Beatrice Tramontano

2. Pius II, Nicholas of Cusa, and the Crusade to Retake Constantinople and Jerusalem   35
   Nathan Ron

3. The Political Peace of Luis Vives and the Religious Peace of Pico della Mirandola: Philosophical Perspectives between Italy and Spain   59
   Manuel López Forjas and Veronica Tartabini

4. Peace, Prophecy, and the Apocalyptic Expectation: Girolamo Benivieni's Letter to Clement VII   90
   Maria Fallica

5. The Ambiguities of Erasmus's Religious Peace: A Reading of *De amabili ecclesiae concordia* (1533)   134
   Ludovico Battista

6. *Specula Pacis*: Cosmopolitan Pacifism in Desiderius Erasmus and Thomas More   167
   Antonello Mori and Antonio Senneca

7 Peace in the Material World: Objects as Meeting Points for
   Islamic and Christian Traditions in Late Sixteenth-Century Spain   187
   Francisco J. Moreno Díaz del Campo

8 Political and Religious Moderates in the French Wars of Religion
   and the Revolt of the Netherlands: A Comparative Perspective   214
   Alberto Hernández Pérez

9 Religious Co-existence in Malta, 1530–1798   241
   Frans Ciappara

10 Tolerance, Peace, and Otherness in Spanish Jesuit Thought of the
   Baroque Period   269
   David Martín López

11 "Tiered Tolerance": Protestants and the "Other" after 1685   296
   Nora Baker

12 Religious Freedom and History of Religions in Benjamin
   Constant   324
   Roberto Celada Ballanti

Index   341

Foreword

Alessandro Saggioro

The Covid-19 pandemic has drastically limited the possibility of face-to-face encounters and the use of archives and libraries, thus hindering academic research as much as any other sector of our life. Such a historical moment could have become a sort of "year zero" for humanity, bringing a new start, fresh visions, and perspectives, had it not been for the terrible conflict that broke out in Europe on February 24, 2022. Since its very beginning, the war Russia unleashed against Ukraine has revived the nuclear threat, which seemed to have vanished forever at the end of the last century—the "short century," according to Hobsbawm's famous definition. The times we are living through, however, seem rather to belong to the "long century" that began in year 1 of the new millennium, one day in September, with a violent attack on the World Trade Center, and continued with the consequent pre-emptive war on terror, labelled as the "Enduring Freedom" campaign and its dramatic consequences world-wide.

Humanity was not particularly peaceful before 2001—in fact, wars too often occurred throughout its history—but the magnitude of conflicts in the current millennium is such that they affect the whole world, causing the apparent failure of pacifism and compromising peaceful global coexistence. At the same time, many voices from religious communities and leaders around the world advocate a new approach to peace. A permanent call for responsibility stands against the roar of guns and weapons. During their meeting in Bahrain on November 3, 2022, Pope Francis, the Grand Imam of al-Azhar, Muhammad Ahmad al-Tayyeb, and their host, King Hamad bin Isa al Khalifa, sounded a unique call for peace, namely, that peace is best achieved both within and between religions, as a way to build a global accord involving the entire humanity. The event follows relevant public statements, such as the Document on Human Fraternity for World Peace and Living Together, signed by Pope Francis and the Grand Imam al-Tayyeb on February 4, 2019, and the Declaration of the Kingdom of Bahrain, launched in 2017 and promoted on a large scale by King Hamad bin Isa al Khalifa. Both documents evoke peace as the antidote to a long history of wars in which interactions between religions have long been conflictual and disruptive. The issue has once more proven to be paramount in the light of the tragic events that have recently taken place in the Middle East, where a supposedly insurmountable religious hatred has too long been used as an alibi for violence and destruction. Therefore, now more than ever, there is an urgent need to reflect on peace from a religious perspective, focusing on the understanding of interreligious dialogue as a privileged path to mutual recognition and peace.

The concept of the present book series rests on these historical premises. It has been conceived as a meeting place that will develop through several calls inviting international researchers to debate the theme of peace, specifically regarding religion. While the book series addresses the theme of religions and peace studies, it will also include disciplines and approaches enabling this field to adopt an open and critical stance, such as anthropology, sociology, political science, history of religions, philosophy, and law, without neglecting historical-literary and historical-artistic studies. A cluster of complex issues will also articulate this series: border and boundaries; identity, alterity, and diversity; narratives and politics; concepts and material symbols, and many others.

Over the past twenty years, it has become increasingly urgent to reflect not only on conflict but also on peaceful coexistence, reconciliation, and building long-lasting positive relationships. These themes often carry religious dimensions with foundational and legitimizing functions. Working on the concept of peace cannot be taken as either a simple task or a cliché. While the world of professional peacemakers—especially politicians and governments—dramatically fails its mandate, peace risks becoming a mere rhetorical expedient. In an age when one cannot ignore the watchwords of sustainability, dialogue, and mediation, religions have the chance to overcome the bias that surrounds them and play an increasingly important role in pacification processes.

Peace studies, or peace and conflict studies, are understood here as a broad category of disciplines and approaches whose task is to analyze the developments of the concept of peace and its concrete implementations throughout history. Religious dynamics are part and parcel of peace and conflict in all times and places; this alone further increases the list of potential research interests for the present book series. Religious traditions represent a starting point for reasoning about peace, especially when one considers them in broader terms, as breeding grounds for cultural products whose poetics, aesthetics, and politics range from a steady attachment to tradition to the discovery of new and original developments. Through religious traditions, human creativity shapes new social and cultural trends and values; it is the task of scholars to decipher the behavioural shifts associated with these new aspects and understand their unprecedented intellectual and scientific challenges.

This volume, the first in the series Religions and Peace Studies, focuses on the early modern era, a period in which historiographical debates became foundational for religious discourses on peace. This age witnessed not only the explosive conflict between competing confessions, all exclusively claiming institutional or charismatic authority, but also the emergence of minoritarian cosmopolitan and irenic thinking, illustrated by figures such as Nicholas of Cusa and Desiderius Erasmus.

The epistemological approach of the volume consists in disambiguating the performative aspect of peace discourses of the fifteenth to eighteenth centuries. It seeks to achieve this by acknowledging both the limits of peace discourses as being utopic, teleologic or even partially violent, and their lasting impact on the intellectual, cultural, political, and social life in Europe and beyond. Analysing ideological stances, cultural practices, peace treaties, and archive records, the chapters in this volume draft models of peace and tolerance, inspired by a vision of religion as capable of transcending its narrow boundaries and meeting the demands of the "others." Modernity pushed the religious discourse to simplify and rationalize its dogmatic structure. Stable peace thus became the ultimate goal of religion in Europe. According to the editors, the historian's task consists of a double movement, as they attempt to demonstrate in this volume. On the one hand, they show the partiality and fragility of the peace discourses in the early modern age, as structural prejudices and personal weaknesses marred their followers. On the other hand, the volume explores the performative value of these discourses in shaping self-representations, models of coexistence and, lastly, laws and doctrines.

The focus on early modern Europe is meant to be an inspirational starting point. What are pacifism, nonviolence, and mediation theory developments in other cultural contexts and continents? How did intellectuals and ruling elites reflect on the value of peaceful coexistence? To what extent has daily coexistence been affected by dominant ideas and ideologies and to what extent has it contributed to changing them from below? Which ideas and practices have we inherited from the great empires of the past through the global transformations that took place over time? These are just a few questions aiming to stimulate further reflection and writing, foster interdisciplinarity, and encourage other scholars to break new research grounds.

Author biography

Alessandro Saggioro is Full Professor in History of Religions at Sapienza University of Rome, Italy. He is the editor-in-chief of *Studi e Materiali di Storia delle Religioni*, a peer-review journal founded in 1924. The main research topics of his publications are the experimental teaching of the history of religions proposed in Italian schools, historiography and methodology of comparative religion, the relationship between performance and religion between Christianity and paganism and the relationship of Identity and Otherness. He is currently devoted to the study of the Late Antiquity and of Religious Pluralism; his latest works are focused in particular on the Codex of Theodosius II.

The Crux of Peace: An Introduction

Maria Fallica

The historian's perspective, even when confronted with the pressing relevance of war and the imperative aspiration for peace in the contemporary world, frequently comes back, almost irresistibly, to early modern Europe, as a decisive place for understanding the problems at stake in the building of the concept and practice of peace in conflictual and pluralistic societies.[1] In a sense, the conflicts and the attempts at resolution, the utopias and the philosophical models of the sixteenth to the eighteenth centuries still represent models, archetypal structures, or theoretical *cruces*.

This volume assesses the narratives of peace in our age against the backdrop of violent and contradictory contexts, measuring their ambivalence in regard to the absolute demands of theological and political entities and the price they paid for pragmatic and interested motives. The volume proposes a multidimensional view on the narratives that presided over the intrareligious exchange and the processes of peace-building, combining historical-critical analysis of documents, archive research, and comparative history with analysis of the world of objects. In doing so, it deals with selected historical figures, formulas of peace, images and objects, which represent turning points and milestones along the way. Some of them are unavoidable points of reference in the narratives of peace; thus, Nicholas of Cusa (analyzed in the essays by Beatrice Tramontano and Nathan Ron) and Desiderius Erasmus (Ludovico Battista, Antonello Mori and Antonio Senneca) are studied in their contribution to an emerging peace discourse, attempting to read them against the grain, revealing the fractures and aporias of their perspectives, as well as the political and ecclesiological stances underlying their choices.

1. See at least Lazzarini 2020.

The role of European Humanism is further explored through Luis Vives's political and religious ideal of peace, nourished by an Italian heritage (Manuel López Forjas and Veronica Tartabini) and the foundational utopia of Thomas More (Antonello Mori and Antonio Senneca). With the poet Girolamo Benivieni and his master Girolamo Savonarola (Maria Fallica), a very different rhetoric of peace emerges, in its apocalyptic violence and political allegiances. In the context of the intolerant policy of the Hispanic monarchy in the sixteenth century, the world of objects allows us to glimpse the everyday life of the Moriscos, the degree of assimilation to which they were subjected, and the resistance which it met (Francisco J. Moreno Díaz del Campo). In a similar fashion, early modern Malta is an important observation point for testing and re-assessing the cohabitation of Christians, Muslims, and Jews on a border (Frans Ciappara).

The study of the idea and practice of tolerance has historically been linked with the intolerant explosion of the wars of religion and the counter-attempts to build confessional states capable of tolerance or at least coexistence, as we see comparatively in the case of France and the Netherlands (Alberto Hernández Pérez). Likewise, the volume explores two different contexts which, for different reasons, have been frequently evoked by historians as germinal *loci* of a discourse of peaceful coexistence and toleration, questioning their actual impact and value. On the one hand, the relevance of the reflection of religious minorities on tolerance and non-violence is here studied in the writings of Huguenot refugees of the late seventeenth to eighteenth centuries and in connection with Pierre Bayle's legacy (Nora Baker). On the other hand, the theorization of the appropriate encounter with the religious "other" and the political theory of just war and peace is studied in the thought of Jesuit writers (David Martín López).

Lastly, the volume closes with an essay by Roberto Celada Ballanti, who introduces the work on ancient polytheism by Benjamin Constant, enlisting it in the religious-liberal tradition that we have seen throughout the volume, from Cusanus to Kant and Constant, as a trajectory oriented toward religious freedom and peaceful recognition of the other.[2]

---

2. On this see also the very important monograph by Celada Ballanti (2009).

As it is already possible to discern thanks to this brief summary, peace is here considered as a relational and liminal value, which was the subject of utopian visions and eschatological appeals, and which had to be negotiated with other guiding principles and moral demands and could be accosted to concepts such as acceptance, tolerance ("tiered" tolerance, in the words of Nora Baker) or, on the other side of the scale, "fighting concordism,"[3] delegitimization of doctrinal divisions,[4] obedience to the state, or forced acquiescence and submission. In this period, the image of the enemy was expanded and amplified in proportion to the widening of global contacts and accordingly to a growing disciplinary attitude.[5]

The intuition of the difficult combination of different and compelling values was in fact often expressed with figures of the impossible, of which the most powerful and best-known is perhaps the kiss between Peace and Justice, which, since its appearance in the Hebrew Bible (Ps. 85:10) and its large employ in Christian theology, liturgy and art, suggested a fullness of grace. In the early modern age, this embrace, was, on the one hand, apocalyptically prophesized as the coming of the kingdom, and therefore never fully disposable and materialized in a concrete *civitas terrena*; on the other, the incipient coming of the King of Peace or the Angelic Pope or the Holy Emperor or the triumph of Florence were expected and repeatedly announced as the actual, imminent coming of redemption and the meeting of opposites. Peace in the early modern age is, in a word, a dialectic concept.

Europe the self-tormentor: a plea for peace from a self-destructive body

On January 22, 1543, the Spanish doctor Andrés de Laguna gave a solemn oration in the presence of the dignitaries of the city of Cologne,

---

3. This term is used by Martínez Gómez to speak of Pico della Mirandola's aspiration of peace which fights and subsumes wrong interpretations in the biblical, Chaldean, and Persian sacred books (see Lopéz Forjas and Tartabini, this volume: p. 73); here I employ it in a more general way, alluding to the dialectic nature of many types of concordisms.
4. See Johannes Cochlaeus, *Consyderatio de futuro Concordiae*, analyzed in Battista's essay, this volume: pp. 156–57.
5. Andretta 2009: 32.

in a university class arranged for mourning, at sundown. An old, tearful, amputee beggar, almost at the end of her life, mourns her wretched state in dialogue with the doctor who has revived her. The woman is Europe, tormenting herself and mourning her fall from grace: *Europa heautentimorumene: es decir, que míseramente a sí misma se atormenta y lamenta su propia desgracia*. The *topos* of the personification of grieving Europe is here declined with particular effectiveness as the denunciation of inner laceration and dissension: if the Athenian Menedemus—the *Heauton timoroumenos* of Terentius's comedy—punished himself for having wronged his son, Europe laments a more hurtful damage, brought to her by her children, who, thirsting for blood, assault her and gnaw at her liver, relentlessly and viciously.[6] As Lopéz Forjas and Tartabini remind us in this volume, Laguna's work attests to the rich heritage of Erasmus's teaching in Spain, in the form of the condemnation of the scandal of Christian princes at war with one another and in the appeal for a renewed Christian republic. Peace is the remedy prescribed by the physician, Laguna, to be administered by princes and bishops, who would build a *res publica christiana*, capable of standing against the Ottoman threat. Laguna's Europe stands on the edge of a precipice: "completely void and bursting apart, fixing her eyes to the ground, thinking of nothing but the rope and the abyss."[7] The overturning of the image of *Europa triumphans* in the *Europa deplorans*[8] is here accompanied by a growing consciousness of the self-destructive nature of European societies, a mother devoured by her children. The remedy is incarnated in paternal and healing figures, such as Laguna, *typus* of the Emperor and the civil and religious authorities who are called to heal the ill and self-damaging body.

If the remedy had turned out to be partial and defective, the image of Christian Europe as a self-harming *corpus*, incapable of peace, would have evoked in our eyes, as readers from the twenty-first century, the self-denunciation which has been made in the last centuries of the destructive power of the "West" and the tendency to critically assess its heritage, to deconstruct its result and come out from itself. If, in the words of

6. Laguna 2001: 144.
7. Laguna 2001: 132, translated in Kaiser 2020: 40.
8. Kaiser 2020: 50–51.

Marcel Gauchet, Christianity is "a religion for departing from religion,"[9] the self-contestation of Europe coming from Erasmus and his followers all throughout Europe can be seen as a first occurrence of this dynamic, in which a religious discourse contests its own presuppositions with the aim of a greater adherence to its ideal aspirations: thus, "the religious identity of belonging is criticized, retracted, to revive beyond it that promise that expands the same identity beyond itself."[10] Peace is thus conceived outside the border: outside religion?

The religious liberal tradition and peace: trajectories and problems

Narratives of Peace in Religious Discourses opens with Tramontano's analysis of Nicholas Cusanus's momentous vision of Christianity as a religion capable of self-emptying and rationalization that, in his ideal, could mean a radical openness to the other, thanks to its acknowledgment of the contingency of every conjecture. The line of thought opened by Cusanus and Erasmus, imbued with the legacy of the Christian Platonism of Origen, goes in the direction of the universalization of a transcendental principle that surpasses and relativizes every historical manifestation of religion and identifies and categorizes religion as an autonomous and rational category. In the words of Italian historian Marco Maria Olivetti, the modern age is one in which *religio* and *fides christiana* are distinguished and differentiated and the categorization of religion takes place along with the constitution of related specialized knowledge.[11] The concept of peace in western Christianity underwent a similar process, in the progressive juridicization of Gospel values that had started, at least since Augustine, to problematically distinguish between *iura coeli* and *iura fori*[12] and that meant an operation of separation which made peace a secularized object, which was carved out from its religious horizon which, however, continued to nourish it and inform its ideal utopian nature.

9. Gauchet 1997: 101.
10. Lettieri 2011: 28 (my translation).
11. Olivetti 1995; see also Tramontano, this volume: p. 32.
12. Lettieri 2011: 43.

One of the most defining moments of this parable of separation was the Peace of Augsburg (1555), which, as the historian and philosopher Reinhart Koselleck has argued, aimed to determine the condition for a secure and stable peace, capable of holding even if, as it was then more and more obvious, the religious parties would never be reconciled:

> Henceforth peace and religious unity were no longer identical—peace meant that the fronts of religious civil war were to be shut down, frozen in situ. Only with difficulty can we today assess how monstrous this imposition seemed at that time. This compromise born of necessity concealed within itself however a new principle, that of 'Politics', which in the following century was to set itself in motion. [...] peace became possible only when religious potential was used up or exhausted, that is at the point at which it was possible to politically restrict or neutralise it. And this disclosed a new and unorthodox future.[13]

The equivalence of peace with reason, already prepared in the "liberal" tradition from Cusanus to Erasmus, reaches one of its clearest definitions in Kant's thought. Kant's ideal of universal hospitality, jurisdictionally founded, was based on the moral obligation to move towards perpetual peace. The pacification of society is closely linked to law, creating a (republican) society that the citizens can accept as legitimate: as Jürgen Habermas writes, for Kant, "the abolition of war is a command of reason. Practical reason first brings the moral veto to bear against systematic killing."[14] The many critiques which the Kantian proposal encountered are usefully reconstructed in the same essay by Habermas:

> Although he recognized the divisive force of religious differences, he immediately qualified this with the remark that, although there may exist different sacred texts and historical creeds, "there can be only one single religion holding for all human beings and in all times." Kant was so deeply influenced by an abstract notion of enlightenment that he was blind to the explosive force of nationalism. The highly influential political consciousness of ethnic membership in communities of shared language and descent was just awakening in Kant's time. During the nineteenth century, it would assume the form

---

13. Koselleck 2004: 14.
14. Habermas 2006: 121.

of national consciousness and not only cause calamities in Europe but also contribute to the imperialist expansion of the industrialized states. Kant shared with his contemporaries the "humanist" conviction of the superiority of European civilization and the white race. He failed to grasp the import of the selectivity of a particularistic international law that was tailored to a handful of privileged states and Christian nations. Only these nations recognized each other as possessing equal rights and they divided up the rest of the world among themselves into spheres of influence for colonial and missionary purposes. [Lastly,] Kant was not yet aware of the importance of the fact that European international law remained embedded in a common Christian culture.[15]

Habermas's recollection is important as it summarizes that philosophical and historiographical effort of deconstructing the narrative of peace as the teleologically driven conquest of European civilization, as Hernández Pérez puts it in this volume. Therefore, the ambiguous and colonialist aspect of our history of the narratives of peace is broadly dealt with in the volume, avoiding commonplace celebrations of alleged "forerunners" of contemporary values or sticking to overexposed historiographical assumptions. Thus, for instance, Ron's essay reminds us how the irenic attitude of Cusanus did not exclude a crusading spirit, which led him to an open and harsh attack on Muhammad; Battista's essay shows how in Johannes Cochlaeus's Catholic reception of Erasmus, concordism could be a polemical device for fighting divisions in the Church and delegitimizing the other and their "heretical" options, following Erasmus's anti-Lutheran attitude. The history of the narratives of peace and tolerance is a history of ambivalent projects, of which the volume identifies lines of fractures, approximations, and incoherencies.

Peace as interrupted *polemos*: a place for the victims

Frans Ciappara, thanks to his survey of the Archive of the Roman Inquisition in Malta, offers us a glance at the tragic life of Anna, a Bosnian slave of Giovanni Vassallo in Malta, forcibly baptized, who was sent to the Inquisitor for her doubts on the faith imposed upon her

---

15. Habermas 2006: 145–46.

and ended up taking her own life in 1700.[16] As historians, we find ourselves again and again, as Carlo Ginzburg pointed out in connection with his studies on witchcraft trials,[17] in the position of the Inquisitors: even as we try to give voice to the victims, we cannot but share the point of view of the Inquisitors, as they were the only ones who told Anna's story and controlled her memory. Our knowledge is fragmented and profoundly influenced by the cultural codex of the documents that we read, as well as our cultural prejudices; her life and death, as well as the innumerable accounts of slaves' lives in Europe and the Mediterranean, testify as prosecution witnesses in any history of the concept of peace and toleration.

Almost a century later, the scathing image which famously opens Kant's *Zum ewigen Frieden* (1795) well represents the ambivalent nature of the aspiration for peace in western societies: the signboard of a Dutch innkeeper that was illustrated with a picture of a graveyard, with the inscription "perpetual peace."[18] The acknowledgment of the utopian and somehow deadly nature of many invocations for peace is necessary and foundational for the building of an alternative option. Therefore, the galley ship, a recurrent topic in our volume, is in this sense a revealing *locus* of the ambiguities of this era: it was evidence of a reciprocal and harsh subjection on the coasts of the Mediterranean Sea and a place of a tentative, yet imperfect recognition of the religious other.

A material peace: resistance, coexistence, peace

This volume often takes an alternative route when looking at the narratives and discourses on peace and toleration, following the recent progress of the so-called "material turn" in history and making it dialogue with the history of ideas and the analysis of the rhetorical formulas of peace; therefore, the volume attempts to make objects tell their stories and reveal different perspectives.

Moriscos dresses are one of the protagonists of Moreno's study of late sixteenth-century Spain; they represent an object of specific regulations,

16. AIM, Proc. 95A, ff. 160r–89v; see this volume: p. 255.
17. Ginzburg 2012.
18. Kant 1991: 93.

as they were feared by the Crown as the last vestiges of Islamic identity, and testify to shifts in identities, resistance to assimilation and shared experience. Peace could very well mean the forced sharing of material habits.

The long description made by the Jesuit Luis de Guzmán of the Japanese visitors to Madrid is striking in its attention to the dresses, a sign of an alterity that was so distant from the cultural codex of the observer as to deserve their full attention and a complete report. This attention to alterity is put in contrast by Martín López with a well-known 1586 Augsburg engraving that represents four Japanese ambassadors, whose dresses and appearance are almost fully westernized[19]: only their cropped hair maintains a vestige of their diversity, a sign of unconscious resistance to assimilation. Thus, the material turn drives us back to the question already implicit in the previous pages: is it possible to describe and found a peace that does not disfigure the other and preserve their irrefutable alterity?

Peace as a heretical option

Celada Ballanti reminds us in his essay of the definition made by the sociologist of religions Peter L. Berger, who identified the hermeneutical act as the free, "heretical" option connotating the modern age. Heresy is here not the mark of condemnation imparted by an entity in a position of power to a minority or oppressed individuals, but a synonym of choice, a deviation from tradition and the corruption of time. We can conclude that peace in the modern age is a heretical force: often defended by minorities, in a relation of deconstruction and indissoluble bond with its religious tradition, incoherent with its moral demands. A feeble messianic force,[20] whose kingdom has yet to come.

---

19. See infra, p. 291.
20. The reference is naturally to Benjamin's "weak messianic force" (Benjamin 2003).

Author biography

Maria Fallica (PhD, Sapienza University of Rome) is a post-doctoral researcher at Sapienza University of Rome. Her research interests lie in the reception of the Fathers of the Church in the modern age, the history of the Reformations, the Italian Reformation of the sixteenth century, and the history of methodism. Her most recent publications are *The Protestant Origen: Polemical Use and Theological Appropriation of Origen in 16th Century Patristic Anthologies* (Münster: Aschendorff, 2022) and *Il metodismo via media della Riforma. Progresso e tradizione nella* Christian Library *di Wesley* (Rome: Carocci, 2022).

References

Andretta, S. (2009), "Note sulla natura dell'immagine del nemico in età moderna tra identità e alterità," in F. Cantù, G. Di Febo, and R. Moro (eds.), *L'immagine del nemico. Storia, ideologia e rappresentazione tra età moderna e età contemporanea*, 31–40. Rome: Viella.

Benjamin, W. (2003), "On the Concept of History," in idem, *Selected Writings, Vol. 4, 1938–1940*, edited and translated by H. Eiland and M. W. Jennings, 389–400. Cambridge, MA: Harvard University Press (German original edition: *Gesammelte Schriften*, Frankfurt: Suhrkamp Verlag, 1972).

Celada Ballanti, R. (2009), *Pensiero religioso liberale: lineamenti, figure, prospettive*. Brescia: Morcelliana.

Gauchet, M. (1997), *The Disenchantment of the World: A Political History of Religion*, translated by O. Burge. Princeton: Princeton University Press (French original edition *Le désenchantement du monde*, Paris: Editions Gallimard, 1985).

Ginzburg, C. (2012), *Threads and Traces: True False Fictive*. Berkeley and Los Angeles: University of California Press.

Habermas, J. (2006), *The Divided West*, edited and translated by C. Cronin. Cambridge: Polity Press (German original edition: *Der gespaltene Westen*, Frankfurt: Suhrkamp Verlag, 2004).

Kaiser, R. (2020), "Tota caduca et dehiscens—Europe's Critical Condition in Andrés Laguna's *Europa* (1543)," in N. Detering et al. (eds.), *Contesting Europe: Comparative Perspectives on Early Modern Discourses on Europe, 1400–1800*, 39–53. Leiden: Brill.

Kant, I. (1991), *Perpetual Peace: A Philosophical Sketch* (*Zum ewigen Frieden. Ein philosophischer Entwurf*), in idem, *Political Writings*, translated by

H. B. Nisbet, edited by Hans S. Reiss, 2nd ed., 93–130. New York: Cambridge University Press.

Koselleck, R. (2004), *Futures Past: On the Semantics of Historical Time*, translated by K. Tribe. New York: Columbia University Press (German original edition: *Vergangene Zukunft. Zur Semantik geschichtlicher Zeiten*, Frankfurt: Suhrkamp Verlag, 1979).

Laguna, A. (2001), *Europa heautentimorumene: es decir, que míseramente a sí misma se atormenta y lamenta su propia desgracia*, edited by M. Á. Gonzalez Manjarrez. Valladolid: Junta de Castilla y Leon.

Lazzarini, I., ed. (2020), *A Cultural History of Peace in the Renaissance*. London: Bloomsbury.

Lettieri, G. (2011), "Un dispositivo cristiano nell'idea di democrazia? Materiali per una metodologia della storia del cristianesimo," in A. Zambarbieri and G. Otranto (eds.), *Cristianesimo e democrazia*, 19–134. Bari: Edipuglia.

Chapter 1

Theological and Philosophical Bases for Dialogue between Religions in Cusanus's *De pace fidei*

Beatrice Tramontano

Introduction

The observation of the fecundity of questions that Cusanus faces in *De pace fidei* (1453) shows its epochal aspect, first of all because it was written in an extremely complex historical period, on the threshold of Modernity, at a time of great theological disputes within Christianity, upset by the problematic relations with the Church of the East. The historical context is in no doubt fundamental to understanding Cusanus's work, because 1453 in particular is a key year for its dramatic nature: the taking of Constantinople by the Turks, comparable in its impact on Christianity to that which had been the sack of Rome, is the extreme point of an enormous political and identity crisis. When in fact, on May 29, Sultan Mohammed II conquers Constantinople, the news of the fall of the city spreads rapidly in the West and arouses a real trauma in the political and intellectual elite, who see this as the prelude to an imminent clash of civilizations that would lead to the destruction of Christianity.[1] The loss of Byzantium means in fact many different things to humanists, because it represents the end of a great and glorious empire, a major blow to Christendom, and the loss of a rich heritage of art, architecture, and

---

1. Peroli 2017: 103.

scholarship. After the events of 1453, most humanists come to call the Turks "barbarians," and many see them as a threat to high culture, considering them as the latest and most dangerous of the barbarian hordes to menace European security since late antiquity.[2]

While in order to respond to this crisis Pope Nicholas V invokes the crusade, hoping for the salvation of the "Second Rome," Cusanus tries to follow the path of theological-philosophical research, placing the question of the relationship between the various religious denominations at the center of his ecclesiastical-political commitment and his speculative activity. In this moment Cusanus is bishop of Bressanone, and the relationship between different religious faiths is at the center of his ecclesiatical-political interests and speculative activity, as it was since the beginning of his ecclesiastical career; in fact Cusanus had attended numerous important events for Christianity, such as the unionist Council of Basel-Ferrara-Firenze, aimed at the reunification of the Church of the East and of the West, and he had tried to mediate the difficult relations with the Islamic world, going to Constantinople in 1437 as papal representative, and returning to Italy with a delegation composed of the Emperor of the East, the Patriarch, and some intellectuals of Greek and Byzantine culture. Beyond these fundamental and significative historical facts, what is interesting and innovative in Cusanus's work is the theological-philosophical elaboration that goes along with his "political" commitment, structuring and grounding the unique modalities through which it is possible to think about dialogue between religions and tolerance at a historical and political level.

Structure of the work

De pace fidei presents the reader with a sort of Universal Religious Council that takes place in Heaven in the presence of God. The celestial setting refers us to a vision that, as Cusanus informs us in the opening, would have kidnapped a very pious man, shaken by the news coming from Constantinople and describing atrocities and violences committed

---

2. Bisaha 1999: 185–93.

in the name of faith, showing him the only way to be able to realize a "perpetual peace" (*perpetua pax*) among peoples:³

> There was a certain man who, having formerly seen the sites in the regions of Constantinople, was inflamed with zeal for God as a result of those deeds that were reported to have been perpetrated at Constantinople most recently and most cruelly by the King of the Turks. Consequently, with many groanings he beseeched the Creator of all, because of His kindness, to restrain the persecution that was raging more fiercely than usual on account of the difference of rite between the [two] religions.⁴

In this assembly of saints the wise men of all cultures and religions are called to participate in order to find, through the questioning of the Word, Peter and Paul, the basis for the pacification of all the different existing religious confessions.

The assembly of saints in which the dialogue takes place reflects on a transcendent level the cusanian idea of the Church as *concordantia*, as a unitary organism in reciprocal vital interaction between the members and leaders at all levels, and towards which authority is functionally oriented as service. Cusanus emphasizes in fact the Church as *communio fidelium* that lives of the Holy Spirit, promoter of harmony not only on a personal level, but also on the level of structures, so that the principle of the fundamental collegiality of the Church, which finds its most genuine expression in the council as the true representative of the universal Church and supreme subject of power and authority, is not opposed, but is harmoniously integrated with the principle of primacy seen in its more pastoral than juridical dimension.⁵

The attempt to achieve peace between religions is conceived and realized through the idea of faith, in a specific way already evident from

3. Maurizi 2011: 181.
4. All English translations in this contribution are taken from Hopkins 2001: "Fuit ex hiis, quae apud Constantinopolim proxime saevissime acta per Turkorum regem divulgabantur, quidam vir zelo Dei accensus, qui loca illarum regionum aliquando viderat, ut pluribus gemitibus oraret omnium creatorem quod persecutionem, quae ob diversum ritum religionum plus solito saevit, sua pietate moderaretur" (*De pace fidei*, 1, 1).
5. Gaia 1971: 64–65.

the title: *fidei* is a subjective genitive, showing at the first aspect how the search for peace is inscribed and possible by its nature only within the theological discourse, because *fides* is considered the only essential possibility of trust in peace, as the realization of every confessional elaboration. Cusanus's discourse is, in fact, developed through the different confessions, at a theological level, with the aim to show how the concept of peace is intrinsically connected with the idea of religion, because peace cannot be found through an escape from religion, but rather with an implementation of religion(s) itself, finding in each one the own faith that lives in each historical religion and of which each is an expression.

The attempt is to construct a dialogue between faiths that doesn't want to reach a kind of uniformity between them, but on the contrary that wants to find the same idea of *truth* that can be found in every confession, enhancing and not eliminating the differences. The cusanian theoretical proposal differs in fact from the apologetic position which aims at the conversion of all religious denominations to a specific religion, because it is not a matter of embracing another faith, different from the one professed so far, but of finding the one and the same faith that is presupposed in all of them: "You will [all] find to be everywhere presupposed not a faith that is other but a faith that is one and the same."[6]

The same mental experiment of the kidnapping of the author wants to underline how the analysis of peace is elaborated at a deep philosophical and theological level, even if *De pace fidei* is born with the aim of responding to a concrete historical problem; this philosophical-theological elaboration wants to be valid in fact as a universal way to consider existence and relations between different religions. Cusanus assumes peace as a real methodological principle, at a historical level, but he derives it from the ontological thesis of the fundamental *concordantia* between beings: his religious ecumenism has very strong theological and philosophical bases.

---

6. "Non aliam fidem, sed eandem unicam undique presupponi reperietis" (*De pace fidei*, 4, 10, 11–12); Monaco 2014: 418.

Contractio and *coniectura*

The theological and philosophical bases that structure *De pace fidei* come from Cusanus's enormous work *De docta ignorantia* (1440), connected with his treatise *De coniecturis* (1442). In this sense we can refer to Cassirer's interpretation that connects *De docta ignorantia* to *De pace fidei*, juxtaposing the theory of cosmos of the former to the philosophical-religious one of the latter. Even if, considered from the point of view of content, the two texts move in completely different spheres, yet they are only different reflections of the same and unique underlying systematic conception: in the same way in which previously deductions were drawn from the principle of *docta ignorantia* for the science of the world, from the same principle deductions are now drawn for the science of God.[7]

Cusanus conceives an idea of Universe that unhinges the scholastic metaphysical conception of substance. There is no entity that can be conceived as isolated, or connected to others only "externally": "Consider more closely and you will see that each actually existing thing is tranquil because of the fact that in it all things are it and that in God it is God. You see that there is a marvelous oneness of things, an admirable equality, and a most wonderful union, so that all things are in all things. You also understand that for this reason there arises a difference and a union of things."[8] The idea of relation is in this way fundamental for his ontology, structuring the *communio* that brings together the totality of beings: in this reciprocal relation it is contained in the Unity of God, characterized itself by the relational dynamic of Trinity.

Universe is therefore "one. Its oneness is contracted by plurality, so that it is oneness in plurality. And because Absolute Oneness is first and the oneness of the universe is derived from it, the oneness of the universe will be a second oneness, consisting of a plurality."[9] In this sense, the

---

7. Cassirer 2012: 32–33.
8. "Considera attentius et videbis, quomodo quaelibet res actu existens ex eo quiescit, quia omnia in ipso sunt ipsum et ipsum in Deo Deus. Mirabilem rerum unitatem, admirandam aequalitatem et mirabilissimam vides connexionem, ut omnia sint in omnibus. Rerum etiam diversitatem et connexionem in hoc exoriri intelligis" (*De docta ignorantia*, II, V, 120).
9. "[…] comperimus unum, cuius unitas contracta est per pluralitatem, ut sit unitas in pluralitate. Et quia unitas absoluta est prima et unitas universi ab ista, erit unitas

medieval construction of cosmos is inverted, because there is no more hierarchy and Universe has no longer a omogenous, stable center; multiplicity belongs to the Absolute, participating in it as a finite *contractio* of the infinite essence of God, and because of this belonging every essence in the cosmos shares with the Absolute its identity, but also its difference. If God is in fact the absolute Unity, the Universe is a contracted Unity, full of finite realities, being an inadequate and phenomenal representation of the Unity of God. Inside the contingent world man participates of the spiritual nature of God at the maximum degree, through the mediation of Christ that represents the principle, means and fulfillment of creation.

What is interesting in Cusanus's theory is that this ontological thesis is applied to religion: as God expresses Himself in multiple things, the Truth expresses Itself in the different empirical religions. Man has in fact an incomplete knowledge of the nature of God, and so he adores Him in an incomplete way, with different religions that approach the Divinity but that can't understand It completely. This is because Finite and Infinite have an asymmetric relation, which becomes evident in the nature of beings, in which identity and difference live together, getting closer to the absolute idea of identity and difference, but never reaching it. In the universe of creatures differences are in fact expressions of the totality, and consequently the totality of the degrees is contained in the absolute: the possibility of concordance between religions therefore derives from the possibility of including the different degrees and manifestations of the finite beings in the mystery of God, expressed paradoxically in the idea of *complicatio-explicatio* and *coincidentia oppositorum*.

There is here a paradox that lies at the heart of the Infinite and of its (non)relationship with the Finite: singularity is called to itself by the invocation of an Other that is, at the same time, absolute Identity and absolute Difference.[10] This paradox at an ontological level reflects the way in which human reason approaches the Absolute; as in the Universe the finite creature can approach the Infinity without reaching it, so at

---

universi secunda unitas, quae in quadam pluralitate consistit" (*De docta ignorantia*, II, VI, 123).
10. Maurizi 2011: 196.

a gnoseological level the rational knowledge of God is achieved only through the *coniectura*.

The term *coniectura* refers to the Origenian concept; Origen of Alexandria is surely an author that influences Cusanus, mostly through the mediation of Origenian authors such as Pseudo-Dionysius and Gregory of Nyssa, and of the mystic tradition of Eriugena and Eckhart. In this sense Cusanus belongs to the authors of the fifteenth and sixteenth century influenced by Origenism, particularly in the Florentine neo-Platonic context. *De docta ignorantia* re-proposes the Origenian interpretation of worship in Spirit and Truth as transcendence of all types, untiring mystical progress towards the mystery of God: true Christianity is an entirely spiritual Christianity, which, while confessing the Truth and the necessity of the mediation of the Church and its dogmas, transcends them towards the intuition of the paradox of God, beyond any idolatrously fixed, finite understanding.[11]

Coniectura is a positive affirmation, participating in the Truth, having with it an essential relationship and representing a positive expression of it:

> Therefore, a surmise is a positive assertion that partakes—with a degree of otherness—of truth as it is [in itself]. However, just as by means of the oneness-of-reason the senses experience their own otherness and make surmises by freeing from precise oneness assertions about perceptible objects, so reason, by means of its root-oneness, viz., by means of the light of intelligence, discovers its own otherness and its falling away from preciseness into surmise. Similarly, intelligence, insofar as it is a power near [to God], rejoices that by the aid of Divine Oneness it makes surmises in its own very clear way.[12]

---

11. Lettieri 2000: 309–310.
12. "Coniectura igitur est positiva assertio, in alteritate veritatem, uti est, participans. Quemadmodum vero sensus in unitate rationis suam alteritatem experitur et assertiones sensibiles ab unitate praecisionis absolvendo coniecturas facit, ita ratio in radicali unitate sua, in ipso scilicet intelligentiae lumine, suam alteritatem et casum a praecisione in coniecturam invenit, sic et intelligentia ipsa, ut propinqua potentia, in unitate divina se suo quidem clarissimo modo gaudet coniecturari" (*De coniecturis*, I, 11, 57).

This participation takes place *in alteritate*, because the Truth is grasped not in its totality but through the contingency, starting from a point of view and a perspective always singular, finite, particular. The unique and infinite *veritas* is expressed in the plurality of conjectures through the singularity, the individuality of the knowing subjects and the limited and finite modes of their cognitive faculties, but this does not mean that it multiplies or divides into parts, maintaining on the contrary its absolute indivisibility, unity, and simplicity.

In the Cusanian metaphysical and gnoseological vision individuality and singularity do not have a negative meaning, but a positive one, constituting the way in which the One and the Truth can be participated in and revealed. Finiteness and particularity acquire a productive sense because they are not an obstacle, but represent our openness to the Truth; there is, in fact, a circularity between the unique, infinite, and transcendent Truth, and conjectures, always plural, finite, and singular:[13]

> Let one who keeps in mind these statements make a surmise about participation in the following way. Since whatever can be partaken of is partaken of only with a degree of otherness, it will have to be partaken of in fourfoldness; for oneness both goes forth from itself into otherness and exists in a fourfold way. Whatever is partaken of by something else cannot be received either maximally or minimally or equally. Moreover, since oneness's simplicity is not partaken of insofar as it is simple but is partaken of otherwise, it is partaken of with a degree of compositeness, so to speak, or with a falling away from that simplicity—i.e., with a degree of difference from simplicity. Therefore, simplicity, since it is simplicity, is not partaken of in parts but in the way in which what-is-simple can be partaken of according to itself as a whole. However, since oneness's simplicity is unimpartible maximally, minimally, and equally (for it is partaken of, as it is, [only] by means of a coincidence, as is shown in Learned Ignorance), it will have to be partaken of with a certain fourfoldness that falls short of maximality, minimality, and equality. Therefore, oneness is partaken of not insofar as it is an enfolding simplicity or insofar as it is unfolded in otherness but insofar as its changeable and unfolding power-to-be-partaken-of is understood (by means of

---

13. Monaco 2013: 86–87.

a certain coincidence) as a mode-of-power of the enfolding, unpartakeable oneness.[14]

In this way knowledge is reached by all different experiences as different modalities of opening or assimilation of the "true," yet complementary since they are all oriented to the one and only eternal Truth; each "modal apprehension" of the truth can amend itself from its own partiality and unilaterality only in the mutual comparison, or mutual verification, with each other perspective. It is therefore not by chance that Cusanus affirms that "what must be said cannot be expressed suitably; hence, an expansive number of words is quite useful."[15] This point is fundamental in order to understand *De pace fidei*, and its possibility of thinking about a rational agreement between different religions: if knowledge of Truth occurs from an individual, finite, conjectural perspective, which can only be multiple, then the multiple points of view that approach the Truth from a finite point of view can only be all legitimate. It is necessary to underline this ontological and gnoseological structure in order to see in a clear way how Cusanus's discourse about peace is structured and strengthened by a rational philosophical elaboration.

The connection between this ontological structure and the possibility of peace between religion is expressed in the messenger's words, just at the beginning, which represents the central core of Cusanus's idea: "If

---

14. "Haec tenens participationis coniecturam hac via efficiat. Omne enim participabile, cum non nisi in alteritate participetur, in quaternitate participari necesse erit. Pergit enim unitas a se in alteritatem et quaternario subsistit. Omne, quod in alio participatur, nec maxime nec minime nec aequaliter poterit recipi. Ipsa etiam unitatis simplicitas, cum non, uti est simplex, sed aliter participetur, in quadam, ut ita dixerim, compositione aut casu ab ea ipsa simplicitate, hoc est in simplicitatis alteritate, participatur. Non igitur participatur simplicitas secundum partem, cum sit simplicitas, sed modo, quo participabile est simplex secundum se totum. Quoniam autem incommunicabilis est maxime, minime atque aequaliter ipsa unitatis simplicitas—ita enim, uti est, participaretur per coincidentiam, ut in Docta ignorantia aperitur –, hinc in quadam quaternitate a maximitate, minimitate atque aequalitate cadente participari necesse est. Non igitur participatur unitas, ut est complicans simplicitas nec ut est alterata explicatio, sed ut alterabilis eius participabilitas explicatoria quasi modus quidam virtutis ipsius complicativae imparticipabilis unitatis per quandam coincidentiam intelligitur" (*De coniecturis*, 1, 11, 58).
15. Cuozzo 2012: 131: "Nam quod dicendum est, convenienter exprimi nequit. Hinc multiplicatio sermonum perutilis est" (*De mente*, IV, 74).

You will deign to do the foregoing, the sword will cease, as will also the malice of hatred and all evils; and all [men] will know that there is only one religion in a variety of rites."[16] At a speculative level this statement is fundamental: here Cusanus affirms that for the different confessions it is not a question of adapting to a single religion, to a single given Truth because, as we have seen, not one of them can reach the absolute knowledge of the Infinite. As a consequence, each religious faith does not deny, indeed solicits, the plurality of the various historical expressions, indivisible from the Truth but at the same time never identifiable with it, because the Truth of Revelation exceeds the cognitive capacity of man.

If God, elusive, is an excessive reality, then all the historical realities are approximations to the Truth, and consequently relativized; for this reason, different religious faiths can be plural and multiple and are possible together, because in any case they remain conjectural. The thesis of conjectures is used at a historical-political level, to allow the conception of a plurality as long as it does not claim to be absolutized and remains in the contingency, in which the Truth of Revelation cannot be totally expressed, but on the contrary includes all the sensitive manifestations beyond the principle of contradiction.

Here lies a fundamental ontological structure, defining the conjectural aspect of human knowledge, that approaches the Truth as a polygon inscribed in a circle approaches the circumference, without ever being able to touch it:

> Therefore, it is not the case that by means of likenesses a finite intellect can precisely attain the truth about things. For truth is not something more or something less but is something indivisible. Whatever is not truth cannot measure truth precisely. (By comparison, a noncircle [cannot measure] a circle, whose being is something indivisible.) Hence, the intellect, which is not truth, never comprehends truth so precisely that truth cannot be comprehended infinitely more precisely. For the intellect is to truth as [an inscribed] polygon is to [the inscribing] circle. The more angles the inscribed polygon has the more similar it is to the circle. However, even if the number of

---

16. "Si sic facere dignaberis, cessabit gladius et odii livor, et quaeque mala; et cognoscent omnes quomodo non est nisi religio una in rituum varietate" (*De pace fidei*, 1, 6).

> its angles is increased *ad infinitum*, the polygon never becomes equal [to the circle] unless it is resolved into an identity with the circle.¹⁷

This simple and prospective character of human knowledge is not, however, a limit, but rather the possibility of opening up to the unconditional because the multiple, the difference, the otherness are not distant from the One; on the contrary, through multiplicity and difference, the reality of the One becomes visible in its being an ontological link between the different creatures. The unity of God is equality with itself and co-implication of the multiple, the nexus between unity and equality and the nexus of divine unity-equality with the creature. In this sense, the Trinity does not simply mean plurality, but the relationship between the Absolute and the contingency.

This Cusanian gnoseological theory, however, is absolutely not to be considered as a form of relativism or subjectivism, because it is not the reality to be relative, or even not to be able to be affirmed, but only the points of view on the only Truth to be different and multiple; but in this difference is expressed the close connection between the finite world and the Truth, showing again how much multiplicity is strictly connected with Unity. Starting from here, it is clear how the variety of rites cannot be considered as something negative representing, on the contrary, the impossibility of manifesting the transcendence of God, but at the same time the possibility of witnessing His greatness through the pluralization of the forms of expression of the Divine and of Truth: "Once this [fact] is admitted, the varieties of rites will not be disturbing, for they were instituted and received as perceptible signs of true faith. Now, the signs [themselves] admit of change, though the signified object does not."¹⁸

---

17. "Non potest igitur finitus intellectus rerum veritatem per similitudinem praecise attingere. Veritas enim non est nec plus nec minus, in quodam indivisibili consistens, quam omne non ipsum verum existens praecise mensurare non potest; sicut nec circulum, cuius esse in quodam indivisibili consistit, non-circulus. Intellectus igitur, qui non est veritas, numquam veritatem adeo praecise comprehendit, quin per infinitum praecisius comprehendi possit, habens se ad veritatem sicut polygonia ad circulum, quae quanto inscripta plurium angulorum fuerit, tanto similior circulo, numquam tamen efficitur aequalis, etiam si angulos in infinitum multiplicaverit, nisi in identitatem cum circulo se resolvat" (*De docta ignorantia*, I, 3, 10).
18. "Quo admisso non turbabunt varietates illae rituum. Nam ut signa sensibilia veritatis fidei sunt instituta et recepta. Signa autem mutationem capiunt, non signatum" (*De pace fidei*, 16, 55).

The Neoplatonic and mystic aspect

The idea of conjectural knowledge asserts the impossibility of defining God in an affirmative way, because according to His nature He is subtracted from any possibility of being defined in a way that is not conjectural and contingent; this means that God can't be defined with a name because all the names are conjectural, and they exemplify Him without saying what He is in Himself.

The name of the Trinity itself is a conjecture that reveals God as the dialectic law of unity, separation, and connection: it is evident how much the Neoplatonic model acts here, and the Christian Gnostic and Johannine model of the eternal, secret, and sapiential articulation of God and of the relationship that the Son has with created humanity. The Neoplatonic system acts in Cusanus's vision as an ontology that finds in reality a unitive force, an active energy, with respect to which multiplicity and becoming are constituted as an effect of return, being realities identical to themselves only insofar as they participate in the One, like a weakened echo of the infinite Unity; this same structure incessantly in action cannot be understood from the outside, "represented" and "objectified" on a plane of immanence.[19] So, negation is more able than affirmation to express God's nature: "And so, the theology of negation is so necessary for the theology of affirmation that without it God would not be worshiped as the Infinite God but, rather, as a creature. And such worship is idolatry; it ascribes to the image that which befits only the reality itself. Hence, it will be useful to set down a few more things about negative theology."[20]

The important element of *theologia negativa* shows how Cusanus roots his theological and philosophical elaboration in the mystic tradition of Pseudo-Dionysius the Areopagite, the School of Chartres, and Meister Eckhart. Cusanus's Christianity becomes in this way a speculative and mystic elaboration that finds its origins already a long time before, in the Christian Alexandrine tradition: the first occurrences of the term "mystic"

---

19. Maurizi 2011: 189.
20. "Et ita theologia negationis adeo necessaria est quoad aliam affirmationis, ut sine illa Deus non coleretur ut Deus infinitus, sed potius ut creatura; et talis cultura idolatria est, quae hoc imagini tribuit, quod tantum convenit veritati. Hinc utile erit adhuc parum de negativa theologia submittere" (*De docta ignorantia*, I, 26, 86).

are for the most part attested in the Alexandrian context (already from Philo), first of all in the Valentinians, then in Clement, Origen, and then in the Origenian Eusebius of Caesarea. Christian theology becomes properly mystical when it becomes Alexandrian, that is, speculative, assuming a Platonic ontological configuration (also culminating in a Platonic me-ontology): mysticism is that theology that penetrates into the intimacy of the secrets of God, no longer historical-economic, but ontological, intelligible, grasping the absolute transcendence, then the absolute main simplicity, which is beyond the same *ousia*.[21]

The influence of this Christian tradition continues in authors such as Pseudo-Dionysius and Meister Eckhart, becoming references for Cusanus himself, who fits into this tradition, and it is evident since the philosophical elaboration of *De docta ignorantia*:

> For all beings participate in Being. Therefore, if from all beings participation is removed, there remains most simple Being itself, which is the Essence (*essentia*) of all things. And we see such Being only in most learned ignorance; for when I remove from my mind all the things which participate in Being, it seems that nothing remains. Hence, the great Dionysius says that our understanding of God draws near to nothing rather than to something. But sacred ignorance teaches me that that which seems to the intellect to be nothing is the incomprehensible Maximum.[22]

Here *Deus absconditus* is the object of that "negative knowledge" which is *docta ignorantia*, an object that is at the same time "known and ignored"; *intellectus*, in fact, "believing" firmly in what is absurd and paradoxical, transforms what for *ratio* is absolutely unthinkable, and therefore a source of bewilderment and disbelief, into absolute necessity, revealing *ignorantia* to be the object of God's gift,[23] through the

21. Lettieri 2017: 85–86.
22. "Omnia enim entia entitatem participant. Sublata igitur ab omnibus entibus participatione remanet ipsa simplicissima entitas, quae est essentia omnium. Et non conspicimus ipsam talem entitatem nisi in doctissima ignorantia, quoniam, cum omnia participantia entitatem ab animo removeo, nihil remanere videtur. Et propterea magnus Dionysius dicit intellectum Dei magis accedere ad nihil quam ad aliquid. Sacra autem ignorantia me instruit hoc, quod intellectui nihil videtur, esse maximum incomprehensibile" (De docta ignorantia, I, 17, 51).
23. Cuozzo 2012: 78.

fundamental role of *fides*. It is impossible to conceive God and represent Him in His essence, and also to define Him through positive definitions and names, that risk reducing God to something finite and contingent:

> And so, from these considerations it is evident that the affirmative names we ascribe to God befit Him [only] infinitesimally. For such [names] are ascribed to Him in accordance with something found in created things. Therefore, since any such particular or discrete thing, or thing having an opposite, can befit God only very minutely: affirmations are scarcely fitting, as Dionysius says. For example, if you call God "Truth," falsity is the contradistinction; if you call Him "Virtue," vice is the contradistinction; if you call Him "Substance," accident is the contradistinction; and so on. But since God is not a substance which is not all things and to which something is opposed, and is not a truth which is not all things without opposition, these particular names cannot befit Him except very infinitesimally. For it is not the case that any affirmations—which posit in Him, as it were, something of what they signify—can befit Him who is not some particular thing more than He is all things. Therefore, if affirmative names befit God, they befit Him only in relation to created things.[24]

As a consequence, trying to define the essence of God through the multiplicity of images and creatures is part of an idolatrous attitude of religion that, as in the dialogue the Word explains to the Hindu about the *simulacra*, wants to absolutize its own image of God, exchanging what is only one of the possible formulations with the divine Truth in its precision, transforming what is one of the possible ways, and intrinsically therefore imperfect, in a claim of absolute understanding of the divine

---

24. "Est itaque ex hoc manifestum nomina affirmativa, quae Deo attribuimus, per infinitum diminute sibi convenire; nam talia secundum aliquid, quod in creaturis reperitur, sibi attribuuntur. Cum igitur Deo nihil tale particulare, discretum, habens oppositum sibi nisi diminutissime convenire possit, hinc affirmationes sunt incompactae, ut ait Dionysius. Nam si dicis ipsum veritatem, occurrit falsitas; si dicis virtutem, occurrit vitium; si dicis substantiam, occurrit accidens; et ita de reliquis. Cum autem ipse non sit substantia, quae non sit omnia et cui nihil opponitur, et non sit veritas, quae non sit omnia absque oppositione, non possunt illa particularia nomina nisi diminute valde per infinitum sibi convenire. Omnes enim affirmationes, quasi in ipso aliquid sui significati ponentes, illi convenire non possunt, qui non est plus aliquid quam omnia. Et propterea nomina affirmativa, si sibi conveniunt, non nisi in respectu ad creaturas conveniunt" (*De docta ignorantia*, I, 24, 78–79).

mystery. It is precisely this mystery of God that must be maintained, in order to not misunderstand His essence as *Deus absconditus*, and this is what different religions have to do, to avoid the risk of falling into an idolatrous representation, and remembering that

> You, then, who are the giver of life and of existence, are the one who is seen to be sought in different ways in different rites, and You are named in different names; for as You are [in Yourself] You remain unknown and ineffable to all. For You who are infinite power are not any of the things You created; nor can the creature comprehend the concept of Your infinity, since there is no comparative relation of the finite to the Infinite.[25]

The possibility of thinking concord between religions is thus expressed entirely in the recognition that religious symbols, doctrinal elaborations and dogmatic formulas, and the various institutional formulas only find meaning by maintaining the reference to a foundation that cannot be expressed through historical languages, which are certainly necessary and significant, but which are at the same time a reference, a figure of another surplus, that does not exhaust the meaning, but rather increases it further. In this sense Cusanus theorizes a relativization of the rite as a necessary passage to salvation, in view of the exaltation of faith as an essential and necessary element and that is common to all religions.

The authenticity of every religious tradition and of the historical forms in which it expresses itself such as its symbols, rites, and its doctrinal patrimony consists in strictly conjugating participation, in expressing the experience of a participation without, however, understanding it as a closed event, as the place of an absolute and exclusive definition, and the praxis of the *communio* is the form in which this dialectic can be effectively preserved and witnessed. The basic intention of *De pace fidei* consists in this way precisely in recalling the different historical faiths, faced with the tragic experience of their conflicts, to an awareness of their

---

25. "Tu ergo, qui es dator vitae et esse, es ille qui in diversis ritibus differenter quaeri videris et in diversis nominibus nominaris, quoniam uti es manes omnibus incognitus et ineffabilis. Non enim qui infinita virtus es, aliquod eorum es quae creasti, nec potest creatura infinitatis tuae conceptum comprehendere, cum finiti and infinitum nulla sit proportio" (*De pace fidei*, 1, 5).

participatory status, of this tension between participation and deferral to the Truth that is at the foundation of every authentic religious conscience.[26]

Trinity and Christology

In order to theorize a conciliation between different faiths there are some theological aspects to face, first of all that of Trinity. It seems, at a first view, an impossible theoretical point on which to create agreement, because neither Jews nor Muslims can agree on this Christian dogma. To address this, Cusanus simply reiterates the doctrine of the Trinity from *De docta ignorantia*, again emphasizing how the ineffability of divine infinity informs the Trinitarian structure of God's work as Creator, and presenting Christ as the manifestation of the equality through which God establishes the difference of the world. Muslim and Jewish critiques of the Trinity are interpreted as the consequence of an obviously misguided idea of a plurality of gods, whereas everyone in the heavenly council agrees that to reject the Trinity as it is here explained would be to isolate God and creation from one another, thus nullifying the idea of divine fecundity and creativity. Understandably, the latter is a position nobody wants to defend.[27] Even on this question, which seems to be the thorniest in the discussion between the monotheisms—the concept of the Trinity—it is possible to find an agreement, because God himself is beyond this concept, being beyond all the possible determinations, and therefore being one and triune, accepting in Himself the unity and multiplicity, equality and difference, in a dialectic inconceivable to the "simple" human reason.

Again, in the dialogue with the Hindu, Trinity is called into question regarding polytheism, because from a non-Christian point of view thinking about plurality inside the divine nature seems to be very problematic. The trinitarian faith would seem to be contradictory insofar as it affirms the plurality of the principle and the three trinitarian persons would not be, then, to be understood as God in an absolute sense, but gods by participation.[28]

26. Peroli 2017: 120.
27. Alfsvåg 2014: 55.
28. Bidese 2010: 100.

But in reality "As Creator, God is triune and one; as Infinite, He is neither triune nor one nor any of those things that can be spoken of. For the names that are ascribed to God are taken from creatures, since in Himself God is ineffable and beyond all that can be named or spoken of."[29] The worshipers of God must worship Him as *principium universi*, in which we can find multiplicity, inequality, and division of parts; so it is not the divine nature that is characterized by multiplicity, but its manifestation in finite creation, that anyway participate in the infinite Essence. Trinity is of course inconceivable even by Judaism and Islam, but in Cusanus's elaboration it becomes acceptable because it represents fecundity and divine creative virtue (*fecunditas simplicissima*), showing how relationship is the modality through which the divine principle expresses Himself.

The Incarnation itself is explained by a philosophical argument that makes Christ a symbol of union between the finite and the infinite. This is not a simplistic apologetic operation, because Cusanus finds in the Christian Revelation the core of the dialectic between the essence of God and the whole finite world related to Him, and to His abyssal infinity. The theological-religious idea of the Cusanian Christology consists therefore in considering Christ as the realization of the human search for God, and this realization happens to man not as something foreign, something absolutely unknown, but as a confrontation with what man must be and for this reason can be: the spiritual nature united to the creator.

Christ, or rather the idea of the Incarnation of God, is therefore in this way presupposed in every religion—at least as an implicit need for thinking about the transcendence—regardless of whether this is conscious or not at all. It builds the heart of the *una religio* that according to Cusanus can be expressed in a multiplicity of rites and uses. Cusanus does not place Christianity and the other religions in opposition to one another, but he considers Christian Revelation to be the realization, the fulfillment of these religions, to which all men and all religions aspire. In this way Christianity shows itself to be an enormous hermeneutic elaboration that makes it possible to be open to plurality and difference, through a

---

29. "Deus, ut creator, est trinus et unus; ut infinitus, nec trinus nec unus nec quicquam eorum quae dici possunt. Nam nomina quae Deo attribuuntur, sumuntur a creaturis, cum ipse sit in se ineffabilis et super omne quod nominari aut dici posset" (*De pace fidei*, 7, 21, 9–12).

dynamic of "rationalization" and "overcoming" of the structure of dogma as the exclusive and closed order of Truth. The speculative structure that develops the argument of an achievable peace between religions is therefore theological, and at its core inevitably Christian.

Christianity as hermeneutic "relativization"

Christianity represents the possibility of thinking about otherness and difference in a dialogical way, through a process of "mediation" and "harmonization" of all the other theological structures. Cusanus does not want to make an empirical synthesis between the different doctrines, but rather to delineate the original unity of them in diversity, due to the concept of *presupositio fidei*. Now we no longer have a large number of simple "heterodoxies" in the face of a universally valid and universally binding "orthodoxy," but otherness, the *eteron*, is recognized as the foundational moment of the *doxa* itself. The verity, which in itself remains elusive and unattainable, can be known only in its otherness. From this conception springs for Cusanus a truly extraordinary "tolerance," which is anything but indifference, since the plurality of forms of faith is not accepted as a mere empirical coexistence, but constitutes a speculative requirement founded on the basis of the theory of knowledge.[30]

The attempt to recompose the crisis, internal to Christianity and in the confrontation of Christianity with other faiths (in particular, Islam) passes through this openness, also in a historical key, towards a plurality whereby Christianity, Judaism, and Islam reveal themselves as modes of manifestation of the same Truth, modes that are all true because they are contingent and not absolute, and therefore able to live together. The rationalization carried out with regard to Christianity allows the mediation and harmonization of a plurality of theological analyses, so that the hermeneutic and allegorical mechanism of Origenian universalization is used to include even at a historical level monotheism and polytheism, activating a radically innovative, pluralist, tolerant, humanist perspective, with a strong speculative element. In this sense the destiny of Christianity itself is that of the *kenosis* of its dogmatic-exclusiveness aspects, to assert itself in its own spirituality through an infinite search for the intuition of the

---

30. Cassirer 2012: 34.

Truth of the paradox of God, which can therefore overcome the external datum, whether it be the *dogma* or the ecclesiastical structure.

In this mechanism of "relativization" Christianity itself is implied, revealing itself as a hermeneutic system capable of making openness to plurality and difference possible: the possibility of thinking about otherness and difference in a dialogical way is in itself contained in the Christian theological framework, which in its deployment makes this dialectic possible. Here lies the great Origenian tradition, an enormous and complex allegorical elaboration to which Cusanus belongs and from which he derives his own theology. Cusanus's philosophical thought is in fact nourished by the Origenian system, by that option of questioning dogma as the exclusive order of Truth, without which it would be impossible for him to elaborate a thought of the dialectic between identity and difference as internal to Christianity itself and as the inversion of authentic theology. An obvious example of this is the resumption of the Origenian thesis of the Eucharist as a conceptual and figurative place which, deprived of its material structure, remains a sign, a symbol that exalts the message of salvation beyond ritual manifestations, because "This sacrament, insofar as it pertains to the perceptible signs (provided faith itself be maintained) is not of such necessity that there is no salvation without it."[31]

In this dynamic of "rationalization," even if it is evident that Cusanus's theology maintains a transcendental and revelatory structure, an ambiguity may arise in this elaboration of Christianity: there could be the risk, in fact, of weakening the revealing message, the ontological difference between creator and creature, and therefore in general the most important dogmas of Christian religion. This is the criticism that, for example, Johann Wenck makes of Cusanus in *De ignota literatura* (1441), in particular focusing on the idea that in God, as *infinita Unitas*, creator and creature have the same ontological essence.

Conclusion

I started this contribution by saying that Cusanus's *De pace fidei* shows an epochal aspect, situating itself on the threshold of Modernity; in this

---

31. "Hoc sacramentum, prout est in sensibilis signis habita fide, non est sic necessitatis, quod sine eo non sit salus" (*De pace fidei*, 18).

sense, I do not intend in any way to juxtapose the idea of tolerance that emerges from the work with that of a modern-enlightenment matrix. Cusanus is in fact inserted in a Christian theological tradition, and I think it is necessary to contextualize the Cusanian discourse, without yielding to the temptation to project it forward with modern categories.

It is evident that Cusanus cannot think about a possible conciliation through the removal of the truth of faith, and the relativization, for example, of theological dogmas such as Revelation or Incarnation; in this sense it is not possible to speak of tolerance as understood, for example, in its modern rationalistic matrix. This is all the more true due to the fact that, as I have tried to show before, the analysis of concordance between religions and the attainment of tolerance takes place through a mechanism of thought internal to the Christian theological device, which produces this attainment because of its theological structure.

Cusanian elaboration is therefore all the more complex precisely because, starting from the assumption of not ignoring the deepest and most proper theological elements of every religion, tries to find a meeting point precisely on the theological level itself, thus making the analysis more fruitful and speculatively complex. Indeed, it is precisely through the affirmation of fundamental theological points common to all religions that it is possible to find a point of understanding. Presenting itself as the condition of possibility for conciliation, Christianity can be interpreted in this text in two different ways: on one hand, as coincident with the only and true religion that brings the message of salvation, and on the other hand, as a religion of reason that can therefore allow the conciliation between faiths only if it eliminates the revealing elements that exceed rational understanding.

It is obvious that, in the end, Christianity makes possible the mediation of differences. But the rationalization of critical and discordant points does not mean, therefore, that other religions, which would therefore be called to embrace its dogmas, are brought back to Christianity; on the contrary, Christianity makes reconciliation possible precisely because it activates towards itself the same dynamic of emptying and rationalization that it uses towards other religions, thus allowing the landing at a meeting point. And, of course, at the end of the dialogue all the participants discover that they agree about the fundamental messages of faith, beyond the exterior and historical cults.

The strength of Christian theology, therefore, lies in its discursive capacity, which knows that it does not possess Truth, and that it must remain inattainable: if no representation of Truth coincides with Truth itself, then no theological elaboration can be valid as absolute knowledge. Ultimately this reflects what happens on the ontological level, where the affirmation of conjectural ignorance paradoxically enhances the affirmation of the greatness of divine unity. The presence of difference in relation to otherness is not a problem, because on an ontological level the relationship is structured in this way, in the relationship between identity and difference in which openness to the other constitutes identity itself, reflecting the multiplicity of divine manifestations in creation.

A fundamental element in Cusanus's Christianity is in fact its mechanism of questioning dogma, without which it would be impossible to elaborate a thought of the dialectic between identity and difference as internal to Christianity itself and as a stronger manifestation of authentic theology. Cusanus's construction can be considered a rational investigation of religion as an object and therefore, following Marco M. Olivetti, the possibility of thinking about religions (not by chance the term is plural) and of a faith as an expression of the dynamic of distinction between religion and *fides christiana* in the modern era that also occurs internally to Christianity, and not only in apologetic function (assuming the controversy of the opponent), but also in irenic function; in this sense Cusanus shows himself as a thinker leaning toward modernity.[32]

Starting from the historical problem of *De pace fidei*, Christian identity is inevitably forced to confront itself with the theme of difference, of the irreducible otherness that puts it in question, but Cusanus shows how this confrontation with the other is in reality inherent in the structure of Christianity itself, characterized by a dialogic dynamic. Christian religion appears, unlike the others, to be intrinsically addressed to the theological, but the discursive force of theology is not at all unveiling; it does not represent the Truth at all, because no theology can be valid as *scientia dei*.[33]

32. Olivetti 1995.
33. Cacciari 1994: 151–52.

Author biography

Beatrice Tramontano's (PhD, Sapienza University of Rome) research deals with the topic of multiculturalism in Western liberal democraticies, with a focus on the comparison of the philosophical theories of Charles Taylor and Jürgen Habermas, and focusing on certain aspects of multicultural societies such as religious pluralism, the relationship between religions and public space, secularization and post-secularism, and the question of recognition and individual and collective rights within the liberal-democratic normative system. She has published articles on the developments and critiques of the multicultural model by interculturalism, postcolonial studies and feminist theory as well as the relationship between multiculturalism and immigration in European societies.

References

Primary sources

Cusanus, N. (1971), *De pace fidei*, in P. Gaia (ed.), *Opere religiose*. Turin: Utet.
Cusanus, N. (2017), *De docta ignorantia*, in E. Peroli (ed.), *Opere filosofiche, teologiche e matematiche*. Milan: Bompiani.
Cusanus, N. (2017), *De mente*, in E. Peroli (ed.), *Opere filosofiche, teologiche e matematiche*. Milan: Bompiani.
Cusanus, N. (2017), *De coniecturis*, in E. Peroli (ed.), *Opere filosofiche, teologiche e matematiche*. Milan: Bompiani.

Secondary sources

Alfsvåg, K. (2014), "Divine Difference and Religious Unity: On the Relation between *De Docta Ignorantia, De Pace Fidei* and *Cribratio Alkorani*," in I. C. Levy, R. George-Tvrtković, and D. Duclow (eds.), *Nicholas of Cusa and Islam: Polemic and Dialogue in the Late Middle Ages*, 49–67. Leiden: Brill.
Bidese, E. (2010), "Il 'pneuma' nel De pace fidei di Niccolò Cusano," in *Lo Spirito e il potere. Questioni di pneumatologia politica* [*The Spirit and Power: On Political Pneumatology*], *Politica e religione. Annuario di teologia politica/Yearbook of Political Theology*, vol. 11, Morcelliana, 95–114.
Bisaha, N. (1999), "'New Barbarian' or Worthy Adversary? Humanist Constructs of the Ottoman Turks in Fifteenth-Century Italy," in D. R. Blanks and

M. Frassetto (eds.), *Western Views of Islam in Medieval and Early Modern Europe: Perception of Other*, 185–205. London: Palgrave Macmillan.

Cacciari, M. (1994), *Geofilosofia dell'Europa*. Milan: Adelphi.

Cassirer, E. (2012), *Individuo e cosmo nella filosofia del Rinascimento*, translated by G. Targia. Torino: Bollati Boringhieri (German original edition *Individuum und Kosmos in der Philosophie der Renaissance*, Leipzig; Berlin: B. G. Teubner, 1927).

Cuozzo, G. (2012), *Mystice Videre. Esperienza religiosa e pensiero speculativo in Cusano*, Mimesis (Bibliotheca Cusana n. 1). Milan: Udine.

Gaia, P., ed. (1971), *Opere religiose di Nicolò Cusano*. Turin: UTET.

Hopkins, J. (2001), *Complete Philosophical and Theological Treatises of Nicholas of Cusa*, vol. 1. Minneapolis: The Arthur J. Banning Press.

Lettieri, G. (2000), "Origenismo (in Occidente, sec. VII–XVIII)," in A. Monaci Castagno (ed.), *Origene. Dizionario. La cultura, il pensiero, le opere*, 307–322. Rome: Città Nuova.

Lettieri, G. (2017), "Più a fondo. L'ontologia apocalittica valentiniana e le origini della teologia mistica cristiana," in I. Adinolfi et al. (eds.), *L'anti-Babele. Sulla mistica degli antichi e dei moderni*, 71–116. Genova: Il nuovo melangolo.

Maurizi, M. (2011), "Tra utopia e ontologia. La questione della pace in Cusano," in F. Bonicalzi (ed.), *Pensare la pace. Il legame imprendibile*, 181–98. Milan: Jaca Book.

Monaco, D. (2013), *Cusano e la pace della fede*. Rome: Città Nuova.

Monaco, D. (2014), "Il Dio nascosto e la pluralità delle religioni: il *De Pace Fidei* di Nicolò Cusano," in M. Coppola, G. Fernicola, and L. Pappalardo (eds.), *Il dialogo filosofico tra le religioni nel pensiero tardo-antico, medievale e umanistico*, 415–28. Rome: Città Nuova Editrice.

Olivetti, M. M. (1995), "Filosofia della religione," in Rossi P. (ed.), *La filosofia*, vol. I: *Le filosofie speciali*, 137–220. Turin: Utet.

Peroli, E. (2017), "Niccolò Cusano e il dialogo tra le religioni," in G. Caponigro (ed.), *Figli di Abramo. Il dialogo fra religioni cinquant'anni dopo "Nostra aetate"*, 103–22. Pisa: ETS.

Chapter 2

Pius II, Nicholas of Cusa, and the Crusade to Retake Constantinople and Jerusalem

Nathan Ron

Introduction: Retaking the Second Rome

Mehmed II did not stop at Constantinople but continued to expand his domains in the Balkans. At Belgrade, the sultan was stalled for a while in 1456, when a crusading force, commissioned by Pope Calixtus III and headed by Janos Hunyadi and John Capistran, overran the sultan's camp and forced him to retreat.[1] The victory impacted Christendom, and Calixtus III wrote in a letter that he was now expecting "not only the recovery of Constantinople but also the liberation of Europe, Asia and the Holy Land."[2] Pope Calixtus III died in 1458, and Aeneas Sylvius Piccolomini, a Sienese humanist turned prelate, was elected as Pope Pius II (r. 1458–1464). He is well known as the pope who took great pains to wage a crusade against the Turks, dedicating himself to this task, and nearly succeeding. Was this crusade limited to retaking Constantinople, or did it also aim to take the Holy Land, similarly to the crusades of old?

---

1. Inalcik 1989: 311–53 (322–24); Babinger 1978: 137–50. On Capistran's role, see Housley 2004: 94–115. I am indebted to Thomas M. Izbicki for drawing attention to important texts employed in this article and for his comments and insights.
2. Setton 1978: 183 n. 89 (Letter of August 1456 to Archbishop Antonino Forcillioni of Florence).

To a considerable extent, there was an alteration of the crusade ideal in fifteenth- to sixteenth-century Europe. As Norman Housley has pointed out, the crusading strategy changed. Although maintaining the ideal of liberating the Holy Land, it also became an instrument of the papacy to be used for other purposes.[3] Thus, James Hankins argues that the fifteenth-century crusades differed from those of the classical period in having as their primary goal, not conquering the Holy Land, but the recovery of Constantinople.[4] Pius II's abortive crusade has been taken as evidence for this point of view. But while Pius II's persistence on the goal of retaking Constantinople and his placing himself as head of the crusading expedition is well known and often discussed, the conquest of the Holy Land as part of this crusade, or at least as an option, is not discussed or even mentioned by historians.[5] Exceptional in this regard is Benjamin Weber who emphasizes the focal place of the retaking of Jerusalem in the papal strategy concerning crusades that were planned or initiated by fifteenth-century popes. Thus, "crusade could not be limited to a defensive war in the Aegean or on the Danube. War against the Ottomans was a secular affair, led by the princes and supported by the Papacy. But papal projects had to go further, and they remained focused on Jerusalem."[6]

The bulk of the sources, in particular official documents such as papal bulls, refer to the recovery of Constantinople and the defense of Christendom against the Ottoman menace as the goals of Pius II's crusade. Thus, the proclamation of the crusade, in the bull *Ecclesiam Christi*, of January 14, 1460, issued by Pius II at the closing of the Mantua congress, specifies the following target:

> In the first place, following the custom of our predecessors, who proclaimed general expeditions either to liberate the Holy Land, or against other unbelievers, we declare a general war and expedition against the very perfidious Turks, the most vicious of our God's

---

3. Housley 2018: 9; Housley 1992: 46–48; Setton 1978: 149–60, 200–270.
4. Hankins 1995: 111–207 (113).
5. E.g. (others than the items specified above): Monfasani 2019: 97; Bisaha 2004a: 40; Bisaha 2008: 123–24; Bisaha 2004b: 140.
6. Weber 2017: 11–44 (23). See also ibid.: 33: "The growth of the Ottoman threat against Western Christendom necessitated a transfer of the military front toward the Aegean and the Balkans. But the primary objective of the crusades, the Holy Land, did not disappear."

enemies, a war that is to be taken up and fought by all Christ's faithful over a period of three years, and to which each and every Christian alike is summoned to contribute according to their ability.[7]

Constantinople is not specifically mentioned, but a general war against the Turks meant, first and foremost, the recovering of the Second Rome. Would that be all? Was not the conquest of the Holy Land part of the plan, or at least an option earnestly considered?

Jerusalem next

Indeed, at that time the Holy Land was not under Ottoman rule, and was governed by the Mameluke Sultanate based in Egypt, while the crusade was to be waged against the Ottoman Turks. However, certain sources do have the Holy Land as a desirable goal and even an objective of this crusade. In some of his orations, delivered before and after the fall of Constantinople to the Ottomans in 1453, Aeneas Sylvius Piccolomini, the future Pope Pius II, advocated a crusade all the way to Jerusalem, Constantinople being the major goal en route. Moreover, at the Congress of Mantua in 1459, under his authority as Pope Pius II, a congress that marked a significant step toward the crusade, he called for the taking of Jerusalem. Shortly after the coronation of the Emperor Frederick III (r. 1452–1493) in Rome, Piccolomini delivered there his oration *Moyses vir Dei* (April 24, 1452), in which he implored Pope Nicholas V, on the emperor's behalf, to wage a crusade with the aim of retaking the territories lost to the Turks and the Saracens, Jerusalem included. Piccolomini was lamenting the poor situation of Jerusalem and the holy places under Saracen rule, a situation that left a shocked impact on the emperor, who had gone on a pilgrimage to the Holy Land in 1493.

7. Cotta-Schønberg 2019e: 45 [3]: "In primis generale bellum atque expeditionem contra perfidissimos Turchos, Dei nostri accerrimos hostes, more praedecessorum nostrorum, qui generales expeditiones, vel ad liberandum Terram Sanctam, vel contra alios infideles indixerunt, ab omnibus Christifidelibus triennio duraturum, gerendum ac suscipiendum esse, decernimus, omnes et singulos Christianos ad praesidium ejus belli pariter pro viribus invitantes, decernentes pariter in tantae necessitatis articulo unumquemque pro viribus et secundum quotum infra dicendum ex suis facultatibus debere conferre." See also Housley 2012a: 220; Housley 2012b: 78.

You may imagine how he felt when he saw those revolting, filthy, and criminal Saracens lording it over the holy places in their possession. What could he say other than the words of the prophet: O God, the heathens are come into thy inheritance, they have defiled thy holy temple: they have made Jerusalem as a place to keep fruit. And again: How doth the city sit solitary that was full of people! How is the mistress of the Gentiles become as a widow: the princes of provinces made tributary! Oh, how deeply moved was the emperor by the oppression of this city and by the abject state of the Christians living across the sea.[8]

Although an explicit call to take the city is absent in this paragraph, the crusading spirit is strongly felt, as well as Piccolomini's desire to bring the holy city and its sacred sites under Christian possession. The oration contains other references dealing with former crusades to the Holy Land that, according to Piccolomini, should serve as a source of inspiration for the present planned crusade. Significantly, there are also specific references to Assyrians, Egyptians, and Saracens as distinct from the Turks.

So, it will not be difficult to summon a crusade, and there will be great hope of victory. His Imperial Majesty knows the Assyrian and Egyptian people to be weak, impotent, and effeminate, warlike neither in temperament nor in planning [...] Who will fear the Turks in their robes and turbans or the Egyptians in their flowing garments? Speaking to King Ezekias, Arsaces likened them to a broken staff of

8. Cotta-Schønberg 2019a: 52 [9 EV]: "At cum spurcidos illic Saracenos, immundos, horridos, sceleratos dominari videret, veniebat in mentem: tactus dolore cordis intrinsecus. Nil aliud dicere potuit quam propheticum illud: O Deus, venerunt gentes in haereditatem tuam, polluerunt templum sanctum tuum, posuerunt Jerusalem in pomorum custodiam. Et iterum, sicut alius propheta clamat: Quomodo sedet sola civitas plena populo, facta est vidua domina gentium, princeps provinciarum est sub tributo. Proh quantum urgebat angebatque Fridericum illius sanctae civitatis indigna servitus, et illorum, qui trans mare sunt, Christianorum oppressio." Also Cotta-Schønberg 2019a: 52 [9 IV/FV]: "Sed quo animo tunc fuisse arbitraris, cum spurcidos illic Saracenos, immundos, horridos dominari videret, sanctissima loca possidentes? Quid aliud dicere poterat nisi propheticum illud: Deus, venerunt gentes in haereditatem tuam, polluerunt templum sanctum tuum, posuerunt Jerusalem in pomorum custodiam. Et iterum: Quomodo sedet sola civitas plena populo, facta est vidua domina gentium, princeps provinciarum facta est sub tributo. Pro quantum urgebat Caesarem haec civitatis oppressio, et illorum, qui sunt trans mare, Christianorum conculcatio."

reeds. If our armies were beaten by them in former times, it was not because of their strength or their military skills, but because of their numbers. If the forces of the Christians are so numerous that they cannot be physically overwhelmed by the mass of Saracens—which is the very meaning of the word crusade (*passagium*), then victory will certainly be in our hands, just like former examples show us.⁹

Throughout his orations, when Piccolomini refers to Assyrians and Egyptians he means the Mameluke Sultanate, which in his time ruled Syria and Egypt, and the Holy Land between. Saracens, in his terminology, means Muslims other than Turks. Thus, his much-desired crusade was aimed not just against Turks but also at conquering the Holy Land. Piccolomini's oration *Quamvis omnibus* of 16 May 1454, delivered at Regensburg, uses, again, the authority and mindfulness of the Emperor Friedrich III on the issue of the Holy Land.

> And you, great nobles, dukes, margraves, and knights, whose courage equals your nobility, you His Imperial Majesty urges to call to mind not only the recent and lamentable fall of Constantinople, but also those old injuries that may now barely be healed. Consider how God [must love] Jerusalem and his Holy Land where he lived for more than thirty years, as a man together with other men, a land that he ennobled with his miracles and dedicated with his own blood, and where the first flowers of the resurrection appeared. And now those who hate the lifegiving cross occupy that Holy Land, that blessed land, that land overflowing with milk and honey, the workplace of our salvation! Our enemies are in possession of the Holy City, and scoundrels trample the pious and holy places that were empurpled by the blood of the immaculate lamb.¹⁰

9. Cotta-Schønberg 2019a: 78–79 [22 IV/FV]: "Non erit ergo difficile convocare passagium, nec rursus spes magna victoriae deerit. Novit majestas imperatoria: Assyriorum Aegyptiorumque gentem imbecilles, inermes, effeminatique sunt, neque animo, neque consilio martiales […] Quis tunicatos mitratosque Turcos aut brachatos timeat Aegyptios, quos Arsaces, ad Ezechiam regem loquens, baculo arundineo confractoque comparavit. Quod si aliquando nostri exercitus ab eis victi1 sunt, neque viribus, neque rei militaris peritiae, sed numerositati hostium hostium ascribendum est. Quod si Christianorum copiae tot fuerint, ut opprimi Saracenorum multitudine nequeant, quod passagii nomen exposcit, certa in manibus erit victoria, sicut prisca exempla nos instruunt."
10. Cotta-Schønberg 2019b: 48 [18]: "Vos autem, magnanimi proceres, duces, marchiones, equites, quos non minus alti cordis quam clari sanguinis crediderim,

Thus, the oration is a plea for a joint European crusade against the Turks, aiming not only at preventing the Turks from expanding into Europe, but also at retaking territories formerly lost to the Turks and the Saracens, including Jerusalem. In his oration *Constantinopolitana clades* delivered on October 15, 1454, Piccolomini envisioned a crusade to liberate Jerusalem following the crusaders of old, in which Duke Geoffroy of Lorraine together with a force of Germans, some French, and a few Italians "passed through Hungary, entered Greece [...] and reached Jerusalem [...] His army is reported to have had 200,000 soldiers—and Germany can muster much greater forces than that."[11] In this oration, Piccolomini explains that there are many ways to Heaven, but at present the easiest and the most glorious road is to take up arms against the Turks, "the infidel enemies of our celestial fatherland, of the eternal city, Jerusalem on high, and to make war with pure and constant hearts. I believe that now you understand, Princes, the war I am advocating is not only just, but also useful."[12]

In this oration, Piccolomini is employing another historic example, trying to convince his listeners of their ability to get to Jerusalem: "Therefore Konrad let the Saxons and other neighbors stay at home so that they could fight the Prussians and other barbarians while he himself went to Jerusalem together with the Rhenish, the Swabians, the

---

commonitos efficit Caesarea majestas, ne Constantinopolitanam cladem dumtaxat, quae recens est et supra modum dolenda, sed vetusta quoque vulnera, et jam vix curabilia, ante mentis oculos revocetis cogitetisque quomodo Deus coeli Hierosolymam terram suam, in qua visus est, et annis supra XXX homo cum hominibus conversatus; suam utique, quam illustrativt miraculis, quam proprio sanguine dedicavit, in qua primi resurrectionis flores apparuerunt. En Terram Sanctam, terram benedictam, terram lacte et melle fluentem, officinamque nostrae salutis osores occupant vivificae crucis. Sacrosanctam civitatem nostri possident hostes, pia ac sacratissima loca agni immaculati purpurata cruore sceleratissimi calcant pede."

11. Cotta-Schønberg 2019c: 104 [38] [FV]: "paucis Italis Hungariam percurrisse, Graeciam [...] Jerosolymam pervenisse [...] In ejus exercitu ducenta millia pugnatorum fuisse traduntur, atqui multo majores copias sola Germania cogere potest."
12. Cotta-Schønberg 2019c: 86 [30] [EV]: "caelestis patriae nostrae et aeternae civitatis, supernae Jerusalem, perfidos inimicos arma sumentes puris et constantibus animis bellum geramus. Cognoscitis, ut arbitror, jam, principes, hujus belli, quod suademus, non honestatem modo, verum etiam utilitatem."

Franconians, and the Barbarians. The same you can do now."[13] At the Congress of Mantua, which marks a significant milestone toward materializing his crusading plan, Pius II clearly expressed his intention regarding Jerusalem:

> But you, unhappy and miserable Christians, have been deprived of the tomb of our God and the noble City of Jerusalem. Let us pass over Alexandria, Thebes, Memphis, and all of Egypt. Let us be silent about Antioch [...] But that Jerusalem, mother of the Old and New Testament, is now in the power of our enemies, we cannot lament and mourn enough: no effort must be spared to recover it and no war refused.[14]

Another reference to Jerusalem which might perhaps indicate that the Holy Land was part of the crusading plan is Louis XI's offer to Pius II through his envoys in March 1462. The king of France—in order to win Pius II's support or neutrality regarding the king's demands in Italy—promised to strengthen the crusade by sending to Greece, to fight the Turks, 40,000 horsemen and 30,000 archers, "a force which could easily drive Mahomet from Europe and recover for a second time Syria and the most holy sepulchre of Christ."[15] We may well doubt the king's sincerity—the number of soldiers seems far too high to be true—just as Pius II did in his *Commentaries*.[16] However, the fact the king saw the potential expedition as targeting the Holy Land is telling. Presumably, the king would not have declared this force as sufficiently strong to take the Holy Land had he not thought that Pius II aimed at taking it.

---

13. Cotta-Schønberg 2019c: 112 [42] [FV]: "Conradus autem, dimissis Saxonibus et ceteris vicinis, qui domi cum Prutenis ac reliquis barbaris decertarent, ipse cum Rhenanis, Suevis, Franconibus, ac Baioariis Jerosolymam penetravit. Idem et nunc vobis agere licet."
14. Cotta-Schønberg 2019d: 69 [13 cont.]: "Vos vero infelices ac miserrimi Christiani, sepulchro Dei vestri et urbe clarissima Hierosolymorum privati estis. Tacemus Alexandriam, Thebas, Memphim, et omnem Aegyptum. Tacemus Antiochiam... Hierosolymam veteris ac novi testamenti matrem in hostium esse potestate satis flere ac dolere non possumus, pro qua recuperanda nullus labor evitari deberet, nullum declinari bellum."
15. Setton 1978: 232 (based on *Comm.* VII, 13).
16. Ibid.

Researchers who focus on Piccolomini's crusading agenda tend to describe him as "the greatest crusading pope of the Renaissance," "the most militant crusader of the fifteenth century," and emphasize that "his crusading program was ambitious and he vowed to lead the crusade in person."[17] Pius II is also said to have been motivated by a belligerent drive linked with personal ambition to win a classically oriented *gloria* and to have been filled with "noble thoughts of leadership, driven by personal ambition and fame."[18] Importantly, Pius II found in Julius Caesar's *Commentarii* the models according to which he shaped his self-image in his own Commentaries. By borrowing and refashioning Caesarean elements, "Pius helped to cast himself in his Commentaries as a just, wise, and all powerful monarch—temporal and spiritual alike—and as a trusted and talented commander in war."[19] However, these researchers overlook a most significant element, which fits very well with their evaluations, namely Pius II's desire and intention to conquer Jerusalem following the retaking of Constantinople. Pius II's ambition and crusading drive motivated him to aim deep into the east, far beyond Constantinople. Some fifty years later, Pope Leo X (r. 1513–1521) sought a crusade, and worked, diplomatically and politically, to achieve it. During almost all his years in office he pursued a truce between the rulers of Europe and the formation of a united Christian force to launch a crusade headed by the emperor, or alternatively the king of France, to take Constantinople and wipe out the Turkish menace of the Ottoman empire.[20] Officially, this was not a crusade to take the Holy Land. However, in 1516–17 the Ottoman Turks defeated the Mamelukes and took Syria and Egypt, the Holy Land included. From this time on, Leo X's increased efforts to wage a crusade against the Turks may well have referred to the conquest of the Holy Land, although no such goal was officially set. For Erasmus, the determined anti-crusading protagonist, this was unthinkable. Using weighty arguments, he shattered the quasi-legitimacy of this crusade, of any crusade, and of any indulgences to finance it.

---

17. Hankins 1995: 128–30; the last quote is from Housley 2006: 135–36.
18. Von Martels 2003: 222.
19. O'Brien 2009: 1057–1097 (1060).
20. Setton 1978: 142–72.

We have heard so often of crusading expeditions, of recovering the Holy Land; we have seen so often the red cross emblazoned with the triple crown, and the red chest beside it; we have heard so often the sainted sermons promising the earth; we have heard so often of doughty deeds and boundless hopes—and the only thing to triumph has been money. Therefore, since the proverb warns that it is quite shameful to trip over the same stone twice, how can we, who have been misled thirty times over, believe any more promises however splendid, when we have been blatantly fooled so often? This very question has almost led the public to reject indulgences altogether.[21]

Erasmus harshly renounced the wrongdoings associated with the financing of past crusades and in particular the selling of indulgences and accepting of donations in return for futile promises. The idea of defending Europe by "freeing" Jerusalem would have been strongly condemned and utterly rejected by Erasmus. In this regard, Erasmus's moral perspective stands out in comparison to Cusanus. Tom Izbicki, who has studied Cusanus's active role in the distribution of papal indulgences in Germany during the early 1450s, concludes that there is no evidence pointing to the involvement of Cusanus in the distribution of indulgences for financing Pius II's crusade, yet Cusanus never questioned the actual value of indulgences. Cusanus's proclamation of spiritual favors contributed to the negative reception of these concessions and their financial aspects. "In the long run, the German sense of grievance over indulgences as sources of papal revenue, and the poor reputation of the Roman curia north of the Alps provided fertile ground for Martin Luther at the outbreak of the

---

21. CWE 64: 246–47; ASD V-3: 65–66: "Toties audiuimus cruciatam expeditionem, recuperationem terrae sanctae, toties vidimus rubram crucem, triplici corona insignitam, cum rubro scrinio, toties audiuimus sacrosanctas conciones omnia pollicentes, toties acta praeclara, spes amplissimas, nec aliud triumphatum est quam pecunia. Itaque, quum prouerbio moneamur, esse turpissimum bis ad eundem lapidem impingere, nos plus tricies falsi, qui possums fidere promissis quamlibet splendidis toties aperte delusi? Eadem res in totum prope alienauit animas hominum ab indulgentiis." For Erasmus's anti-Crusade attitude as allegedly indicating moderation, see Bisaha 2004b: 175; Schwoebel 1967: 225. Despite his objection to the institution of Crusade, Erasmus's attitude toward Islam was not necessarily moderate, see Ron 2014.

Reformation."²² Contrarily, Erasmus strongly denounces this form of fundraising, stressing that a great amount of the funds never reached their destination but rather found their way into the coffers of greedy popes, cardinals, monks and princes, while the rank and file was licenced to take plunder in lieu of their pay.²³ However, it should be remembered that Erasmus preached and wrote his anti-crusading teachings more than half a century after the fall of the second Rome. For him, this cataclysmic event was not a living memory but an established fact, unlike Pius II's and Cusanus's perception of this disaster. Therefore, as a peace-pursuing intellectual, Erasmus could not treat the waging of a war against the Turks, in his own time, as a justified defensive war.

The crusading spirit of Nicholas of Cusa

Morimichi Watanabe has wondered what Cusanus would have done had he arrived in Ancona in 1464 for the scheduled departure of the crusading fleet: "Could he willingly support the crusade, though he had always believed in peace? If so, how would he have convinced himself to take such a position?"²⁴ Watanabe himself came up with some hypothetical answers, yet none of them touches upon Cusanus's active involvement in and ideological support of the crusade.²⁵ Even Housley, who should be credited for observing Cusanus's support of the crusade,²⁶ overlooked some evidence, to be discussed further on, which testifies not just to Cusanus's support of or desire for the crusade, but to his active and willing involvement in getting it underway. Inevitably, Cusanus's *De pace fidei* (1453), an irenic response to Ottoman conquest of the Second

---

22. Izbicki 2019a: 81–95 (citation on 95). The study is based on *Acta Cusana* (edited at present by J. Helmrath and T. Woelki, formerly by E. Meuthen and H. Hallauer).
23. ASD V-3: 64; CWE 64: 246: "I am not unaware of the excuses many people make for this attitude. This charade, they say, has been played out too often by the Roman pontiffs, and the outcome has always been farcical: either nothing has been done or the situation has deteriorated. The money collected, they say, has stuck fast in the hands of popes, cardinals, monks, generals, and princes; the common soldiers are licensed to take plunder in lieu of their pay."
24. Watanabe 2014: 16.
25. Ibid.
26. Housley 2017: 643–67.

Rome, creates the impression that a man of peace, unlinked in any way to a crusade, authored this work. *De pace fidei* messages a belief in the close relationships of all faiths, predominantly Christianity and Islam. Furthermore, Cusanus considered the formation of a universal religion, which could be accepted by all believers.

> [...] and all [men] will know that there is only one religion in a variety of rites. But perchance this difference of rites cannot be eliminated; or perhaps it is not expedient [that it be eliminated], in order that the diversity may make for an increase of devotion, since each region will devote more careful attention to making its ceremonies more 'favorable,' as it were, to You, the King. If so, then at least let there be one religion—just as You are one—and one true worship of You as Sovereign.[27]

The different speakers of the different religions in the *De pace fidei* conduct a non-polemical philosophical and theological discussion, in which the spirit of positive inclusiveness, tolerance, and optimism are predominant.

Furthermore, in his concluding lines, Cusanus linked his universal religion to perpetual peace, since such a religion would end religious conflicts and wars and establish concord and consensus instead: "Moreover, [He commanded] that thereafter [these wise men], having full power [to speak] for all [in their respective nations], assemble in Jerusalem, as being a common center, and in the names of all [their countrymen] accept a single faith and establish a perpetual peace with respect thereto, so that the Creator of all, who is blessed forever, may be praised in peace."[28] *De*

---

27. All translations into English are from Hopkins's standard works. Hopkins 2001: 635; *De pace fidei*, I, 7, 10–15: "et cognoscent omnes quomodo non est nisi religio una in rituum varietate. Quod si forte haec differentia rituum tolli non poterit aut non expedit, ut diversitas sit devotionis adauctio quando quaelibet regio suis cerimoniis quasi tibi regi religio et unus latriae cultus."
28. Hopkins 2001: 670; *De pace fidei*, XIX, 62, 20–63, 5: "Et mandatum est per Regem regum ut sapientes redeant et ad unitatem veri cultus nationes inducant, et quod administratorii spiritus illos ducant et eis assistant et deinde cum plena omnium potestate in Iherusalem quasi ad centrum commune confluant et omnium nominibus unam fidem acceptent et super ipsa perpetuam pacem firment, ut in pace creator omnium laudetur in saecula benedictus. Amen."

pace fidei is defined, *inter alia*, as expounding Cusanus's Christocentric and Platonic-panoramic prayer for religious peace.[29]

Housley thinks that *De pace fidei* is a profoundly original text, yet it misdirected its readers to conclude from it that Cusanus rejected the crusade against the Turks. Housley ascribes to Cusanus a crusading desire even before 1453, already in the 1430s.[30] Indeed, aside from Pope Pius II, whose initiative this crusade was, Cusanus played one of the most important roles in materializing the crusading plan. He was engaged in the crusade to the extent that he was present in Mantua at the congress convened by Pius II, and took part in addressing and welcoming leaders of high rank who attended the Congress.[31] Thus, as we saw, his warm welcome of Albert, margrave of Brandenburg, the glorified combatant and general (the "German Achilles") who was about to reinforce Pius II's crusading expedition. When Albert came to Mantua, "the cardinal of *San Pietro* left the ranks and went out to meet him," and the Pope praised Albert "for his prompt and generous promises of support against the Turks," and endowed him with money and expensive gifts. Pius also conferred on Albert a sword and a cap ornamented with pearls.[32] This is a demonstration of Cusanus's warm and open support of the crusade. But even before the Mantua congress convened, shortly after the fall of Constantinople to the Ottomans, Cusanus was already involved in preparations for a crusade.[33] In May 1454, at the Diet of Regensburg, Cusanus enthusiastically supported a crusade against the Turks. According to Piccolomini's account, "gravely and at length he addressed the location of the fallen city, the

---

29. Hollmann 2017: 177 (for the citation).
30. Housley 2017: 659, 662.
31. Perhaps for just a brief time before taking his place as papal vicar *in temporalibus* for Rome in 1459. See Izbicki 2019b: 97–112 (107, n. 58).
32. *Comm.* III, 45, 3: "Huic Mantuam venienti cardinalis Sancti Petri extra ordinem occurit [...] laudavitque magnificis verbis, qui sua opera contra Turchos alacri et magno animo promisisset." The gifts are mentioned too. This piece of evidence, which passed Housley's attention, I presented at the Watanabe Lecture and Symposium on Cusanus, the Qur'an, and the *Cribratio alkorani*, held by the Cusanus American Society, September 29–30, 2018, at the United Lutheran Seminary, Gettysburg, Penn., USA. It is integrated in Ron 2019: 113–36, and Izbicki 2019b: 97–112.
33. Housley 2017: 664–65. See also Piccolomini's oration *Quamvis omnibus* (May 16, 1454, Regensburg), where Pius mentions (twice) Cusanus's engagement in recruiting the King of France to the crusade.

ways of its people, the power of the Turks and their military methods. And while he did not deny that the Greeks deserved all they had suffered, he nevertheless exhorted the Christians vehemently to avenge the injuries to their savior."[34] This knowledge of Constantinople he acquired after being sent there by Pope Eugene IV to negotiate with the Emperor John VIII Palaeologus on the union of the Greek and Roman churches. Cusanus spent several months in the city in 1437.[35]

Piccolomini's Regensburg oration provides more evidence, ignored or overlooked by researchers, on Cusanus's involvement. Piccolomini asserts: "According to the Most Reverend Cardinal, the Most Christian King of France follows the example of his forefathers and has sent a letter to the Supreme Pontiff in which he promises that he, too, will take up arms if he hears that the Germans have declared war on the Turks."[36] Cusanus and the king of France are mentioned again further on, in the same oration and context: "The Most Christian King of France follows in the footsteps of his forefathers and has, as we heard some days ago from my Most Reverend Lord, the Cardinal, sent a letter to the Supreme Pontiff in which he promises to join the German nation in the defense of the Faith."[37] Following the Diet, Cusanus wrote a letter (May 24, 1454) to John Capistran claiming that the conflict between the Teutonic Knights and the king of Poland was an obstacle to the crusade.[38] That Cusanus was informed and therefore aware of the Turkish threat we learn also from three letters dating from 1457–1458—including a letter from Piccolomini to Cusanus, referring to the possibility of war against the Turks—that were recently published.[39] These letters contain, *inter alia*, short notices

---

34. Housley 2017: 664, citing Meuthen 1972: 2: 491.
35. Halff 2020: 91–151 (92–93); Halff 2019: 15–28; Watanabe 2011: 284–93.
36. Cotta-Schønberg 2019b: 54 [24]: "Rex autem Franciae Christianissimus, majorum suorum vestigia premens, teste reverendissimo cardinali, summo pontifici litteras dedit, quibus sese arma sumpturum pollicetur, si Germanos indixisse Turchis bellum cognoverit."
37. Cotta-Schønberg 2019b: 88 [45]: "Rex autem Franciae Christianissimus, suorum majorum vestigia sequens, ut ex reverendissimo domino meo cardinali superioribus diebus audistis, summo pontifici litteras dedit, per quas se cum Germanica natione ad defensionem fidei concursurum pollicetur."
38. *Acta Cusana* 2016 [Helmrath and Woelki, eds.]: 700–701.
39. *Acta Cusana* 2020 [Helmrath and Woelki, eds.]: 1544–46 (Nr. 5256), 1601–1602 (Nr. 5338), 1880 (Nr. 5697).

on the Turkish menace in general and references to the danger of the Turks pushing deeper into Europe.

Arguably, Cusanus's support of the crusade was not just the result of following the commands of his pope. He worked for it willingly and wholeheartedly. In particular, his active participation in the Congress of Mantua, even if brief, is telling and should not be underestimated.[40]

Cribratio Alkorani and crusading spirit

In 1461, on the pope's request, Cusanus published *Cribratio alkorani*. Notwithstanding the complex and complicated methodology of the *Cribratio*, and despite the disagreements among researchers on the nature of the *Cribratio*, and particularly on its linkage, if any exists at all, to the *De pace fidei*, there can be no doubt about two essential elements of the *Cribratio*, which reflect Cusanus's non-irenic approach, to say the least.[41] First and foremost, Cusanus attacks Muhammad, which in itself implies severely degrading Islam, or even refuting it altogether. Muhammad is denigrated and discredited throughout the *Cribratio*. Thus, the refutative attitude of the *Cribratio* toward Islam is reflected in the prologue of book I, where Cusanus refers to the Qur'an as a book of foolish errors: "I inquired whether any of the Greeks had written against these foolish errors."[42] Further on, in the same prologue, Cusanus testifies: "At length, I urged Brother Dionysius the Carthusian to write against the Koran."[43] In book I of the *Cribratio*, Cusanus portrays Muhammad as an ignorant who

40. Such an underestimation is implied from Izbicki 2019b: 107: "Evidence for Cusanus' support of the anti-Turkish crusade following 1453 is sparse […] Cusanus was at Mantua briefly, probably before taking his place as papal vicar *in temporalibus* for Rome in 1459."
41. On the *Cribratio*, see the special issue of *Revista Española de Filosofía Medieval* 26/1 (2019), titled "Responding to the Qur'an: Cusanus, his Contemporaries and Successors" (Duclow et al. 2019). See also Burton et al. 2019; Izbicki et al. 2019; Levy et al. 2014. For more literature, see Watanabe 2014: 7–19; Aikin and Aleksander 2013: 219–35; Meuthen 2010; Watanabe 2004: 3–24; Izbicki 1999: 175–83; Biechler 1999: 185–202; Hopkins 1994; Biechler and Bond 1990.
42. Hopkins 2001: 965; *Cribratio alkorani*, prologus: 5: "Quaesivi, si quis Graecorum scripsisset contra illas ineptias."
43. Hopkins 2001: 966; *Cribratio alkorani*, prologus: 6: "Demum concitavi fratrem Dionysium Carthusiensem, ut scriberet contra Alkoranum." It was commissioned

was guided by Satan ("prince of this world"), deceived and manipulated by the Jews, and the Qur'an is defined by Cusanus as deceitful.[44]

In the latter part of the work, particularly in chapter 19 of Book II, entitled "An Invective against the Qur'an," Cusanus engages in particularly harsh denigrations of Muhammad and the Qur'an.[45] Some of the chapter titles of part III read as follow:

> II. Muhammad did not know what ought to be done and what ought to be believed; and he left behind nothing firm. III. Why those who believe the Koran are called "saved ones"; and that the sword is teacher. VIII. The goal of Muhammad's work was his own exaltation. IX. At times Muhammad writes that Christ is God and man; at times, that He is only a man. Similarly, at times [he writes] that God is one; at times, that He is more than one. X. Muhammad continually changes [his views], as [is instanced] in his examples. XIV. The covenant between God and Abraham excludes the Ismaelites, and it concludes in Christ, the Mediator. XV. Only the Christian, who adores Trinity-in-oneness, can be a descendant of Abraham. XVI. Arabs are altogether ignorant of the law of Abraham, and they are persecutors of it.[46]

In writing this, Cusanus was following a medieval polemical routine, adopting what Norman Daniel details as the Christian medieval attack on Muhammad as a prophet, including pointing to contradictions in the

---

by Cusanus during his papal legation through Germany in 1451–1452. See Mougel 1896: 56–62; Ocker 2004: 132–33; Izbicki 2019a: 81–95.

44. Hopkins 2001: 976; *Cribratio alkorani*, I: 23–24.
45. Hopkins 2001: 1045–1048; *Cribratio alkorani*, II: 124–28 (*Invectio Contra Alkoranum*); Watanabe 2014: 13.
46. Hopkins 2001: 973–74; *Cribratio alkorani*, prologus: 19–20: "II. Quod Mahumetus ignoravit, quid agendum et sentiendum, et nihil firmi reliquit. III. Cur dicuntur salvati credentes Alkoranum; et quod gladius est magister. VIII. Quod finis operis Mahumeti fuit sui exaltatio. IX. Quod Mahumetus nunc scribat Christum deum et hominem, nunc hominem tantum, sic nunc singularem deum, nunc pluralem. X. Quod Mahumetus continue variat, ut in exemplis. XIV. Quod pactum dei et Abrahae excludit Ismaelitas et in Christo mediatore concluditur. XV. Quod non nisi Christianus trinitatem in unitate adorans Abrahae filius esse possit. XVI. Quod Arabes legem Abrahae penitus ignorent et eius sint persecutores."

Qur'an. This was typical of Christian polemicists' belief that they could discredit Islam by discrediting Muhammad.[47]

Sharp anti-Muhammad elements appear in a work Cusanus wrote before the *Cribratio*. In the sermon which he gave on August 24, 1456 he praised the recent Christian victory over the Turks at Belgrade. Cusanus describes Muhammad as a "pseudo-prophet" and explains the positive references to the Gospels in the Qur'an as the beguiling deception of Satan, emphasizing the doctrinal divergence of denying the crucifixion. Thus, Muhammad praised Christ and the Gospel "but posited false insights while promising paradisiac lust of flesh and body. And since the cross of Christ is the ultimate spiritual testimony of conceiving the Gospel [...] therefore it seems that Satan induced Mohamed's doctrine to people so that the head of evil, the son of perdition, will spring out of it and constitute himself as the enemy of the cross of Christ."[48]

In another sermon, given a year earlier in 1455, Cusanus refers to the Book of Revelation, chapter 13, and identifies Muhammad as the beast, preceding the Antichrist: "The first beast rising up from the water or the sea can be understood as Muhammad [...] and the second is the Antichrist."[49] One should not underestimate Cusanus's earnestness when he consistently and harshly condemns Muhammad, a condemnation that is literally equal to the theological refutation of the Qur'an and of Islam itself. And of course, Muhammad's evils and wrongdoing resulted from his being manipulated and deceived by the Jews. Who else?

The second non-irenic aspect of the *Cribratio* is Cusanus's attitude toward Islam as the religion of the sword. In the *Cribratio*, and only there, Cusanus defines Islam as a religion of the sword and accuses Muhammad of responsibility for this. One of the chapter titles of the *Cribratio* states

47. Daniel 1993: 100–130 (ch. III); Hoeppner Moran Cruz 1999: 55–82 (66).
48. Sermo CCXL *Laudans invocabo*, Nicolaus Cusanus 2002: 229 (the translation to English is mine): "sed apposuit falsum intellectum promittens paradisum voluptatis secundum carnem et delicias corporales. Et quoniam crux Christi est ultimum testimonium spiritualis intelligentiae evangelii [...] ideo doctrinam Mahometh diabolus videtur hominibus persuasisse, ut ex ipsa veniret caput malitiae filius perditionis, qui se inimicum crucis Christi constitueret." See Hankins 1995: 128 (n. 49); O'Malley 1979: 234, nn. 156–57; Euler 2014: 20–29 (27).
49. Nicolaus Cusanus, Sermo CCX, *Iterum Venturus est*: 38–39 (the translation to English is mine): "Primam bestiam de aqua seu mari ascendentem posse Mahimmet intelligi [...] et secundum bestiam esse antichristum." See Van der Meer 2009: 321.

"that the sword is teacher."⁵⁰ Thus, Muslims forced their religion on Christians by the threat of the sword: "And countless apostate Christians and Arab Christians and Christians who being of the same law as the Arabs pretend to be of the Arab sect because of fear of the sword."⁵¹ Cusanus went as far as to proclaim that the sword is the final decisive proof of whatever is read in the Qur'an. In another part of the text he has Muhammad saying: "We have destroyed, says God, cities before the eyes of those who have not believed. And neither would you believe miracles, except by the sword."⁵² According to Cusanus, Muhammad strove for domination to be gained by the force of the sword:

> But you have seemed to me, Oh Muhammad, to have sought—under the pretext of religion—the power of dominating. For you reduce all [matters] to the sword; and even by the sword you strive to obtain tribute [...] Does anyone fail to understand that the goal of your religion—that your zeal and the rite [prescribed] by your law—tends only toward your dominating?⁵³

Accordingly, Muhammad founded and headed a warlike religion aiming for domination and expansion. This might have been true in light of the central role of Jihad among the teachings of the Qur'an and in light of the Islamic drive to fulfill it during the Middle Ages since the rise of

---

50. Hopkins 2001: 973; *Cribratio alkorani*, alius prologus: 19: "et quod gladius est magister."
51. Hopkins 2001: 979; *Cribratio alkorani*, I, 29: "Multi etiam Christiani sub principibus sectae Arabum Christo devotius serviunt et infiniti Christiani renegati et Arabes et eiusdem legis cum ipsis timore gladii."
52. Hopkins 2001: 1061; *Cribratio alkorani*, III: 137–38: "Est igitur ultima resolutio probationis omnium, quae in Alkoran leguntur, gladius [...] Respondit: Destruximus—inquit deus—civitates ante eos, qui non crediderunt; nec etiam vos miraculis crederetis nisi per gladium."
53. Hopkins 2001: 1068; *Cribratio alkorani*, III, 148: "Sed visus es mihi, o Mahumete, praetextu religionis dominandi potentatum quaesivisse; omnia enim in gladium resolvis et gladio saltem ad tributum pervenire contendis. Persuasisti quemlibet in sua lege salvari posse ac quod deus fidelium constantiam diligat, variantes vero nequaquam. Deinde accipis gladium quasi illos velis ad varietatem compellere, quos animasti constantes manere, sed das optionem ipsis, ut vel varient vel tributum solvant. Quis non intelligit finem tuae religionis zelum et ritum tuae legis tantum ad hoc tendere, ut domineris?" See Aikin and Aleksander 2013: 223.

Muhammad.⁵⁴ However, Norman Daniel was right in pointing out that Christians adopted this view of Islam as religion of the sword "while at the same time enthusiastically embracing the almost identical doctrines of Crusade."⁵⁵ This doctrine was embraced not only by Pius II but by Cusanus too. Readers of Cusanus, and perhaps scholars in particular, should take notice of it.

Conclusion

Pius II was not far from leading a crusade to Constantinople. If successful, the crusade was apparently to proceed to Jerusalem. Cusanus willingly assisted in attempting to set this crusade in motion. His crusading spirit is manifested *inter alia* by his presence in Mantua and his hearty welcome of key *personae*, such as Albert III, margrave of Brandenburg, who arrived to express their support of the crusade or reaffirm their promise of participation. Although documented in Pius II's commentaries, this significant piece of evidence has until recently been overlooked by researchers. Cusanus's treatment of Islam, in his *Cribratio alkorani*, as a religion of the sword, and his harsh denigration of Muhammad, resonate with his crusading spirit. But even if Cusanus was captivated by this spirit at an early stage of his career, perhaps as early as the 1430s, even then we should not consider the *Cribratio* as a sort of continuation or completion of *De pace fidei*.⁵⁶ John Monfasani is right in defining the *Cribratio* as a serious work of refutation.⁵⁷ In his harsh denigration of Muhammad, Cusanus was following a medieval polemical routine, adopting the Christian medieval pattern of attacking Muhammad. Christian polemicists wished to discredit Islam by discrediting Muhammad, and Cusanus followed suit. Moreover, similarly to such polemicists, who were also crusading enthusiasts, and to

---

54. The teachings of Jihad are found in Surahs 2, 4–5, 8–9, 11, 13–14, 22, 25, 29, 36, 38–39, 41, 44, 60, 73, 86, 120. For the meaning and role of Jihad in Islam, see Lewis 1991: 71–90; Daniel 1993: 131–57 (ch. IV); Lewis and Churchill 2008: 145–54; Bonner 2006.
55. Daniel 1993: 131.
56. As opposed to Meuthen 2010: 130: "Sifting the Qur'an (*Cribratio Alkorani*) presents similar thoughts [to *De pace fidei*]," and Valkenberg 2014: 35: "we meet here an eschatological vision of interreligious harmony" (sic!).
57. Monfasani 2019: 104–105.

Pius II, Cusanus not only supported a crusade against the Turks but linked himself to a holy war that also targeted Jerusalem—an objective, second to Constantinople, that Pius II as head of a full-scale crusade was to reach. As far as the Holy Land was concerned, this was to be a war that Erasmus would have harshly denounced, just as he condemned more than half a century later Leo X's plan to wage a crusade against the Turks. Cusanus, cardinal and polymath, a valued philosopher and theologian, the author of the irenic *De pace fidei*, was not unattached to the crusading project of his time. Apparently, the respect and appreciation we tend to feel for Cusanus, due to his philosophical works and the scholarly reputation he earned, make it difficult for us to identify and admit the anti-Muslim nature of his *Cribratio* as well as his devotion to the crusade. However, he worked with Pius II to set a large-scale crusade in motion which, if successful, would attempt to reach Jerusalem. Fortunately, this non-defensive war never materialized.

Author biography

Nathan Ron is a research fellow at the School of History, University of Haifa, Israel. He is the author of five books: *Erasmus and the "Other": On Turks, Jews, Amerindians and Indigenous Peoples* (New York: Palgrave Macmillan, 2019); *Erasmus: Intellectual of the 16th Century* (New York: Palgrave Macmillan, 2021); *Erasmus, the Turks, and Islam* (Tel Aviv: Resling, 2022) (in Hebrew); *Nicholas of Cusa and Muhammad: A Critical Revisit* (New York: Peter Lang, 2023); *Erasmus and the Jews: Humanism and Antisemitism in Early Modern Europe* (Haifa: Pardes Publishing, 2023) (in Hebrew). Ron is the author of numerous articles, among them: "Erasmus' Attitude toward Islam in Light of Nicholas of Cusa's *De pace fidei* and *Cribratio Alkorani*," *Revista Española de Filosofía Medieval* 26/1 (2019): 113–36; and (with Thomas Izbicki) "Nicholas of Cusa and the Ottoman Threat to Christendom," *Medieval Encounters* 28 (2022): 129–47.

References

Primary sources

Cusanus, N. (2002), *Opera omnia iussu et auctoritate Academiae litterarum heidelbergensis ad codicum fidem edita: Sermones IV (1455–1463)*, edited by E. Hoffmann and R. Klibansky. Hamburg: Felix Meiner.

Erasmus, D. (1969–), *Opera Omnia* (=ASD). Amsterdam: Elsevier.

Erasmus, D. (1974–), *Collected Works of Erasmus* (=CWE). Toronto: University of Toronto Press.

Hopkins, J., trans. (2001), *Complete Philosophical and Theological Treatises of Nicholas of Cusa*, 2 vols. Minneapolis: The Arthur J. Banning Press.

Pius II (2003–2007), *Commentaries*, edited by M. Meserve and M. Simonetta, 2 vols. Cambridge, MA: Harvard University Press.

Secondary sources

Aikin, S. F., and J. Aleksander (2013), "Nicholas of Cusa's *De pace fidei* and the Meta-exclusivism of Religious Pluralism," *International Journal for Philosophy of Religion* 74: 219–35. https://doi.org/10.1007/s11153-012-9367-0

Babinger, F. (1978), *Mehmed the Conqueror and His Time*. Princeton: Princeton University Press.

Biechler, J. E. (1999), "A New Face toward Islam: Nicholas of Cusa and John of Segovia," in G. Christianson and T. M. Izbicki (eds.), *Nicholas of Cusa: In Search of God and Wisdom*, 185–202. Leiden: Brill.

Biechler, J. E., and H. L. Bond (1990), *Nicholas of Cusa on Interreligious Harmony: Text, Concordance and Translation of* De Pace Fidei. Lewiston, NY: Edwin Mellen Press.

Bisaha, N. (2004a), "Pope Pius II and the Crusade," in N. Housley (ed.), *Crusading in the Fifteenth Century: Message and Impact*, 39–52. New York: Palgrave Macmillan.

Bisaha, N. (2004b), *Creating East and West: Renaissance Humanists and the Ottoman Turks*. Philadelphia: University of Pennsylvania Press.

Bisaha, N. (2008), "Discourses of Power and Desire: The Letters of Aeneas Sylvius Piccolomini (1453)," in D. E. Bornstein and D. S. Peterson (eds.), *Florence and Beyond: Culture, Society and Politics in Renaissance Italy: Essays in Honour of John M. Najemy*, 121–34. Toronto: Victoria University, Centre for Reformation and Renaissance Studies.

Bonner, M. (2006), *Jihad in Islamic History: Doctrines and Practice*. Princeton: Princeton University Press.

Burton, S. J. G. et al., eds. (2019), *Nicholas of Cusa and the Making of the Early Modern World*. Leiden: Brill.

Cook, D. (2015), *Understanding Jihad*. Oakland: University of California Press.

Cotta-Schønberg, M., ed. and trans. (2019a), *The Oration Moyses vir Dei of Enea Silvio Piccolomini (24 April 1452, Rome)*. Online: https://halshs.archives-ouvertes.fr/halshs-01064759/document.

Cotta-Schønberg, M., ed. and trans. (2019b), *The Oration "Quamvis omnibus" of Enea Silvio Piccolomini (16 May 1454, Regensburg)*. Online: https://hal.archives-ouvertes.fr/hal-01086738/document.

Cotta-Schønberg, M., ed. and trans. (2019c), *The Oration "Constantinopolitana clades" of Enea Silvio Piccolomini (15 October 1454, Frankfurt)*. Online: https://hal.archives-ouvertes.fr/hal-01097147/document.

Cotta-Schønberg, M., ed. and trans. (2019d), *The Oration "Cum bellum hodie" of Pope Pius II (26 September 1459, Mantua)*. Online: https://hal.archives-ouvertes.fr/hal-01184169/document.

Cotta-Schønberg, M., ed. and trans. (2019e), *The Oration "Septimo jam exacto mense" of Pope Pius II (14 January 1460, Mantova)*. Online: https://hal.archives-ouvertes.fr/hal-01187186/document.

Daniel, N. (1993), *Islam and the West: The Making of an Image*. Oxford: Oneworld.

Duclow, D. F. et al. (2019), "Responding to the Qur'an: Cusanus, his Contemporaries and Successors," *Revista Española de Filosofía Medieval* 26/1.

Euler, W. A. (2014), "A Critical Survey of Cusanus's Writings on Islam," in I. C. Levy et al. (eds.), *Nicholas of Cusa and Islam: Polemic and Dialogue in the Late Middle Age*, 20–29. Leiden: Brill.

Halff, M. (2019), "Did Nicholas of Cusa Talk to Muslims? Revisiting Cusanus' Sources for Cribratio Alkorani and Interfaith Dialogue," *Revista Española de Filosofía Medieval* 26/1: 15–28.

Halff, M. (2020), "The Pope's Agents in Constantinopole: Eugenius IV Legation on the Eve of the Council of Ferrara-Florence," *Mediterranea. International Journal on the Transfer of Knowledge* 5: 91–151. https://doi.org/10.21071/mijtk.v5i.12254

Hankins, J. (1995), "Renaissance Crusaders: Humanist Crusade Literature in the Age of Mehmed II," *Dumbarton Oaks Papers* 49: 111–207. https://doi.org/10.2307/1291712

Helmrath J., and T. Woelki, eds. (2016), *Acta Cusana*, vol. 2. Hamburg: Felix Miner.

Helmrath J., and T. Woelki, eds. (2020), *Acta Cusana*, vol. 2, fasc. 6: *1457 Juni–1458 September 30*. Hamburg: Felix Miner.

Hoeppner Moran Cruz, J. A. (1999), "Popular Attitudes toward Islam in Medieval Europe," in D. R. Blanks and M. Frassetto (eds.), *Western Views of Islam in Medieval and Early Modern Europe*, 55–82. New York: St. Martin's Press.

Hollmann, J. (2017), *The Religious Concordance: Nicholas of Cusa and Christian-Muslim Dialogue*. Leiden: Brill.

Hopkins, J. (1994), *A Miscellany on Nicholas of Cusa*. Minneapolis: The Arthur J. Banning Press.

Housley, N. (1992), *The Later Crusades: From Lyons to Alcazar, 1274–1580*. Oxford: Oxford University Press.

Housley, N. (2004), "Giovanni da Capistrano and the Crusade of 1456," in N. Housley (ed.), *Crusading in the Fifteenth Century: Message and Impact*, 94–115. Basingstoke: Palgrave Macmillan.

Housley, N. (2006), *Contesting the Crusades*. Oxford: Blackwell.

Housley, N. (2012a), "Pope Pius II and Crusading," *Crusades* 11/1: 209–247. https://doi.org/10.1080/28327861.2012.12220342

Housley, N. (2012b), *Crusading and the Ottoman Threat, 1453–1505*. Oxford: Oxford University Press.

Housley, N. (2017), "Aeneas Silvius Piccolomini, Nicholas of Cusa, and the Crusade: Conciliar, Imperial, and Papal Authority." *Church History* 86/3: 643–67. https://doi.org/10.1017/S0009640717001275

Housley, N. (2018), *The Ottoman Threat and Crusading on the Eastern Border of Christendom During the 15th Century*. Leiden: Brill.

Inalcik, H. (1989), "The Ottoman Turks and the Crusades, 1451–1522," in H. W. Hazard and N. P. Zacour (eds.), *A History of the Crusade*, vol. 6, 311–53. Madison, WI: University of Wisconsin Press.

Izbicki, T. M. (1999), "The Possibility of Dialogue with Islam in the Fifteenth Century," in G. Christianson and T. M. Izbicki (eds.), *Nicholas of Cusa: In Search of God and Wisdom. Essays in Honor of Morimichi Watanabe by the American Cusanus Society*, 175–83. Leiden: Brill.

Izbicki, T. M. (2019a), "The Legate Grants Indulgences: Cusanus in Germany in 1450–1453," in T. M. Izbicki et al. (eds.), *Nicholas of Cusa and Times of Transition: Essays in Honor of Gerald Christianson*, 81–95. Leiden: Brill.

Izbicki, T. M. (2019b), "Juan de Torquemada, Nicholas of Cusa and Pius II on the Islamic Promise of Paradise." *Revista Española de Filosofía Medieval* 26/1: 97–112.

Izbicki, T. M. et al., eds. (2019), *Nicholas of Cusa and Times of Transition: Essays in Honor of Gerald Christianson*. Leiden: Brill.

Levy, I. C. et al., eds. (2014), *Nicholas of Cusa and Islam: Polemic and Dialogue in the Late Middle Age*. Leiden: Brill.

Lewis, B. (1991), *The Political Language of Islam*. Chicago and London: University of Chicago Press.

Lewis, B. E., and B. E. Churchill (2008), *Islam: The Religion and the People*. Upper Saddle River, NJ: Pearson Prentice Hall.

Meuthen, E. (1972), "Nikolaus von Kues auf dem Regensburger Reichstag 1454," in Herausgegeben von den Mitarbeitern des Max-Planck-Instituts für Geschichte, *Festschrift für Hermann Heimpel*, 482–99. Göttingen: Vandenhoeck & Ruprecht.

Meuthen, E. (2010), *Nicholas of Cusa: A Sketch for a Biography*, trans. David Crowner and Gerald Christianson. Washington, DC: The Catholic University of America Press.

Monfasani, J. (2019), "Cusanus, the Greeks, and Islam," in T. M. Izbicki et al. (eds.), *Nicholas of Cusa and Times of Transition: Essays in Honor of Gerald Christianson*, 96–112. Leiden: Brill.

Mougel, D. A. (1896), *Denys le Chartreux, 1402–1471. Sa vie, son rôle, une nouvelle édition de ses ouvrages*. Montreuil-sur-Mer: Imprimerie de la Chartreuse de N.-D. des Prés.

O'Brien, E. (2009), "Arms and Letters: Julius Caesar, the *Commentaries* of Pope Pius II, and the Politicization of Papal Imagery." *Renaissance Quarterly* 62: 1057–1097. https://doi.org/10.1086/650023

Ocker, C. (2004), "Contempt for Friars and Jews in Late Medieval Germany," in S. J. McMichael and S. E. Myers (eds.), *Friars and Jews in the Middle Ages and Renaissance*, 119–46. Leiden: Brill.

O'Malley, J. W. (1979), *Praise and Blame in Renaissance Rome: Rhetoric, Doctrine, and Reform in the Sacred Orators of the Papal Court, c. 1450–1521*. Durham, NC: Duke University Press.

Ron, N. (2014), "The Christian Peace of Erasmus," *The European Legacy* 19/1: 27–42. https://doi.org/10.1080/10848770.2013.859793

Ron, N. (2019), "Erasmus' Attitude toward Islam in Light of Nicholas of Cusa's De pace fidei and Cribratio alkorani." *Revista Española de Filosofía Medieval* 26/1: 113–36. https://doi.org/10.21071/refime.v26i1.11846

Schwoebel, R. (1967), *The Shadow of the Crescent: The Renaissance Image of the Turk 1453–1517*. New York: St. Martin's Press.

Setton, K. M. (1978), *The Papacy and the Levant*, vol. II. Philadelphia: American Philosophical Society.

Valkenberg, P. (2014), "Una Religio in Rituum Varietate: Religious Pluralism, the Qur'an, and Nicholas of Cusa," in I. C. Levy, R. George-Tvrtković, and D. F. Duclow (eds.), *Nicholas of Cusa and Islam*, 30–48. Leiden: Brill.

Van der Meer, M. (2009), "World Without End: Nicholas of Cusa's View of Time and Eternity," in A. Alasdair et al. (eds.), *Christian Humanism: Essays in Honour of Arjo Vanderjagt*, 317–37. Leiden: Brill.

Von Martels, Z. (2003), "More Matter and Less Art: Aeneas Silvius Piccolomini and the Delicate Balance between Eloquent Words and Deeds," in Z. von

Martels and A. J. Vanderjagt (eds.), *Pius II—'El Più Expeditivo Pontifice': Selected Studies on Aeneas Silvius Piccolomini (1405–1464)*, 205–27. Leiden: Brill.

Watanabe, M. (2004), "An Appreciation," in C. M. Bellitto et al. (eds.), *Introducing Nicholas of Cusa: A Guide to a Renaissance Man*, 3–24. Mahwah, NJ: Paulist Press.

Watanabe, M. (2011), *Nicholas of Cusa: A Companion to His Life and Times*, ed. G. Christianson and T. M. Izbicki. Farnham: Ashgate.

Watanabe, M. (2014), "Cusanus, Islam, and Religious Tolerance," in I. C. Levy et al. (eds.), *Nicholas of Cusa and Islam: Polemic and Dialogue in the Late Middle Ages*, 9–19. Leiden: Brill.

Weber, B. (2017), "Toward a Global Crusade? The Papacy and the Non-Latin World in the Fifteenth Century," in N. Housley (ed.), *Reconfiguring the Fifteenth-Century Crusade*, 11–44. London: Palgrave Macmillan.

Chapter 3
The Political Peace of Luis Vives and the Religious Peace of Pico della Mirandola: Philosophical Perspectives between Italy and Spain

Manuel Lopéz Forjas and Veronica Tartabini

> Wrath and revenge from men and gods remove,
> far, far too dear to every mortal breast,
> Sweet to the soul, as honey to the taste;
> Gathering like vapors of a noxious kind
> from fiery blood, and darkening the entire mind!
>
> *Iliad*, XVIII, 107ff.

Introduction

The Early Modern European Age is a scene of war and religious unrest. While Charles V of Habsburg (1500–1558) consolidates his power with the restoration of the Holy Roman Empire, so vast that the sun never sets in its dominions, the Council of Trent (1545–1563) tries to defend Catholic orthodoxy against attacks by Protestant states and the Islamic world. These religious wars and conflicts fracture the spirituality of the western world. Peace, thus, becomes an objective of the reflections of the great humanists of the territories most directly involved in the interests of the Church of Rome and the Monarchy of the House of Austria in Madrid:

Italy and Spain. The relationships between these two cultures have never been so intense and interconnected.[1]

There are, above all, three humanists, two Italian and one Spanish, who allow us to reconstruct the complex altarpiece of the cultural connections between these two powers: Marsilio Ficino (Figline Valdarno, 1433–Florence, 1499), Pico della Mirandola (Mirandola, 1463–Florence, 1494) and Juan Luis Vives (Valencia, 1493–Bruges, 1540). Discussing its reception in Spain means addressing the problem of the existence of the Spanish Renaissance.

Renaissance and Humanism between Italy and Spain

It is possible to imagine a humanist current that blew into Spain from Italy, but what must be borne in mind is that this movement was circular. At the beginning of the Cinquecento, the number of Spaniards who traveled to Italy was considerable. Before the success of the Italian centers of knowledge dating back to the pontificate of Martin V (1369–1431) that started with the Council of Constance (1417), the prestigious centers that attracted Castilian university students were Toulouse, Montpellier, and Paris. The largest number of students came from the religious world and this helps us to understand why they preferred ecclesiastical centers to other venues: they wanted to have brilliant careers. It was above all this category that enjoyed constant contact with the papal curia, throughout the pontificate of the so-called antipope Benedict XIII from Avignon (Pedro Martínez de Luna, 1328–1423).[2] With Ottavio di Camillo, let us remember that, thanks to the strategic election of bishops and a reform campaign that spilled over into the structure of Spanish schools, that pope undoubtedly facilitated exchange between those two countries.

With regard to Italy, the Albornoz College of Bologna began gaining recognition and had achieved notoriety in the Iberian context since its foundation in 1367. Later, the whole country got used to being a Renaissance cultural destination. It should be clarified that before this

1. For an in-depth look at the reign of Charles V of Habsburg, see Martínez Millán 2011. Regarding the reign of Felipe II, it is advisable to consult Martínez Millán 1998.
2. Di Camillo 1976: 20–21.

season of changes, ecclesiastical positions were usually granted to aristocratic figures, but from then on they became available to university students, who did not always belong to the nobility. Meanwhile the bishops were trying to find new collaborators among the men of letters to avail themselves of their best skills. The auxiliaries, who accompanied the high officials of the Church on their curial visits, could meet Italian officials and teach their disciplines or their humanistic interests. In this context, we know that there were many Castilians who stayed in Italy a few years, while others moved and hoped to get an important position. All of them acted as catapult centers for other teachers and students to approach Rome in search of an important position next to a prelate or in the Pontifical See. This historical data serves to mark the fact that there were students of Spanish origin who ended up conquered by the charm of the Italian humanist training and wanted to join this cultural movement. The following fact is a fundamental example of the axis that gives stability to our research, namely: the influences between Spain and Italy have never ceased, and especially in the Renaissance period, when they enjoyed perfect circularity.[3]

This data is the fruit of a great academic effort that the Hispanists of recent generations have made to overcome an entire historiographic and anthropological tradition that had put in doubt the existence of the Renaissance in Spain. Even Jacob Burckhardt,[4] despite the extent of his studies which are still a reference, ended up being in part a "victim" of a derogatory reading of Iberian culture at that time which we cannot omit. Ángel Gómez Moreno[5] offers a detailed tour of what was a real confrontation between two lines of investigation: the first one was dedicated to favoring the original contribution of the "civilizing" Germans in the pre-humanist formation process against the Spanish one which was

---

3. Di Camillo 1976: 229–31.
4. See also Byrne 2015: 10.
5. Gómez Moreno 2015: 13–31. The development of the analysis that runs through the pages of this chapter, marked by clarity and exhaustiveness, is our privileged guide to study the criticism against the concept of lack of Renaissance in Spain. Here we share fundamental data to delve into this theoretical problem. From the same author, a less recent text is also recommended: Gómez Moreno 1994. Still, in the introduction to this work, it is possible to discover the complex and rich interweaving of relationships between Italian and Spanish humanists.

seen as "inhuman"; and the second one, occupied in undoing from its base that vision of the events of the Renaissance period. The truth is that there is a culture characterized by splendor that predominated in Spain throughout the Renaissance, at a time when Italian Humanism could take root in that land with unparalleled strength. Let us mention just one example: in the *Novelas ejemplares*, in *La Galatea* and in *Don Quijote*, Miguel de Cervantes (1547–1616) follows an author as a model, that is, the Italian Matteo Bandello (1485–1561). Also, the Marquis of Santillana (1398–1458) and his library with copies of Italian works could be another example.[6] So, let's say with certainty, that there was a Renaissance in Spain. This country was the first to receive Italian Humanism and by adding some characteristics due to its national history, it caused Spanish Humanism to sprout.[7] Ottavio di Camillo explains the following:

> When one examines Renaissance Humanism in Spain, Italian Humanism readily comes to mind because it has long been recognized that this historical phenomenon originated in Italy toward the middle of the fourteenth century and from there spread to the rest of Europe within a period of a century and a half. Documentary evidence from various sources confirms an early diffusion of this movement to Spain and reveals, at the same time, the existence of certain favorable conditions that made the reception of Italian Humanism possible and even necessary.[8]

Let us bear in mind that three waves of Humanism are distinguished, after the early contributions of Francesco Petrarca (1303–1374), Giovanni Boccaccio (1313–1375), and Lino Coluccio Salutati (1332–1406). In the

---

6. Íñigo López de Hurtado de Mendoza, better known as the Marquis of Santillana, stands out for representing in a special way Spanish pre-humanism and for his studies related to the production of Dante Alighieri (1265–1321). To discover the relationship between the Marquis of Santillana and Italy, it is advisable to read Lawrance 1989. Also quoted by Gómez Moreno 2015: 23. Also, in Di Camillo 1976: 67–110.
7. Let us not forget that the Catholic monarchs wanted an Italian tutor for Prince John, Antonio Geraldini (1448 / 1449–1489), and his brother Ambrosio, also known as Marineo Siculus (1444–1536), worked for the greats of Spain. This is an index of a Castilian sensitivity towards humanist training, whose axis was the philological knowledge that spread from Italy at the top of the modern Spanish state. Fontán 1992: 21.
8. Di Camillo 1988: 55.

first half of the fifteenth century, a philological, rhetorical, and grammatical Humanism stands out; whose most eminent representatives were Lorenzo Valla (1407–1457)[9] and Leonardo Bruni (1370–1444). In the second half of that century, another Humanism shaped by the philosophical and theological speculation of Marsilio Ficino and Pico della Mirandola stands out; as did a later Humanism (sixteenth century) and foreign to Italy, with a marked ethical-Christian character and a strong pragmatic and pedagogical projection, embodied by the Valencian Juan Luis Vives, the Englishman Thomas More (1478–1535), and the Frenchman Guillaume Budé (1467–1540).[10] But one element is perceived that unites all the ingredients and all the waves that we have just listed: the dignity of man, based on his divine origin. Starting from that common divine root, humanists demonstrated the need for peace between every type of man and civilization. After this necessary panorama to justify the communion between Italy and Spain, let's discuss Ficino's Neoplatonism, the peace wanted by his student Pico and his reception in the land of the Habsburgs.

Pico della Mirandola and religious peace

> I want you to know, that the true man and the Idea of man are one and the same. And yet none of us on earth are real men, while we are separated from God because we are detached from our Idea: which is our form. Divine loving in a pious way will reduce us to that.[11]

---

9. It must be remembered that Lorenzo Valla had a direct link with Spain because he was in the service of Alfonso V of Aragon (1396–1458), accompanying him in his conquest of the kingdom of Naples. In this court, the one who could be remembered as the greatest among Italian humanists, he was able to obtain all the necessary material support to carry out his work as a philologist—an extraordinary example of collaboration between Italy and Spain in favor of the development of European humanism. Reventlow 1999: 22.
10. García Gibert 2010: 238.
11. Ficino 1992: 133. It is important to note the enormous success that the rereading of Plato's *Symposium* had throughout the history of universal philosophy. Directing our attention only to Spanish thought, we highlight, for example, the work of Ortega, which can also be consulted in its Italian translation: Ortega y Gasset 2012. In relation to the Orteguian work focused on the importance of language, it is worth highlighting the reflection on the centrality of the word in *Humanism* by Francisco Rico, who states: "authentic human freedom is exercised through language, through

These words constitute the core of the mystical philosophy of Marsilio Ficino. This author, as is widely known, was the highest representative of the Platonic Academy founded by Cosimo de'Medici (1389–1464) and consolidated by Lorenzo the Magnificent (1449–1492). His work as a humanist focused mainly on the translation from Greek to Latin of the heritage of Plato, the Neo-Platonists and the *Hermetica*. From this point of view, we could recognize a certain similarity between the work performed by Ficino and that developed by the Toledo School of Translators.[12] At the height of the Middle Ages, this Spanish school was dedicated to translating Aristotle and the great authors of the Arab world. Without his intermediary activity, with great probability, the West would have been orphaned of the great classical authorities offered by Antiquity: the Stagirite and his teacher.

Now, the weight of Ficino's production in Italy is unquestionable, but thanks to the in-depth research of Susan Byrne,[13] we know that the same can be legitimately affirmed with respect to Spain. Throughout the sixteenth and seventeenth centuries, Hispanic intellectuals thought of the Italian philosopher as an unquestionable humanist authority.[14] Even King Felipe II had a manuscript of the Platonic translations of the Florentine intellectual in El Escorial.[15] Other Hispanic intellectuals throughout the centuries could not do without the philosophical and philological effort of the author of the *Theologia platonica* (1482): Miguel Servet (1511–1553),[16] Fray Luis de León (1527–1591), Pedro Malón de Chaide (1530–1589), San

---

disciplines, already in civil life, already in contemplation. Because with these tools man can dominate the earth, build society, obtain all knowledge and be, thus, all things (a microcosm), truly realize the divine possibilities promised by having been created in the likeness of God." Rico 1997: 171.

12. We recommend an introduction to the history of Spanish thought with some clarifying data even on medieval times in Martínez Arancón 1986: 27–78. To delve into the subject: Abellán 1979: 210–24.
13. Byrne offers a detailed work on the reception of Marsilio Ficino in Spain, which deals with his presence in the main libraries of the country. Ficino's texts and his translations are analyzed by Byrne 2015. To have an exhaustive map of the content of this enormous research effort, the following review is recommended: Kagay 2019: 671–73.
14. Byrne 2015: 4–5.
15. Byrne 2015: 18.
16. Byrne 2015: 15.

Juan de la Cruz (1542–1591), Cervantes (1547–1616),[17] Luis de Góngora (1561–1627), Sor Juana Inés de la Cruz (1648–1695),[18] Menéndez Pelayo (1856–1912),[19] among many others. Copies of the translation of Plato's complete works[20] and the other Neo-Platonists reassessed by Marsilio circulated in private libraries and in the great study centers of the Hispanic monarchy. For example, Hernando Colón (1488–1539), son of the famous Cristóbal Colón (1451–1506), owned one of the full copies of the commentaries on Dionysus. Diego Hurtado de Mendoza (1504–1575), who was a student in Salamanca and an ambassador in Rome, possessed the handwritten translation of Dantesque *De Monarchia*,[21] signed by Marsilio himself. It should be remembered that Diego was a friend of Saint Teresa of Jesus (1515–1582) and that his library ended up in the hands of Felipe II (1527–1598) in El Escorial.

Johann Heinrich Boeckler recognizes a direct relationship especially between Ficino and two universities on the Iberian Peninsula: Coimbra in Portugal and Alcalá de Henares in Spain.[22] Also, at the University of Salamanca, Ficinian theological texts had their place.[23] At the beginning of the twentieth century, the historian Urbano González de Calle (1879–1966) continued to emphasize that many religious orders, especially the Jesuits, preferred Ficino's Neoplatonism to the Aristotelianism of the then prevailing scholasticism.[24] For example, the Jesuit Juan Andrés (1740–1817) admired the Neoplatonic and Plotinian method of the Italian thinker, against the more sterile scholastic method. According to Byrne, from this aspect, we can discover what the heritage of the Florentine Platonic Academy's teaching was in the thoughts of Pico della Mirandola:

> This is resonant of the first Christian Neoplatonism of the early Common Era, when Church Fathers borrowed from Platonic

17. The study presented on the concepts of Love and Beauty is very interesting, in a comparison between Marsilio Ficino and Miguel de Cervantes, see Byrne 2015: 80–94.
18. Byrne 2015: 61.
19. Byrne 2015: 11.
20. Byrne 2015: 18.
21. Byrne 2015: 24.
22. Byrne 2015: 5.
23. Byrne 2015: 31–32.
24. Byrne 2015: 5.

thought so as to compete with the already-established philosophical schools. It also echoes other Renaissance thinkers, such as Pico della Mirandola (1463–94), who saw philosophy in the service of religion. [...] Ficino, [...] saw "the Platonic doctrine as an authority comparable to that of the divine law" [...], not a rival to Christianity but rather an equal partner, in "complementary roles" with the goal to "unite philosophy and revelation."[25]

Now we can understand the passage from Ficino quoted at the beginning of this reflection, according to what Giuseppe Rensi[26] explains to us. We have to consider this text as the true manifesto of the mystical doctrine of love in the Renaissance. In other words, this writing not only has a literary value, but also a philosophical one because it is an interpretation of Christianity with the conceptual weapons of Platonism. It is a palpable example of incalculable beauty, of the defense of the dignity of man as a result of a dialogue built between God and ancient pagan culture.[27] Pico thus finds his journey to undertake to shape his religious and philosophical peace.

Indeed, Marsilio as well as Pico ended up under suspicion[28] in the territory of the Spanish Inquisition and its "black legend," because they pushed the spread of dangerous doctrines that brought man too close to God. Menéndez Pidal recalled that Plotinus's Neoplatonic translations of magic had an impact on Maimonides (1138–1204) and Miguel Servet. But despite that, as recognized by Benito Jerónimo Feijoo himself (1676–1764),[29] at the beginning of the eighteenth century, Ficino was considered completely orthodox on Spanish soil and his production could be studied without any risk. Thanks to this permission of Iberian Catholicism, perhaps Italian Humanism managed to penetrate the depths of Spanish

25. Byrne 2015: 8.
26. Ficino 1992: 163–66.
27. The information offered by the Protestant theologian Henning Graf Reventlow is very suggestive, underlining the strong interest that Marsilio Ficino nurtured at the same time, both in favor of Platonism and biblical studies. We do know that, at the end of his earthly experience, the Florentine humanist was about to write a commentary on the complete biblical heritage. In line with Ficinian works of Christian orientation, some fragments of his interpretation of the Pauline letters have survived to this day. Reventlow 1999: 39.
28. Byrne 2015: 19.
29. Ibid.

spirituality[30] throughout the Modern Age, leaving its mark on the great Castilian mystics.

Pico and Saint Teresa of Jesus are not incompatible, like Ficino and San Juan de la Cruz[31] or Fray Luis de León,[32] the editor of the first complete Teresian works. From the serenity of the Florentine Academy, an international intellectual and mystical movement is nurtured, whose influence is passed onto the Hispanic empire. It looks to the ancient pagan and Christian world to find a solution to the ills of modern man. A man who has discovered new horizons in the New World and who ends up torn between political, philosophical, and religious wars. In relation to Pico della Mirandola and his conception of peace, we now delve into the consequences of this entire intercultural historical process.

It is easy to imagine the "Prince of Harmony," observing the famous fresco "The School of Athens" by Raphael, despite having been made after his death. In Vatican City, the philosopher would have been ecstatic at the contemplation of all those illustrious thinkers gathered together. Effectively, in *De Ente et Uno* (1491), Pico tries to find an agreement between Platonism and Aristotelianism in conflict in his cultural environment. In *Heptaplus* (1489) and in the famous *Oratio Elegantissima* (1486), he tries to find in Christianity a point of connection between the authors of classical Greek philosophy and the Orientals like Averroes (1126–1198). No one is missing among the eminent protagonists of the history of thought in that immense fresco, except Pico. It must have been a testimony of that rejection that the Holy See herself had directed against him and his desire to achieve religious and, consequently, political peace through an ecumenical council.

Who exactly was Pico of Mirandola and why could we consider him the defender of philosophical and religious peace in the Early Modern Age? With Luis Martínez Gómez, let us remember:

> Count of Concordia, by his noble title, Prince of Concord (Dux Concordiae) reduplicatively surnamed by his contemporary, admirer

---

30. On spirituality and spiritual literature between Italy and Spain in the sixteenth century, see Bertini and Pelazza 1980.
31. For an in-depth look at the connection between Pico della Mirandola and San Juan de la Cruz, see Martínez 2000: 335–72.
32. Byrne 2015: 108.

and friend, at a critical time, Marsilio Ficino, Pico is on the list of men who have felt the need and have glimpsed and dreamed of the possibility of a universal peace, reconciliation or concord, a Leibniz, before *tempus*.³³

With Pico we meet a man whose very existence and training are a hymn to peaceful and enriching interculturality. In fact, this humanist prince studies and creates his works in Bologna (jurisprudence), Ferrara (fine arts), Padua (scholastic philosophy and theology), Florence (Platonism), Pavia, Paris (philosophy), Perugia (studies of the Kabbalah), and Rome.³⁴ Pico comes into contact with all the fundamental theological and philosophical movements of his time: Aristotelianism, Averroism, Scholasticism, Neoplatonism, the Oxford Occamist tradition, the Kabbalistic and magical heritage. He achieves all this while perfectly mastering the languages of the ancient civilizations and confronting the imposing events in their historical context.

It should not be forgotten that Lorenzo the Magnificent died in 1492; Alexander VI (1431–1503) was the new pontiff; Columbus arrived in America; Isabel de Castilla (1451–1504) and Fernando de Aragón (1452–1516) conquered Granada and expelled the Jews from Spain.³⁵ This is the world of our humanist prince, and it is precisely in this world that he sets out in search of peace. He does so by communicating directly with the Hispanic culture. Following Giuseppe Tognon:

> His first real discovery will be that of Arab-Jewish thought which will bind him to the cenacle of those who were spreading it in Italy, Girolamo Ramusio and above all Elia del Medigo. The latter, master and friend, professor of original philosophy, lends himself to a special translation job and provides Pico with some Averroistic commentaries on [Aristotle's] Metaphysics and Meteors, along with numerous "*questiones*" designed to help him in the study of those difficult texts.³⁶

33. Pico della Mirandola 1984: 74.
34. Goñi Zubieta 2020: 186.
35. We appreciate the historical contextualization of Pico's biography, offered by the author in his "*Cuadro cronológico*": Goñi Zubieta 1996: 11–13.
36. Pico della Mirandola 1987: xxi. See also: "Pico's precise pride will be that he was the first to have explicitly mentioned the true Kabbalah among the Latins, and this is incontrovertible at least as regards the name, so much so that the increasingly

In addition, of these Hispanic authors cited, let us bear in mind Flavio Mithridate (1450–1489),[37] *Antonius Cronicus* (1440?–1502),[38] and Spanish Kabbalist Abraham Abulafia (1240–1291).[39] In short, if Ficino had a place in Spain, in the same way, Pico could soak up Hispanic and oriental culture[40] to elaborate his mystical philosophy.[41] The one who will be most in charge of introducing his ideas on Hispanic soil will be an ambassador of excellence: Antonio de Nebrija (1441–1522).[42] He is the most important Spanish grammarian, a humanist trained in Italy under the influence of Lorenzo Valla.[43]

Moreover, in Alcalá de Henares the first translations of Pico's texts introduced by Nebrija were disseminated. It should not be surprising that it is in this prestigious university campus that Pico's position would find favorable ground. Cardinal Cisneros (1436–1517)[44] promoted the translation of the polyglot Bible in this same headquarter while developing his

---

numerous Renaissance Kabbalistic texts only after him will be condemned by the Church with the express qualification of 'kabbalistic.' The heritage known and studied by Pico is that of Kabbalah, handed down in the Spanish Jewish community: Pico made use of it a few years before the expulsion of the Jews from Spain in 1492 and it is interesting to note that he recognized lullism as a kabbalistic method." Pico della Mirandola 1987: xxxvi.

37. "He also met Guglielmo Raimondo di Moncada, a converted Jew from Sicily, known as Flavio Mithridate, a man of controversial personality (he had fled from Rome to Paris because of a murder) who became Pico's Hebrew language teacher and translated for him some texts at the price of gold. According to his nephew Gianfrancesco, after a month, after studying day and night, he learned Hebrew so that, if not perfectly, he was able to write a correct letter." Goñi Zubieta 2020: 34–35.
38. His real name was Antonio Vinciguerra, he was secretary in the Republic of Venice and among his circle of friends he had a great humanist nucleus, including Pico himself who mentions him in the *Oratio*.
39. Goñi Zubieta 2020: 86.
40. For an updated list of Spanish translations of Pico's works, see: Goñi Zubieta 2020: 204.
41. For a reading of the mystical weight of the *Oratio*: Vega 2001: 195–200.
42. About Nebrija and its link with Italian humanism: Di Camillo 1976: 267–98. In addition to Nebrija's mediating role, it is worth remembering at the beginning of the reception of Pico in Spain, also Juan Rodríguez de Pisa and Bachiller Rúa for their early translations. In-depth studies on the subject of the reception of Pico in Hispanic soil and the role developed by these cited authors appear in González Vega 2012: 248–58; 2014: 437–69.
43. Fontán 1992: 18.
44. Fontán 1992: 21.

religious reform in Franciscan aspects, such as Religious Observance. As we saw previously, Ficino's production was already known in Alcalá de Henares. In Alcalá de Henares, Miguel de Cervantes will soon be born, that dreamer of conciliatory literary peace between the values of medieval chivalry and the bloody contrasts of the Early Modern Age.

Now, if Pico's ideas had spread throughout Spain, the Catholic sovereigns would have had problems with their policy of national consolidation, both at the time of driving out the Arab rulers from Andalusia during the Reconquest and at the time of driving out the Jews. It is Carlos Goñi himself, who invites us to remember this aspect, in his recent biography of the Italian author. For the record, one of the staunch enemies of the *Oratio* and his *Apology* was Cardinal Pedro García (1440–1505), counselor of the Kings of Spain, as witnessed by his *Determinaciones Magistrales* published in 1489.[45] Let's take a better look at the reason why the *Oratio* was such a dangerous text as to request the intervention of the Inquisitor Torquemada (1420–1498). Eugenio Garin says: "His dream of a pax fidei, as well as a *pax philosophorum*, could not fail to be suspicious; his appreciation of Jewish thought could not fail to arouse his reaction."[46]

In the introduction of the *900 tesi* that the Tuscan prince dreamed of defending in Rome in front of the Pope, the learned men and all the men who would have wished it, even financing their displacement, wanted to propose a new concept of man and his existential development.[47] Regarding this theoretical passage, Carlos Goñi speaks of *"antropoteísmo"*.[48]

The Tuscan learns to express his opinion in a free, autonomous, and critical way, measuring himself against all the cultures that had populated the face of the earth up to that moment. The dignity of the human being is not questioned, but the theoretical basis from which it has been defended throughout the centuries. According to Pico, man is the beholder of perfect divine creation; the creature that God has placed in the cosmos to admire and appreciate everything else in his universe. Being a limited

---

45. To delve into the figure and the role played by Pedro García, the following is advised: Pico della Mirandola 1987: xl–xli.
46. Pico della Mirandola 1942: 20.
47. Esmorís Galán 2017: 107.
48. Goñi Zubieta 2020: 23.

entity, which needs to be fulfilled, man is paradoxically the most divine creation of God.

Luis Vives, in his *Fabula de Homine*[49] (1518), underlines this point of Pico's and will think of man as a divinity accepted by the other Greek gods. Man is the one who best knows how to act in the great spectacle of the world, requested by Juno to her husband Jupiter. Man is the actor who, disguised as the father of the gods, loses his humanity and becomes total divinity. Most likely, Pico would agree with this humanistic anthropological view. As Alain Guy reminds us,[50] Pérez de Oliva (1495?–1532) will follow the teaching of both of them. In fact, in the *Oratio*, Man is the great miracle of which Mercury spoke to Asclepius and Pico describes his dignity from the classical Greek, Kabbalistic, Hermetic or Christian patristic and Eastern philosophical traditions. All are compatible with the Christian truth, that is, the one that acclaims that a God made man, and offers man the opportunity to become another divinity: the creator of his own existence. All this is revolutionary and aspires to the complete peace of man both with himself and with all the cultures of the world ambassadors of the only truth.

Also, in the *Ente et Uno*, we perceive an analytical method and a similar purpose, trying to get Plato and Aristotle, the Platonists and Aristotelians to find peace and reconciliation. It is not trivial that Garin considers this text as the summit of Pico's lesson. It is interesting to think that María Zambrano (1904–1991), a Spanish author exiled in Rome, heir to Hispanic and Oriental mystical culture and scholar of the Italian Renaissance, thinks of a union of philosophy and poetry in contemporary thought.[51] Her "poetic reason" would have been very compatible with the *Theologia poetica* of Pico and with the *Theologia platonica* of Ficino. Everyone wanted to access the sacred through culture without barriers, to give meaning to human life through the great truths defended under the

---

49. Vives 1988: 153–62.
50. "Eugenio Ímaz quotes him [Hernán Pérez de Oliva] (Luz en la caverna: 213–14) as one of the masters of humanism, devotee of the Renaissance, and connects him with the pioneers of the Roman rebirth, who were Vives and Pico della Mirandola; thanks to the Salamanca rector, the dignity of man, central topic of the new spirit from Petrarca [...] receives its most complete Spanish expression, at the same time of the Erasmian invasion in the Peninsula." Guy 1985: 89. See also Pérez de Oliva 1995.
51. Zambrano 2006.

slogan of the Christianity of peace. From that, we can see how the challenges of the Renaissance are still valid in contemporary society.

Thinking of other parallels, together with Martínez Gómez, we recognize this desire for "concordism" from Pico,[52] *concidentia oppositorum* following Nicholas of Cusa. He wants to go beyond differences, to reach the "vertex" of unity.[53] Like Cusanus, of course, Pico believes in the man who is a reader of the book of the world written by the Creator, with characters that we should all decipher in the harmony of science.[54] The prince of la Mirandola arranges a dialogue between Scotus, St. Thomas, Avempace, Averroes, Alfarabi, Avicenna, Simplicius, Themistius, Theophrastus, Iamblichus, Plotinus, Proclus, St. Augustine, and many others: "The set and result is, in any case, a system of truth distributed in a highly varied multitude of apparently different positions and at opposite times, in the background harmonizable in one unit."[55] It is the epistemological peaceful harmony that yearns to achieve theological, religious, and perhaps political peace. How is it not possible to think about the book *Europe the Self-Tormentor* (1543) by the Spanish doctor Andrés de Laguna (1499–1559),[56] in which he would have wanted to bring all the European princes into a peaceful agreement in favor of the defense of the Christian religion of the Holy Roman Empire of Charles V. At the end: "there is a continuous line that ends in the demand for tolerance in the face of medieval intransigence culminating in the uses of the Roman and Spanish inquisition."[57] Cusanus himself in *De pace fidei* (1453), makes the cries of the:

> inhumanly persecuted which constitutes the base of a celestial Concilium in the highest of the skies; where a Greek, an Italian, an Arab, a Hindu, a Chaldean, a Jew, a Scythian, a Persian, a Syrian, a Spaniard, a German, a Tatar, an Armenian, a Bohemian and an English dialogue and discuss, to which are added Peter, Paul and

---

52. To delve into the concept of concord in Pico, with analytical perspectives open to more disciplines such as art history: Borghesi 2017: 41–54.
53. Martínez Gómez 1984: 78.
54. Martínez Gómez 1984: 82.
55. Martínez Gómez 1984: 79.
56. Laguna 2001.
57. Martínez Gómez 1984: 83.

Christ himself, the Word, who finally is the one to decide the best answer.[58]

To conclude, Pico defends peace, but it makes him tenacious as a warrior. Martínez Gómez speaks of his "fighting concordism," which aspires to achieve peace, passing through victory against the bad interpreters and readers of the biblical, Chaldean, and Persian sacred books.[59] It even seems that the philosopher does not accept anyone who opposes religious faith, because this attitude is an enemy of peace. He is a thinker in favor of reconciliation with deeply Christian roots, in the sense that he seeks a God who is the source of reconciling love and peace. Let's listen to his words:

> Let us also inquire of the just Job, who entered into a life-covenant with God before he himself was brought forth into life, what the most high God requires above all in those tens of hundreds of thousands who attend him. He will answer that it is peace, in accord with what we read him: "He maketh peace in his high places."[60]

A God who wants his peace poured out both in heaven and on earth, we might add. It is probable, if his voice were heard, that it would be an antidote to many of the wars and lacerations that Europe and the world continue to suffer.[61] Luis Vives is the main Spanish humanist and his vision of the political harmony of Erasmian influence offers us an extraordinary example of compatibility between Castilian humanism and Italian humanism. Pico's legacy in Spain did not go unnoticed despite some blockade attempts of the country's political and confessional customs: they won the concerns and achievements of international Renaissance Humanism.

Catholic Concordance in Nicholas of Cusa

As we have seen, Luis Martínez Gómez was successful in recognizing a deep connection between Pico's conception of Christian humanist peace

---

58. Martínez Gómez 1984: 84.
59. Martínez Gómez 1984: 85.
60. Pico della Mirandola 1984: 230.
61. To delve into the cultural influence of the Renaissance in Europe up to contemporary times, see Pico della Mirandola 1984: xliv.

and Nicholas of Cusa's one. Indeed, this author is central to help us understand in depth some fundamental theoretical cores, both of the Prince of Concord and of the Valencian Vives. Let's find out how this connection was developed.

One of the authors who has had the greatest influence in the history of modern thought is Cardinal Nicholas of Cusa. The *docta ignorantia*, of Augustinian origins, expresses deep down an attitude of humility and openness to receive the divine word in order to follow a model of Christian life. In this sense, it is an intellectual predisposition that is oriented towards a calmness of the body and soul along with an inner harmony (in the microcosm) which is necessarily reflected in social life (the macrocosm).[62] From these first theoretical brushstrokes, we began to listen to the voices of Giovanni Pico and Juan Luis Vives.

The philosophy of Cusano seeks peace and concordance among the members of the Church. He reflected it this way throughout his life. He participated in the Council of Basel (1431), where he was in favor of the authority of the Council against those who argued that the highest authority was in the Pope, above the Council. Fearing the danger of schisms, especially taking into account historical experiences, Cusa maintained that the peace of Christendom would only be achieved through the unity of the Church and its members.[63]

Let us remember then that the peace of faith, the *pax fidei*, in this way, consists of the consolidation of the "supremely concordant harmony"[64] among all the congregations. Only in this way can God live in everyone and for everyone. The balance of Christianity is the balance of humanity. It is a single Church, a single body, but as such it has several members. Thus, Cusano strove to write a treatise that would be his most important work: *De concordantia Catholica* (On the Catholic Concordance).

---

62. This interconnection between macrocosm and microcosm is also held by García Gómez 1996: 113 and by Turró 1985: 139. The notion of how we understand macrocosm is expressed by Cusa himself as "Maximality": "human nature is that [nature] which, if it were elevated unto a union with Maximality, would be the fullness of all the perfections of each and every thing [sic]." Nicholas of Cusa 1995, Book III, 3, para. 198: 119.
63. We agree with the Jesuit father José María de Alejandro Lueiro, one of the first to translate Cusa into Spanish: De Alejandro 1981: xiii.
64. Nicholas of Cusa 1995, II, 1, para. 93: 59.

Cusano organized his treatise taking the Holy Scriptures and the Fathers of the Church as sources of authority, highlighting Saint Thomas Aquinas and, above all, Saint Augustine. He also followed the doctrines of Marsilius of Padua, who in his text *Defensor pacis* (The Defender of Peace), had spoken before him about the concordance of the subjects whose articulation was guaranteed by the prince.[65]

Cusa does not place the humanist authors of the Italian Renaissance, who were writing at the same time as him, in his sources, perhaps with the sole exception of Pope Pius II, Aeneas Silvio Piccolomini.[66] The Italian Renaissance had a strong legal tradition that leads to a consolidated constitutional theory. From this point of view too, we could speak of a certain affinity with Pico. For Cusa, by following Aristotle and especially Saint Thomas Aquinas, human beings are born free by nature and are born as subjects full of freedom. The laws, expressed in a legal constitution, are based on natural law, a doctrine that is justified in human reason as inherent to the human being.[67]

The principle of the regulation of customs, to avoid evil and guarantee harmony and universal agreement, is for Cusa, *consensus*: Common sense or *sensus communis*, whose basis is the natural freedom of all human beings, also following natural reason and opening up to the truth revealed by Christ in the Church (*ekklesia*, community), leads one to collectively establish a code of legal law—in this world, in the militant church—to guarantee order, prosperity, and peace. Following the doctrine of Marsilius of Padua, Cusano develops his theory of consensus and of the social pact, which defines it in this way:

> Note that for the convenience of human society, they wish to make a general agreement to obey their kings. Since in a properly-ordered government, an election of the ruler ought to take place by which he is set up as judge of those who elect him, rightly-ordered lords

---

65. Marsilius of Padua (1275–1342) was an important Italian philosopher and in his book *Defensor pacis* (The Defender of Peace) extended the duty of recalling priests and bishops to respect human law. Marsilius of Padua II, 8: 217. For more information, see the text of Bayona Aznar 2006.
66. In fact, Cusa is considered the teacher of Enea Silvio Piccolomini. Leaños 2007: 33.
67. Nicholas of Cusa 1995, Book II, Chapter XIV, para. 130: 98.

and rulers are established by election, and through election they are established as general judges over those who elect them.[68]

From this point of view, natural law is independent and is above the will of princes; rather, it regulates it, and they must legislate in accordance with the principles of justice that emanate from it. Positive law, as we see, is not separate from customary law; rather, it emanates from it and gives it order. Concordance thus implies social union in a harmony that finds its basis in the Church, but at the same time legal peace and its guarantees are derived from it.

The Church is the Mystical Body of Christ[69] and this dimension consists precisely of an ontological order, which is neither figurative nor representative. Unity in the Church finds its maximum expression in what Cusano defends for his time as the most infallible legal authority, the universal council. The law must serve the community and is not directly responsible for generating poverty or servitude among men. Rather, they are caused by ignorance and by not adhering to the law based on the principles of natural law.[70] The law and its correct interpretation are essential to guarantee the well-being of all members of the community. Christian princes, who have Christ as their model, are in charge of procuring peace and justice, the principles of which are revealed and interpreted by the conciliar doctrine of the Catholic Church. Peace, at a ground level, requires a firm hand from the sovereign to apply justice even in a "medicinal" way.[71]

The emperor receives his power from Christ. In the words of Cusa, "Note that the Christian emperor by virtue of his rulership is the vicar of Christ, the King of kings and Lord of lords."[72] The greatness of the emperor does not come from his exploits or his glories, but from his approach to God who has called him a "patron of peace":

68. Ibid., para. 156: 98–99.
69. Ibid., Book II, Chapter XVIII: 118. This aspect is central to understand Pico and his vision of Christianity and also to delve into the development of the history of Spanish thought such as Fray Luis de León. We cite this last author because of his compatibility with Ficino and his student. Regarding this point, consult: Fray Luis de León 2017.
70. Nicholas of Cusa 1995, Book III, Preface, para. 276: 208–209.
71. Ibid., Book III, Preface, para. 286: 212.
72. Ibid., Book III, Chapter V, para. 341: 234.

> I maintain that the authority of the empire is the greatest. For every King and emperor holds public office for the public good. The public good consists in peace, the goal towards which justice and just wars are directed. But the foundation of peace is to direct subjects to their eternal end, and the means to reach that end are the holy precepts of religion. Hence the first duty of the emperor is to observe them.[73]

To close this part on the relationship between the two powers and their role in guaranteeing peace, it must be said, following Cusa, that the purpose of the ecclesiastical hierarchy will be to watch over the magisterium of the Church and the doctrine of the faith, while that of the emperor will be as he says, "the protector [advocatus] of the universal church."[74]

Cusa's project on peace is specified in his later text *De pace fidei* (On the Peace of the Faith). It consists of an ecumenical dialogue following the taking of Constantinople by the Turks. In line with the above, the end of this dialogue is made with the "agreement of religions" and by highlighting the concept of creating a "perpetual peace." As we said, Pico della Mirandola would have supported this deeply humanistic vision of Christian peace as an intercultural and interdenominational communion.

The invasion of the Turks, therefore, and their approach was not exclusively as an interreligious war, but a stage that the militant Church must go through in order to get closer to the fullness of time. In his letter signed in Innsbruck on December 29, 1454 addressed to the Spanish religionist Juan de Segovia,[75] who also had an Italian education and an important role in relations with the Holy See, Cusa did not hesitate to answer him that even in persecutions, peace is possible and also necessary for the glory of the Church: "I firmly believe that persecution is permitted not for death, but for life, not to suppress faith, but for its exaltation, since it is characteristic of the Church to shine under persecution."[76]

---

73. Ibid., Book III, Chapter V, para. 348: 237.
74. Ibid., Book III, Chapter V, para. 351: 238.
75. For an in-depth analysis of the communication between Juan de Segovia and Cusa, see Di Camillo 1976: 197–203.
76. Nicholas of Cusa 1996, II: 97.

Concordance and pacification in Juan Luis Vives

Turning the attention to Spain, the author who developed a doctrine that echoes the ideals of Cusano and Pico was the Valencian humanist Juan Luis Vives, as early as the sixteenth century. He was a friend of Thomas More and Erasmus of Rotterdam[77] and, after studying in Paris, he developed practically all his intellectual work in Flanders. He served in the Court of Charles V of Germany and I of Spain. He tried to defend Catherine of Aragon in her dispute with Henry VIII of England, taking advantage of precisely his position at court. He had a vocation to recover the classical tradition of Latin, with an emphasis on moral and political philosophy based on the historical events of his time.

His political and moral doctrine on peace is found mainly in three great works: his *De subventione pauperum* (*Treatise on provision for the poor*, 1526), *De concordia et discordia in humano genere* (*Between concord and discord*, 1529) and finally, in continuity with the latter, his text *De pacificatione* (On pacification) also from 1529.

However, a few years before the publication of these texts, we already find important exhortations for peace from Vives. In 1522, he addressed a letter to Pope Adrian VI, *De Europeae statu ac tumultibus* ("On the disturbances in Europe"). More than Cusano himself, Vives already writes in a parallel way to his friend Erasmus of Rotterdam, who had published in 1518 *Querela Pacis* (A treatise on the Complaints of Peace). In a conflictive climate for the European monarchies, faced with the spread of the Lutheran Reformation, the consolidation and expansion of the Turkish-Ottoman Empire, Charles V was crowned Emperor in Aachen in 1520, although his official investiture recognized by the Pope would not be until 1530.

Vives is primarily a Christian writer and the sources on which he relies come mostly from Sacred Scripture. Vives addresses the Pope to exhort him as the head of Christianity to pacify religions at a time of turmoil in Europe. At this time war was developing between the monarchy of France and the Habsburg Dynasty, commanded by Charles V. Both were Christian kingdoms, who swore obedience to the Holy See, but at the same time their differences led to the Wars of Italy that ended in 1525

---

77. Consult: Bataillon 1956.

with the Battle of Pavia where the Emperor of Spain emerged triumphant. Faced with these adversities, Vives told Adrian VI:

> It is your mission, Most Holy Father, based on the precepts of our religion, as an interpreter of which you watch over the world, to teach princes and their advisers that this war between brothers and, what is worse, initiated by the same baptism, is unjust, criminal, against law, against piety, just as if the members of the same body fought each other.[78]

The solution that Vives proposed matches that of Nicholas of Cusa: the celebration of a council of all Christendom. How can we not think, also in relation to this, of the dispute alluded to by Pico della Mirandola? The end of its convocation should be based on the common good, appealing to the "love for the harmony of the nations of the entire Europe"[79] that should characterize the Holy Pontiff. Vives openly discusses the notion of a just war and proposes avoiding the fear of risking facing the enmities between the nations of the whole of Europe, in order to resolve their differences.

For his part, to what may look as anticipation of an unsuccessful attempt to bring Henry VIII back to the Roman See, Vives dedicated a text to the King Himself, on the Government of the Kingdom, and on War and Peace in Bruges on October 8, 1525. There he reminded him that the prince is to a state or a kingdom what the soul is to the body[80] and if one is disturbed, it affects the other party in a sensitive way. In the ideal of the formation of princes, peace must be the priority:

> virtue is peaceful, moderate, and not at all fond of revolutions, despising fortune to such an extent that it does not take into account either the body nor the wealth, since it is supported and sustained entirely by the soul. And if Christian piety is added, the whole is the perfection of all the virtues or, rather, the only virtue, which is devoted entirely to retirement and, considering that this life is in a way a journey, easily endures the command of anyone.[81]

---

78. Vives 1992: 19.
79. Vives 1992: 24.
80. Vives 1992: 33.
81. Vives 1992: 37.

Peace is intertwined with Christian *pietas*, from which it must not be separated. The good ruler must not lose sight of divine decrees, which for Cusa came from natural law. Virtue is the source of joy and tranquility and vices are the source of political and social misfortunes. Only the permanence in the one religion—and therefore the one Church—will allow development of the virtues and the act of reaching exemplarity. Vives strongly condemns war and also wants to avoid the mistreatment of citizens, avoiding excessive taxes. If the good ruler applies justice, he guarantees peace among his citizens. If, on the other hand, he does not apply the laws or does so without appealing to harmony, it only generates violence. Vives underlined the title that Henry VIII received from the Holy See—from Pope Leo X—as the "Defender of the Faith," so that he would not forget how he had defended the authority of the pope against the theses of Luther.[82]

The intellectual structure of Vives consists of deducing a philosophical anthropology combined with a social philosophy. The microcosm necessarily affects the macrocosm. The intrinsic good affects the extrinsic and the same happens with evil. This is another point of contact with Pico's philosophical production. Only taking into account those priorities will it be possible to obtain human peace and tranquility, in the words of his first Spanish translator:

> because what God has given to each one, he has not given for him alone, nor for him alone, and because there can be no true piety in us, nor perfect religious and Christian spirit if we do not help each other with joy, as much as we can.[83]

Vives conceives the relief of the poor as an anthropological, ethical, and political task. It requires an awareness of faith and humility. The condition of poverty of man leads him to lose all commendable feelings, to corrupt the laws and exert violence against other people. This philosophy takes into account the care of the body and the spirit. Health is as important as friendship and family values. Virtue, effort, and work are pillars for the development and balance of the community. This is what

---

82. Vives 1992: 48.
83. Nieto Ivarra 1781: vi.

was reflected in Spanish with the name of *liberalidad* (liberality).[84] To benefit others is to benefit oneself, and the health of the republics consists in helping one another. Vives also follows Plato, in his republican ideal of eliminating what is "mine" and what is "yours."[85] The help of the poor, in this sense, is necessary for piety and for the peace of the homeland:

> it is not enough to wish the Good, but to get down to work when the occasion is offered; it is neither decent nor lawful for those who are stimulated by the Divine precepts to stop for human impediments, especially if they follow publicly and privately human and Divine utilities.[86]

The other two works that round off the philosophical project of Vives on the subject at hand expressly deal with harmony and discord in the human race and on pacification. Vives addressed this to Charles V. Faced with the disturbances generated by the European wars, Vives applied the same structure and the same approach that he had already stated in his treatise on provision for the poor. Namely, in order to achieve peace and concord, it is necessary for the emperor to apply the laws with justice, he himself being an example of Christian virtues.

The emperor must achieve concord among the princes, who suffer from being carried away by human forces, opening the way to discord between kingdoms and citizens. As we saw, Laguna's reflection had something in common with this position of Vives. In the Council of the Church, the voice and spirit of Cusano also resounded; it was seen as a necessary means to save the parishioners from the inter-European wars and even religion itself.[87] The role of the emperor, for Vives, would be to achieve the convocation and celebration of the Council.

It is part of human nature to fight the "monster" of discord, to consider man as a "sacred" being[88] who was born to serve God and live in society with other men, having all the divine gifts at his disposal. In his "human dignity" he can fall into disturbances and stop using his intelligence for

---

84. Vives 1781: 26.
85. Vives 1781: 99.
86. Vives 1781: 238.
87. Vives 1997: 55.
88. Vives 1997: 61.

good, degrading himself to the point of being a beast or animal. Pico's echo expressed in the *Oratio*, of his concept of human dignity from its divine origin, is palpable. Man is distinguished from beasts by his particular gifts that God has given him, such as communication, good humor, joy, and affection. When it is carried away by anger and passions, discord is generated, and human life is damaged. Selfishness and ignorance reign and reason is obscured by sin. Here Vives recovers the tradition of Seneca and Saint Augustine, with a view to reestablishing peace and harmony from the heart and inner tranquility, which are always manifested in doing good to others.

Wars, from classical times to Vives's own time, have always denied these dimensions and have been characterized by hunger for personal glory and territorial expansion. Discord causes much damage to the human race, since charity, piety, and beneficence are abandoned. Thus, Vives developed a project to reform the customs within Christendom, before which the emperor had to unite all the scattered members of the mystical body of his kingdoms to restore peace.

Concord implies recovering friendship, kindness, and benevolence. It is an ethical, anthropological call that has strong political and social implications. The stability of the kingdoms depends on it. Peace is in tune with respect for others and the law, respect for oneself, for God, and for the Church. History, as Vives shows throughout the four books of his treatise, has been filled with violence for choosing discord over harmony. They are not equal opposing forces, because harmony is the only one that gives real gains to the human being: "Just as in harmony what is foreign is ours; in the same way in discord we do not really own our personal properties."[89] It is not enough to beg God to give man peace and harmony, but man himself must cooperate and move away from passions and vices. When man eventually experiences this prudence, he follows the precepts of love and stops wishing evil towards himself and towards others. Once again, we have the voice of Pico and his *Oratio*:

> Come back to yourself and love who you truly are, because if you do not detach yourself from yourself and do not abandon yourself, you will easily agree with nature and rise to God, and you will not

---

89. Vives 1997: 166.

turn away from anything but hatred and discord, for nothing you will strive so much as for harmony and love.[90]

In his last text on pacification, Vives recalls that the experience of peace is the requirement to be a true Christian. The denial of oneself, in favor of the salvation of others, is the key to all wisdom and the way to reach Christ. All human values, such as nobility and honor, lived authentically, aim to reestablish harmony and live in it. The model of peace is Christ and his Church[91] and if all the European kingdoms stopped for a moment and remembered that they can only be true Christians if they follow these precepts, there would be no need for wars and they could be unified and ready to prevent invasions like the threat posed at that time by the Turkish army advancing in Europe; which would impose a suffocating lifestyle on Christians, as he described in Vives's other treatise on *Quam misera esset vita christianorum sub turco* ("How miserable the life of Christians would be under the Turks," 1526, although published in 1529).

In all this philosophical work, the trace of Italian Humanism is perceived, even in its deepest roots. In Vives, the voice of Italian humanists and their ideas is heard. Di Camillo underlines:

> Petrarch reproached the scholastics for their barbarous Latin style, as well as their limited idea of education. In open opposition to the "sciences" of the schools, he emphasized the importance of ancient eloquence—moral and literary disciplines for the development of man. His first attacks against the Averroists and against the official teaching given in Paris, Padua and Bologna, where logic and physics predominated over the other disciplines, caused conflicts that would last throughout the 15th and 16th centuries, both in Italy and in Spain, from Coluccio Salutati to Vives.[92]

Fontán adds that Vives embodies one of the three souls that Spanish Humanism develops, after having crossed paths with Italian Humanism. There is a philological Spanish Humanism, the highest expression of which is Antonio de Nebrija; a Hispanic Humanism in defense of

---

90. Vives 1997: 310–11.
91. Vives 1997: 360.
92. Di Camillo 1976: 25–26. This relationship of Vives with the Italian Renaissance is also appreciated in detail in Lentzen 2008 and Bermúdez Vázquez 2010.

Patriotism supported by the Catholic Monarchs[93] and a Spanish, ideological and Christian Humanism whose most relevant author is Vives. It would seem contradictory that a Valencian Judeo-convert, persecuted by the Inquisition of Spain to the point of distancing him from his lands from adolescence onwards, represents one of the most authentic facets of Castilian Humanism. In reality, it is not a paradox, but a faithful representation of the complex fresco that the Renaissance was on Iberian soil.[94]

Conclusion

It is a common journey, the one that unites Petrarch, Cusano, Pico, and Vives. They all had a peaceful and harmonious dialogue with the pagan authors and the Christian Fathers from ancient times to modernity, so that man could find peace in his divine origin surrounded by the Christian God. In detail, the Renaissance and its Humanism find in Giovanni Pico della Mirandola and Juan Luis Vives two extraordinary examples of the achievement of the dignity of the human being as a divine being.

Italy and Spain then began a cultural growth that their intellectual exponents knew how to embody. It was a spiritual growth that made man the greatest discovery of creation and therefore the greatest researcher of peace that only a direct dialogue with a paternal God can guarantee. Ficino made Pico find in Plato and in his followers some guides to reach the mystical peace of the discovery of God. Pico went one step further and found in the most intercultural and confessional concert achieved at that time the key to living peacefully with oneself, with others, and with the God of Christianity. Cusanus advanced his position and prepared Vives's stance. The Valencian humanist politically defended the sacredness of the human being, to propose a method of peace in favor of the needy, the princes, the emperor, and the pope. In short, the Renaissance, in its Italian and Hispanic version, was an unparalleled example of the spectacle of Christianity perceived as a language of peace.

---

93. The Temple of San Pietro in Montorio built by Donato Bramante, at the Royal Academy of Spain in Rome, can be considered an example of the not only political Humanism that the Catholic monarchs tried to promote.
94. Fontán 1992: 21–22.

Author biographies

Manuel López Forjas holds a PhD in Hispanic Studies from the Universidad Autónoma de Madrid, Spain, where he has taught History of Spanish and Latin American thought at the Department of Social Anthropology and Spanish Philosophical Thought. He is a member of the Instituto Universitario La Corte en Europa (IULCE). His research focuses on the intellectual history of Latin America and Spain and the modern history of the Hispanic world. Recently, he has edited some manuscripts from the Spanish philosopher José Ortega y Gasset: "Notas de trabajo de la carpeta Vives," in *Revista de Estudios Orteguianos* 39–43.

Veronica Tartabini is a PhD student of the Department of Social Anthropology and Spanish Philosophical Thought at the Universidad Autónoma de Madrid, Spain. Her research focuses on the reception of Spanish mysticism in Italy—especially on the Discalced Carmelites—including María Zambrano's philosophy. Recent publications include: "Rendere eterno l'istante: misticismo e realismo nel Velázquez di María Zambrano e José Ortega Y Gasset," *B@belonline* 8 (2021): 339–55; "Verso un sapere sul sacro: dal misticismo spagnolo alla ragione poetica," in *Bajo Palabra. Revista de Filosofía*, 251–72; "Pico della Mirandola y Santa Teresa: el camino compartido del Humanismo," at https://theconversation.com/pico-della-mirandola-y-santa-teresa-el-camino-compartido-del-humanismo-175103.

References

Primary sources

Cusanus, N. (1987), *De concordantia catholica o sobre la unión de los católicos*, edited and translated by J. M. de Alejandro Lueiro. Madrid: Centro de Estudios Constitucionales.

Cusanus, N. (1991), *The Catholic Concordance*, edited and translated by P. E. Sigmund. Cambridge: Cambridge University Press.

Cusanus, N. (1994), *De pace fidei and Cribratio alkorani*, translated by J. Hopkins, 2nd ed. Minneapolis: The Arthur J. Banning Press.

Cusanus, N. (1995), *On Learned Ignorance: A Translation and an Appraisal of* De Docta Ignorantia, edited by J. Hopkins. Minneapolis: The Arthur J. Banning Press.
Cusanus, N. (1996), *La paz de la fe. Carta a Juan de Segovia*, edited and translated by V. Sanz Santacruz. Navarra: Cuadernos de Anuario Filosófico.
Ficino, M. (1992), *Sopra lo amore ovvero Convito di Platone*. Milan: ES Biblioteca dell'Eros.
Laguna, A. (2001), *Europa Heautentimorumene, es decir, que míseramente a sí misma se atormenta y lamenta su propia desgracia*, edited by M. Á. González Manjarrés. Valladolid: Junta de Castilla y León Consejería de Educación y Cultura.
León, Fray L. de (2017), *De los nombres de Cristo*, Edición de Cristóbal Cuevas. Madrid: Cátedra Letras Hispánicas.
Marsilius of Padua (2005), *The Defender of the Peace*, edited and translated by A. Brett. Cambridge: Cambridge University Press.
Pico della Mirandola, G. (1942), *De hominis dignitate. Heptaplus. De ente et uno e scritti vari*, edited by E. Garin. Firenze: Vallecchi Editore.
Pico della Mirandola, G. (1984), *Oration on the Dignity of Man*, in E. Cassirer et al. (eds.), *The Renaissance Philosophy of Man. Petrarca. Valla. Ficino. Pico. Pomponazzi. Vives*. Chicago: University of Chicago Press, 223–54.
Pico della Mirandola, G. (1987), *Discorso sulla dignità dell'uomo*, edited by G. Tognon. Brescia: Editrice La Scuola.
Vives, J. L. (1781), *Tratado del socorro de los pobres*, Traducido en castellano. Valencia: Imprenta de Benito Monfort.
Vives, J. L. (1988), *Diálogos y otros escritos*, Introduction, translation and notes by Juan Francisco Alcina. Barcelona: Planeta Autores Hispánicos.
Vives, J. L. (1992), *De Europae dissidiis et republica. Sobre las disensiones de Europa y sobre el Estado*. Valencia: Ajuntament de València.
Vives, J. L. (1997), *De Concordia et Discordia in Humano Genere (Sobre la concordia y la discordia en el genere humano, De Pacificatione (Sobre la Pacificación), Quam misera esset vita christianorum sub turco (Cuán desgraciada sería la vida de los cristianos bajo los turcos)*, Introduction by Valerio del Nero. Valencia: Ajuntament de Valencia.

Secondary sources

Abellán, J. L. (1979), *Historia del Pensamiento Español*, Tomo I, *Metodología e Introducción Histórica*. Madrid: Espasa Calpe.
Bataillon, M. (1956), *Erasmo y España*. México: Fondo de Cultura Económica.

Bayona Aznar, B. (2006), "La paz en la teoría política de Marsilio de Padua," *Contrastes* 11: 45–63. https://doi.org/10.24310/Contrastescontrastes.v11i0.1456

Bermúdez Vázquez, M. (2010), "La relación de Francisco Sánchez con dos importantes representantes del antiaristotelismo renacentista: Juan Luis Vives y Gianfrancesco Pico della Mirandola," *Contrastes* 15: 65–83. https://doi.org/10.24310/Contrastescontrastes.v15i0.1321

Bertini, G. M., and M. A. Pelazza (1980), *Ensayos de Literatura Espiritual Comparada Hispano-italiana (Siglos XV–XVIII)*. Torino: Rosada arti grafiche.

Borghesi, F. (2017), "Il camaleonte in cerca di ordine. Giovanni Pico tra pluralismo religioso e concordia filosofica," in G. Ventura (ed.), *Pico tra cultura e letteratura dell'Umanesimo, Giornata di studi in occasione del 550° anniversario della nascita (1463–2013)*, 41–54. Bologna: Alma Mater Studiorum—Università di Bologna Dipartimento di Filologia Classica e Italianistica Biblioteca "Ezio Raimondi."

Byrne, S. (2015), *Ficino in Spain*. Toronto: University of Toronto Press.

De Alejandro Lueiro, J. M. (1981), "Introducción," in Nicolás de Cusa, *De concordantia catholica o Sobre la Unión de los Católicos*. Madrid: Centro de Estudios Constitucionales, i–xviii.

Di Camillo, O. (1976), *El humanismo castellano del siglo XV*. Valencia: Horizon.

Di Camillo, O. (1988), "Humanism in Spain," in Al. Rabil Jr. (ed.), *Renaissance Humanism: Foundations, Forms, and Legacy*, 55–108. Philadelphia: University of Pennsylvania Press.

Esmorís Galán, L. (2017), "Del mito al logos moderno; Giovanni Pico della Mirandola o el hombre en busca de su imagen," *Logos. Anales del Seminario de Metafísica* 50: 105–127.

Fita, F. (1889), "Pico de la Mirándula y la Inquisición española. Breve inédito de Florencio VIII," *Boletín Real Academia de la Historia* XV: 315–16.

Fontán, A. (1992), *Juan Luis Vives (1492–1540): Humanista. Filósofo, Político*. Valencia: Ajuntament de València.

García Gómez, M. C. (1996), *Hombre y naturaleza: apuntes sobre la antropología renacentista*. Alicante: Universidad de Alicante.

García Gibert, J. (2010), *El viejo humanismo. Exposición y defensa de una tradición*. Madrid: Marcial Pons Historia.

Gómez Moreno, Á. (1994), *España y la Italia de los humanistas: primeros ecos*. Madrid: Gredos.

Gómez Moreno, Á. (2015), "Burckhardt y la forja de un imaginario: España, la nación sin Renacimiento," *eHumanista* 29: 13–31.

González Vega, F. (2012), "Apuntamientos para un estudio de la difusión de Pico en la España renacentista," in A. Steiner-Weber and K. A. E. Enenkel (eds.),

Acta Conventus Neo-Latini Monasteriensis: Proceedings of the Fifteenth International Congress of Neo-Latin Studies, 248–58. Leiden: Brill.

González Vega, F. (2014), "El estilo de una felicidad teológica truncada: las dos Epístolas del bien vivir y treinta y seis Reglas espirituales de Pico della Mirandola en la versión romance del bachiller Pedro de Rúa († 1556)," *eHumanista* 28: 437–69.

Goñi Zubieta, C. (1996), *Pico della Mirandola (1463–1494)*. Madrid: Ediciones del Orto.

Goñi Zubieta, C. (2020), *Pico della Mirandola. Incluye el Discurso sobre la dignidad del hombre. Prólogo de Jaume Casals*. Barcelona: Arpa.

Guy, A. (1985), *Historia de la Filosofía Española*. Barcelona: Anthropos.

Kagay, D. J. (2019), "Ficino in Spain. Susan Byrne. Toronto: University of Toronto Press, 2015," *Sixteenth Century Journal* 50/2: 671–73.

Lawrance, J. N. H. (1989), *Un episodio del proto-humanismo español. Tres opúsculos de Nuño de Guzmán y Giannozzo Manetti*. Salamanca: Diputación de Salamanca.

Leaños, J. (2007), *Piccolomini in Iberia: Influencias Italianas en el Génesis de la Literatura Sentimental Española*. Maryland: Scripta Humanistica.

Lentzen, M. (2008), "A proposito dell'Oratio de hominis dignitate di Giovanni Pico della Mirandola e delle Fabula de homine di Juan Luis Vives," in L. Secchi Tarugi (ed.), *Il concetto di libertà nel Rinascimento. Atti del XVIII Convegno Internazionale (Chianciano-Pienza 17–20 Iuglio 2006)*, 401–411. Quaderni della Rassegna, 52. Firenze: Franco-Cesati.

Martínez (OCD), E. (2000), "San Juan de la Cruz: para una recreación del humanismo renacentista más allá de la modernidad," *Revista de Espiritualidad* 59: 335–72.

Martínez Arancón, A. (1986), *Historia de la filosofía española*. Madrid: Ediciones Libertarias.

Martínez Gómez, L. (1984), *Introducción*, in Pico de la Mirandola, *De la dignidad del hombre. Con dos apéndices: Carta a Hermolao Bárbaro y Del ente y el uno*, 13–97. Madrid: Editora Nacional.

Martínez Millán, J., ed. (1998), *Felipe II (1527–1598): Europa y la Monarquía Católica, Congreso Internacional: Felipe II (1598–1998), Europa dividida, la monarquía católica de Felipe II: Universidad Autónoma de Madrid 20–23 abril 1998*. Madrid: Editorial Parteluz.

Martínez Millán, J., ed. (2011), *Carlos V y la Quiebra del humanismo político en Europa, 1530–1558: Congreso internacional: Madrid 3–6 de julio de 2000*. Madrid: Sociedad Estatal para la Conmemoración de los Centenarios de Felipe II y Carlos V.

Nieto Ivarra, J. G. (1781), "Aviso al lector," in J. L. Vives, *Tratado del socorro de los pobres*, i–xxxiv. Valencia: Imprenta de Benito Monfort.

Ortega y Gasset, J. (2012), *Appunti per un commento al Convivio di Platone*, edited by P. Piro. Milan: Mimesis Filosofie.
Pérez de Oliva, H. (1995), *Diálogo de la dignidad del hombre*. Madrid: Cátedra.
Reventlow, H. G. (1999), *Storia dell'interpretazione biblica. Rinascimento, Riforma, Umanesimo*, V. III, Italian translation by E. Gatti. Casale Monferrato: Piemme.
Rico, F. (1997), *El sueño del humanismo (De Petrarca a Erasmo)*. Madrid: Alianza Universidad.
Turró, S. (1985), *Descartes, del hermetismo a la nueva ciencia*. Barcelona: Anthropos.
Vega, M. J. (2001), "La solitaria oscuridad del padre. El Dios de las tinieblas en la Oratio de Dignitate Hominis de Pico della Mirandola," *Quaderns de Italià* 6: 195–200. https://doi.org/10.5565/rev/qdi.66
Zambrano, M. (2006), *Filosofía y Poesía*. México: Fondo de Cultura Económica.

Chapter 4

Peace, Prophecy, and the Apocalyptic Expectation: Girolamo Benivieni's Letter to Clement VII[1]

Maria Fallica

> Righteousness looked from the sky. And seeing this marriage of the Son of God with human nature, and wishing to come to that banquet, she took leave of God and descended forthwith to earth, shouting and singing, *Gloria in excelsis Deo*. And lo, from the other part of heaven came a woman in a simple, white, and pure dress who was most beautiful and graceful, and with great haste she ran towards Righteousness, and they kissed each other; and thus, *Iustitia et pax obsculate sunt*. And forthwith one of them, who was Lady Peace, said, *Et in terra pax hominibus bone voluntatis*.[2]

> Dinanzi alla tua faccia vengon due vaghe et belle Donne l'una Pieta l'altra Iustitia: con queste due sorelle che così l'una abraccia l'altra: che indivisa è loro amiticia porton Pace et Letitia.

> *Pax, pax, et non erit pax.*[3]

---

1. I would like to thank Lorenzo Geri, Michele Lodone, and Marcello Simonetta for their valuable suggestions on the manuscript. Moreover, my sincere gratitude goes to Kenneth Gouwens for his generous help in reviewing my English and for his thorough and informed scholarly opinion. All the remaining errors are sadly mine.
2. Translation by Hatfield 1995: 90. On peace as a legal institution and its signs and formal gestures, from the Middle Ages to the Early Modern Age, see Niccoli 2007: 70–123.
3. Benivieni 1500: CXVI[r].

In analyzing the crisis of Italy (1494–1530), scholars have understandably given detailed attention to war and warfare, an emphasis justified both by the military and political strife on the peninsula and by the centrality of warfare in the writings of Machiavelli. The popularity of apocalyptic prophecy in precisely those decades, amply documented by Marjorie Reeves[4] and others, has often been linked to this strife, which called out for explanation in cities such as Florence and Rome, each of which had come to see itself as a new Jerusalem in the making. How did present scourges figure into the divine plan? Girolamo Savonarola, the Dominican friar who governed and divided Florence with his preaching, would often repeat the words of the prophet Jeremiah, who introduced the Lord's denunciation of the enemies of His chosen people: "They dress the wound of my people as though it were not serious. 'Peace, peace,' they say, when there is no peace" (Jer. 6:14). Learned enemies of the city go on philosophizing, saying "there will be peace," when it is clear "that Italy is not in a position to be exempt from the scourge and have peace."[5] God's urging in Jeremiah, in the past tense in the Latin Vulgate (*Et curabant contritionem filiæ populi mei cum ignominia, dicentes: Pax, pax! et non erat pax*) is adapted in Savonarola's works, where the verb *esse* is intended in the future, the tense of prophetic vision; a vision that is still subject to the change made possible by repentance and conversion.

Pax, the people cry out. *Non erit pax*, the prophet replies. *Pax*, the philosophers meditate. *Non erit pax*, history replies. Machiavelli, the theorist (and attempted implementer) of a model of a state in which it was possible both "to love peace and to know how to make war,"[6] alluded to this Savonarolan commonplace when he wrote to Francesco Vettori on August 26, 1513, "I believe the friar who said: 'Peace, peace, and there will be no peace.' I admit to you that every peace is difficult."[7]

---

4. Reeves 1992.
5. Cf. Savonarola 1955, I: 300.
6. Machiavelli 1989: 580. The quotation belongs to the *Art of War*, I, 108: "amare la pace e saper fare la guerra."
7. Machiavelli 1989: 923 ("Io credo al frate che diceva 'Pax, pax, et non erit pax', et cedovi che ogni pace è difficile"). On this theme in Florentine sixteenth-century preachers, see Francesco da Montepulciano's homily, edited in Lodone 2021: 197–228, 225: "Tu di' pur pace, pace, e parti si posi ogni cosa. Ma quando tu crederai che ogni cosa sia determinata, allora ogni cosa germinerà guerra, fame e pestilentia."

The present chapter analyzes the call for peace made by Girolamo Benivieni in his letter to Pope Clement VII after the victorious and grueling siege of Florence in 1530. Through the analysis of Benivieni's letter, I will interpret his appropriation of Savonarola's memory as part of an attempt at reconciling his close personal relationship with the letter's addressee, the second Medici pope, with his never-betrayed discipleship of Savonarola.

Girolamo Benivieni between Savonarola and the Medici

After ten months of devastating siege, in August 1530 the Republic of Florence capitulated to the forces of Emperor Charles V, who in 1529 had forged a lasting alliance with Pope Clement VII. The city's fortune, as well as the hopes and fears of its most notable citizens, were now in the hands of the pontiff, who quickly set about restoring Medicean dominion over Florence. It is in this context that an earnest and authoritative appeal came to the pope from one of the most distinguished Florentine intellectuals, one with profound ties to the forces which moved the city: the then 77-year-old Girolamo Benivieni (1453–1542), intimate since his youth with the Medici family.

Girolamo, son of Paolo Benivieni and brother of Antonio and Domenico,[8] was one of the most distinguished Florentine citizens of his time:[9] in his long life, he overcame several tides of political turbulence, managing to remain faithful to the memory of Savonarola, thanks to being politically moderate and being close with key figures in the Medici family (above all, Cardinal Giulio de' Medici, the future Pope Clement VII, but also, within the *popolani* branch of the Medici family, Giovanni di Pierfrancesco and his wife Caterina Sforza), and in the Salviati family.[10]

Similarly, already in the fourteenth century, Rupescissa: Lodone 2021: 231. My thanks to Michele Lodone for this helpful comparison.

8. Antonio is considered a founder of modern pathological anatomy; Domenico was a philosopher and ardent defender of Savonarola; see Stefanutti 1966 and Vasoli 1966a.
9. The family is praised in Poliziano's elegy dedicated to Antonio, the physician: see Del Lungo 1867: 236–38.
10. Benivieni was in 1505 the arbiter of the financial dispute between Caterina, the widow of Giovanni, and her brother-in-law Lorenzo, on the inheritance of Giovanni;

One of the most influential historians of Savonarola's life and legacy, Donald Weinstein, describes Benivieni as a "troubled spirit" and traces his development from being "one of the bright lights of Lorenzo's *brigata* of poets, close to Lorenzo's murdered brother Giuliano, friend and pupil of Marsilio Ficino, Angelo Poliziano, and Giovanni Pico—in short, the very epitome of the Laurentian courtier-*literatus*," to being, through his songs and writings, the "chief publicist of the Savonarolan movement."[11] An important vernacular poet in his own right, he benefited from fervent allegiance to friends more illustrious and brilliant than he, whose memory he defended, cultivated, and sustained: above all, the prodigious young philosopher Giovanni Pico della Mirandola,[12] and, of course, Girolamo Savonarola. Benivieni was intimately linked with both, in deeds and writings, illuminating and translating their doctrines to the vast public. In fact, hermeneutic activity was crucial to the production of Benivieni, who was an exegete and self-exegete, as the *Commento* (1500) on his own songs testifies. This hermeneutical circle famously entailed[13] Pico's *Commento* on Benivieni's *Canzona dell'Amor celeste e divino*, which is a major testimony of the *docta amicitia* which joined the two, who were also united in their approach to Savonarola's preaching and doctrines. Benivieni soon became one of the closest followers of the friar, composing several songs for the movement,[14] translating into the vernacular some key texts of Savonarola (such as *Della semplicità della vita cristiana*, the second version of the letter to Pope Alexander VI; the *Epistola dell'umiltà* was translated from the vernacular into Latin)[15] and prefacing the Latin

---

he was later invited in 1524 by Clement VII and Jacopo Salviati to tutor Giovanni delle Bande Nere's son Cosimo, the future duke: he declined the role due to his poor health, but the invitation shows how highly he was held in esteem. The support and patronage of Lucrezia de' Medici was fundamental in Benivieni's life, as shown in the surviving letters between the two. Benivieni drafted the letter by Lucrezia in which she asked her brother the Pope to support the project of transferring Dante's bones in Florence; see Pugliese 1970; Roush 2002; Tomas 2017.

11. Weinstein 2011: 205. On Benivieni's poetical works, see Di Benedetto 2020.
12. On this crucial relationship see above all Pugliese 2003.
13. Leporatti 2011: 374.
14. *Viva nei nostri cuori, viva o Firenze*, which was sung on Palm Sunday 1496; *Da che tu ci hai Signore*, performed on Carnival 1497 for the bonfire of the vanities; *Venite ecco il Signore*, planned for the failed bonfire of Lent 1497.
15. Pugliese 1996; Vasoli 1966b.

version of the *Compendium revelationum* (1495).[16] He was amongst the notable Florentines who petitioned the pope for mercy in 1497, in an appeal to acknowledge the fact that from the doctrine of Savonarola always came true salvation and peace for the city,[17] and he was admonished after Savonarola's burning.[18] Benivieni's devotion was recognized by his selection as the custodian of several relics of the friar,[19] a collection of his sermons, and an account of the last declarations of Savonarola and his companions before his death.[20] His allegiances remained very clear throughout his life: then again, as Carlo Dionisotti writes, he was a man "non naturalmente docile: era anzi di una purissima e durissima tempra."[21] However, his position in Florence after the fall of the Piagnone republic and the restoration of the Medici was guaranteed by his high political connections and the moderate stance which he always took in the midst of agitated times despite the radicalism of other Piagnoni.

His pro-Medicean stance was clear on the occasion of Cardinal Giovanni de' Medici's elevation to the papal throne in 1513: Benivieni

16. Cf. Crucitti 1974: 431–32.
17. See Filipepi 2020: 113: "Noi, cittadini infrascripti, a corrobatione delle sopradette cose, a Vostra Santità per gli detti religiosi et venerandi Padri esposte et narrate, attestiamo essere la sincera e indubitata verità che dalla dottrina del detto P. f. Girolamo, nella nostra città predicata, non la destrutione ma la vera salute e pace sempre è proceduta. Per la qual cosa, con ogni debita humiltà, preghiamo Vostra Santità si degni il detto Padre dalle dette censure liberare […]. Il che per la sua solita clemenza facendo, siamo certissimi, non solo la gloria et honore di Dio doverne risultare, ma la salute et spirituale et corporale, con la universal pace et vera unione di tutta la nostra e vostra città."
18. See the document published by Re 1906: 372 (ASF, May–August 1498, n. 110, cc. 95^b–96).
19. Re 1906: 113.
20. Pugliese 1981. Pugliese 1996: 312 prefers to interpret the relics kept by Benivieni as being the sermons by Savonarola, identified with ms. 480 in the museum of San Marco, studied by Verde 1992, which bears the name of Benivieni as the owner.
21. Dionisotti 1980: 349. Here Dionisotti is writing about the *questione della lingua*, in which, contrary to Ridolfi's opinion, Benivieni did not adhere meekly to Bembo's dictate and correct his edition of the *Commento*: his opinion on the matter was clear and in favor of the vivacious, living Florentine language. Di Benedetto 2011 proposes a solution to the problem posed by the revision of the *Commento*, which, as Ridolfi noted, is in line with Bembo's dictates: Di Benedetto 2011 tentatively argues that the handwritten revision was not made by Girolamo but by his nephew Lorenzo Benivieni.

dedicated to him a *frottola In renovatione ecclesiae*, a poem for the renovation of the Church, which Caterina Re brilliantly summarized as "the Savonarolan dream laid at the feet of a Medici."[22] Six years later, when Benivieni gathered his literary production for a volume of *Opera* published by Giunti, he placed this composition in Pope Leo's honor at the very end.[23] This choice is striking, for, as Roberto Leporatti has demonstrated, the *frottola* appears only in the printed version, whereas in the autograph codex (which attests Benivieni's editorial work prior to printing), in the section of the *laude*, the song *Vergine casta* still appeared, a laud written by Savonarola *nella presente ruina della chiesa militante di Christo*. As Leporatti argues, the prudent omission from the printed collection of such a strong and polemical text is counterbalanced by the addition of the *frottola*, which articulates the same themes and principles, but does so in such a way that they are not an invective but instead a prophecy.[24] The conventional pastoral scene presents the sheep threatened by wolves, and the coming of a lion from Judah's tribe whose roar alone scares off the predators: of course this is Leo, whose Florentine origins are proudly blazoned, who will unify the flock of the faithful. The song transmutes its metaphor in the equally traditional image of the ship, almost destroyed on account of the corruption of recent pontiffs. Leo is urged, too, to care for the Church, his naked Spouse, covering her with his mantle.[25]

Thus Benivieni identifies the pope as the *pastor angelicus*: the elusive object of a long series of millenarian expectations since at least the fourteenth century.[26] The election of Giovanni de' Medici as pope both increased the prominence of this theme and intensified the urgency of discrediting others who were thought possibly to be this longed-for pastor.

The capacity of ecclesiastical authority to embrace (and arguably coopt) millenarian belief is eloquently attested in many speeches made

---

22. Re 1906: 135: "il sogno savonaroliano deposto ai piedi di un Medici."
23. Benivieni 1519: it includes the *Commento* of his Canzone by Pico, a *Bucolica*, a section of humanistic lyrics from his early years and a section of religious poetry with the vulgarization of the psalms, the *laudi*, the *stanze* and the *frottole*.
24. Leporatti 2010: 204.
25. Benivieni 1522: 201^r.
26. See at least Vasoli 2000.

at the Fifth Lateran Council.[27] However, papal advocates were keenly sensitive to the threat posed by any whose claims to inspiration led them to attack the institution of the Church. Thus Sharon Leftley writes:

> the prediction of an imminent millennium, even in relatively radical forms, was not enough to lead 'prophets' into trouble. [...] Their views seem to have been countenanced as long as two conditions were met: that they did not claim direct revelation, and did not attack the structure and hierarchy of the Church. Where conflict did arise it seems to have centred around these two themes: the nature of the revelation, and their attitude to ecclesiastical authority.[28]

Leo was vigilant in opposing a range of religious figures who could be construed as Savonarolan—that is, as appropriating a direct, personal, and charismatically derived personal authority—such as Pietro Bernardino and Teodoro, who both attributed to themselves the title of angelic pope and were the scapegoats in the condemnation of Savonarolan tendencies in 1515 Florence.[29] A brief from Leo X to his cousin Giulio praised the swift action against the two by the Florentine church and associated them with Savonarola: an association strongly rebuffed by most Savonarolans.[30]

Also in 1515, Benivieni copied a very brief tract (recently edited by Olga Zorzi Pugliese)[31] which was supposedly taken from an old book of prophecies written by a lord Obehut of the Counts of Paris, and copied by a brother Abbias in Paris; Josephine Jungić weighs the possibility that Benivieni himself wrote the prophecy, whilst Pugliese prefers to attribute it to Giorgio Benigno Salviati, the author of the *Apocalypsis nova*.[32] The prophecy, which in the text is delivered by the angel Uriel, is taken to describe the destruction of Florence and Italy by a French king, who in 1517 would assault Genoa and F.[lorence]. Upon seeing these events, the

---

27. Leftley 1999: 123.
28. Leftley 1999: 126.
29. Lodone 2019.
30. See Polizzotto 1994 and Rusconi 2010.
31. Pugliese 1986.
32. The name of the supposed author of the *Apocalypsis*, that of Beatus Amadeus, is inscribed in the heading of the covering folio: Pugliese 1986: 128. Jungić 1997 identifies the copying of this manuscript as a moment of loss of faith on Benivieni's part regarding Leo X.

pope would die and be succeeded by a most holy pastor, who would collaborate with the king of France. This prophecy is well in line with a relevant strand of Florentine millenarianism, which, already in the fourteenth century, put together world renewal, the ascent of a spiritual Church, and the leadership of a French king, a second Charlemagne.[33] It evidences Benivieni's steadfast hope of a spiritual reform that would be sustained by political force. It should be noted, finally, that Benivieni's careful scrutiny of the traditions regarding the angelic pope is at the heart of his interest in Angelo Clareno's *Chronicon*, a text he annotated extensively.[34]

A call for mercy: Girolamo to Giulio

Already during his tenure as archbishop of Florence (1508–1513), Giulio de' Medici "followed a policy of cultivating the support of former Savonarolans by offering them high posts in the archiepiscopal curia and by inviting their advice."[35] Following the return of the Medici to power there in 1512 and Giulio's elevation to the cardinalate the following year, his influence on the Florentine church increased, and his policy of accommodation continued. Giulio was personally close to many devout reformers, such as the Camaldolese monk Paolo Giustiniani, author with Vincenzo Quirini of the famous *Libellus ad Leonem X* and Benivieni's correspondent.[36] The historian Jacopo Nardi, a close friend of Benivieni[37] and also a Savonarolan, describes Cardinal Giulio as honorably conversing with learned and pious men such as Benivieni in the Medici's garden

---

33. Weinstein 1970: 52.
34. Pugliese 1980. See Reeves 2000: 402: "it was in the circle of Fra Liberato and Fra Angelo Clareno that the first set of fifteen *Vaticinia de summis pontificibus*, the *Liber de Flore*, and its accompanying smaller tracts originated. These were men whose fortunes had risen and fallen with the succession of popes, who had been raised to a pitch of high expectation by Celestine V and cast into the depths by his successor. For them the immediate juxtaposition of good and evil was a close reality. It was easy to believe that the final drama of history would be played out in such terms—by an abomination of desolation followed instantly by an angelic *renovatio*."
35. Weinstein 1970: 351.
36. Dall'Aglio 2006b: 72.
37. Benivieni unsuccessfully tried to intercede for Nardi in 1530 after the restoration of the Medici: Nardi's important role in the Last Republic of Florence was punished with exile; see Dall'Aglio 2012.

next to San Lorenzo in Florence: it was the time, as Nardi bitterly recognizes, in which the city was governed with the utmost semblance of civility and freedom and the utmost dissembling of princedom.[38] An episode in these civil and pleasant conversations is recounted twice in our sources. According to the version in the *Vita* of Benivieni written by his nephew, Antonio (1533–1598), at a banquet (perhaps in 1522)[39] Cardinal Giulio asked: "Girolamo, you profess to believe in the Friar, [so] how you can also be our friend and intimate?" Benivieni replied, "in the manner of Gamaliel to the Scribes":

> Monsignor mine, if the Friar's work is human, it will resolve itself quickly on its own; but if it is of God, then no matter what men might do, it will move ahead. But your Excellency need not ever fear the Friar's friends and disciples, who quietly await the miracle that God might work. Rather guard yourself well against these dissatisfied whisperers around you who, insatiable, never cease to trouble others with their impious machinations and to vent their excessive appetites.[40]

The episode of Gamaliel to which Benivieni here alludes (described in Acts 5:34-39) is a perfect example of apocalyptic reasoning. Truth is history, and God's action in it: if the friar's work is from God, it will move ahead as a charismatic force that human opposition cannot quash. This argument would be present in the background of Benivieni's 1530 letter. Jacopo Pitti provides a somewhat different version of the episode: Benivieni says

> I do not deny, Your Excellency, that I am one of the Friar's followers or that I—like all good men in this city—desire our common

---

38. Nardi 1858.
39. Roush 2006.
40. English translation by Roush 2006: 4; here the Italian version of Antonio Benivieni, ff. 41r–41v: "Monsignore mio, se l'opera del Frate è humana, la si risolverà presto per se stessa; se l'è di Dio, che ché gli homini se ne facciano, l'andrà per certo innanzi. Ma Vossignoria Illustrissima non tema già mai delli amici et devoti del Frate, essi aspettando il miracolo e che Dio Operi, quieti se ne stanno. Guardisi bene ella da alcuni di questi mormoratori inquieti che l'ha d'attorno, i quali, sempre insatiabili, non restano o resteranno già mai di travagliare, e nuovi e vasti concetti concependo altrui sollevare per compimento e sfogo dei loro smoderati appetiti."

freedom; but neither I nor any of them will commit a felony on that account, nor will they ever take up arms against the state: we shall fervently pray God and yourself to grant it to us.[41]

Benivieni's prompt answer guaranteed him the final say in the debate; and, as his nephew said, he was "allowed to keep his own opinion and innate liberty" (*opinione e natia libertà*).[42] This episode is very significant insofar as it recalls the image of the liberal and open debate which Giulio de' Medici wanted to promote and the relevant role of Benivieni in Florence, which is the essential context for understanding the 1530 letter and the peculiar position of Benivieni as pro-Medicean, yet at the same time a faithful follower of Savonarola. The political climate promoted by Cardinal Giulio in those years made this conjunction possible.

As Giorgio Caravale's studies have shown, the teaching and protection, respectively, of Benivieni and Cardinal Giulio were the premise for the Savonarolian conversion of Lancillotto Politi, who, while following the Papal court between Bologna and Florence, discovered Savonarola's writings and chose to enter the Dominican order.[43] In 1520, Benivieni penned the preface to a virulent polemic against Luther by Politi, who had now assumed the name Ambrogio Catarino.[44] Benivieni commended the author's effort to eradicate the error, but declared freely his hope for Luther's repentance and reconciliation with the Catholic Church: charitable sentiments, as Dionisotti writes, which were not the norm in Catholic Europe in those days.[45] However, we must not forget that the choice of Benivieni to compose the preface for this work—which was one of the

41. English translation by Polizzotto 1994: 250, slightly modified; see Pitti 1842: 123: "Io non niego, monsignore illustrissimo, di non [sic] essere dei seguaci del Frate; ed insieme con tutti gli uomini dabbene di questa città, desiderare la libertà comune; ma né io, né coloro faranno per tal conto fellonia, né verranno le armi contro allo stato giammai: pregheremo bene Dio e voi, che ne la conceda, per mantenerla in pubblico giustamente e con fede, e in privato con industria e parsimonia."
42. English translation by Roush 2006: 5.
43. Possibly in Benivieni's house: Catarino himself says that he was the guest of a *piagnone*, where he read Savonarola's works: Caravale (2007: 19) argues that it could have been Benivieni, since we know that he was a protector of Politi in those years.
44. Girolamo Benivieni to Antonio Negusantio in Politi 1956: 1. On the *Apologia*, see Preston 2003 and Caravale 2007.
45. Dionisotti 1980: 210.

first responses to Luther, written at the urgent request of a powerful circle in Florence, a city effectively ruled by the Pope's cousin—evidences on the one hand the circle's complete trust and high regard for the old Savonarolan, and on the other that he was taking a clear stance against Luther.[46] This position was not unique to Benivieni; on the contrary, as Massimo Firpo argued, after some early enthusiasm, many Piagnoni feared and rejected Lutheran contaminations, which would have risked betraying their original inspiration and facilitating their political marginalization.[47] Luther's own appropriation of the figure of Savonarola complicated matters.[48] The connection Savonarola–Luther was later made by Politi himself, who would recant his earlier positions in a virulent accusation of the friar,[49] the *Discorso contra la dottrina et le profetie di fra Girolamo Savonarola* (1548).

Coming back to Benivieni's relationship with Giulio de' Medici, the latter was probably the addressee of a letter (recently published by Olga Zorzi Pugliese) written to a newly elevated pope: the closeness exhibited by the letter, which uses the second person, is much more plausible for Clement VII than Leo X, Pugliese argues with ample reason.[50] The letter, thus dated 1523, congratulates Clement on his accession to the papal throne and expresses sentiments of closeness and solidarity with the pope, who must now sail the vast sea in a ship that is almost submerged. Benivieni dares to remind him of the high duties and sacred tasks of the Papacy, and that the *patrimonium Christi*—which many popes before him dispersed in vain, considering it their property—is not Clement's, but is given for the frugal sustenance of the pope and his household, and the restoration and preserving of the Church's status; all that remains belongs

46. Lazzerini 2013 prefers to stress the elements of Benivieni's spirituality which in his opinion signal a closeness to an evangelical orientation; I think the general theological-political choices made by Benivieni make this improbable.
47. Firpo 1997: 343.
48. See Luther 1524.
49. See Dall'Aglio 2006a; Caravale 2007. Faldi 1994 claims that Benivieni, at the end of his life, was convinced of the fallacious nature of Savonarola's prophecies; Faldi sustains his arguments on a disputed passage of Politi's *Discorso*, which is not at all a reliable source and reports Benivieni's words on the last moments of Savonarola's life second-hand. Re (1906: 115–17) had already denied this hypothesis and Pugliese (1996: 311 n. 14) disproves Faldi's argument.
50. Letter published by Pugliese 1970: 285–87.

to the poor of Christ. If the appeal to sobriety and charity is nothing new or particularly relevant in the words of a religiously rigorous man, the emphases are interesting as they are in line with Florentine spirituality as exemplified, for instance, by the saintly bishop of Florence, Antonino Pierozzi (1389–1452), whose process of canonization was a top priority for the Medici popes, since 1515, the success of which was due to Cardinal Giulio's commitment.[51] The spiritual economy of earthly riches, to be expiated by the rich with charity and almsgivings, and in turn rewarded by prayers from the poor, was at the core of the spirituality of a mercantile city like Florence.[52] Benivieni fervently urges the pope to rescue his flock from the wolves through his actions and example, for otherwise the ruin of the state and loss of faith will certainly occur.[53] The pope is urged to choose not the way of pleasure but the way of God; he, Benivieni,

---

51. See Mussolin 2012.
52. See for instance a passage from his *Summa Theologica*, quoted in Kent 2000: 134: "The Divine Providence, which disposes of everything appropriately, permits some to be lacking in temporal goods, so that in the patient suffering of their poverty they may acquire eternal life. To others he gives an abundance, not in order that they may dissipate it on dogs, falcons, and horses, extravagant clothing, games, banquets, etc... but so that of this property, given to them by God, they should take what they need for themselves, and give the rest to His poor, and by the virtue of charity be received into the eternal tabernacles through the prayers of the poor." Pierozzi's Thomistic moral and economic vision were wildly popular and the *Summa* was a bestseller.
53. Pugliese 1970: 285–86: "Scimus enim te non ignorare quae sint pontificatus qua cura, quo labore, qua sollicitudine, et diligentia ea omnia administranda tibi sint. Nosti, scio, verum et legitimum pastorem animam propriam, hoc est vitam ipsam corporalem, pro ovibus fuerit, exponere oportere. Nec te preterit patrimonium Christi, ante hoc pontifices suum putaverunt et ut suum perperam disperserunt, esse tuum sed tibi datum ut in victum et vestitum tuum et familiae tuae (et hunc quidem secundum decentiam status tui perquam parcum et honestum), partim in reparationem et conservationem status Ecclesiae, caetera pauperum sunt Christi, repetenturque in illa die magna iudicii ab his, qui eum in alios turpes vel superfluos usus converterunt. Scitor igitur, beatissime in hoc te Deum excitasse, et ad hoc te culmen evexisse ut gregem benigne, non desecas, sed ex eorum luporum faucibus eripias, curia, nec dicam malignitate, nonnullorum pastorum qui ante Christi ovile non per ostium sed aliunde ascenderunt, crudeliter eumque in omni sanctitate vitae et doctrina custodias, et Ecclesiae suae sanctae incolumen representes. Si enim et tu eiusmodi pastorum viam missum tibi gregem (quod absit a sanctitate tua) eisdem quibus atque exemplis perderes et mactares, nulli christianorum dubium actum esset de re publica Christiana, cum omne vitium in precipiti et fides Christi perperam pene extincta sit."

a humble servant, dares to pronounce these words moved by that love which, even if you "drive it out with a pitchfork," to use Horace's words, "it will come back, winning over ignorant confident scorn."[54] Even in a conventional letter, the candor of Benivieni's words, directed as they are to the vicar of Christ, attest to his sincerity and courage in advocating for the common good of the Florentines.

Their relationship seems to have prospered in the years of Clement's papacy; Benivieni used personal connections to send his homages to the pope, as on March 17, 1525, when he wrote to Francesco Fortunati, the tutor of Giovanni delle Bande Nere and *pievano* of Cascina, asking him to remind Clement that *quando iustitia et pax obsculatae sunt, veritas de terra exorta est, et iustitia de coelo prospexit*.[55] The prophecy of Psalm 85.10-11 (= Vulgate 84.11-12) was a helpful reminder in a moment of disaster and dismay, when the pope was coming to terms with the defeat of his allies in the Battle of Pavia.

In the *Canzone exhortatoria a disporsi alla susceptione de le gratie promesse come disopra alla città di Firenze III*, Benivieni's song from the Savonarolan period, which would later be included in the 1500 *Commento*, the faithful are urged to stride forward on "spiritual feet," to acknowledge that Christ is the King of Florence who comes "with the right foot of mercy and the left foot of justice," to judge the city in respect of the spiritual and temporal government. The *canzone* proceeds in the second stanza to introduce two women, "sisters and daughters of God," Mercy and Justice, intimately joined, who bring peace and joy to the soul. These four *ancille* (Mercy, Justice, Peace, Joy) are at the court of the Virgin Mary, who precedes her Son. Benivieni's auto-exegesis comments that the soul must prepare six *mansiones* to host the mystical Spouse:[56] the

54. Pugliese 1970: 287: "Obsecro sanctitatem tuam excuset presumptionem, vel potius stultitiam meam, meus erga te amor quem 'furca expellas licet, tamen usque recurrit, et mala perrumpit furtim fastigia victor'." The quotation is from Hor. *Ep*. I, X, 24–25, but Benivieni replaces the original word "naturam" with "amor."
55. Letter published by Re 1906: 347.
56. Benivieni 1500: CXVI^r: "il che mysticamente ci insinua che a uolere riceuere epso sposo bisogna che la anima prepari in prima dentro da se sei mansione. Una alla Iustitia: et questa si fa rendendo a ciascuno quello che e suo; Verbi gratia: alla ragione el freno della sensualità: allo intellecto lo imperio della ragione: a Dio se medesimo: al proximo secondo la instantia delle sue necessita etiam insino alla vita corporale. L'altra alla pieta o uero misericordia: et questa si apparecchia retrahendo

way to peace is prepared by the renunciation of all passions and human affections and by coming to God, who is peace. In the *canzone* there is the continuous fluctuation between the complete interiorization of the coming of the Lord and intimations that Christ would actually come to Florence, which God "hauendola nuouamente electa per sua l'ha ancora in uno certo modo reedificata dandole una nuoua forma di uiuere di reggere et di governare."[57] Benivieni recalls in the *Commento* how Florence had been given the particular gift of a prophet, who was mocked and ridiculed and who had shown how to overcome adversities. The mystical vision can be linked to a sermon preached by Savonarola on Christmas Eve 1493, which connects the vision of Psalm 85 with the Nativity scene and presents Mercy, Truth, Righteousness, and Peace as heavenly women who attended Christ's birth. One of the sermons on the book of Haggai in 1495 describes the kiss of righteousness and peace as it took place in Florence, a testimony of God's love and mercy for his city: "the scourge was coming from one side and mercy met her halfway, et *iustitia et pax obsculatae sunt*, and they embrace and God has shown his mercy and his justice and has saved you."[58] The eschatological embrace of heavenly virtues prophesized in the Psalm is happening, right now. Not without reason has this imaginary lexicon been connected with Botticelli's *Mystic Nativity*,[59] which is in this interpretation another proof of Botticelli's reliance on his Savonarolan beliefs besides his *Mystic Crucifixion*. Therefore, Benivieni's greeting to the pope is anything but conventional, and it hints

---

se medesimo et la propria sua anima da e suoi più capitali inimici cioè da e vitii et da peccati et sovvenendo al proximo con parole et con opere secondo la exigentia de suoi bisogni. La terza alla pace: et questa si prepara extirpando da se tutti e desideri et tutte le affectione terrene: et reducendosi in Dio el quale e epsa pace. La quarta alla iocundita ouero letitia; et questa si fa purgando la mente e contemplando spesso e benefici di Dio, maxime quello della incarnatione della Croce et della morte di Cristo insieme con la gloria che Dio ha preparata a coloro che lo amano. La quinta ad epsa uergine gloriosa: et questa fabrica col martello della humilita: Quia respexit dominus humilitatem ancille sue. La sexta et ultima ad epso sposo: et questa si edifica et fa sopra tutte le altre perfecta per le mani di Amore: Quia deus charitas est: et qui manet in charitate in deo manet et deus in eo."

57. Benivieni 1500: CXVII^r.
58. My translation; Savonarola 1965: 133–34.
59. Hatfield 1995.

at the hopes concentrated in his figure.⁶⁰ Benivieni would ask Clement not only to be the head of a spiritual renovation of the Church, but also to deliver peace to Florence in one of the most dramatic moments of her history.

A *piagnone* to the triumphant pope: the 1530 letter

Benivieni's letter to Pope Clement, imploring his mercy on Florence, was well known in his times, as it was also summarized in Jacopo Nardi and Benedetto Varchi and alluded to by Gianfrancesco Pico.⁶¹ It was published in the appendix of Milanesi's edition of Varchi's *Storie* in 1857–58 and then in a single edition in 1858, on the basis of two manuscripts, Riccard. 2710 and BNF II II 437, where Milanesi found a preface to the letter attributed to Nardi. Catarina Re saw other manuscripts of the letter including a copy in the Vatican Library (Barb. Lat. 1535) and gave a description of these texts.⁶² Pugliese has demonstrated that Benivieni used his copy of some Latin sermons of Savonarola, most probably manuscript 480 of the Museo of San Marco,⁶³ as a source for passages he later encapsulated in

---

60. It was not the first case of one of Savonarola's followers who decided to write to Clement and disclose to him his role in the coming millennium. There exists a letter by Francesco de' Ricci, ostensibly written in the beginning of 1527, but clearly dated after the Sack, in which the ascension to power of the Medici family and their double accession to the papal throne were willed by God, but they had to flee Florence. The failure of Leo in doing so meant that he was struck down by God. Clement, therefore, could be the angelic pope who would lead Florence to the mystical Jerusalem. See Polizzotto 1994.
61. Nardi 1858, I: 97: "Essendo egli poi d'età di ottant'anni mandò a papa Clemente VII in calendi di novembre 1530, poscia che mediante l'esercito ecclesiastico e imperiale detto papa aveva preso il dominio della sua patria, avvertendo sua santità, e confortandola a tener sospeso il suo giudicio circa le cose del prefato fra Girolamo, non solamente per questo particolar vaticinio, ma per molte altre cose che il detto Girolamo raccontava, secondo sé, degne di molta considerazione. Confortava medesimamente detto papa che, avendo ricevuto da Dio così bella vittoria, dovesse costituire nella sua patria un giusto e santo e laudabil governo, secondo che da Dio ne aveva la potestà. Ma della epistola del Benivieni, la quale ho veduto tutta, basti aver detto insino a qui."
62. Re 1906: 116–17, n. 3.
63. The codex contains the drafts of the *Sermones Quadragesimales* of the year 1491, preached in Santa Maria del Fiore; the material was taken up again

the epistle. This is proved by the index, handwritten by Benivieni, which indicated some quotations from the sermons: two of them can be found in the epistle, in a passage where Benivieni mentions his ownership of Latin sermons by the friar.[64] Pugliese casts doubt on the attribution of the prefatory epistle to Nardi, which was accepted by Re, on the basis that there is no record of this letter in Nardi's list of works; neither does the moral emphasis of the preface seem to be in line with Nardi's expressed political interests. Pugliese proposes instead the name of Antonio Beccaria from Ferrara (d. 1543), who plagiarized various works of Savonarola, an attribution that remains to be verified on the basis of the handwriting. Pugliese calls for a new, critical edition of the letter (the present one was based only on two manuscripts out of a total of fifteen) that could solve the problem of a small lacuna,[65] attain better stylistic consistency, and eliminate some supplementary quotations from Savonarola's works which appear to have been made by later commentators.[66] The occasional mistakes on the date of one or the other of Savonarola's sermons, already noted by Roberto Ridolfi,[67] can be attributed to the method of quotation, which, as Benivieni admitted, often relied on his memory. For now, we can only rely on Milanesi's edition of the letter. It does, however, readily allow us to understand Benivieni's plea to the pope and his attempt at

---

for the preaching of Lent 1496 and 1497. Almost all the codex is handwritten by Girolamo Savonarola, and it contains annotations by other hands (certainly the ones of the two Benivieni brothers, Girolamo and Domenico). See Savonarola 2001 and http://www.mirabileweb.it/manuscript/firenze-museo-di-san-marco-bibliotecadel-convento-manuscript/205059.

64. Pugliese 1996: 312–13; Savonarola 2001: 371–72 has the list of the *notabilia* handwritten by Girolamo Benivieni on the lapel of f. 1 of the codex; on the last page of the manuscript there is a list of propositions written by Domenico Benivieni. As recognized by Pugliese, *ibidem*, two of these *notabilia* were incorporated in the letter: *Cogita ergo qualis et quanta erit haec persecutio*, notation made to a sermon of 1492, and *Turcus veniet contra nos et christianitatem capiet a quo capta liberabitur*, notation made to the XX sermon of Lent 1491. Other six *notabilia* were not included in the text of the letter.
65. Benivieni 1858: 20, after "e che e popoli."
66. There is also an almost certain gloss, which reports a quotation from Philippe de Commynes (Benivieni 1858: 21: "Monsignor Argentone istorico franzese"): Pugliese 1996: 314 says that this type of quotation is outside Benivieni's writing habits.
67. Ridolfi 1974: 2.

presenting Savonarola's prophecy as a vital instrument for reading the signs of the times and the present needs of Florence.

In Milanesi's 1858 edition, the letter is 24 pages long and is dated November 1, 1530. It opens with a Latin *exordium*[68] which pays honor to the pope and depicts the writer as an old man close to death,[69] called to give an account of his administration of the time spent on earth and to present it to Christ's tribunal. If the debt accumulated with God is beyond repair, however, the debt due to the pope, Benivieni argues, has to be satisfied. This prologue is remarkably reminiscent of the habit of medieval merchants of dedicating a separate entry in their accounting books for "God's account" (*il conto di messer Domineddio*), which went to charity; Cosimo the Elder had such a book, and, as Dale Kent says, "the common notion of 'God's account' shows how vividly Florentines conceived spiritual debts on the model of their worldly obligations [...] The ingrained habit of balancing credits with debits shaped devout Florentine merchants' views of the economy of salvation."[70] Benivieni's spiritual debt *vis-à-vis* Clement, even if already partially paid back, is now rewarded from time to time with a coin which, Benivieni fears, could be considered counterfeit.[71] The authenticity and veracity of the coin with which he is

---

68. Benivieni 1858: 11: "Sanctissime ac Beatissime Pater, post pedum oscula beatorum. Octuaginta annos natum, ipsa me aetas admonet, ut sarcinulas colligam, antequam e vita discedam." Pugliese 1996: 317 recalls how the discovery of a Latin version of the letter, kept in the Dominican convent of Santa Sabina, Rome, made her think that the vernacular version was a translation, and this exordium was the last trace of the original Latin. However, upon close analysis, she concluded that the Latin version is in fact a later translation. This Latin solemn exordium is just a rhetorical convention quite usual in the epistolary habits of this age.
69. The age indicated by Benivieni (80) is slightly exaggerated, no doubt for a pathetic effect.
70. Kent 2000: 133.
71. Benivieni 1858: 12: "è ben vero che io ho più volte messo mano alla scarsella, numerata la pecunia, e fattone un legato per mandarla alla Beatitudine Vostra, e da tal debito liberarmi; e poi in su lo spaccio del fante, ho mutato pensiero, come quello che occupato da un certo timore, e da una certa sapienza umana, ho dubitato che la pecunia con la quale io posso e debbo pagare questo debito, non sia reputata falsa: e così non solo non satisfare all'obbligo mio con grazia della Beatitudine Vostra, ma più presto riportarne qualche odio o indignazione; se odio però si può interporre fra la sincerità dell'animo mio e la benignità della Santità Vostra, la quale Iddio sa se io l'amo quanto me medesimo: e questo amore, se io erro, è quello che mi fa errare."

paying is the real content of the letter, which will be judged by the standard which sets gold aside from hoax, silver from lead: namely, time and God's judgment. This criterion for assessing reliability and truthfulness is the same as the famous conversation between Benivieni and Cardinal Giulio, which Benivieni comes to recall to his patron: "Your Holiness could remember what I told You some years ago about the subject of Friar Girolamo Savonarola and the things which he prophesized; I urged You to leave judgement to God, *qui solus scrutator est cordium*; this is a safer resolution than judging ourselves, especially in the negative." That is because, if he was who he claimed to be, namely, a man "sent by God to announce the scourge which we have since seen, and have experienced with such great ruin, and are experiencing. [...] It must be said, too, that he was one of the great men whom the Christian religion has had since Christ's coming; and so if, on the contrary, he deceived all, he was the most wicked man in the world, as he himself posits and maintains on many occasions in his writings; it is much safer, however, to delegate judgement to God."[72] The clear reference made by Benivieni is to that dialogue with Cardinal Giulio recounted in the sources cited above, in which he had already defended his loyalty to the friar and suggested the proof of time for a better judgment on his life and deeds. Time has passed, and the letter itself is a first example of this evaluation of the trustworthiness of Savonarola's words and their applicability to the present. Benivieni recalls how he first doubted Savonarola's intentions, and how he was convinced by the constant familiarity with him, alongside Giovanni Pico della Mirandola and Benivieni's brother Domenico, which showed Savonarola's doctrine, goodness, and integrity of life. Benivieni claims that he has always ultimately entrusted to God the judgment on

---

72. My translation, Benivieni 1858: 12–13: "La Santità Vostra si può ricordare di quello che io gli dissi già più anni sono di Fra Girolamo Savonarola, e delle cose da lui predette; confortandola a rimetterne il giudizio a Dio, *qui solus scrutator est cordium*; parendomi più sicuro partito, che farne giudizio noi, massimamente in male; perché, se pur poi e' fussi stato quello che ei diceva d'essere, cioè mandato da Dio a denunziare a tutta Italia il flagello, che noi abbiamo di poi visto, e con tanta nostra rovina provato, et proviamo; [...] bisogna dire che dall'avvento di Cristo in poi, ei sia stato uno dei grandi uomini che abbi auto la religione cristiana; così come per l'opposito s'egli ingannava e' popoli, il più tristo uomo del mondo: come lui medesimo in più luoghi delle sue predicazioni allega e afferma: e però, è molto più sicuro il rimetterne il giudizio a Dio."

the friar and has never condemned the unconvinced, knowing that the faith in these things is not a matter of human free will, because the Spirit blows where He wills. Therefore, remembering the opinions of many, who thought that Savonarola's treatment was the cause of the divine punishment of Florence, Benivieni offers to the pope a collection of Savonarola's prophecies, placing before him "what I have heard, read, and observed, amongst those things which can deservedly turn the mind of everyone, and, if not absolutely to judge this the truth, then at least to suspend judgement."[73] Benivieni's suggestion to ultimately leave judgment to God is not simply an indication of cautious prudence, born out of political necessity, but an apocalyptic marker, a symptom of a mentality which assigns to the Spirit the freedom of electing and disowning, a supreme liberty which leaves the faithful in hope, expectation, and trembling. However, Savonarola's life and doctrine, Benivieni argues, did not need any defense: if there was sin in him, it was very well hidden, and his doctrine was the same as Christ's. Thus, Benivieni chooses not to engage at all in the accusations hurled at Savonarola during his life, that he was a heretic and schismatic, not even judging them worthy of mention. The true proving ground is the verification of his prophecies, which Benivieni states as the true aim of the letter, and for which he resorts to the treasure of his memory. Lastly, before getting into the subject, without naming names, Benivieni polemicizes against those who have minutely examined the friar's writings so as to make them useful in staking out their own positions. He affirms that he has never done so owing to the certainty that faith in these matters is not man-made, and vain disputations are more likely to produce scandal than anything else. This seems on the one hand a self-defense, on the part of a renowned man of letters and prominent follower of Savonarola, for having until then remained quiet and not having taken a position in writing on the friar; on the other hand, it looks to be an attack on polemics either for or against Savonarola, which by their very nature are incapable of being faithful to the friar's teachings.

---

73. My translation, Benivieni 1858: 14: "A me basta satisfare al debito mio, che è mettere innanzi alla Santità Vostra quello che io ho udito, letto e osservato di quelle cose che possono meritatamente inchinar lo animo di ciascuno, e se non a giudicare assolutamente questa verità, almanco a sospendere il giudizio."

When introducing Savonarola's prophecies, Benivieni draws a distinction, as Savonarola usually did,[74] between the absolute and the conditional: absolute prophecies are immutable, written in God's mind, and will inevitably be fulfilled; conditional prophecies, in contrast, depend upon secondary causes and are therefore variable and subject to human influence. Benivieni recalls that four of Savonarola's prophecies were absolute: the scourge of Italy and especially Rome, the Church's renewal, the conversion of Turks and Moors, and Florence's fortune. Leaving aside the scourge of Italy, which, as Benivieni said, is plain for all to see, the other prophecies, even if absolute and therefore bound to happen, are conditional with respect to the timing of their fulfillment: Fra Girolamo's opinion was that they were very near, for example in the case of the conversion of Turks and Moors, but this was only his evaluation. His apocalyptic impulse is here diffused in time dilation, a time-tested strategy for dealing with the tardiness of the eschatological events that was invoked already in apostolic times.

Coming back to his memories of the encounter with Savonarola, Benivieni recalls how he, along with his brother Domenico and Count Giovanni Pico della Mirandola, went to listen to the friar's preaching, and were presented with sound doctrine, yet were offended by "the manner of his preaching, his gestures, and the pronunciation."[75] The topos here expounded is the contradiction between the humble, virulent, and simple preaching of the friar, which was at odds with the refined, humanistic sermons pronounced in Florence in his days. One of the friar's major opponents, Fra Mariano da Genazzano, who preached in the church of Santo Spirito, is mentioned: the contraposition between Savonarola's simple and effective style and the Augustinian's articulate and polished sermons was promoted by Lorenzo the Magnificent, who tried unsuccessfully to offer an alternative to the friar's preaching in his first years in Florence.[76] It should be noted how Savonarola promoted this image of himself, and the comparison with the young and almost unarmed David against Goliath: for instance, in the draft of sermon 5 of the first Sunday

---

74. See for instance Savonarola 1955, I: 288 (sermon XXII on Ezekiel, February 22, 1497).
75. My translation, Benivieni 1858: 17.
76. Cf. Pellegrini 2020: 59.

of Lent in 1491, preserved in the already quoted ms. 480, and marked by Girolamo Benivieni with a note, Savonarola wrote: *veniet David, idest chorus aliquorum, pulcher aspectu et manu fortis. Non in armis regalibus sed in paupertate extrema; non in philosophia et rhetorica sed in simplicitate etc. non in superbia mundi sed in humilitate etc.*[77] Afterwards, Savonarola himself annotated in a *postilla* that he had not pronounced the prophecy; instead, he had urged himself to be like David (*hanc prophetiam dimissi et hortatus sum ut essem sicut David*[78]). Benivieni annotated the prophecy of the coming of a new David, clearly interested in one of the crucial figures of the Florentine imaginary field, appropriated by the Medici and by Savonarola.

Then, Benivieni introduces the narration of the true prophecies that Savonarola had uttered anticipating Charles VIII's coming: the deaths of Pope Innocent VIII and Lorenzo the Magnificent, the expulsion of the Medici and the new government in Florence. Excluding the first one, these events were foretold in private to some citizens whom Benivieni mentions and who were his sources. Some pages are now devoted to establishing Savonarola's credentials as a true prophet, mentioning different successful prophecies, quoting from his memories and from his manuscripts. Benivieni's letter also singles out Savonarola's prophecy of the Sack of Rome, foreshadowed in the second homily on Ezekiel (December 4, 1496), which announces the coming of people from the cloud,[79] angry and cold people, bloodthirsty, lustful and rapacious;[80] as is widely known, and as Benivieni claims to have read in intercepted correspondence between

---

77. Savonarola 2001: 28.
78. Savonarola 2001: 34.
79. Aquilo, the north wind; cf. Aug. *Conf.* 10, 36, 59, where Lucifer is said to have placed his throne in the Aquilo, so that humanity could serve him in a cold darkness. The devil is cold for his sin, argues Savonarola in this homily. Cf. Savonarola 1955: 17–28.
80. Benivieni 1858: 22: "E verrà la nube dalla parte dell'Aquilone, che saranno gente fredda e arrabbiata, e con superbia tornerà dentro questa nube, che significa che egli aranno desiderio di sangue, di concupiscenzia e di roba; scoppierà di fuore, perché arderanno molte ville, città e castella. Il fuoco sarà il fuoco della carestia, e il fuoco ancora della pestilenzia, che involgerà molta gente. Firenze, se tu farai bene, questa nube e questo fuoco ti andranno attorno, e diràgli Iddio: non andar più là, va' di qua: e così sarai liberata." Cf. Savonarola 1955: 17–28.

the enemy's forces, the Landsknechts were directed first to Florence, then decided to go directly to Rome.

Benivieni also recalls an episode which directly involved him, when Piero de' Medici attempted to come back to Florence in arms (1497): Benivieni, very alarmed, was sent to Savonarola by one of the city's leading citizens, and the friar, smiling, answered with the words of Jesus to Peter, *modicae fidei, quare dubitasti?*, promising that Piero would quickly depart, as in fact happened.[81] Savonarola, Benivieni continues, often prophesized pestilence and famine, two recurring events in the history of the city: a fact that enables him to digress and present his ocular witness of the tragedy of the siege of Florence. Benivieni comments in detail on the desperate situation of the city, listing the exorbitant costs of food in those terrible days, and offers his own reading of the events of August 1530, with the negotiation for the surrender and the attempted dismissal by the magistrature of the Ten of the Florentine General Captain, Malatesta Baglioni. For Benivieni, the surrender is proof of divine benevolence, as it spared the city the fate that had befallen Rome only three years before. He portrays Baglioni, who had betrayed the city in a secret agreement with the pope, in a surprisingly good light: all the city implores Baglioni not to leave it in disorder and danger, and the captain pronounces words of repentance and ultimately allows the surrender. The fatal day, August 8, 1530, is the nadir of disorder, the utmost chaos from which God draws good: namely, the surrender of the city, which now must receive the kind of government which Clement will be pleased to ordain for it. Benivieni recalls Savonarola's sermon XXV on Micah,[82] which presents God with

---

81. Benivieni 1858: 23–24.
82. Benivieni 1858: 28: "Nell'ultimo capitolo della venticinquesima predica sopra Michea, sono queste parole: 'O Signore, tu mi pari fatto simile al figolo che fa vasi, e piglia la terra e mettela in su la ruota e girala, e fa un vaso; e quando egli l'ha presso che fatto, trova un sasso, e cerca di cavarlo, e acconciarlo; e quando vede pur di non lo poter cavare, e acconciarlo, gli dà della mano e guastalo e scompiglia ogni cosa, e butta quel sasso in terra, e ripiglia poi della altra terra e rifà quel vaso buono.' E poche parole di sotto soggiugne: 'Così dico a te, Firenze, se tu non vorrai intendere, egli si scompiglierà un tratto ogni cosa, e farassi un disordine dal quale nascerà poi un grande ordine'." Cf. Savonarola 1962: 2: 295–96, here the passage which is not quoted in Benivieni's text: "Al tempo del diluvio tu trovasti e' vasi cattivi pieni di sassi, tu scompigliasti ogni cosa in tutto el mondo, e poi rifacesti buoni vasi. *Quis Deus similis tui?* 'Quale Dio si truova simile a te?' Chi è quello che possa intendere

the biblical image of the potter, who tries with a stone to modify the clay pot when it is almost finished but, when that fails, throws the pot on the ground, and then takes up some other clay to remold the vessel. Benivieni appropriates the image and sees its fulfillment on August 8, 1530, when God

> has thrown the clay down from the wheel onto the ground, and thrown everything in disorder, so that, as I believe, he will take the clay up again from the ground, purified and rough-hewn, and place it atop the wheel of his divine providence, making of it a pot of that kind eternally ordained by his divine will for the salvation, peace, and glory of this troubled city (*ha questo presente giorno otto d'agosto 1530, dato, come è noto a ogni uomo, di mano alla terra, buttatola giù dalla ruota, e scompigliato ogni cosa, per ripigliare, com'io credo, della terra di nuovo, e poi purgata che l'arà, e tolto via tutti gli impedimenti, porla sopra la ruota della sua divina provvidenza, e farne un vaso tale, quale egli ha nel consiglio di sua Divina Maestà ab eterno ordinato, per salute pace e gloria di questa tribolata città*).[83]

Everything upside down: prophecy and apocalyptic under siege

The overturning of Florence, the pot of clay in the hands of God, the unhappy potter who decides to destroy his creation and start again, represents in my opinion the best way to understand Benivieni's stance and its ambiguities, which perplexed even his interlocutors at the time. How was it possible to maintain a staunch fidelity to Savonarola's preaching

---

li tuoi iudici? Al tempo de Giudei, quante volte scompigliasti ogni cosa, e poi racconciasti! Così a te, Firenze, se tu non vorrai intendere, e' si scompiglierà un tratto ogni cosa e farassi uno disordine, dal quale nascerà poi uno grande ordine: picchia quello, ammazza quello altro: e assetterassi poi ogni cosa." I think that here maybe Benivieni had in mind sermon 12 of Lent 1491, contained in ms. 480, which he marked with a *nota* which is not directly included in the letter (*Si amas filios non ne.fare alcuno prete: necabitur ad filo della spada*: Savonarola 2001: 371): in the draft of the sermon Savonarola wrote: *Ecce: coram senioribus et sacerdotibus sum et dico vobis quod Dominus confringet hoc vas Italiae et praesertim in hac parte* (Savonarola 2001: 74). On the violence against priests, see Lerner 2004.

83. Benivieni 1858: 28.

and at the same time to welcome the government of a Medicean pope?[84] I believe the answer lies in the ambiguities inherent in the apocalyptic mentality itself, as nourished in Savonarola not primarily by the medieval tradition[85] but by the Bible itself. The image of the potter clearly exemplifies this background: it is a prophetic image, very well-grounded in Jewish thought.[86] In Isaiah 29:16 it indicates the unfathomable nature of God's will, and the prophet chastises the arrogance of the creature that challenges the absolute power of the Maker (*You turn things upside down, as if the potter were thought to be like the clay! Shall what is formed say to the one who formed it, "You did not make me"? Can the pot say to the potter, "You know nothing"?*). In the Epistle to the Romans (9:20-21), the apostle Paul invokes the image to drive home God's absolute, unconditional, creative freedom to change the object of his election, now electing those who had been rejected and rejecting those who had been chosen.[87] If the Pauline God who wills to overturn the economy of salvation is at the heart of Savonarola's mentality, the closest parallel for the image in the Savonarolan homily and in its actualization in Benivieni is chapter 18 of Jeremiah, where the scene is set at the potter's house:[88] the Lord reminds the children of Israel that they are clay, with which He can do as he pleases, as the potter who starts a new creation when the first one is damaged. The divine call to repentance envisages and threatens the possibility of the overturning of election, and the punishment of the unfaithful people. Paul would read this overturning of election and God's change of heart as it happened in Christ, in an economy of salvation which however providentially gives a decisive role to Israel, the rejected vessel.

84. See on this Dall'Aglio 2005.
85. Which, however, was very important, as proved by Weinstein, in Savonarola's identification with Florence and her elected destiny: see Weinstein 1970; Weinstein 2011.
86. Cf. James Dunn's commentary on Romans, which comments on Rom. 9:20-21 that "The idea of a creator is also present in wider Greek thought but the idea here is characteristically Jewish, particularly the thought of God as creator having a continuing oversight and responsibility for his creation such that the possibility of the creature answering back is even conceivable (contrast the Greek idea of "fate") [...] The potter with his clay ($\pi\eta\lambda\acute{o}\varsigma$) was a popular image for God as Creator in Jewish thought (Ps 2:9; Isa 29:16; 41:25; 45:9; Jer 18:1-6; Sir 33:13; T. Naph. 2.2, 4; 1QS 11.22)" (Dunn 1988: 545–46).
87. Lettieri 2009: 80, my paraphrase.
88. Jer. 18:1-10.

In the economy of the salvation of Florence, the city of Christ,[89] the dramatic events of August 1530 are the moment of total reversal: God has broken the old damaged and corrupted vase, to give way to a new creation. The image is unfurled plainly by Benivieni himself, who declares that the vase is "the reform of Florence's good government" ("la riforma del buon governo di Firenze");[90] the clay is the Florentine citizenry, responsible for the botched molding of the vase; God's hand is His grace and *adiutorium*; and the stone is the obstinacy and perverted will of those who hamper God's work. With these premises, God's remedy has been to give over the wheel into the hands of the pope, for the peace and glory of Florence. We see, then, that Benivieni's high, millenarian hopes for the destiny of Florence are not abandoned, but redirected. God works in disorder, from which He draws good: the city is now clay, from which Clement can work in a truly demiurgic way. Thus Benivieni writes:

> May His Divine Majesty grant to Your Beatitude the grace to give [a government to Florence] in the way and form which is most useful for the peace and salvation of this people, steadiness and strength and progress and dominion of the city, and the perpetual glory and honor of Your Holiness' most excellent House: provided that you lay the foundations and build the form of government upon the stone of which is written, *Petra autem erat Christus*, this cannot fail to be optimal.[91]

The Florentine Republic, whose end is here described in providential terms, was enflamed and sustained by a civic religion that included the Savonarolan conviction that the city had been elected by God and freed by Him from its usurpers. Consider in this context the famous observation of Francesco Guicciardini, that the obstinate faith of the Florentines in a

---

89. On this, once again, see Weinstein 1970, who describes the emergence of a civic "myth of Florence" as divinely elected and head of Italy's renovation; Weinstein also underlines Benivieni's role in this narrative: "All peoples and all nations, wrote Benivieni, would conform to the one true religion of Florence, and the world would be united in one sheepfold under a single shepherd. In the new age Florence would extend her hegemony in a benevolent *imperio* because she was the city of the elect and of the true religion." The reference is to Benivieni 1500: CXIII^v.
90. Benivieni 1858: 28.
91. My translation; Benivieni 1858: 29.

victorious future made them resist for months under siege, when no one would have believed they could do it even for days: this "due to the faith that they cannot perish, according to the prediction of Brother Jerome of Ferrara."[92] Varchi gives us a revealing glimpse of the hopes and apocalyptic anticipations of Benivieni in the last days of the Florentine Republic: he, with other noble Florentine citizens, believed that the city would be saved at the very last moment, when the situation would appear desperate and without solution: only then would the angels save the city with swords.[93] The moment of utmost abjection and humiliation is the moment of redemption; the rescue will come immediately after the disaster, the cross right before the resurrection: these are true markers of apocalyptic thinking, old and new.

Angels with swords did not appear: the one who did appear was the Medici pope, preceded by the imperial army. Here we can see the ambiguity of the apocalyptic expectation, which needs to read the signs of the times, to interpret them as the revelation of the divine message, and therefore tends to sacralize immanence. The denunciation of the corruption, injustice, and evil of this world cannot fail to project its hopes on historical figures as tools of redemption: for Savonarola, this was Charles VIII; for Benivieni, Pope Clement (and Leo before him). This means a paradoxical balance between the ecstatic challenge of consolidated ecclesiastical and political structures and a principle of stabilization of the message, apologetic defense and certification of its truthful status, and promise of "a hundredfold here below."[94] In this sense, I think, one can overcome the tensions which have been assumed in scholarly

---

92. See Guicciardini 1965: 40.
93. Varchi 1841: 452: "senzachè non vi mancavano di quegli, i quali erano o di sì gran bontà, o di sì poco intelletto, che dalle parole mossi delle prediche di fra Girolamo, le quali chiamavano profezie, quanto più i nemici stringevano Firenze, tanto si rallegravano essi maggiormente, avendo per fermo, che quando la città fosse in termine ridotta, ch'ella più rimedio nessuno non avesse, né forza umana potesse in verun modo difenderla, allora finalmente, e non prima, dovessero essere mandati dal cielo in sulle mura gli angioli a liberarla miracolosamente colle spade; né erano questi che ciò credevano uomini di volgo solamente e idioti, ma eziandio nobilissimi, come Giuliano Capponi, e letterati, come Girolamo Benivieni." On Varchi, see at least Simoncelli 2006 and Lo Re 2006.
94. See Matt. 19:28-29.

debates on Savonarola, between prophecy and apocalypticism:[95] both are moments of the same phenomenon, inherent to its dualism. In this sense, the Old Testament prophets do not suffice to explain Savonarola's stance, which is rooted in the nature of Jesus's messianism, characterized by the reclaimed elective, direct, and visionary intimacy with God, which announces the arrival of a new kingdom, declares the divisive nature of his preaching, and asks for a lifechanging adherence to his followers. This apocalyptic nature[96] of Jesus's mission is mediated through successive historical revivals which build new, stable religious identities. In the Jesus movement an ecstatic, apocalyptic, and disruptive moment coexists with a principle of orthodoxy which requires the establishment of a new identity and mystical body. While orthodox, this expectation is at the same time radically polemic with respect to the established order: it entails instituting a new, victorious order, which creates new heavens

95. This opposition is, for instance, very marked in Paolo Prodi's refined analysis of Savonarola's teaching: he sees apocalypticism as a position which comes down as an ecstatic stand-by, whilst prophecy is an active stance which expresses itself as "giunto di congiunzione tra Dio e l'uomo, tra il potere e la sua contestazione, tra il presente e il futuro all'interno della storia" (Prodi 1998: 210). This recalls Martin Buber's (1957) description of the two as opposite *Geistererscheinungen*: one, that of the prophet, which intervenes in history, demanding a momentous decision from his hearers, and the other one, which substantially complies with reality in an acquiescence with present reality, drawing a future of redemption and perfection.
96. Here I depend on Lettieri 2018b: 55, who defines thus Jesus's apocalypticism and his heresy: "la pretesa eretica gesuana mi pare propriamente apocalittica, in quanto a) fondata sulla pretesa di accogliere direttamente, senza intermediari istituzionali, la rivelazione di Dio, di cui Gesù possiede una visione diretta; b) incentrata sulla visione dell'imminente avvento del nuovo eone, distruttivo nei confronti del vecchio eone; c) caratterizzata dall'azione esorcistica di Gesù, che in Spirito sottrae al demonio, visto ormai cadere dal cielo, il suo potere sugli uomini di Israele e sul 'mondo'; d) prospettata come rivelazione ultimativa, che pone l'aut aut tra un'incredulità dannatrice e la fede salvifica, non surrogabile dal culto o dalla meditazione della Legge; e) connessa alla ridefinizione delle gerarchie religiose giudaiche, con l'esaltazione di Gesù/Figlio dell'uomo quale probabile messia escatologico e dei dodici come suoi governanti corrispondenti alle dodici tribù di Israele. Questo dispositivo apocalittico, portato da Gesù al centro del sistema religioso giudaico, nel Tempio, diviene sovversivo ed eretico, proprio perché fondato sulla pretesa di possedere una potenza dello Spirito sovraordinata a quella di sacerdoti, scribi, farisei, potenze politiche, quindi di impersonificare la volontà ultima di Dio nei confronti della storia di Israele."

and a new earth.[97] In Savonarola, prophetic denunciation and millenarian announcement of triumph are parts of a whole. And Benivieni, at once an apologist of the prophet and a pragmatic Medicean, is also profoundly immersed in apocalyptic thinking: for instance, his constant appeal to Gamaliel's proof (i.e., if it is from God, we shall see that from its fruit, its visible action on earth) opens up the possibility to be proved wrong. Apocalyptic thinking at its most sophisticated becomes exquisitely contorted, for it must allow room for the operation of the unfathomable and at times hidden nature of God's will, which may confound human reason and hopes.[98] Therefore, Benivieni, as a citizen under siege in the sunset of the Florentine Republic, could not fail to wait for the sign to come from heaven and utter an appeal, at once hopeful and tragic, to the predestined winner.

Peace as an apocalyptic sign in Savonarola

The apocalyptic mentality which we have ascribed both to Savonarola and to Benivieni is the key to understanding the concept of peace in these authors. Historians have mentioned the ambiguity and complexity of Savonarola's notion of peace, which is crucial to understanding his

---

97. Cf. Lettieri 2019a: 359: "La nozione protocristiana di eresia è di origine e sostanza eminentemente apocalittica, dipendente a) dalla pretesa di incarnare un'idea di rivelazione nuova e definitiva, salvificamente critica (κρίσις è giudizio ultimo), innovativa o distruttiva di Dio; b) dalla consapevolezza di difendere questa rivelazione dall'aggressione demoniaca, che mira a dividere, confondere, ingannare la comunità eletta. Si tratta di due facce inseparabili della stessa medaglia: la nuova luce trova la resistenza delle tenebre, vecchie e nuove, interne ed esterne. E questo in duplice senso: a) intesa in senso elettivo, eresia significa contestazione liberante della violenza dominante, religiosa e politica; desiderio di comunità carismatica, di avvento del Regno."
98. It would be interesting to compare this attitude to the one expressed after the 1527 Sack of Rome by the Illirian bishop Joannes Staphyleus, as described in Gouwens 2012: 98–100. Staphyleus's oration to the Rota in 1528 transforms the visions of doom of the Sack into a providential possibility for penance and pardon. Egidio da Viterbo is another possible parallel to Benivieni's letter: whilst in his *Schechina* the critical role in the providential plan is played by Charles V, the apocalyptic mechanism is the same: "present evidence of decline indicates, paradoxically, imminent renewal" (Gouwens 2012: 103).

thought. The most famous meaning of this word in Savonarola is probably "pace universale," a key theological-political concept: this universal peace meant a general amnesty for all the Mediceans (as was in fact passed on March 1495 as a Law on Peace and Amnesty), and was intended, in accordance with Paul's words to the Corinthians, to *make everything new and let the old depart* (2 Cor. 5:17). Peace unites the city and makes it secure and fearsome to its enemies. It has to be obtained through penance and prayers, so that, if Florence observes Savonarola's dictates, God can be her Physician, the *medico*,[99] who will take the place unjustly usurped by the Medici. Here we see the plasticity of the theological role of healer: Savonarola took on this role himself, denying it to his adversaries; the two Medici popes would then forcefully claim for themselves the role of healer of the Church and Italy.

The ability to promote peace in the city was the first success claimed by Savonarola: the events of November 1494 testified to this gift. The Florentine embassy received by Charles VIII, who was menacingly encamped in Pisa and had declared his intention to come to Florence, notably included Savonarola, who had a private meeting with the king. On the same day, a popular riot forced Piero de' Medici to leave the city. Savonarola claimed that the pacific nature of the revolution, a first in Florentine history, was made possible by the preparation of penance and fasting he had proposed, which mitigated God's wrath.[100] The universal peace meant the end of partisanship and divisions and the passing of good laws. The legislative action was accompanied by the prophetic glance towards a glorious future. The idea of a universal peace was figuratively represented in the vision which Savonarola narrated in the *Compendium of Revelations*: he arrived at the gate of Paradise, carrying a crown as a gift to the Virgin Mary, made by the Florentines with their prayers and deeds. "The tiny hearts at the peak of the crown surmounted by a cross represent the union of love and also the universal peace recently established among the citizens of Florence."[101]

---

99. Savonarola 2006: 162.
100. On this see Pellegrini 2020: 86–90.
101. Weinstein 2011: 149.

Savonarola's providential role is vindicated in the letter to Pope Alexander VI on October 16, 1495.[102] Accordingly, peace is the sign, the litmus test of the veracity of Savonarola's doctrine: "if those who follow the doctrine I preach acquire peace, as experience proves, it is a sign that it is the divine law, and that I preach nothing but the Gospel law or a doctrine which proceeds from God."[103] The same thing is reiterated in *A Dialogue concerning Prophetic Truth*, which states that, as according to Gal. 5:22-23, the fruit of the Spirit is love, joy, peace, patience and so on, and so his teaching, if faithfully obeyed, bears the fruit of "the full incomparable joy and peace in the house of the Lord."[104] In the letter to Pope Alexander VI (June 25, 1497), coming shortly after the papal excommunication of May 13, 1497, and written on the occasion of the murder of the pope's son Giovanni, Duke of Gandia, peace is equated with faith:

> faith, supported by innumerable miracles and the divine works of the most famous men, by prophecies as well as arguments and doctrines, and continually strengthened by the blood of countless martyrs, is the one and only true peace and consolation of the human heart. [...] The just man is one who lives in faith, as the Lord attests, Who says: "My just one shall live in his faith." Blessed, therefore, is the one who is called by the Lord to this grace of faith, without which no one can have peace, as Isaiah says: There is no peace for the wicked, says the Lord my God.[105]

Here Savonarola boldly equates peace with faith, faith in the truth prophesied by him. The second part of the letter is even clearer, as Job's words ("But who has opposed God and had peace"?) are defiantly proposed to the pope, declaring that all "things which I have prophesied and prophesy are true and from God." Even in a letter intended as consolation to the grieving pope, the peace proposed is the one prophesized by Savonarola himself.

---

102. Cf. Savonarola 2006: 271–72: "in the city of Florence peace has followed upon my words, which, if it had not followed, all Italy would have been perturbed, because the city of Florence, agitated by sedition and massacres, as much intestine as external, would have collapsed."
103. Savonarola 2006: 289.
104. Savonarola 2006: 101.
105. Savonarola 2006: 300.

Peace is a crucial part of millenarian expectations, which define themselves as the expectation of an imminent advent of a new world on earth before the end of time, characterized by justice, peace, and abundance.[106] A popular patristic etymology of Jerusalem was *visio pacis*, a vision of peace.[107] In Joachim of Flora, "the central message remained his affirmation of a real—though incomplete—achievement of peace and beatitude within history."[108] A reign of peace and justice coming after God's scourge was expected by the "positive" stream of the apocalyptic movements, as Weinstein calls it.[109] Most prophecies connected with the "myth of Florence" announced a reign of peace.[110]

Savonarola's preaching since the arrival of Charles VIII is marked by the millenarian announcement of a new Jerusalem, which is to be holy and peaceful and triumphant on earth. His appropriation of this common theme, which had a solid scriptural and popular basis to the point of appearing almost banal, is marked by a profound scriptural insight that radicalizes the ambiguity characteristic of this concept. First of all, the positioning of a principle of pacification and justice entails a dialectic with those who oppose this principle: as Machiavelli would notice, the friar preaching neatly divided "them" from "us," "two companies [*stiere*]: one which serves under God, namely, himself and his followers; the other under the Devil, namely, his opponents."[111] In Savonarola's terms: "quello cittadino che non vuole e ricusa questa pace […] debba esser fatto rebelle, che è contrario al bene commune della città."[112] God's kingdom is a plenitude that has yet to come: this means a temporary split between present reality and the forthcoming kingdom. Christ will be its king, but he is not reigning now, because the city has not repented. God will violently overthrow the impious, as his messenger announces. As

---

106. For the patristic concept of the millennium and the exegesis of Revelation 20, see Simonetti 2007. The exact positioning of the sabbath age, within or outside history, was a debated subject among Christians; the reign of peace could often have such materialistic traits that distinguished it clearly from the kingdom of saints prophesized in Revelation 20; see Reeves 2000: 295–305.
107. Cf. Origen, *Hom. in Ier.* 3.2; 9.2; Aug., *Psal.* 64.4.
108. Reeves 1993: 305.
109. Weinstein 1970: 93.
110. Weinstein 1970: 56–58.
111. Machiavelli 2004: 87.
112. Savonarola 1965: 245.

recognized by Jean-Louis Fournel and Jean-Claude Zancarini, "quand le frère crie 'Pace, dico, pace, Firenze,' il définit donc, en même temps, la nécessité de combattre ceux qui ne manqueront pas de s'opposer à cette paix nécessaire: à l'intérieur du discours de paix se développe immédiatement et nécessairement un discours de guerre."[113] The apocalyptic discourse opens up a dialectic between the two forces at play, characterized by polarization, and following Revelation 3:15, it rejects the lukewarm.[114]

This polarization goes to extremes both in the radical violence of its language and in the range of enemies which it identifies. For instance, in the Renovation Sermon of January 13, 1495 on the Psalms, Savonarola declares that it is necessary to fight against the half-hearted and against the twofold wisdom (*duplex sapientia*) of the New and the Old Testament: this fight is much harsher now than in Christ's times, Savonarola comments, because then there was only the Old Testament, and those who erred, believed they were doing good. In other words, then, there was only one established system of orthodoxy, whereas now, there are philosophy[115] and the Scriptures, which allow the tepid to hide; if Christ should return now, he would be crucified a second time.[116] The revelation of the truth in Christ provokes new and more radical evil.

The audacity of these words clarifies better than anything else the magnitude of the crisis in the theological and political system founded by Savonarola. The traditional Christian language of the spiritual war, which in a long tradition of Christian exegesis served to disempower the violence of the Old Testament writings, is stretched to extremes, often

---

113. Fournel and Zancarini 2002: 57.
114. Fournel and Zancarini 2002: 59.
115. Savonarola was not opposed to philosophy in itself, as his strong philosophical formation proves; however, the refutation of worldly wisdom is an essential part of apocalyptic thinking.
116. Savonarola 1974: 265 (January 13, 1495, *Renovation Sermon*): "Da poi che ti cominciai questo Apocalisse abbiamo avute di molte contradizioni: parte ne sai tu, parte Dio, parte gli angeli suoi. Bisogna combattere contra i tiepidi, et contra duplicem sapientiam idest contra la sapienza del nuovo e vecchio Testamento, contra duplicem scientiam contra la filosofia e le scritture sacre, et contra duplicem malitiam idest contra il male che fanno oggidì i tiepidi, e che conoscono che fanno male e vogliono farlo. Il che non fu così al tempo di Cristo, perché v' era solamente il Testamento vecchio; e, se erravano, credevano far bene. E però ti dico che, se Cristo oggi tornasse quaggiù un'altra volta, di nuovo sarebbe crocifisso."

stepping out of metaphor.[117] In the twenty-second homily on Micah (August 28, 1496), a sermon quoted by Benivieni in his letter, Savonarola justifies theologically the invocation of evil:[118] "the philosophers" say that evil is a privation of goodness, namely, evil is nothing; if the just man conforms to his nature, he would not err. When someone desires an evil, such as fornication, they desire this evil per accidens, desiring some good such as pleasure. Therefore, if the just man desires the scourge (*flagello*) to bring back humanity to good living (*ben vivere*), he desires it *per accidens*: and this evil *per accidens* is desired also by God, who cannot err, and has used many times this evil for the conversion of humanity. If God cannot err using evil *per accidens*, so Savonarola also cannot err. The Virgin herself ordered Saint Mercury to take up arms and kill emperor Julian; the prophets and the saints always prayed for the scourge to come soon. The sermon continues with the well-known invocation "spada, spada; carestia, carestia: pestilenzia, pestilenzia. Vieni, Signore, vieni presto." With the posture of one who speaks from a *locus terribilis*,[119] Savonarola's apocalyptic invocation calls at the same moment for the scourge and the Lord. Therefore, even peace could be a deceptive signal, as remarked by Savonarola, for instance, in his sermon XXIII on Haggai (December 28, 1494), where he states that "among all the things in any category, there is always one of that category which holds the first place and is superior to the others. [...] If we speak of the contemplative life, we say that in this category it is truth which always has the greatest force. Truth has this nature: that in peace it is overcome if it sits idly and is not set in motion, but in war, where it is contradicted, it wakes up and in the end wins all."[120] Truth needs war, not peace, to win all. The prevalence of peace can be suspicious in the sense denounced by the First Letter to the Thessalonians, which describes the day of the Lord as a thief coming in the night (*while people are saying, "Peace and safety," destruction will come on them suddenly, as labor pains on a pregnant woman, and they will not escape*, 1 Thess. 5:3); therefore, true peace is to desire to suffer

117. Fournel and Zancarini 2002: 68–69.
118. Savonarola 1962, 2: 197–201.
119. "Questo loco ha terribile investitura; bisogna fare qua a modo del Signore": Savonarola 1962, 2: 63.
120. Savonarola 2006: 165.

for Christ.[121] Even more clearly, "dove è unione senza contraddizione, quivi non è Dio."[122] Therefore, "noi faremo guerra di fuora, ma la pace nostra sarà dentro al cuore":[123] we will fight outwardly, but our peace will be inside. In this new Jerusalem, Righteousness and Peace are kissing in the midst of war.

An old man asking for peace: some conclusions

One of the last episodes narrated in Benivieni's letter of 1530 is the prophecy by Friar Girolamo of a new pope named Clement, under whom Florence would suffer great tribulations, but God would ultimately help her.[124] According to Gianfrancesco Pico della Mirandola, Benivieni himself was the source of this prophecy after Savonarola's death.[125] The letter closes with the prophecy of the barbers who will "shave" Italy and punish her, namely, the king of France, the Spanish army along with the Landsknechts, and either the Turks or the Lutherans (this last referent, Benivieni says, is not yet clear). Last would come pestilence: may God be satisfied with these punishments and placate himself, leaving Florence and Christianity in peace.

Benivieni's fate after the end of the siege and of the Republic was not easy; we know from a letter to Jacopo Salviati (October 1530) published by Re, of the benevolence of the pope towards the old man, which he tried to use in favor of his Savonarolan friends.[126] It is the same letter in which

---

121. Savonarola 2001: 22–27.
122. Savonarola 1984: 239.
123. Savonarola 1974: 185. See on this Palumbo 2002.
124. Benivieni 1858: 32: "La notte precedente il dì della morte di Fra Girolamo, Iacopo Nicolini uno degli uomini deputati a far compagnia alli condannati a morte, parlando col detto Fra Girolamo, in fra l'altre cose ch'ei disse aver ritratte da lui, fu che Firenze avrebbe grandi tribulazioni, ma che le maggiori sarebbero quando nella Chiesa di Dio regnasse un pontefice chiamato Clemente, ma che la città non dubitasse, che Iddio l'aiuterebbe." On this episode, see Simonetta 2014: 254–55.
125. Pico della Mirandola 1999: 150: "Hoc mihi ex ore ipsius Iacobi Hieronymus Benivienius vir probus et prudens manu sua literis testatus est." On the relationship between the Benivieni's family (Domenico in particular) and Gianfrancesco, see Garfagnini 2000.
126. Re 1906: 348: "ho ricevuto per parte di N. S. molto amorevole salute, delle quali certamente ho preso tanto maggior piacere, quanto elle mi rendono più certo dello

he reveals to his powerful protector his pitiful economic and political situation: after being considered by the Republicans as too Medicean, now he is considered too Savonarolan, and thus fined.[127] However, Benivieni was part of the council of 200 in 1532 under Alessandro de' Medici's government, clearly being still considered a prominent and influential citizen. Florence would not return to her pristine freedom, neither would Clement show himself merciful with his enemies; but the return to power of the Medici would mean, at least, peace for the exhausted city.[128]

Benivieni's path is the perilous one of a man confronted by two powerful theological-political alternatives: Savonarola's prophetic utterance, which shows Florence as the divinely elected citadel crowned by Christ the King, and the Medici popes' construction, which, coming from Florence, had conquered Rome and overcome the disaster of the Sack, taking back power in the city. I have argued that it can be misleading to read these alternatives as polar opposites, positing a black and white opposition between prophecy and hegemony, apocalypse and power. On the contrary, Girolamo Benivieni's life and thought attest how closely intertwined and mutually influencing these two visions could be.

The ascent of the Medici to ecclesiastical power since the fifteenth century was characterized by an appropriation of the imaginary field: they had presented their role in a messianic fashion, winning their unique and constitutionally challenging supremacy in the city with their capacity for harnessing the religious field. From the appropriation of the figure of David and Moses to the skillful use of the cult of the Magi, the figure of a messianic leader coming from Florence was not Savonarola's exclusively, but was widely used by the Medici, and would even be invoked

---

    amore di sua S.tà verso di me, polvere e cenere; e veramente, attese le condizioni de' tempi, la grandezza de' pericoli, gli affanni, le continue molestie e innumerabili cure e sollecitudini che di necessità bisogna che si ravolghino intorno alla mente sua non è certo poco segno d'amore ch'elle non abino avuto forza di cancellare la memoria mia del libro suo: ringraziate, prego, la sua B.ne a mio nome, e a lei mi raccomandate."

127. Ibid.: "grazia ne abino quelli che mi hanno avuto a giudicare come poco amico di quello stato, così come ora gli amici de' Medici, giudicandomi forse ancora loro poco amico dello stato presente, mi hanno computato nel numero di 300 cittadini a pagare di presente ducati 110 per uno, e rimanere obligati a ducati 260 per uomo."

128. On the flourishing of biographical writings after the political victory of the Medici, see Bramanti 2017: 67–93.

to court their favor by a political thinker and playwright distinctly not known for his piety.[129]

Moreover, both the Medici and Savonarola were capable of going beyond the metaphor:[130] their political action strictly paralleled their occupation of the symbolic field. In their unwavering quest first for a Florentine cardinal and then for a papal dynasty, they attracted and manipulated the yearning for an angelic pope. Savonarola occupied, in a sense, the same metaphorical space, identifying himself with David or Moses, preaching a war that was not only spiritual, and escalating an opposition to the pope which meant a projection as judge of the supreme spiritual authority of the West; in a sense, a substitution. This capacity is in a sense a secularized *accomodatio*, the capacity of adaptation to times, places, and the recipient. In other terms, it is the problem of the "riscontro," as Machiavelli theorized it; namely, the correspondence and conformity between the human action and its context in time.[131] Machiavelli himself had polemically noted how Savonarola adapted his political actions to time and context in his famous March 1498 letter: Savonarola "acts in

---

129. Such as in Niccolò Machiavelli, on whose "courtship" of the Medicean favor see Gaetano Lettieri's studies (see in particular on this theme Lettieri 2017a; Lettieri 2017b; Lettieri 2018a; Lettieri 2018b): my work is deeply indebted to his reading of these decisive decades and his analysis of Medicean messianism. Lettieri 2019b sees Machiavelli's *Mandragola* as a systematic sacred parody of the mystical marriage between Christ and the church, identifying the true recipient of the comedy as Leo X himself, already exalted and invoked in *Prince* XXVI as the political-military" head" of the redemption of languishing Italy. Lettieri 2021 shows the complex relationship between the images of the *Mandragola* and the religious symbolism of Savonarola, identifying in the little red crosses of the Piagnoni a direct influence on Machiavelli's comedy.
130. See on this Cacciari 1998: 233–34: "Spaccato in due è il mondo che Savonarola rappresenta: da una parte i suoi seguaci, 'optimi', schiera che 'militava sotto Iddio'; dall'altra i suoi avversari, 'scelleratissimi', 'sotto el diavolo'; buoni son esclusivamente quelli che lo seguono, 'perversi' quelli che lo combattono. E questi bisogna 'amazare', come Mosè ammazzò un egiziano: 'O Egiptio, io ti vo' dare una coltellata...' ('scoprendo e vitii loro', intende dire il domenicano—ma in simili forme di comunicazione è proprio l'immagine a contare!). Per l'occhio di Machiavelli è retorica, è colore, son bugie [...] ma anche infinitamente di più: sono i tratti tipici del linguaggio demagogico, le forme per 'appellarsi' alla moltitudine per *persuaderla* all'azione rivoluzionaria."
131. Galli 2014.

accordance with the times and colors his lies accordingly";[132] strikingly, however, this capacity of adaptation is precisely what Machiavelli recommends to the prince.[133]

Expressed in a formula, they all governed with *Paternostri*.[134] All of them tried to occupy the center, the new Jerusalem, whether it was Florence or Rome. This is not to say that the means to obtain peace and power were the same for Cardinal Giulio de' Medici, Girolamo Savonarola, Pope Leo, and the Florentine Republicans of 1527–30. However, they were all occupied in the theological-political project of constructing a way to peace, which had always as its concomitant the taking of power. In the Medici popes' policy, peace encompassed both the *libertas Ecclesiae* and their family's primacy in Florence; in Savonarola's preaching, peace began with the general mutual pardon and was crowned by the offer of the city to the Virgin, in the hands of the friar. None of these is the idealistic construction of philosophers: and Girolamo Benivieni, a hopeful realist, knew that the believer had to ask for signs from history itself. A change was imminent: that much was clear. Who would incarnate this change, history would tell, and the prophets and their followers would indicate.

132. English translation in Machiavelli 2004: 10.
133. See Najemy 1999: 680: "But was Machiavelli not—at least some part of him—in admiration of the friar's dexterity and flexibility, of his skill in using and interpreting religion, biblical texts, and even the image of Moses, to the advantage of a political cause with which Machiavelli later identified—the restored republic whose second chancellor he soon became? Indeed, fifteen years later Machiavelli compared Savonarola's attempt to introduce new ordini to the similar aims of legendary lawgivers, including Moses himself. The flexibility of interpretation and the ability to adapt to circumstances that he saw in Savonarola are precisely what he would emphasize still later in the example of the Roman consul Papirius who skillfully interpreted both the falsified report of the chicken-handlers and the religious customs of the Samnites in order to build the confidence of his troops. Machiavelli makes clear his admiration of the consul's willingness to hide or distort the auspices when he thought it necessary 'to make the result correspond to the prophecy.' He likewise recognized and, I suspect, admired a similar ability in Savonarola and considered it 'religion well used.' Savonarola, no less than the Romans, understood the ineluctable necessity of interpreting religion." On another important Machiavelli's passage on Savonarola (*Discorsi* I, 1) see Lodone 2011.
134. I modeled this on the famous sentence attributed to Cosimo the Elder, reported by Machiavelli (*Istorie fiorentine*, VII, 6), which denied the possibility of governing through prayers. Here my reference is paradoxical, hoping to indicate a theological-political field that all the actors tried to occupy, with the weapons at their disposal.

Author biography

Maria Fallica (PhD, Sapienza University of Rome) is a Marie Skłodowska-Curie Global Fellow at Sapienza University of Rome. Her research interests lie in the reception of the Fathers of the Church in the modern age, the history of the Reformations, the Italian Reformation of the sixteenth century, and the history of methodism. Her most recent publications are *The Protestant Origen: Polemical Use and Theological Appropriation of Origen in 16th Century Patristic Anthologies* (Münster: Aschendorff, 2022) and *Il metodismo via media della Riforma. Progresso e tradizione nella* Christian Library *di Wesley* (Rome: Carocci, 2022).

References

Primary sources

Benivieni, A., il Giovane (n.d.), *Vita di Girolamo Benivieni*. Firenze: Archivio di Stato. Archivio Leonetti Mannucci Gianni, Codice 43 (MS BNF II.I.91).

Benivieni, G. (1500), *Commento di Hieronymo Benivieni a più sue canzone et sonetti dello Amore et della Belleza Divina*. Firenze: Tubini.

Benivieni, G. (1519; 1522), *Opere di Hieronymo Benivieni*. Firenze: Giunta.

Benivieni, G. (1858), *Epistola a papa Clemente VII, con una prefazione attribuita a Jacopo Nardi*. Firenze: Le Monnier.

Del Lungo, I. (1867), *Prose volgari inedite e poesie latine e greche edite e inedite di A. Poliziano*. Firenze: Barbera.

Filipepi, S. (2020), *Estratto della Cronaca novamente scoperto nell'Archivio Vaticano*. Spoleto: Centro Italiano di Studi sull'Alto Medioevo.

Guicciardini, F. (1965), *Maxims and Reflections of a Renaissance Statesman (Ricordi)*, translated by M. Domandi. New York and London: Harper.

Luther, M. (1524), *Meditatio pia et erudita Hieronymi Savonarolae a Papa exusti, super Psalmos Miserere me, et In te Domine speravi*. Strasbourg: [Herwagen].

Machiavelli, N. (1989), *The Chief Works and Others*, 5th edn, vol. 2, translated by Allan Gilbert. Durham, NC and London: Duke University Press.

Machiavelli, N. (2004), *Machiavelli and His Friends: Their Personal Correspondence*, 2nd ed. Dekalb, IL: Northern Illinois University Press.

Nardi, J. (1858), *Istorie della città di Firenze*, edited by L. Arbib. Firenze: Società Editrice delle Storie del Nardi e del Varchi.

Pico della Mirandola, G. (1999), *Vita Hieronymi Savonarolae*, edited by E. Schisto. Firenze: Olschki.

Pitti, J. (1842), *Istoria fiorentina*, edited by L. F. Polidori. Firenze: Viesseux.

Politi, L. [Ambrosius Catharinus] (1956), *Apologia pro veritate Catholicae et apostolicae fidei ac doctrinae adversus impia ac valde pestifera Martini Lutheri dogmata, 1520*, ed. J. Schweizer. Münster in Westfalen: Aschendorff.

Rupescissa, G. da (2015), *Vade mecum in tribulatione*, edited by E. Tealdi. Milan: Vita e pensiero.

Savonarola, G. (1955), *Prediche sopra Ezechiele*, edited by R. Ridolfi, 2 vols. Rome: Belardetti.

Savonarola, G. (1957), *Prediche sopra Giobbe*, edited by R. Ridolfi, 2 vols. Rome: Belardetti.

Savonarola, G. (1962), *Prediche sopra Ruth e Michea*, edited by V. Romano, 2 vols. Rome: Belardetti.

Savonarola, G. (1965), *Prediche sopra Aggeo con Il Trattato circa il reggimento del governo della città di Firenze*, edited by L. Firpo. Rome: Belardetti.

Savonarola, G. (1974), *Prediche sopra i Salmi*, edited by V. Romano, vol. 2. Rome: Belardetti.

Savonarola, G. (1984), *Lettere e scritti apologetici*, edited by R. Ridolfi et al. Rome: Belardetti.

Savonarola, G. (2001), *Il Quaresimale del 1491. La certezza profetica di un mondo nuovo*, edited by A. Verde and E. Giaconi. Firenze: Edizioni del Galluzzo.

Savonarola, G. (2006), *Selected Writings: Religion and Politics, 1490–1498*, translated by A. Borelli and M. Pastore Passaro. New Haven and London: Yale University Press.

Varchi, B. (1841), *Storia fiorentina* [1547–1565], edited by L. Arbib, vol. 2. Firenze: Società Editrice della Storia del Nardi e del Varchi.

Secondary sources

Bramanti, V. (2017), *Uomini e libri del Cinquecento fiorentino*. Manziana (Rome): Vecchiarelli Editore.

Buber, M. (1957), "Prophecy, Apocalyptic, and the Historical Hour," in idem, *Pointing the Way*, translated by M. Friedman, 192–207. New York: Harper & Row.

Cacciari, M. (1998), "Inimicizia fraterna. Teologia e politica in Savonarola," *Micromega* 4: 225–38.

Caravale, G. (2007), *Sulle tracce dell'eresia. Ambrogio Catarino Politi (1484–1553)*. Firenze: Olschki.

Crucitti, A. (1974), "Nota critica," in G. Savonarola, *Compendio di rivelazioni. Testo volgare e latino e Dialogus de veritate prophetica*, edited by A. Crucitti, 377–456. Rome: Belardetti.

Dall'Aglio, S. (2005), *Savonarola e il savonarolismo*. Bari: Cacucci.
Dall'Aglio, S. (2006a), "Catarino contro Savonarola: reazioni e polemiche," *Archivio Storico Italiano* 164: 55–127.
Dall'Aglio, S. (2006b), *L'eremita e il sinodo. Paolo Giustiniani e l'offensiva medicea contro Girolamo Savonarola (1516–1517)*. Firenze: Edizioni del Galluzzo.
Dall'Aglio, S. (2012), "Nardi, Jacopo," in *Dizionario Biografico degli Italiani*, vol. 12. Online at: https://www.treccani.it/enciclopedia/jacopo-nardi_(Dizionario-Biografico)/.
Di Benedetto, S. (2011), "Girolamo Benivieni e la questione della lingua: alcune considerazioni sulle correzioni al Commento del 1500," in *ACME. Annali della Facoltà di Lettere e Filosofia dell'Università degli Studi di Milano*, vol. LXIV/II. Online at: https://www.ledonline.it/acme/allegati/Acme-11-II_09_Benedetto.pdf.
Di Benedetto, S. (2020), *Depurare le tenebre delli amorosi miei versi: la lirica di Girolamo Benivieni*. Firenze: Olschki.
Dionisotti, C. (1980), *Machiavellerie. Storia e fortuna di Machiavelli*. Torin: Einaudi.
Dunn, J. D. G. (1988), *World Biblical Commentary. Romans 9–16*. Nashville: Thomas Nelson.
Faldi, L. (1994), "Una conversione savonaroliana. Ambrogio Catarino Politi: Il suo ingresso e i primi anni nell'Ordine Domenicano," *Vivens homo* 5: 553–74.
Firpo, M. (1997), *Gli affreschi di Pontormo a San Lorenzo. Eresia, politica e cultura nella Firenze di Cosimo I*. Torino: Einaudi.
Fournel, J.-L., and J.-C. Zancarini (2002), *La politique de l'expérience: Savonarole, Guicciardini et le républicanisme florentin*. Alessandria: Edizioni dell'Orso.
Galli, C. (2014), *s.v.* "Riscontro," in *Enciclopedia machiavelliana*. Online at: https://www.treccani.it/enciclopedia/riscontro_%28Enciclopedia-machiavelliana%29/.
Garfagnini, G. C. (2000), "Il messaggio profetico di Savonarola e la sua recezione. Domenico Benivieni e Gianfrancesco Pico," in idem, *"Questa è la terra tua." Savonarola e Firenze*, 191–204. Firenze: Sismel Edizioni del Galluzzo.
Gouwens, K. (2012), "Humanists, Historians, and the Fullness of Time in Renaissance Rome," in J. Burke (ed.), *Rethinking the High Renaissance: The Culture of the Visual Arts in Early Sixteenth-Century Rome*, 95–110. Farnham: Ashgate.
Hatfield, R. (1995), "Botticelli's *Mystic Nativity*, Savonarola and the Millennium," *Journal of the Warburg and Courtauld Institutes* 58/1: 88–114. https://doi.org/10.2307/751506

Jungić, J. (1997), "Savonarolan Prophecy in Leonardo's *Allegory with Wolf and Eagle*," *Journal of the Warburg and Courtauld Institutes* 60/1: 253–60. https://doi.org/10.2307/751235

Kent, D. V. (2000), *Cosimo de' Medici and the Florentine Renaissance: The Patron's Oeuvre*. London and New Haven: Yale University Press.

Lazzerini, L. (2013), *Teologia del Miserere. Da Savonarola al Beneficio di Cristo 1490–1543*. Torino: Rosenberg & Sellier.

Leftley, S. (1999), "The Millennium in Renaissance Italy: A Persecuted Belief?" *Renaissance Studies* 13/2: 117–29. https://www.jstor.org/stable/i24412730

Leporatti, R. (2010), "Formazione di una raccolta: le Opere di Girolamo Benivieni," in M. A. Terzoli et al. (eds.), *Letteratura e filologia fra Svizzera e Italia: studi in onore di Guglielmo Gorni: volume II*, 177–244. Rome: Edizioni di storia e letteratura.

Leporatti, R. (2011), "Girolamo Benivieni tra il commento di Pico della Mirandola e l'autocommento," in R. Leporatti and M. Danzi (eds.), *Il Poeta e il suo pubblico. Lettura e commento dei testi lirici nel Cinquecento Convegno internazionale di Studi (Ginevra, 15–17 maggio 2008)*, 373–97. Geneva: Droz.

Lerner, R. E. (2004), "Medieval Millenarism and Violence," in *Pace e guerra nel basso medioevo: Atti del XL Convegno storico internazionale, Todi, 12–14 ottobre 2003*, 37–52. Spoleto: Fondazione Centro italiano di studi sull'alto Medioevo.

Lettieri, G. (2009), *Il nodo cristiano. Dono e libertà dal Nuovo Testamento all'VIII secolo*. Rome: self-published.

Lettieri, G. (2017a), "Nove tesi sull'ultimo Machiavelli," *Humanitas* 72/5–6: 1034–1089.

Lettieri, G. (2017b), "Machiavelli interprete antiluterano di Erasmo. L'Esortazione alla penitenza (1525) epitome del De immensa Dei Misericordia (1524)," *Giornale critico di storia delle idee. Mimesis* 2: 27–103.

Lettieri, G. (2018a), "Machiavelli in gioco. Un agente segreto papale a Venezia," *Studi e Materiali di Storia delle Religioni* 84/2: 688–729.

Lettieri, G. (2018b), "L'eresia originaria e le sue alterazioni. I—La matrice giudaico-apocalittica dell'eresia di Gesù," *B@belonline* 4 = *Pensare l'eresia. Tra origine e attualità*, 26–78.

Lettieri, G. (2019a), "L'eresia originaria e le sue alterazioni. II—Definizione giovannea e dispositivo dialettico di un'idea cristiana," *B@belonline* 5: 339–78.

Lettieri, G. (2019b), "Il Cantico dei cantici chiave della Mandragola. Callimaco figura del papa mediceo, voltando carta tra lettera erotica e allegoria cristologico-politica," in A. Guidi (ed.), *Niccolò Machiavelli. Dai 'castellucci di San Casciano alla comunicazione politica contemporanea*, 43–100. Manziana: Vecchiarelli Editore.

Lettieri, G. (2021), "Lo 'spiraculo' di Machiavelli e 'le mandragole' di Savonarola: Due misconosciute metafore cristologico-politiche," *Studi e Materiali di Storia delle Religioni* 87/1: 285–321.

Lodone, M. (2011), "Savonarola e Machiavelli: Una nota su Discorsi, I 11," *Interpres* XXX: 284–98.

Lodone, M. (2019), *s.v.* "Teodoro," in *Dizionario Biografico degli Italiani*, vol. 95. Online at: https://www.treccani.it/enciclopedia/teodoro_%28Dizionario-Biografico%29/.

Lodone, M. (2021), *I segni della fine. Storia di un predicatore nell'Italia del Rinascimento*. Rome: Viella.

Lo Re, S. (2006), *La crisi della libertà fiorentina. Alle origini della formazione politica e intellettuale di Benedetto Varchi e Piero Vettori*. Rome: Edizioni di Storia e Letteratura.

Mussolin, M. (2012), "La promozione del culto di sant'Antonino al tempo di Leone X e Clemente VII e i progetti di Antonio da Sangallo il Giovane per la chiesa di San Marco," in L. Cinelli and M. P. Paoli (eds.), *Antonino Pierozzi OP (1389–1459). La figura e l'opera di un santo arcivescovo nell'Europa del Quattrocento. Atti del Convegno internazionale di studi storici (Firenze, 25–28 novembre 2009)*, 509–532. Firenze: Edizioni Nerbini.

Najemy, J. M. (1999), "Papirius and the Chickens, or Machiavelli on the Necessity of Interpreting Religion," *Journal of the History of Ideas* 60/4: 659–81. https://doi.org/10.1353/jhi.1999.0041

Niccoli, O. (2007), *Perdonare. Idee, pratiche, rituali in Italia tra Cinque e Seicento*. Rome: Laterza.

Palumbo, M. (2002), "In margine alla questione savonaroliana," *Laboratoire italien* 3. Online at: https://journals.openedition.org/laboratoireitalien/371#bodyftn25.

Pellegrini, M. (2020), *Savonarola. Profezia e martirio nell'età delle guerre d'Italia*. Rome: Salerno Editrice.

Polizzotto, L. (1994), *The Elect Nation: The Savonarolan Movement in Florence, 1494–1545*. Oxford: Clarendon Press.

Preston, P. (2003), "Catharinus versus Luther, 1521," *History* 88: 364–78. https://doi.org/10.1111/1468-229X.00267

Prodi, P. (1998), "Profezia e utopia nella genesi della democrazia occidentale," in G. C. Garfagnini (ed.), *Savonarola. Democrazia tirannide profezia*, 199–211. Firenze: Edizioni del Galluzzo.

Pugliese, O. Zorzi (1970), "Girolamo Benivieni: umanista riformatore (dalla corrispondenza inedita)," *Bibliofilia* 72/3: 253–88.

Pugliese, O. Zorzi (1980), "Il 'Chronicon' di Angelo Clareno nel Rinascimento: volgarizzamento postillato da Girolamo Benivieni," *Archivum franciscanum historicum* 73: 514–26.

Pugliese, O. Zorzi (1981), "A Last Testimony by Savonarola and His Companions," *Renaissance Quarterly* 34/1: 1–10. https://doi.org/10.2307/2861159

Pugliese, O. Zorzi (1986), "Apocalyptic and Dantesque Elements in a Franciscan Prophecy of the Renaissance," in P. Pulsiano (ed.), *Proceedings of the PMR Conference*, vol. 10, 127–35. Villanova, PA: Villanova University.

Pugliese, O. Zorzi (1996), "Girolamo Benivieni seguace e difensore del Savonarola: considerazioni sul problema testuale dell'epistola a Clemente VII (1530)," in G. C. Garfagnini (ed.), *Studi savonaroliani. Verso il V centenario; Atti del primo seminario di studi, Firenze, 14–15 gennaio 1995*, 309–318. Firenze: Sismel.

Pugliese, O. Zorzi (2003), "Girolamo Benivieni, amico e collaboratore di Giovanni Pico della Mirandola: la sua traduzione inedita del commento al Pater noster," *Bibliothèque d'Humanisme et Renaissance* 65/2: 347–69.

Re, C. (1906), *Girolamo Benivieni fiorentino: Cenni sulla vita e sulle opere*. Città di Castello: Lapi.

Reeves, M., ed. (1992), *Prophetic Rome in the High Renaissance Period*. Oxford: Clarendon Press.

Reeves, M. (2000), *The Influence of Prophecy in the Later Middle Ages: A Study in Joachimism*, 2nd ed. Oxford: Clarendon Press.

Ridolfi, R. (1974), *Vita di Girolamo Savonarola*, 4th ed., 2 vols. Firenze: Sansoni.

Roush, S. (2002), "Dante as Piagnone Prophet: Girolamo Benivieni's 'Cantico in laude di Dante' (1506)," *Renaissance Quarterly* 55/1: 49–80. https://doi.org/10.2307/1512532

Roush, S. (2006), "Piagnone Exemplarity and the Florentine Literary Canon in the Vita di Girolamo Benivieni," *Quaderni d'Italianistica* 27/1: 3–20. https://doi.org/10.33137/q.i..v27i1.8974

Rusconi, R. (2010), *Santo Padre: La santità del papa da san Pietro a Giovanni Paolo II*. Rome: Viella.

Simoncelli, P. (2006), *Fuoriuscitismo repubblicano fiorentino, 1530–54: 1530–37*, vol. 1. Rome: Franco Angeli.

Simonetta, A. (2014), *Volpi e leoni. I Medici, Machiavelli e la rovina d'Italia*. Milan: Bompiani.

Simonetti, M. (2007), *s.v.* "Millenarismo," in A. Di Berardino (ed.), *Nuovo Dizionario patristico e di antichità cristiane*, 2nd ed., 3280–82. Genova: Marietti.

Stefanutti, U. (1966), "Benivieni, Antonio," in *Dizionario Biografico degli Italiani*, vol. 8. Online at https://www.treccani.it/enciclopedia/antonio-benivieni_%28Dizionario-Biografico%29/.

Tomas, N. R. (2017), *The Medici Women: Gender and Power in Renaissance Florence*, 2nd ed. London and New York: Routledge.

Vasoli, C. (1966a), "Benivieni, Domenico," in *Dizionario Biografico degli Italiani*, vol. 8. Online at https://www.treccani.it/enciclopedia/domenico-benivieni_(Dizionario-Biografico)/.

Vasoli, C. (1966b), "Benivieni, Girolamo," in *Dizionario Biografico degli Italiani*, vol. 8. Online at https://www.treccani.it/enciclopedia/girolamo-benivieni_%28Dizionario-Biografico%29/.

Vasoli, C. (2000), "L'immagine sognata: il 'papa angelico,'" in L. Fiorani and A. Prosperi (eds.), *Roma, la città del papa. Vita civile e religiosa dal giubileo di Bonifacio VIII al giubileo di papa Wojtyła*, 73–109. Torino: Einaudi.

Verde, A. F. (1992), "Fra Girolamo Savonarola e Lorenzo de' Medici. Il quaresimale in S. Lorenzo del 1492," *Archivio Storico Italiano*, "Studi su Lorenzo dei Medici e il secolo XV," 150/2: 493–605.

Weinstein, D. (1970), *Savonarola and Florence: Prophecy and Patriotism in the Renaissance*. Princeton: Princeton University Press.

Weinstein, D. (2011), *Savonarola: The Rise and Fall of a Renaissance Prophet*. New Haven and London: Yale University Press.

Chapter 5

The Ambiguities of Erasmus's Religious Peace: A Reading of *De amabili ecclesiae concordia* (1533)

Ludovico Battista

Introduction

The topic of concord or religious peace is widely debated by Erasmus scholars,[1] but has occasionally been subject to considerable misinterpretation. Because of its equivocal generality, the problem of religious peace has sometimes been identified with the mere ethical and tolerant kerygma of Erasmian Christianity: Erasmus was contrary to every dogmatic "strictness" and reluctant to propose his own spiritual convictions in an assertive manner; for example, by defining doctrinal boundaries too rigidly. Even though he was persuaded of the need for spiritual reforms, Erasmus was at the same time a lover of peace, inspired by the search for a moderate position and for conciliation with tradition, which could only be progressively and gradually improved. The topic of religious concord

---

1. For a general overview of the link between Erasmus's religious humanism, spiritual reformism, and reflections on peace, see Padberg 1969; Tracy 1978; Olin 1979; Dust 1987. For a description of the theme of peace as religious irenicism rather than "pacifism," see Ron 2014. A preliminary clarification: in this chapter, I am focusing on the problem of religious concord, which is obviously to be distinguished from that of political "peace" and which concerns Erasmus's strategy for reaching a point of convergence with respect to and as a resolution for the doctrinal controversies of his time.

has thus been interpreted as stemming from Erasmus's character and from his carefulness, moderation, and intellectual flexibility.[2]

However, such an approach runs the risk of undervaluing the ideological and polemical scope of the reflection on religious *concordia*. Even the topic of "peace" implies fundamental exegetical, theological, and doctrinal choices that are anything but innocent or neutral, as Erasmus himself was well aware, since he knew how to skillfully bring out or conceal their inner "critical nature" according to the circumstances. One exemplary moment is undoubtedly his dispute with Luther. Scholars have to some extent considered this debate to be inconsistent with the irenicism of Erasmus, which would never have allowed him to take part in a "doctrinal" dispute of this kind, because of a postulated empathy with the Reformers. Or, conversely, they have minimized its critical aspects by remarking on the zetetic, non-assertive, problematizing attitude even in works such as *De Libero Arbitrio* (1524). By taking these approaches, however, scholars have fallen victim to the argumentative trap set by the author, becoming confused by his dissimulation in a series of statements that use irenicism, dogmatic relativism, and the topic of concord precisely as weapons *against* Luther, according to a shrewd theological position.[3] The theme of religious peace thus also deserves further attention that inquires into whether it is possible to identify in it an ideological and theological background that—far from being purely irenic—is consciously anti-Lutheran in its aim. In other words: Is not the question of peace a way of neutralizing the effects of the Reformation; that is, of reintegrating them into the Catholic context, and thus of contesting to Luther and his followers the leadership of a process of Church reform?

A survey of this topic would require numerous references. Here I consider only one of Erasmus's last texts, a commentary on Psalm 83 entitled

---

2. See two fundamental and classic studies of the interpretation of Erasmus's 'oscillating' positioning: Cf. Huizinga 1984; Mann Philips 1949. More recently, Barral-Baron 2014 insisted on the dramatic nature of this flexibility. For an analysis of the link between the problem of tolerance and the question of rhetoric connected to the problem of *adiaphora* and *consensus* cf. Remer 1996: 43–103.
3. See Torsini 2000: 1–77, whose excellent critical analysis of the text highlights this aspect.

De sarcienda Ecclesiae concordia (1533).⁴ Dedicated to the problem of concord, this work is one of the most illustrative examples of Erasmus's anti-Lutheran strategy and one of the clearest in countering the positions advanced by the Reformation.

Luther as Korah

Written in response to numerous appeals that Erasmus take a position on the religious debate and in order to suggest a way of achieving a peaceful resolution to the conflict,⁵ *De amabili ecclesiae concordia* was published in Basel in July 1533 and dedicated to Julius von Pflug, a younger theologian who was his correspondent and admirer and also the bishop of Naumburg and counsellor to Charles V.⁶ The emperor had instructed Pflug to find a way to pacify Germany and as a solution he explicitly asked for Erasmus's support. *De amabili*'s dedication letter thus reveals a specific agenda: it is not a vague appeal for a reconciliation to be built on a generic basis, but an oriented political project supporting the idea of a common Council of the Church, that indicates the center—both theological and institutional: the Erasmianism of the Imperial Court⁷ together with the Roman Papacy—around which to reunite a Christianity that had been torn by divisions. This aspect of the work clearly emerges from its conclusion, in which Erasmus addresses first the Emperor Charles and Ferdinand, king of the Romans and king of Hungary and Bohemia, then the kings of France and England, and finally Pope Clement VII, whose

4. *De sarcienda Ecclesiae concordia liber*, Basel: H. Frobenius et N. Episcopius, 1533; now edited in ASD V, 3: 245–313: English translation by Raymond Himelick (1971), *Erasmus and the Seamless Coat of Jesus: On Restoring the Unity of the Church. With Selections from the Letters and Ecclesiastes*, Lafayette, IN: Purdue University Studies: 26–109. For a synthetic analysis see Kantzenbach 1957: 82–87 and Pollet 1969.
5. On the problem of religious dialogues, see Honée 1993: 1–30; Honée 1997: 65–75.
6. Cf. Pollet 1990: 222–27; *Contemporaries of Erasmus*, III: 77–78. It is important to remember Pflug's role in drafting—a decade later, after the victory over the Schmalkaldics at Mühlberg in 1547—a formula for addressing abuses in sacred matters as part of preparing a confession of faith that could win both Protestant and Catholic estates over to the side of the emperor.
7. About the relationship with Charles V, cf. Tracy 1978; Tracy 1996; Halkin 1974: 301–319.

character would allow the most equitable terms possible after the restoration of peace.[8]

At first sight, we must note that in this work Erasmus seems to be trying to minimize the doctrinal divergences with the reformers. For instance, albeit with some detachment, he seems to accept some Lutheran theological expressions relating to grace and divine forgiveness, though always harmonizing them within the framework of his own humanistic and Origenian conception of the infinite mercy of God. Erasmus asserts, for example, that without mercy there can be no access to the *atrium* of the Church, and that consequently this access consists in faith: "The means of access to the Church is faith, without which baptism means nothing; but no one bestows faith on himself. It is the gift of God, by which God goes before and draws to Christ His elect."[9] He thus explicitly states that everything that man possesses is freely given through Christ:

> Whatever God bestows on us is bestowed through and on account of the Son, not on account of the good works we have performed. "We all offend in many things." He alone is the Lamb innocent of every stain. Therefore God our Defender, if our countenance—our conscience, that is—offends you, look instead upon the countenance of your Son whom you love unexceptionably, and through His merits grant us what we ourselves do not deserve.[10]

Moreover, albeit ambiguously, he proposes to set aside the question of free will:

> Argument over freedom of the will is more likely to produce briars than fruit. [...] Meanwhile, it is sufficient to agree among ourselves that man can do nothing through his own powers; if he can do

---

8. Cf. Himelick 1971: 97; ASD V, 3: 312, ll. 928–930.
9. Himelick 1971: 65; ASD V, 3: 288, ll. 38–40: "Aditus in Ecclesiam fides est, sine qua nihil prodest baptismus. At fidem nemo sibi largitur, Dei donum est, quo Deus quos vult preuenit et ad Christum trahit."
10. Himelick 1971: 74; ASD V, 3: 295, ll. 289–95: "Quicquid Deus largitur nobis, per Filium ac propter Filium largitur, non propter opera iusticiae, quae fecimus nos. Nos enim in multis offendimus omnes. Solus ille agnus est omnis expers maculae. Ergo protector noster Deus, si tuos oculos offendit facies, hoc est, conscientia nostra, respice in faciem Christi Filii tui, quem sine exceptione diligis, per illius merita nobis largire, quod ipsi non meremur."

anything, he owes it all to the grace by whose gift we are whatever we are. Thus, in all matters we may recognize our own frailty and give praise to the Lord's mercy.[11]

Such statements reveal a conciliatory aim, and even an apparent acknowledgment of some Lutheran claims: present-day critical inquiry has therefore emphasized this search for a mediating position and a reforming equilibrium within the crisis triggered by the Lutheran protest. However, an analysis of the overall framework of the commentary should balance this aspect by highlighting some macroscopic *critical* and *polemical* aspects that give a completely different meaning to Erasmus's words. The first of these is the very peculiar choice of psalm, the title of which reads: "For the conclusion, a psalm of the sons of Korah for the wine presses." The question about the title and the overall meaning of the psalm becomes the focus of Erasmus's exegesis and commentary.

The episode concerning Korah recalled by Erasmus is contained in the book of Numbers, chapter 16. Here is narrated the seditious and schismatic protest of the Levites Korah, Dathan, and Abiram, who rebelled against and challenged Moses and Aaron for the leadership of the community and the priesthood.[12] For this illegitimate and subversive act, God had punished them by causing them to plunge into the abyss.[13] From a symbolic point of view, the story has a clear anti-schismatic meaning: since the *Decretum Gratiani*, the episode had symbolized the legitimacy of condemning as heretics those who rebel against the authority of the

---

11. Himelick 1971: 86; ASD V, 3: 304, ll. 625–30: "De libero arbitrio spinosa est verius quam frugifera disputatio. Et si quid de hoc quaerendum est, in theologicis diatribis sobrie discutiatur. Interim inter nos illud conuenire satis est hominem ex suis viribus nihil posse, et si quid vlla in re potest totum eius deberi gratiae, cuius munere sumus quicquid sumus, vt in omnibus agnoscamus imbecillitatem nostram et glorificemus Domini misericordiam."
12. Num. 16:1: "Korah son of Izhar, the son of Kohath, the son of Levi, and certain Reubenites—Dathan and Abiram, sons of Eliab, and On son of Peleth—became insolent and rose up against Moses."
13. Num. 16:31-33: "As soon as he finished saying all this, the ground under them split apart and the earth opened its mouth and swallowed them and their households, and all those associated with Korah, together with their possessions. They went down alive into the realm of the dead, with everything they owned; the earth closed over them, and they perished and were gone from the community."

legitimate priesthood and the ecclesiastical structure.[14] Although Korah and his followers recognize the same God of Israel and do not contest any orthodox dogma, they are to be considered heretics and excluded from salvation for not having obeyed the religious and political authority, that of Moses. Erasmus's strategy is clear: by arguing for the absence of any radically heterodox doctrine asserted by Protestants, or at least the possible compatibility of their theological position with the Catholic Church, Erasmus aims at emphasizing the fundamental error that condemns them; that is, having separated themselves from the *atria* of the Church and having wanted to build *their own* tabernacles, which has led to their being struck down by the wrath of God. Erasmus's call for reconciliation is repeated several times and could not be more explicit in his critical address to Protestants:

> Let us reflect on the folly of so detesting the practices of certain popes or priests or monks that we ourselves become worse than they are; for anyone who abandons the fellowship of the Church and moves into heresy or schism is worse than one who leads an indecent life in sound beliefs.[15]

We must also remember that the episode of Korah's rebellion and punishment had played a central role in the centralizing and monocratic ideology of the Renaissance Papacy and in the anti-conciliarist strategy of papal exaltation during the fifteenth century, which employed the figure of Moses.[16] In 1439, in one of the first sessions of the Council

---

14. *Causa VII, Quaestio* I, C IX: "Perditionem sibi adquirunt qui ab episcopis recedentes unitatem ecclesiae scindunt: Nam et Chore, et Dathan, et Abiron cum sacerdote Aaron et Moyse eundem Deum nouerant, pari lege et religione uiuentes unum et uerum Deum, qui colendus atque inuocandus fuerat, inuocabant: tamen quia loci sui ministerium transgressi et contra Aaron sacerdotem, qui sacerdotium legitimum dignatione Dei atque ordinatione perceperat, sacrificandi sibi licentiam uendicauerunt, diuinitus percussi penas statim pro illicitis conatibus penderunt, nec potuerunt rata esse et proficere sacrificia irreligiose et illicite contra ius diuinae dispositionis oblata."
15. Himelick 1971: 82; ASD V, 3: 301, ll. 512–15: "Reputemus, quam sit stultum sic odisse mores quorundam Pontificum aut sacerdotum ac monachorum, vt ipsi fiamus illis deteriores. Deterior enim est, qui recedit ab ecclesiae consortio et in haeresim aut in schisma demigrat, quam qui impure viuit saluis dogmatibus."
16. Cf. Stinger 1983: 201–23; Lettieri 2021: 287–88; Lettieri 2023a; Lettieri 2023b.

of Florence, reacting to the anti-papal positions of the Council of Basel, Eugene IV promulgated the bull *Moyses vir Dei*. The figure of the pontiff as the new Moses was exalted to reaffirm the pope's role as the only *caput* of the Church, against any conciliarist and divisive temptation, which was represented by Korah, Dathan, and Abiram.[17] Beginning with this bull, the celebration of Mosaic symbolism became an ideological element strongly characterizing the history of the fifteenth-century and early sixteenth-century Papacy. Some other examples include the Oratio Moyses vir Dei of 1452 by Enea Silvio Piccolomini[18] and the lateral frescoes of the Sistine Chapel (1481–1482) commissioned by Sixtus IV,[19] in which the *Punishment of the Sons of Korah* by Botticelli is dominant

17. "recedite a tabernaculis hominum impiorum, maxime cum longe amplior sit plebs christiana quam illa tunc iudeorum, ecclesia sanctior quam sinagoga, et christi vicarius ipso Moyse auctoritate et dignitate superior. Quam Basiliensium impietatem dudum previdere cepimus, [....] Decernimus etiam et declaramus omnes et singulos predictos fuisse et esse schismaticos et hereticos, et ultra penas in prefato Ferrariensi concilio declaratas, tanquam tales cum omnibus eorum fautoribus vel defensoribus, cuiuscunque status, conditionis, et gradus ecclesiastici vel secularis exiterint, etiam si cardinalatus, patriarcali, archiepiscopali, episcopali, abbatiali, aut alia quavis dignitate prefulgeant, ut cum predictis Chore, Dathan et Abiron meritam accipiant portionem (Nm 16), penis condignis omnino puniendos" (Alberigo et al. 2013: 529–59).
18. Cf. Cotta-Schønberg 2019.
19. Cf. Ettlinger 1965: 105–19: "To the Fathers and early commentators of the Bible Corah's rebellion had been a straightforward example of heresy [...] But during the fifteenth century this argument was somewhat changed and its terms became more specific. Corah's disobedience was likened to disobedience to the Pope. [...] If the Corah story could be used in this fashion in order to confound the adherents of the conciliar theory, Sixtus IV had good reason to make use of it in his own cause. Throughout his pontificate he was under the constant threat of various plans aiming at the convocation of a new Council of the Church and he had to be on his guard, even though none of these schemes succeeded." Moreover, one should recall an important polemical text, the *Dissentio inter sanctissimum Dominum Nostrum Papam et Florentinos suborta* (1478), in which Pope Sixtus IV replied to the anti-papal Medici propaganda document "*Florentina Synodus.*" In it, the events of the Old Testament and Jewish history were used ideologically to vindicate papal authority and the legitimate repression of the schismatics. Recently Daniels (2013) identified Platina as the author of the *Dissentio* because of the extensive use of Josephus Flavius's *Antiquities*: Lorenzo the Magnificent is identified with Saul, Ahab, Nimrod, etc., and the text concludes with a curse against him that quotes the speech that Moses is said to have addressed to Korah.

and positioned opposite to the other major symbol of papal authority, *The Delivery of the Keys to Saint Peter*, painted by Perugino.

It therefore seems difficult to imagine that, in an exhortation aimed at the concord and unity of the Church, Erasmus was not aware that the reference to the punishment of the sons of Korah entailed a tribute to papal authority and the endorsement of his power as the basis of the ecclesiastical structure. This encomiastic aspect was also strategically necessary to balance the plea for a conciliar solution of the religious controversies. It was therefore not simply a matter of choosing a psalm "dealing with the loveliness of peace and concord within the Church"![20]

Erasmus wisely succeeds in dissimulating the polemical violence expressed by the Korah episode; in fact, he dwells rather on Numbers 26:11: "But Korah's sons did not die." Remembering that God had mercy on the sons of Korah, he poses the question in the form of an invitation to reconciliation: he emphasizes that the sons do not bear the faults of the fathers, so that those who have strayed can—by abandoning their father, Luther!—still be saved at any time if they reconcile with the Church and do penance for the errors they committed. In any case, it would be a mistake not to identify a wise rhetorical strategy in the commentary, whose transparent irenicism and search for a path of dialogue does not and cannot completely conceal Erasmus's clear stance in favor of the Roman Church and the papal authority, which are defended at least implicitly.

Erasmus begins with the historical explanation of the title: the three psalms dedicated to the presses (eighth, eightieth, and eighty-third) referred to the three Jewish festivals of Passover, Pentecost, and Scenopegia, or the tent of tabernacles, as the Pseudo-Jerome's *Breviarium in psalmos*[21] shows. For exegesis, he uses its Origenistic and mystical interpretation of the festivities: the feast of tabernacles, celebrated in September in front of the wine presses, allegorically indicates the gathering of the Catholic Church as a gift of the Spirit (the wine of the harvest); that is, the fulfillment of the Jewish celebrations in the message of Christ's resurrection (symbolized in the number 8).[22] The need for an allegorical interpretation

---

20. As Himelick said in his *Introduction* to the text: cf. Himelick 1971: 3.
21. This work is a collection of writings by Origen, Eusebius of Caesarea, Hilary, and Jerome, put together by an unknown compiler of the ninth to tenth century: *Breviarium in psalmos*, PL 26, 801–1346.
22. Cf. Breviarium in psalmos, PL 26, 1058–1059; 1070.

is also underlined by Erasmus's polemic against the pagan conception of the feasts: celebrating does not mean giving in to human passions, vices, and obscene desires—in the eyes of God this is madness—as it did for the pagans, but rather, it means understanding the edifying sense of the Christian message in a spiritual and moral light.

This introduction allows Erasmus to interpret the episode of Korah and his sons in an immediately symbolic and edifying key, with an irenic and spiritual, rather than anti-heretical, purpose. The true ultimate typological reference of the three addressees of the three psalms mentioned (David, Asaph, and the sons of Korah) is Christ, but in what sense can Christ be called the "son" of the schismatic Hebrew Korah? Rather than simply referring to the allegorical etymology of Korah as Calvary, as Augustine did, Erasmus emphasizes that the expression is not absurd even from a historical-typological point of view: in terms of the flesh, Christ drew his origin from the people of Israel, who were obstinately rebellious against God, but from whom God desired to draw spiritual salvation anyway. Therefore, Erasmus underlines that God granted salvation to the descendants of Korah, who, having converted and repented, renounced the crimes of their father:

> Nevertheless, Scripture graces with praise the posterity of Korah, with the name of the forebear whose impiety made more lustrous the piety of the sons; although they had been bound by the strictest obligations of nature to this author of rebellion, nevertheless the love of religion in them took precedence over natural sentiment, inasmuch as they either—as seems likely—came to their senses and, loyal to Moses, separated themselves from their father [...] Therefore, since God does not charge sons with what their parents have done unless they themselves copy their actions. [...] But it is a finer thing to see the descendants of evil men achieve outstanding virtue than a good man born of good parents. [...] [God] does not make us responsible for transgressions that we regretted and of which we did penance.[23]

23. Himelick 1971: 36–37 (translation modified by me); ASD V, 3: 264–65, ll. 211–35: "Et tamen Scriptura laudis gratia notat posteros Core, progenitoris nomine, cuius impietas illustrauit filiorum pietatem, qui, cum essent arctissimis naturae vinculis astricti seditionis autori, tamen in illis affectum naturae vicit amor religionis. Siquidem vt est probabilis coniectura, aut auscultantes Mosi resipuerunt separaruntque se a patre, aut sic apud illud remanserunt, vt impio proposito nequaquam

Thus, Erasmus succeeds at the same time in a double aim: on the one hand, to offer an irenic and not openly controversial use of the episode, by inviting his readers not to reject those who have momentarily turned away from the true tabernacle: all Christian believers must recognize themselves as sons of Korah because they are all sinners. On the other hand, Erasmus nonetheless places emphasis on the duty to abandon one's heretical fathers, thus implicitly stressing the need for the repentance, penance, and reintegration of those who have challenged the authority of the legitimate priesthood of Moses/Pope.

> Korah, Dathan, Abiron, and On tried to divide the tabernacle, just as heretics and schismatics have always tried to split apart the Church; and just as the prompt wrath of God fell upon those who, even though warned, refused to give up the madness of their impious deeds and turbulent endeavours, so doubtless the flames of hell await these others. Regarded in this light, we must all be sons of Korah in the sense that a son must not, in spite of religious faith, cleave to father, or brother to brother, or wife to husband, or son-in-law to father-in-law; but we must all withdraw from the tents of the wicked, if not bodily, surely in the matter of this discord of minds. If any error steals upon us through our thoughtlessness, let us listen to Moses and, once advised, follow the better ways.[24]

This is revealing of an overall Origenian reading of the key theme of the tabernacles; that is, an interpretation of the Church in anti-Lutheran terms as something universal and progressive, a community on the move made by believers who—all of them, though in their different degrees—advance

---

assentirentur [...] Ergo quum Deus non imputet parentum commissa filiis nisi facta illorum imitentur [...] Sed pulchrius est ex malis prognatos virtute claros euadere, quam si quis bonus nascatur ex bonis. [...] Non imputat nobis nostra delicta, quorum semel poenituit."

24. Himelick 1971: 37–38; ASD V, 3: 265, ll. 244–53: "Core, Dathan, Abiron et Hon conati sunt diuidere tabernaculum, quemadmodum heretici ac schismatici semper conati sunt ecclesiam discindere; sed vt in illos praesens ira Dei desaeuiit, ita qui moniti nolunt ab impiis sectis ac seditiosis conatibus resipiscere, hos sine dubio manet gehennae incendium. Atque in simili rerum statu oportet omnes esse filios Core, vt nec filius contra pietatem adhaereat patri, nec frater fratri, nec vxor marito, nec gener soecero, sed ab impiorum tabernaculis secedendum est, si non corpore, certe animorum dissensione; et si quid erroris per incogitantiam obrepsit, auscultemus Mosi et moniti meliora sequamur."

in the spiritual deepening of their relationship with God.[25] Foundational to this interpretation are the metaphors of the exodus and the tent as authentic dimensions of the Church: the place of God's revelation is not a stable building, the Temple in which it is claimed that His presence is enclosed, delimiting an absolute inside and outside of religious identity, but the temporary and wandering tabernacle, never permanently fixed, always imperfect and continuously progressing in faith and charity.[26] The heretic is therefore condemned not on the basis of some absolute and ultimate definition of religious dogma; that is, for his disobedience to orthodoxy, but rather for having wished to establish *his own* tabernacles, where he claims to exclusively "possess" an authentic relationship with God, abandoning the dynamic, imperfect, and progressive dimension of the only Church, which instead charitably welcomes all men of good will.

The problem is claiming to define a single truth that excludes all others. Erasmus understood that to proclaim there could be only one meaning of the Scripture meant causing the indiscriminate proliferation of sects. The heretic is someone who, while considering himself a defender of the true religion, invents new dogmas, beliefs, and conventions to split the Church and create a stumbling block to the other believers. Or, as the example of the Arians against Athanasius shows, the heretic is one who fails to fulfil the precept of mutual charity and Christian peace by seeking to have his brother unjustly condemned. The true Christian, on the other hand, does not seek to give scandal to his brother, but proceeds in charity and seeks concord. Against Luther, Erasmus points out that while it is true that the authenticity of religious worship is spiritual, interior, and hidden, this is not to say that the Church is *entirely invisible*:

> What some people say, that the Church is invisible, is not altogether false. Only God looks into human hearts and truly knows who are His own. Nevertheless, there are many kinds of evidence for surmising where the Church of God is, and where the synagogue of Satan.[27]

25. On the theme of progress in the Origenian tradition, see Fallica, Jacobsen, and Lettieri 2022.
26. Cf. Origen 1921. See also Godin 1982.
27. Himelick 1971: 43; ASD V, 3: 270, ll. 400–403: "Nec omnino falsum est, quod dicunt quidam inuisibilem esse ecclesiam. Solus enim Deus introspicit corda hominum, ac vere nouit, qui sint ipsius. Multis tamen argumentis saepe deprehenditur vbi sit ecclesia Dei, vbi synagoga Satanae." Although unbalanced and conditioned

It is difficult to deny the systematic delegitimization of the Lutheran schism. Lutherans are those who, claiming to constitute their own tabernacle, do not accept participation in common spiritual progress, and do not recognize themselves as weak, humble, and progressing in faith like others:

> "*I have chosen to be a nobody in the house of my God rather than to live in the tents of sinners.*" What is it to be a nobody? To lie on the threshold or in the waiting-room and to be despised, the lot of beggars. But so great is the majesty and bliss of the Church that what is most abject in it far surpasses all the attractions of the world. Just as in the heavenly Jerusalem are many mansions of which the meanest is better than all the palaces of kings, so in the Church, as in a great house, are vessels of various kinds, some more splendid than others, but the cheapest of them more precious than the whole world.[28]

The fundamental accusation against the schismatics is that they are "proud": Erasmus argues that many heresiarchs were motivated by mere personal ambition and the inability to humbly accept their role in the Church.[29] In this sense, Erasmus makes an anti-Lutheran exaltation

---

by a confessional perspective, I nevertheless find this observation by Hentze worthy of interest: "Auch wenn für Erasmus der vornehmliche Teil der Kirche, die *praecipua pars*, verborgen ist, da niemand seines Heils und seiner Rechtfertigung absolut sicher sein kann, ist die Kirche dennoch sichtbar. Das zeigt sich, wenn er z.B. von der Autorität der Kirche spricht. Er betont ausdrücklich, es sei das die Autorität der römischen Kirche, der er folge. Diese Autorität ist für ihn nicht irgendeine vage, undefinierbare Größe, sondern die *publica auctoritas* der Kirchenleitung" (Hentze 1974: 70).

28. Himelick 1971: 77; ASD V, 3: 296–97, ll. 358–65: "Elegi abiectus esse in domo Dei mei, magis quam habitare in tabernaculis peccatorum." Quid est abiectum esse? Iacere in limine aut vestibulo et conculcari. Quod mendicorum est. Tanta autem est ecclesiae maiestas et felicitas, vt quod in ea contemptissimum est, longe praestet omnibus mundi splendoribus. Sicut in coelesti Hierosolyma multae sunt mansiones, quarum infima tamen potior est omnibus regum palatiis, sic in ecclesia velut in magna domo diuersi generis vasa sunt, quorum aliud est alio honoratius, et tamen quod in his vilissimum est, preciosius est vniverso mundo."

29. "Here the Prophet, incidentally, exposes the reason why many men either do not enter the Church, or leave it, or, once ejected for a sin, are reluctant to return. Those who are puffed up by worldly success are unwilling to deflate their camel humps in order to pass through the lowly entrance. We learn from accounts of the past that numerous heresiarchs were occasioned by the fact that they were not promoted to the

of penance as the imitation of Christ's self-humiliation: the authentic experience of faith should correspond only to a practical act of self-spoliation, self-criticism, and obedience, consequent on acknowledging legitimate religious authority.

> That man dear to God, the Emperor Theodosius, understood this when he preferred to put aside all the confused noise of empire and enter into the humble role of penitent rather than not be in the house of the Lord. Those very penitents, miserable in garb, weakened by fasting, worn out by tears and remorse, who lie just like beggars on the threshold of God's house, are much more fortunate than those who, with Satan as master, are reigning in the tents of wickedness, inasmuch as these penitents, if they are sincere, can be outside of the Church in body while inside it in mind or spirit.[30]

The last part of *De amabili* consists in a moralistic warning to those who behold the mote in the brother's eye but do not see the beam in their own. Erasmus calls for balance in judging and criticizing the Church: although there is imperfection, vice, and sin everywhere, it is a source of discord to examine only the faults of others without also recognizing their virtues. Rather, every individual and group in the Church must exercise its duty according to conscience: this means the ecclesiastics, the princes, and the people in the same measure. It is necessary to begin from a strict (but not angry!) analysis of faults, starting with the most common ones, in order to slowly correct and eliminate them, without fractures or scandals, which would have counterproductive effects.

---

augustness of a bishopric" [*Hic obiter Propheta aperit fontem, quam ob rem plerique mortales, vel non accedunt ad ecclesiam, vel recedunt ab ecclesia, vel eiecti ob culpam grauantur redire. Qui tument honoribus mundanis, nolunt deponere cameli gibbos, vt per humile ingrediantur ostium. Et ex historiis discimus complures haeresiarchas esse factos, quod ad episcopi dignitatem non admouerentur*] (Himelick 1971: 77; ASD V, 3: 297, ll. 372–77).

30. Himelick 1971: 78; ASD V, 3: 298, ll. 391–97: "Vidit haec illi Deo charus Theodosius imperator, qui maluit vniuersum imperii strepitum deponere et in abiectum poenitentium ire locum, quam non esse in domo Domini. Illi ipsi poenitentes cultu squalidi, ieiuniis attenuati, lachrymis et moerore confecti, qui tanquam mendici iacent in limine domus Dei, multo feliciores sunt, quam qui sub Satana regnant in tentoriis impietatis. Siquidem hi, si modo vere poenitet, licet corpore sint extra domum ecclesiae, animo sunt intus."

And many [faults] steal upon us little by little as the occasion offers and have to be got rid of little by little as the occasion offers and if it can be done without a desperate upset. If not, they should be disregarded until time itself offers a more favourable opportunity. The same kind of adroitness must be used in dealing with dogmas.[31]

"Condescension" (*sygkatabasis*) is needed to iron out doctrinal differences, and so this "effort of rapprochement" must be made "without disturbing basic principles" while considering "human frailty," "in order that man may be gradually brought to a more perfect state."[32] In any case, to eradicate the causes of dissent imposes a certain degree of sceptical suspension of judgment: freedom of choice should be allowed as regards everything that is not essential and must be accepted or tolerated, at least until a Council rules to the contrary.

It is therefore necessary not to weaken Erasmus's argument by reducing it to a simple plea for reciprocal moderation. What underlies the statement concerning the duty to "*dissimulare*," to disregard not only the vices of the Church but even its errors in matters of dogma, is the subordination and relativization of the value of theological assertions, reduced to mere instruments of spiritual formation, to conjectural degrees of the ever-elusive divine truth that allows personal, ethical-religious progress towards perfection, and which can never conflict with the precept of concord and reciprocal charity.[33]

---

31. Himelick 1971: 84; ASD V, 3: 302, ll. 572–75: "Pleraque paulatim ac per occasionem irrepserunt, ea paulatim ac per occasionem tollenda sunt, si fieri queat absque graui tumultu; sin minus, dissimulanda, donec ipsa dies porrigat occasionem commodiorem. Eadem dexteritate vtendum est in dogmatibus."
32. Himelick 1971: 86; ASD V, 3: 304, ll. 617–20. Cf. Kantzenbach 1957: 87: "Das Zauberwort in alle Schwierigkeiten heißt 'Sygkatabasis.' […] Drei Punkte scheinen Bedeutung für die Zukunft zu haben: 1. Der doppelte Kirchenbegriff, 2. Der Begriff (*implicite*) der *Akineta* und 3. Der Begriff der *Sygkatabasis* bzw. Akkomodatio." About the doctrine of the *accomodatio* or "condescension," cf. Walter 1991: 42–53; Hoffmann 1994: 106–12; 148–51; 177–84.
33. "*Commoditas* is, in first place, the reason on account of which a metaphor moves from one meaning to another: 'Metaphor transfers by means of similitude a word from its particular significance to another for the sake of any benefit.' The purpose for this translation is to accommodate speech to hearers in such a way that they understand what is in their best interest, what is useful and advantageous for them in their particular circumstances. Accordingly the intent and goal of persuasive

Erasmus dwells on the necessary "temperate relationship between the (cognitive) force and the object"; that is, between the spiritual degree of the creature and the divine theophany: directing one's gaze directly towards the sun would mean being blinded by it and not respecting the proportions between one's ability to see and the divine object. The sun represents the origin and the teleological goal of the soul's ascending path, the unitary source that drives the human eye towards ever higher realities, but divine revelation passes through many intermediate gradations which, although imperfect and only progressively more "adequate," are nevertheless legitimate and necessary because they are appropriate to the degree to which each intellect is seeking God.[34]

The Origenian doctrine of theophanies thus represents a clearly anti-Lutheran argument: defining an absolute dogmatic heart of Christian faith may be counterproductive and a stumbling block. Within such an Origenian conception of *accomodatio*, or *sygkatabasis*, important is the believer's aptitude to transform the object of his beliefs into spiritual nourishment; that is, to transform it into authentic religious experience and moral action. For this reason, the exact definition of the dogmatic object is of secondary importance, while its performative capacity to nourish the believer's practical life is primary.

Consistent with this gradualist conception, Erasmus affirms the positive value of even the superstitious forms of common devotion. Indeed, if the faith is the authentic desire to please God, even those who practice a naïve or simpler religiosity participate in the Church's progression towards perfection.

> Some devout people are disposed to believe that the prayers and good works of the living help the dead, especially if they were scrupulous about doing these things while the deceased were living. [...] There is also the conviction of some religious people that saints, male and

---

rhetoric, *utilitas*, is based on providing advantageous things and removing disadvantageous things. In sacred rhetoric, moreover, the intended benefit for the hearers acquires a more excellent quality as *commodum* encourages them to move from the flesh to the spirit and to advance in piety" (Hoffmann 1994: 183).

34. Himelick 1971: 48; ASD V, 3: 273, ll. 538–41: "Requiritur moderata cognatio inter potentiam et obiectum. Alioqui si quod sensui obiicitur, careat modo, sensum obruit; veluti sol nulla nube temperatus, si intendas oculos, corrumpit visum, et sonitus immodicus adducit surditatem."

female, [...] even now have some influence with Him. Superstition [...] ought to be exposed; but devout and ingenuous feeling must be sustained, even if it is attended by a certain amount of error.[35]

Even the most superstitious forms of religiosity, such as the worship of images or saints, are sometimes inspired by "a certain overflowing of love,"[36] and therefore cannot displease God. The natural desire for God is basically good, so that naïve spontaneity saves superstitious ritual as an initial and providential level of worship. If what defines Christianity is love and spiritual brotherhood, then any apocalyptic logic of overturning the "legalistic" mediation of the sacred is neutralized; just as is also avoided any dualistic logic of identifying the Church in the elective act of God's gift of grace, which would condemn the human "mediation" to being an emptied and anti-Christic image of the divine truth.

Although for Erasmus the Roman Church is full of moral vices, this does not necessarily lead to it being condemned as anti-Christic (not even in its head and leadership): to do so would mean splitting the community, scandalizing one's brother in the faith and claiming to judge him by denying him the possibility of advancing down his own naïve path towards God.[37]

---

35. Himelick 1971: 87–88; ASD V, 3: 305, ll. 654–70: "Pii cuiusdam affectus est credere preces ac bona opera viuentium prodesse defunctis, praesertim si haec illi, dum viuerent, facienda curarunt. [...] Religiosi item affectus est credere sanctos et sanctas [...] nunc quoque nonnihil apud eum posse. [...] Superstitio quam fateor in inuocatione cultuque diuorum esse plurimam, coarguenda est; pius ac simplex affectus interdum tolerandus est, etiam si sit cum aliquo coniunctus errore."
36. Himelick 1971: 89; ASD V, 3: 306, ll. 702–704: "Hic affectus Deo non potest ingratus esse, qui non e superstitione, sed ab abundantia quadam amoris proficiscitur."
37. "Accomodation in Scripture, both as an accommodation of the word to the reader and of the reader to the word is for Erasmus analogous to accommodation in education as such, both as the accommodation of the teacher to the student and of the student to the subject matter. [...] Respect for each person's individuality and natural gifts marks an education that is liberal because it enables formation by evocation instead of enforced conformity, by emulation rather than by competition. [...] The teacher's love and respect for the student, derives, we conclude, from the dynamic of participation and separation, that is, from their freedom to accommodate themselves while at the same time keeping distance on account of their authority. In this way, they imitate God's relation to humanity" (Hoffmann 1994: 111–12).

The Catholic reception

The history of the reception of *De amabili* is significant with respect to the goal that Erasmus had set himself: it received widespread attention and enjoyed numerous reprints throughout Europe, at least seven in the following years; it was translated into German both by Wolfgang Capito and Georg Witzel, a former Lutheran who had returned to the ranks of Roman Catholicism.[38] In other words, it immediately represented a common starting point—on both sides of the controversy—fostering dialogue aimed at reconciliation and restoration of the Church's unity. Capito, a humanist and friend of Erasmus, but pro-Reformation, dedicated his translation of the text to the Archbishop of Mainz, Albert.[39] Although in his introduction he was obviously cautious in defining a doctrinal lowest common denominator and in sharing with Erasmus all the concessions that the evangelicals would have to make, he pointed out the possibility of accepting Erasmus's proposal for reconciliation in order to safeguard the essential principle of Christian love through an admission of fault by both parties. As Friedrich Kantzenbach has already noted, Capito, in his *Commentary on the Prophet Hosea*, followed a strategy of recognizing an evangelical heart in the Roman tradition and of massively recovering patristic theological *loci* according to a "Catholic" desire to mediate between the extremes of the dispute. Moreover, at the same time as Capito's translation, his companion Martin Bucer was publishing an essay in preparation for the Council, which—although reaffirming some of the fixed points of the reformist side—was evidently inspired by Erasmian ideas.[40]

---

38. Cf. Kantzenbach 1957: 90–92; Stupperich 1986: 254–55; Rummel and Hunt 2000: 3–4; Rummel 2000: 129–30.
39. Albert was also indirectly the cause of Luther's revolt: he and his territories had been granted the "scandalous" preaching of indulgences for the factory of St. Peter, which was entrusted to the Dominican John Tetzel.
40. Cf. Kantzenbach 1957: 90–91. "Capito added, moreover, that evangelicals could not accept prayers for the dead; Erasmus had advised to bear with those who believed in their efficacy. Both agreed that belief in the intercession of the saints was acceptable, if it did not involve superstition, and on the use of images, if it did not involve idolatry. Erasmus, however, made further concessions: [...]. Capito did not reject confession out of hand, but objected to its being made obligatory. The two men also disagreed on the nature of the mass" (Rummel 2000: 135).

And on the Catholic side? So far, the historiographical tradition has mostly underlined the diffidence with which the Roman Church received Erasmus's work. For example, Erika Rummel has pointed out that Catholic controversialists criticized Erasmus's proposal because it would have required too many concessions to the reformist side.[41] One may remember the later polemics of the Louvanian theologian Jacques Masson, whose writing against Erasmus, *Adversus Erasmi librum de sarcienda ecclesiae concordia*, remained unfinished after Masson's death and was only published in 1555 on the initiative of his nephew.[42] In addition to this, Erika Rummel and Laura Hunt studied the reaction of Pier Paolo Vergerio, papal legate at Ferdinand's court beginning in the spring of 1533, who in a draft addressed to King Ferdinand (undated, but probably close to a letter that Vergerio wrote to the papal secretary Pietro Carnesecchi on November 5, 1533) hurled a violent invective against the Dutchman.[43] He stated that Erasmus was not a friend of Rome: ("è stato invero poco amico della santa fede, si leggono tra dotti le composition di M. Iacobo Stunica, del Principe di Carpi, di Augustino Steuco").[44] Erasmus was said to have repeated charges against the Church by criticizing confession, which he maintained was not "of ancient custom"; the power of the pontiff, which did not date back to the early Church;[45] and the "sacred ceremonies, the profession of monks, ecclesiastical decrees." He therefore concluded that Erasmus shared, with Luther himself, Valla's pestiferous heritage, namely the questioning of the power of the pontiff:

> ha fatto molto peggio che vedendono i tumulti, le ruine, le strage concitate da tanti noui heretici, Erasmo con tanta sua eloquentia et tanta dottrina non s'ha mai voluto opponer, et reprimer il mal crescente—che dico io opponersi!—esso colludeua con quei spiriti tartarei sequaci di Luthero, esso con i suoi scritti, esso con la sua

---

41. Cf. Rummel 2000: 130–31. "In 1533 Cochlaeus reported that Erasmus' Concord had given offense to Catholic churchmen. He mentioned in particular the reaction of church leaders in Scotland, where he had sent a copy: 'The bishops and monks do not like his books, but reject them as suspect'" (Rummel 2000: 130).
42. The text is in Latomus 1550: 172–82.
43. Edited in Rummel and Hunt 2000: 14–19.
44. Rummel and Hunt 2000: 14.
45. Damasus "was called high priest, and not high bishop [*fu detto sommo sacerdote, et non sommo episcopo*]" (Rummel and Hunt 2000: 15).

auttorita gli ha aiutati, onde accortamente disse gia il Signor Alberto da Carpi, che Erasmo Lutherizaua, et Luthero Erasmizaua.[46]

Other critical judgments can be found in the correspondence between Cochlaeus and Aleander: in a letter from Dresden dated April 23, 1534, Cochlaeus told Aleander of the accusations made against Erasmus's writings.[47] On closer inspection, however, the reactions of the high curial world of the Catholic Church seem to have been more complex than has been noted, and in some very significant cases were openly favorable. We shall consider that in the same exchange in which Cochlaeus refers to the criticism of Erasmus, he himself pointed out (defending the book) that in any case the *"libellum de concordia"* would have been far more detestable to the Lutherans. Cochlaeus was concerned that the criticisms should not lead Erasmus to support the Protestants.

> Ex parte nostra plerique clamitant contra libellum de concordia, quem tamen nobis tolerabiliorem puto quam haereticis. Certe nollem eum virum injuriis a parte nostra in transversum agi. Malignissime cavillatur in eum Lutherus: in quo enim illum judicat, seipsum condemnat.[48]

While Erasmus's proposal had caused some perplexity, it was nevertheless read and appreciated in the highest spheres of the ecclesiastical hierarchy. A resounding confirmation comes from a letter to Erasmus himself. On May 16, 1534, Giovanni Danieli—a member of Cajetan's household[49]—sent a short note to the humanist, which probably accompanied a lost letter from Cajetan himself.[50] Here Danieli mentioned that Erasmus's work *De amabili Concordia* had been read and widely appreciated by the pope and by the cardinal himself:

---

46. Rummel and Hunt 2000: 15.
47. *Letter from Cochlaeus to Aleander, Ex Dresda 23 Aprilis 1534*, in Friedensburg 1888: 247–49.
48. Ibid., 249.
49. *Contemporaries of Erasmus*, I: 376.
50. *Letter from John Danielis to Erasmus, 16 May 1534*, n. 2935, in Allen X: 385–86; English translation by Clarence H. Miller: 286.

> Both of your letters, my venerable master, were greatly pleasing both to the cardinal and to the pope, and both of them are extremely well disposed towards you. Concerning the cardinal, I can testify from what I saw and heard from him when I was with him and read him both your letter and your book concerning amiable concord. As for the pope, when I spoke to the cardinal today about the subject matter of the said book, he told me, among other things, that the pope very carefully read your letter to the cardinal and a copy of it in German, which pleased him greatly, and that, when he had heard the testimony of the cardinal about the book, he was most enthusiastic and remained very favourably disposed towards you.[51]

Cajetan had not only read and appreciated the pamphlet but, having communicated its contents to the pontiff, had witnessed his rejoicing, his *exultare*, and his expression of affection for Erasmus. In short, the pope—assisted by Cajetan, the great anti-Lutheran controversialist, the figure behind *Exurge Domine*—had fully approved! The postscript also said that some people in Rome had criticized the work, but that Cajetan had publicly defended it by directly dismantling the objections against it.

> Before I had seen the aforesaid book by you, some people here found fault with it, saying that Erasmus allowed complete freedom for anyone to indulge in his own judgement, an objection that afterwards in my presence the cardinal most thoroughly refuted.[52]

That Erasmus's written works supported the Roman Catholic Church was evident to the top curial offices; its anti-Lutheran scope and its use of

---

51. *Contemporaries of Erasmus* XX: 286; Allen X: 386, ll. 1–10: "Reverende mi domine, ambe epistole vestre fuerunt gratissime et cardinali et pontifici, et vterque est propensissime erga vos voluntatis. Et de cardinali quidem testificari possum ex visis et ab eo auditis, coram quo legi et litteras et libellum de amabili concordia. De Pontifice, cum hodie loquerer cardinali de negocio dicti libelli, inter cetera dixit mihi cardinalis, pontificem accuratissime perlegisse epistolam vestram ad cardinalem et exemplum illius alterius germanice, easque ei perplacuisse, et audito testimonio cardinalis de libello totum exultasse et remansisse optime erga vos affectum."
52. *Contemporaries of Erasmus* XX: 286; Allen X: 386, ll. 18–20: "Antequam vidissem prenominatum libellum vestrum, quidam hic reprehendebant eum, dicentes Erasmum in totum permittere vnicuique in suo sensu abundare, quam obiectionem postea me presente cardinalis optime diluit. Certo scio nunc eos futuros equiores etc." On the reception of Erasmus in the Roman curia, see Schätti 1954; Gerbhardt 1966.

religious codes with apologetic aims were fully acknowledged. Erasmus's work also left traces in the later writings of the Roman side of the controversy. On close inspection, one can find possible references to the work of *De amabili ecclesiae concordia* in several Roman treatises, especially in the years of preparation for the Council. In 1535, Cochlaeus published the *Dialogus de tollenda in fide et religione discordia per concilium generale*, a text that clearly echoed Erasmus's proposal for a reconciliation with the Protestants.[53] Pursuant to the typically humanistic and Erasmian form of a dialogue, three characters confront each other in a polite way: Petreius, the strict defender of Roman orthodoxy and the Papacy; Paceus, the Erasmian theologian, who—inclined to peace—tries to minimize and resolve the disagreements; and Arenius, who defends the Lutheran sect but can be persuaded by his two interlocutors. Cochlaeus was clearly subordinating the perspective of Paceus, presented as a skeptical character who was not inclined to dogmatic definition, to the authority of Petreius, who was able to understand the theses of Arenio and Paceus and to persuade them of the truth of Catholic doctrine and the error of Lutheran formulas. Anyway, it was undeniable that the Erasmian methodology of dialogue had been resumed, in which the "heretical" position was recognized and corrected through the strategic use of doubt, hypotheses, and rational reasoning. It should also be noted that, among the many examples of virtuous prelates of the Church, Erasmus himself was the first to be listed, before Sadoleto, Budé, and Vives.[54]

In another essay written against Sturm, the *Aequitatis Discussio super Consilio delectorum Cardinalium* (1538),[55] Cochlaeus confirms the

---

53. Cochlaeus 1545a: 65–96. Cf. Kantzenbach 1957: 144–48.
54. "Quanto magis nunc tempore salutis & gratiae credendum est, plusquam Septem Milia uirorum, inter Ecclesiae Praelatos, non in una duntaxa prouincia parua, qualis Iudaea fuit, sed in multis ac magnis per Orbem terrae prouinciis & regnis, reperiri posse, qui & uerbo & exemplo bene praesunt, atque de die in diem meritis & uirtutibus proficiunt & clarescunt & apud deum & apud homines? Quot rogo & quantos posset numerare unus Erasmus Roterodamus, doctiss. Episcopos, aliosque probatae uitae atque doctrinae ueros Ecclesiasticos, literarum commercio sibi cognitos? Quot Sadoletus? Quot Budaeus? Quot Viues? Quot alii clarissimi atque doctissimi uiri innumeri? Absit igitur, ut sancta Mater Ecclesia, cui datus est spiritus ueritatis ut cum ipsa maneat in aeternum, sit temporibus nostris usque adeo sterilis & effoeta" (Cochlaeus 1545a: 72r).
55. Cochlaeus 1931.

pro-Erasmian position of an important part of the Roman curia, stating that the early condemnation of the *Colloquia* produced by the latest curial document about the Church's reform, *De emendanda ecclesia*, was not an interdiction against all of Erasmus's writings, but was merely a caution about one of them from a pedagogical point of view; it was clear that this critique was in any case far less heavy than the harsh criticism Luther had addressed to Erasmus:

> Deinde ais: "Quid tam vanuum est, quam Erasmi colloquia tollere et pro sacris nugas doceri?"—At non tolluntur Erasmi colloquia prorsus et omnino, sed prohibentur praelegi pueris: forsitan propterea, quod minus religiose alicubi ludunt et loquuntur de ueneratione sanctorum, de votis monasticis et de externis ceremoniis, quae hoc tempore plus satis irreligiose contemnuntur et conculcantur a plerisque sectis. Et cur illos Erasmi amicos ita reprehendis, cum idipsum iam pridem censuerit Lutherus, quem probas? Ipse enim non solum colloquia, sed et alia Erasmi opuscula e scholis eiicienda esse sancivit, uelut impia et irreligiosa.[56]

In January 1545, the Ingolstadt editor Alexander Weißenhorn published another significant text by Cochlaeus, the *Consyderatio Iohannis Cochlaei, de futuro concordiae in religione tractatu, Vuormatiae habendo*,[57] dedicated to Cardinal Ercole Gonzaga, who was invited to support—together with the College of Cardinals and the Pope—the imperial attempt to propose convening a general Council on German soil in order to settle the Lutheran controversy and avoid Protestant defection.[58]

56. Cochlaeus 1931: 18–19.
57. Cochlaeus 1545b.
58. Cochlaeus 1545b: A2v–A3r: "Quoniam uero pars protestantium Principum ac statuum potius Nationale quam Generale desyderat Concilium, ac dilati hactenus Generalis Concilii moram inuidiose imputare solet summo Pontifici Coetuique Cardinalium, et Ecclesiasticos Imperii Principes ac status dissidentiae, tanquam pessimam habeant causam, iactanter arguit, uisum est mihi operae praecium atque etiam necessarium esse hac de re ad Rev. et Illust. Celsitudinem uestram scribere, tanquam ad Principem et Cardinalem summae authoritatis pietatisque & sapientiae, qui ut loco et situ, ita et gratia ac beneuolentia Germanis nobis propinquior est, Quem hoc scripto supplici deuotione maxime rogatum uolo, ut apud sedem Apostolicam diligenter adiuuet pios ac necessarios Cesareae Maiestatis conatus, ad promouendum et celebrandum primo quoque tempore in Germanica natione generale Concilium, ne forte per Nationale Concilium Germania a caeteris fidei Catholicae nationibus tota

This work too is clearly dependent on that of Erasmus. Cochlaeus's fundamental accusation is against the pride of Luther and his followers, who dare to claim that a concord between Catholics and Lutherans in doctrinal matters is impossible, and that their schism is desired by God:

> Concionatores uero eorum, qui diabolo instigante antiquas haereses in lucem protulerunt, ac nouum schisma excitauerunt, probe sciunt, suum regnum et autoritatem non nisi in discordia consistere, audent uel aperte scribere, quod impossibile sit, inter nos et illos in fide et religione concordiam fieri, seque certos esse, quod hoc schisma eorum Deo placeat. Ideo patronis suis ubique dissuadent, ne concordiae tractatum nobiscum ineant, talesque proponunt fraudulenter articulos, quos a nobis minime concedi posse probe sciunt [...].[59]

Furthermore, Cochlaeus explicitly referred to the episode of Korah and Moses as scriptural demonstration of the illegitimacy of any schism and separation from the Church:

> Miserabilis profecto et horrenda est caecitas eorum, quibus talia persuaderi possunt, ut ex animo credant ea esse uera, Cum tot sint passim in utroque Testamento Scripturarum loci, qui schismata damnant ac maxime reprehendunt, Quod essem aliud fuit scelus Chore Datan et Abyron, propter quod uiui per abruptos terrae hiatus in inferna descenderunt, nisi quod contra Moysen et Aaron schisma suscitarunt?[60]

In order to make clear his condemnation of the blindness of the schismatics, God inflicted on them the most horrendous and frightening punishment: to be plunged directly into the abyss. As for Erasmus, Luther's fundamental error is thus a sin against charity, accomplished by lacerating the unity of the Church:

> Et audet nunc suis persuadere Lutherus, se certum esse, quod suum hoc schisma Deo placeat, qui antea publice testatus est non semel, impium esse quodcunque Bohoemorum schisma, etiamsi ius

---

in iis quae fidei et religionis antiquae sunt, deficiat, irrecuperabileque detrimentum patiatur."

59. Cochlaeus 1545b: A3v.
60. Cochlaeus 1545b: A4v.

diuinum staret pro eis, eo quod summum ius diuinum sit charitas, contra quam est omne in fide et religione schisma.[61]

The reference to Erasmus and his writing on free will was consequently explicit:

> Ego breuissime interrogans, an ipsi reuelatum esset, eoque id impudenter affirmante, ulterius quaesiui, quo nam signo aut miraculo id nobis, ut credere debeamus, probaret, nihil habuit os impudens amplius, quo illud Pauli dictum sibi arrogaret, Recte enim in eum dixit aliquando doctissimus uir Erasmus Roterodamus, quod uel equum claudum sanare nequeat, tantum abest ut ullo claruerit unquam miraculo impius iste omnis sanctimoniae conspurcator et hostis.[62]

Despite the harsh tones, Cochlaeus's text nevertheless invites appeasement. The quotations from Cochlaeus—from the 1530s until this last text of 1545—clearly show how the theme of concord was understood in an ideological and controversial sense as a way of countering and delegitimizing doctrinal divisions within the Church.[63] Furthermore, it was also a

---

61. Cochlaeus 1545b: B1v.
62. Cochlaeus 1545b: D2v.
63. "Für Cochlaeus ist Erasmus, mit dem er auch freundschaftlichen Briefwechsel gepflogen hat, eine der Hauptautoritäten in der Bekämpfung Luthers. Schon der Untertitel seiner Kommentare zeigt das an: unter den Instanzen und Personen, auf die sich das Werk stützen will, ist Erasmus einziger namentlich genannt. Seine Polemik gegen Luther hat er gründlich gelesen, besonders die Schrift vom freien Willen, den *Hyperaspistes*, den *Ecclesiastes*, und die *Purgatio adversus epistolam... Lutheri* von 1534. Er verwendet diese Schriften in langen Zitaten immer wieder für seinen eigenen Kampf. Für ihn ist Erasmus nichts anders als der aufrechte, von keinerlei Zweifel angefochtene Streiter für die rechtgläubige Kirke. Mit allerlei Schmeicheleien habe Luther versucht, ihn auf seine Seite zu locken. Aber vergebens, Erasmus habe sich ihm nicht zugewandt, ja er sei der gewaltigste Kämpfer gegen di Sektierer geworden. Luther haben ihn überhören wollen, sei ihm ängstlich aus dem Wege gegangen. Und als es ihm schließlich haben stehen müssen, sei er alsbald kläglich zusammengesunken unter den Hieben des Gelehrten. Hernach hebe er sich nur noch aufs Schimpfen und Schmälen verlegt, so arg, dass Erasmus seinen Brief an Amsdorf nur als das Schreiben eines seiner Sinne nicht Mächtigen habe ansehen können. Als Grundlage der *katholischen* Lutherbiographik finden wir also ein klares und positives Bild: Erasmus als der alle Häretiker niederschmetternde Herkules—ein Bild, das in der Durchführung der Trienter Beschlüsse sie bald zerschlagen sollte" (Flitner 1952: 47–48).

way to promote a Council that would have as its aim to define the search for a meeting point between the different positions. The ambiguity of the German Catholic reception of this text, which was both trying to respond to and neutralize the demands for reform, is therefore evident.

Another example of Erasmus's influence on the Roman Catholic theologians, and one that could testify to the same ambiguities about the attempts at concord and reconciliation with the Lutheran side, is offered in a text by Friedrich Nausea. In 1540, during the Worms *Colloquia*, he published in Mainz the *Hortatio ad ineundam in Christiana Religione Concordiam*, a brief exhortation directly addressed to the theologians and orators gathered for the *Colloquia*, inviting them to preserve the concord essential to Christian faith.[64] To make this possible, Nausea invited everyone to trust in the mercy of Christ, and to convert with a sincere feeling towards God, according to Erasmus's precept of moderation and spiritual interiorization:

> Vbi maluerimus ea dissimulare, quam exagitare, quae minore religionis incommodo dissimulantur. Quandoquidem manum doctam requirant et arteficem omnia ea, quae grauiora sunt, quam ut dissimulare oporteat paulatim, et per occasionem tollenda sunt, quae per occasionem irrepserunt, ne sit alioquin grauis exoriturus tumultus. Nec enim conducit (ut aiebat ille magnus Erasmus Roterodamus) ad concordiam, in sinistram retorquere partem, quae dicta sunt ambigue, aut deprauare per calumniam, quae pie dicta sunt.[65]

The non-coincidental recurrence of the Erasmian word *dissimulare*, as a key term for achieving de-escalation of the controversy, must also be underlined. The reference to the *De amabili concordia* was thus evoked in the immediate aftermath, with the idea of a possible "synkatabasis" or *condescensio* to methodically reconstitute the necessary unanimity and return to moving forward together within a unified Church. Nausea pointed out that, in order to do so, the Church should not renounce those

64. Nausea 1540.
65. Nausea 1540: B1r. Note the perfect terminological correspondence with Erasmus's text: cf. Himelick 1971: 84; ASD V, 3: 302, ll. 572–75: "Pleraque paulatim ac per occasionem irrepserunt, ea paulatim ac per occasionem tollenda sunt, si fieri queat absque graui tumultu; sin minus, dissimulanda, donec ipsa dies porrigat occasionem commodiorem. Eadem dexteritate vtendum est in dogmatibus."

things that have been transmitted with greater authority and that are confirmed by secular use and consensus.

> Quando uix aeque conducat resartiendae concordiae, quam condescensio quaedam, quam Graeci *synkatabasin* nominant. Quam seruabimus ubi nos mutuo, utpote una pars alteri nonnihil accommodauerimus, nec funiculum contentionis adeo tetenderimus, ut utraque pars in tergum rupto fune, sit casura. Superest igitur, ut positis opinionum et affectuum dissidiis, eodem sensu, eademque sententia iam tandem incumbamus ad sartiendam Ecclesiae concordiam.[66]

The danger of continuing in a state of contention and constantly pulling on one's own side of the rope is that it may break the rope and cause everyone to fall to the ground. Precisely for this reason, concord must become an unavoidable requirement of dialogue, which passes through mutual accommodation. One must know how to "come down together" to the lowest common denominator of faith: but this is also evidently a cutting operation aimed at the very roots of Lutheran theological provocation. Such a short and consequential piece of writing, whose aim was to create an ideological and political manifesto for the *Colloquia*, confirms that Erasmus's work was perfectly functional for Catholic projects because the Church understood its own structural ambivalence and therefore its political capacity to mediate with the Reformers, while at the same time reaffirming a number of firm opinions from the Catholic perspective.

Conclusions: an ideological war

At the end of this brief analysis, it seems possible to conclude that several dominant historiographical interpretations have systematically underestimated the ideological and polemical horizon of Erasmus's writings on concord and peace, thus neglecting the importance of its Catholic reception. In addition, the definitive litmus test for an anti-Lutheran interpretation of the *De amabili ecclesiae concordia* is provided by Luther himself, who openly criticized and rejected it as a papist manifesto.

---

66. Nausea 1540: B1r-v.

In 1534, the Lutheran Antonius Corvinus wrote the dialogue *Dissertatio quatenus expediat Erasmi de sarcienda ecclesiae concordia rationem sequi*. In this conversation, two interlocutors faced each other: Julianus set out all the points of the Erasmian position, and Corvinus himself expressed his own opinions by defending the basic assumptions of the Reformation, starting with criticism of the Papacy as a tyranny of conscience, of the priesthood as a satanic invention, and so on. Although critical and polemical, the work depicted a desire for a dialogue with Erasmus's thought. While reproaching the Dutchman for his inconsistency, Corvinus underlined his respect for him as the humanist who freed Germany from barbarism.[67] In a later edition of 1534,[68] Luther was asked to add a preface to the text: though Luther substantially supported Corvinus's verdict, he strongly sharpened the author's criticisms of Erasmus, thus offering us a document describing his reaction to the question of the religious concord that was animating the theological and religious debates of the time.

Luther understood that the theme of the *concordia* was slippery and was in the service of a strategy of neutralizing his own main theological positions. He therefore denounced Erasmus's position as a dangerous corruption of Christian conscience and truth, which cannot tolerate compromise on the subject of faith. First of all, for Luther a distinction must be made between the *concordia fidei* and *concordia caritatis*. From the point of view of charity, it is our duty to do everything for our neighbour, to observe peace and harmony. However, the point of view of faith is different: it does not struggle, like charity, with flesh and blood, but with desperate and evil spirits, whose malice is obstinate. In other words, there can be no peace or concord or friendship with the devil and with darkness.

---

67. Kanztenbach 1957: 88–89; Rummel 2000: 133: "He expresses surprise to find a reform-minded man like Erasmus turned into an enemy of the evangelicals. Julianus defends 'his friend' Erasmus, noting that he had engaged in polemic with Luther unwillingly [...] Corvinus disapproves of obliging friends in such serious matters, but Julianus insists that Erasmus had no alternative [...] Corvinus supports only a qualified irenicism [...] There was no place for lenience in doctrinal matters. Julianus, as Erasmus's mouthpiece, refers doctrinal matters to a future Council and, in the meantime, pledges 'to keep away from all sects.' Corvinus, however, rejects the verdict of a Council controlled by Rome."
68. Corvinus 1534.

> Nam doctrina fidei non luctatur cum carne et sanguine sicut Charitas, quae cum hominibus et eorum viciis exercetur, tolerandis, corrigendis, emendandis, quae mutari possunt, et ipsa spem habet perseuerantem vsque ad mortem conuertendi peccatoris. Sed luctatur cum spiritibus nequitiae et desperatis, quorum malitia est obstinata in aeternum, sine vlla spe conuertendi aut mutandi animi. Ideo inter fidem seu doctrinam Christi et Daemonum voluntates, nulla pax, nulla concordia, nulla amicitia tentari debet. Ipse est homicida et pater mendacii, et tam non potest non odisse fidei doctrinam, quam mendacem et nocendi voluntatem non mutare. Quae enim est conuentio Christi et Belial? Quae societas lucis et tenebrarum?[69]

Luther's concern is about whether or not it is possible to define with absolute certainty what is faith, what is truth, and what is vice. According to Luther, Erasmus's position panders to papist impiety because it subordinates the dogmatic level to the ethical level, teaching only dubious and uncertain things and provisional and relative truths, and is not based on the absolute revelation of Christ's grace.[70] Luther grasps exactly what we have tried to show: Erasmus's approach deactivates the anarchic experience of faith as an openness to the gift of grace, defending an economy of rewards and punishments based on the merit of creaturely freedom. To not precisely define the absolute truth of the dogma of salvation by grace means leaving one last space for the pride of human will, which presumes itself to be free and capable of good works.

> Vna est eorum vociferatio, Ecclesia, Ecclesia, Ecclesia, Et Ecclesiam vocant homines, etiam impios, qui supra et contra scripturam sentire et statuere possunt, idque autoritate diuina, Hanc eorum vocem et Erasmus confirmat, Qui vbique Ecclesiam sequi sese promittit. Et interim omnia dubia et incerta docet. Sed si Ecclesiam hoc vocare debemus [...] cur reprenduntur vicia? Cur periclitamur confessione

---

69. Luther, *Praefatio* in Corvinus 1534: A4v.
70. "Vnde et in meo Seruo arbitrio in Erasmi Theologia reprehendi istam Scepticorum sententiam, Necesse est enim in Ecclesia certum dogma, certum verbum Dei haberi, cui certo et secure possimus, credere et in eadem certitudine fidei et uiuere et mori. Quam certitudinem, quia et Erasmus parum curat, et Papistae non docent, sed oderunt et persequuntur, Coire nulla concordia in fide et doctrina potest. Quia Ecclesia hac certa fidei anchora carere non potest, et extra seu supra Verbum Dei, nulla fides substistere potest" (Corvinus 1534: A6v).

> veritatis?[…] Istis ne dicemus, Audiendus est Papa, vt pax constet et concordia, aut incertae sunt relinquendae, suspensa interim sententia, donec aliud Papa decreuerit cum suis?[71]

Erasmus is a papist, and for the sake of peace he wants people to obey the uncertain and doubtful authority of the pope, and not the absolute authority of Christ. Therefore, Luther must reject any attempt at reconciliation as a skeptical and pagan position, an anti-Christic provocation, a denial of salvation by Christ's death and resurrection.

The documents and analyses presented here attempt to highlight the irreconcilable division between Erasmus's Origenian perspective and Luther's apocalyptic and dualistic one. They also aim at clarifying how the theme of peace and concord could not be completely neutral but was freighted with theological perspectives and precise ideological options, as Erasmus's stance in favour of the Roman side had shown. This not only explains why Luther always remained distrustful of and hostile to attempts at doctrinal mediation with Rome, but also explains the ambiguities of the reforming papist party, who were, on the one hand, interested in defending orthodoxy from Protestant attacks, and on the other, in defusing the dispute in order to avoid a radical schism within the Church. As both Erasmus and Luther well understood, under the heading of the question of religious concord, the hermeneutical, exegetical, and dogmatic foundations of the Christian faith were at stake, calling for a choice regarding the deeper essence of the Christian message. Using the terms *pax* and *concordia*, an ideological war was being waged, a dialectic between orthodoxy and heresy. What was being defined was who and what were friends and who and what were foes of the authentic Church.

Author biography

Ludovico Battista (PhD, Sapienza University of Rome) deals with the history of Christianity and the critical relationship between theology and philosophy. His interests focus on the problem of secularization and the genesis of modernity, on the Renaissance and the period of the Reformation (with specific attention to Erasmus and his reception in

---

71. Corvinus 1534: A5v–A6r.

Italy), on the question of political theology since the early Christianity and the patristic reflection. Among his publications are: *Hans Blumenberg e l'autodistruzione del cristianesimo* (Rome: Viella, 2021) and *Le ragioni della religione. Mito, modernità e secolarizzazione in H. Blumenberg and J. Habermas* (Rome: Lithos, 2021).

References

Primary sources

Cochlaeus, J. (1545a), *Dialogus de tollenda in fide et religione discordia per concilium generale* in idem, *In Causa Religionis Miscellaneorvm Libri Tres In Diuersos Tractatus antea non æditos, ac diuersis temporibus, locisq[ue] scriptos digesti*. Ingolstadt [1535].

Cochlaeus, J. (1545b), *Consyderatio Iohannis Cochlaei, de futuro concordiae in religione tractatu, Vuormatiae habendo*. Ingolstadt: Vueyssenhorn.

Cochlaeus, J. (1931), *Aequitatis Discussio super Consilio delectorum Cardinalium (1538)*, edited by P. Hilarius Walter, *Corpus Catholicorum: Werke katholischer Schriftsteller im Zeitalter der Glaubenssspaltung*, Heft 17. Münster in Westfalen: Aschendorffschen Verlagsbuchhandlung.

Corvinus, A. (1534), *Quatenus expediat aeditam recens Erasmi de sarcienda ecclesiae concordia rationem sequi, tantisper dum adparatur Synodus, iuditium Antonii Corvini*. Wittemberg: Schirlentz.

Erasmus, D. (1986), *De sarcienda Ecclesiae concordia liber*, in *Opera Omnia Desideri Erasmi Roterodami*, ASD V, 3: 245–313. Amsterdam: North-Holland Publishing Co. English translation by Raimond Himelick (1971), *Erasmus and the Seamless Coat of Jesus: On Restoring the Unity of the Church. With Selections from the Letters and Ecclesiastes*, 26–109. Lafayette, IN: Purdue University Studies.

Erasmus, D. (1992), *Opus Epistolarium*, edited by P. S. Allen, 2nd ed., 12 vols. Oxford: Oxford University Press, 1906–1958. English translation in *The Correspondence of Erasmus*, 21 vols., "The Collected Works of Erasmus," Toronto: University of Toronto Press, 1974–2021.

Latomus, J. (1550), *Opera*, Bartholomaeus Gravius suis impensis. Louvain: Petri Phalesii ac Martini Rotarii.

Nausea, F. (1540), *Hortatio ad ineundam in Christiana Religione Concordiam*. Moguntiae: Franciscus Behem.

Nausea, F. (1888), "Beiträge zum Briefwechsel der katholischen Gelehrten Deutschlands im Reformationszeitalter. Aus italienischen Archiven und Bibliotheken mitgeteilt von Walter Friedensburg," *Zeitschrift für Kirchengeschichte* XVIII: 233–97.

Origen (1921), *Homiliae in Numeros*, edited by W. A. Baehrens in *Origenes Werke*, VII Band, *Homilien zum Hexateuch in Rufins Übersetzung*, II Teil: *Die Homilien zu Numeri, Josua and Judices*, GCS 30. Leipzig: J.C. Hinrich'sche Buchhandlung.

Secondary sources

Alberigo, G. et al., eds. (2013), *Conciliorum Oecumenicorum Decreta*. Bologna: Centro editoriale dehoniano.

Barral-Baron, M. (2014), *L'Enfer d'Érasme. L'humaniste chrétien face à l'histoire*. Geneva: Droz.

Bietenholz, P. G., ed. (1987), *Contemporaries of Erasmus: A Biographical Register of the Renaissance and Reformation, Volume 3 (N–Z)*. Toronto: University of Toronto Press.

Cotta-Schønberg, M. (2019), *Oration "Moyses vir Dei" of Enea Silvio Piccolomini (24 April 1452, Rome)*, edited and translated by M. von Cotta-Schönberg, 8th ed. (Orations of Enea Silvio Piccolomini / Pope Pius II; 19). https://shs.hal.science/halshs-01064759/document

Daniels, Tobias (2013), *La congiura dei Pazzi: i documenti del conflitto fra Lorenzo de' Medici e Sisto IV. Le bolle di scomunica, la "Florentina Synodus," e la "Dissentio" insorta tra la Santità del Papa e i Fiorentini. Edizione critica e commento*. Firenze: Hoepli.

Dust, P. C. (1987), *Three Renaissance Pacifists: Essays in the Theories of Erasmus, More, and Vives*. New York: Peter Lang.

Ettlinger, L. (1965), *The Sistine Chapel before Michelangelo: Religious Imagery and Papal Primacy*. Oxford: Clarendon Press.

Fallica, M., A. C. Jacobsen, and G. Lettieri, eds. (2022), *Origen and the Origenian Tradition on Progress*. Berlin: Peter Lang.

Flitner, A. (1952), *Erasmus im Urteil seiner Nachwelt. Das literarische Erasmus-Bild von Beatus Rhenanus bis zu Kean Leclerc*. Tübingen: Max Niemeyer.

Friedensburg, W. (1888), "Beiträge zum Briefwechsel der katholischen Gelehrten Deutschlands im Reformationszeitalter. Aus italienischen Archiven und Bibliotheken mitgeteilt von Walter Friedensburg," *Zeitschrift für Kirchengeschichte* XVIII: 233–97.

Gerbhardt, G. (1966), *Die stellung des Erasmus zur römischen Kirche*. Marburg an der Lahn: Oekumenischer Verlag.

Godin, A. (1982), *Érasme lecteur d'Origène*. Geneva: Droz.

Halkin, L. H. (1974), "Érasme entre François Ier et Charles-Quint," *Bullettin de l'Institut historique belge de Rome* XLIV: 301–319.

Hentze, W. (1974), *Kirche und kirchliche Einheit bei Desiderius Erasmus von Rotterdam*. Paderborn: Verlag Bonifacius-Druckerei.

Hoffmann, M. (1994), *Rhetoric and Theology: The Hermeneutic of Erasmus*. Toronto: University of Toronto Press.

Honée, E. (1993), "Die Religionsverhandlungen der Reichstage von Nürnberg (1524), Speyer (1526) und Augsburg (1530) und die Entstehung der Idee eines Religionsgesprächs," *Nederlands archief voor kerkgeschiedenis / Dutch Review of Church History* 73/1: 1–30. https://doi.org/10.1163/002820393X00012

Honée, E. (1997), "Erasmus und die Religionsverhandlungen der deutschen Reichstage (1524–1530)," in M. E. H. N. Mout et al. (eds.), *Erasmianism: Idea and Reality*, 65–75. Amsterdam: Koninklijke Nederlandse Akademie van Wetenschappen.

Huizinga, J. (1984), *Erasmus and the Age of Reformation*. Princeton: Princeton University Press (1st ed. 1924).

Kantzenbach, F. W. (1957), *Das Ringen um die Einheit der Kirche im Jahrhundert der Reformation. Vertreter, Quellen und Motive des "ökumenischen" Gedankens von Erasmus vom Rotterdam bis Georg Calixt*. Stuttgart: Evangelisches Verlagswerk.

Lettieri, G. (2021), "Lo 'spiraculo' di Machiavelli e 'le mandragole' di Savonarola: Due misconosciute metafore cristologico-politiche," *Studi e Materiali di Storia delle Religioni* 87/1: 285–321.

Lettieri, G., ed. (2023a), "El papa, nuevo Moisés. De Eugenio IV a los papas mediceos," *De Medio Aevo* 12/2.

Lettieri, G. (2023b), "Mosè figura papale ne il principe di Machiavelli," in G. M. Barbuto and F. Seller (eds.), *Profezia e politica. Alle origini della Modernità*. Naples: FEDOA.

Mann Phillips, M. (1949), *Erasmus and the Northern Renaissance*. London: Boydell & Brewer.

Olin, J. C. (1979), *Six Essays on Erasmus*. New York: Fordham University Press.

Padberg, R. (1969), "Pax Erasmiana. Das politische Engagement und die 'politische Theologie' des Erasmus von Rotterdam," in J. Coppens (ed.), *Scrinium Erasmianum*, vol. 2, 301–314. Leiden: Brill.

Pollet, J. V. (1969), "Origine et Structure du 'De sarcienda ecclesiae concordia' d'Erasme," in J. Coppens (ed.), *Scrinium Erasmianum*, vol. 2, 183–96. Leiden: Brill.

Pollet, J. V. (1990), *Julius Pflug (1499–1564) et la crise religieuse dans l'Allemagne du XVIe siècle. Essai de synthèse biographique et théologique*. Leiden: Brill.

Remer, G. (1996), *Humanism and the Rhetoric of Toleration*. University Park, PA: Pennsylvania University Press.

Ron, N. (2014), "The Christian Peace of Erasmus," *The European Legacy: Toward New Paradigms* 19/1: 27–42. https://doi.org/10.1080/10848770.2013.859793

Rummel, E. (2000), *The Confessionalization of Humanism in Reformation Germany*. Oxford: Oxford University Press.

Rummel, E., and L. Hunt (2000), "Vergerio's Invective Against Erasmus and the Lutherans: An Autograph in the Biblioteca Marciana," *Nederlands archief voor kerkgeschiedenis / Dutch Review of Church History* 80/1: 1–19. https://doi.org/10.1163/002820392X00752

Schätti, K. (1954), *Erasmus von Rotterdam und die römische Kurie*. Basel: Helbing & Lichtenhahn.

Stinger, C. L. (1983), *The Renaissance in Rome*. Bloomington: Indiana University Press.

Stupperich, R. (1986), *Einleitung* in *De sarcienda Ecclesiae concordia liber*, in *Opera Omnia Desideri Erasmi Roterodami*, ASD V, 3: 245–55. Amsterdam: North-Holland Publishing Co.

Torsini, R. (2000), *I Labirinti del Libero Arbitrio. La discussione tra Erasmo e Lutero*. Firenze: Olschki.

Tracy, J. D. (1978), *The Politics of Erasmus: A Pacifist Intellectual and His Political Milieu*. Toronto: University of Toronto Press.

Tracy, J. D. (1996), *Erasmus of the Low Countries*. Berkeley: University of California Press.

Walter, P. (1991), *Theologie aus dem Geist der Rhetorik. Zur Schriftauslegung des Erasmus von Rotterdam*. Mainz: Matthias Grünewald Verlag.

Chapter 6
Specula Pacis: Cosmopolitan Pacifism in Desiderius Erasmus and Thomas More

Antonello Mori and Antonio Senneca

Introduction

The main contributions to the debate about peace were made by intellectuals such as Desiderius Erasmus and Thomas More, sparked by strong cosmopolitan and pacifist requests. The lives and works of both authors can only be explained in relation to a European context. During the sixteenth century the state-building process, which had begun some two centuries earlier, was completed in Europe. It was a particularly complex period, characterized by several wars and many ethnic and religious tensions. Such a difficult context gave birth to some conceptual paradigms about the concepts of war and peace that would remain as references for the centuries to come.

Erasmus, who considered himself stateless, became the example of a man not tied to any land, who as an intellectual nomad migrated from country to country attracted only by the interests and cultural opportunities that the countries could offer. The entire philosophical-theological production of Erasmus is focused on the idea of peace, largely conditioned by his conception of Christianity. In line with Jesus's teaching Erasmus raises peace to a universal value, but he adds to it a cosmopolitan view dictated by the awareness of being part of an enormous community, that of those who believe in the Word of Christ. Therefore, we should not consider his obsession with peace as mere tolerance, but we must realize that peace itself was the key point of his lifestyle according to the *vera religio*, defining also his ethical, religious, and political framework.[1] These requests are developed in concrete terms in fundamental texts such as *Querela Pacis*, *Dulce bellum inexpertis*, and the *Institutio principis christiani*. The writings are also linked to the situation of perpetual conflict in which Europe was involved during the years of their production. These wars saw Christians fighting each other, something that found no justification—neither religious, nor logical, nor moral—in the eyes of Erasmus. This same topic is treated by Erasmus in *Dulce bellum inexpertis* (1515). In this text, which foreshadows much of the content of the *Querela Pacis*, he produces a dense reflection characterized by pacifism. He observes that the only solution to the death machine developed by the human intellect can be found in the words of Christ and in their true application.

To start the proposed analysis, it is necessary to understand what peace really is. Erasmus tries to answer with a rhetorical question: *quid aliud est pax quam multorum inter ipsos amicitia?*[2] In fact, he considers peace as a gift given by nature to the human being. This is because man is the only animal with powers of reason, a mind participating in divinity, capable of sentimental affection and social union.[3] The harmonious coexistence within the community of men is dictated by the way nature itself has conceived man, that is, as a being who is hairless, weak, defenceless, soft of flesh, thin of skin; in his body there is a lack of what is suited for struggle and violence.[4] Because of this natural law, human beings are bound to reciprocal assistance, therefore "in ipsis statim vitae primordiis perisset hominum genus, nisi conditum propagasset coniugalis concordia; nec enim nasceretur homo et mox natus interiret atque in ipso vitae limine vitam amitteret, nisi obstetricum amica manu, nisi nutricum amica pietas succurret infantulo."[5]

1. About religion and politics in Erasmus see Pasini's article (2013) and Bainton's book (2000).
2. Erasmus 1999: 22.
3. Erasmus 1977: 62.
4. Erasmus 1999: 14.
5. Erasmus 1977: 62. Therefore, "in the very commencement of life, the human race had been extinct, unless conjugal union had continued the race. With difficulty could man be born into the world, or as soon as born would he die, leaving life at the very threshold of existence, unless the friendly hand of the careful matron, and the affectionate assiduities of the nurse, lent their aid to the helpless babe. To preserve the

From these words we can understand that the human being was created to be devoted exclusively to peace, harmony, and universal love. These are the only elements in agreement with his nature. Although this appears as an established truth, man has decided to act otherwise, and even "animantia rationis experitia in suo quaeque genere civiliter concorditerque degunt. [...] Solos homines, quos omnium maxime decebat unanimitas quibusque cum primis opus est ea, neque natura tam aliis in rebus potens et efficax conciliat, nec institutio coniungit, nec tot ex consensu profecturae commoditates conglutinant, nec tantorum denique malorum sensus et experientia in mutuum."[6]

The human being, according to the humanist, appears to choose voluntarily to engage in conflicts and war,[7] although well aware that this choice goes against the logic according to which nature acts, because lions show no fierceness to other lions and the boar does not brandish his deadly tooth against his brother boar.[8]

This behavioral mutation happens with a slow but inevitable process, which Erasmus minutely describes in the central pages of his *Dulce bellum inexpertis*. The author takes us back to the genesis of man, when he was a victim of ferocious beasts and began to devise tricks to counter them, succeeding skillfully thanks to the intellect, an element that distinguishes him from all other creatures. Unfortunately, once the locks have been opened to the deadly river of violence, it overflows and covers all the lands of reason, becoming ever more impetuous and devastating. As a result, man first trained himself to slaughter animals and then to apply the same techniques to his fellow men, justifying this behavior by giving a semblance of justice to the elimination of an enemy. This dragged everyone into a stream of violence that served the interests of

---

      poor infant, Nature has given the fond mother the tenderest attachment to it, so that she loves it even before she sees it." Author's translation.

6.   Erasmus 1977: 63. Even "animals destitute of reason live with their own kind in a state of social amity.[...] Yet man to man, whom, of all created beings, concord would most become, and who stands most in need of it, neither nature, so powerful and irresistible in every thing else, can reconcile; neither human compacts unite; neither the great advantages which would evidently arise from unanimity combine, nor the actual feeling and experience of the dreadful evils of discord cordially endear." Author's translation.

7.   About war in Erasmus see Margolin 1970.

8.   Erasmus 1999: 17.

those who, without any discrimination, sought miserly personal gain and were determined to achieve it by all means.⁹ From these pages emerges a shift from the hoped-for universal peace, that should have governed the lives of people all over the world, to a state in which human beings are in a perpetual struggle within themselves for the most vulgar reasons, fueling a conflict that has grown to such an extent that it has acquired universal and apparently overwhelming proportions.

As mentioned earlier, the hope for peace that the humanist upholds throughout his reflection is deeply connected to the *fides viva* he has in the Word of Christ. Erasmus uses a philological approach to the Scriptures, with the constant mission to purge them of the huge number of posthumous additions that were not congruent with the original message of peace and universal love of Jesus Christ, defined by the prophet Isaiah as the "prince of peace." It is precisely by linking himself to these teachings that the humanist conceives and hopes for a cosmopolitan peace for Europe. Christian kingdoms had been at war with each other for at least a century because human beings, despite having been given instructions to place harmony before everything else,¹⁰ decided of their own free will to violate this most noble dictate and to be subjugated by greed for power, the main reason for wars. These conflicts, according to Erasmus's thought, have an ontological fratricidal component, because they see Christians fighting each other in the name of the same Redeemer and under the banner of the cross.

> Denique quod est omnium absurdissimum, in utrisque castris, in utraque acie crucis signum relucet, in utrisque sacra. Quid hoc monstri est: pugnat crux cum cruce, Christus adversus Christum belligeratur. Hoc signum Christiani nominis hostes terrere solet. Cur nunc oppugnant, quod adorant? Homines non una digni cruce, sed vera.¹¹

---

9. Erasmus 1999: 20.
10. Erasmus 1977: 74.
11. Erasmus 1977: 84. "The absurdest circumstance of all those respecting the use of the cross as a standard is, that you see it glittering and waving high in air in both the contending armies at once. Divine service is also performed to the same Christ in both armies at the same time. What a shocking sight? Lo! crosses dashing against crosses, and Christ on this side firing bullets at Christ on the other; cross against cross, and Christ against Christ. The banner of the cross, significant of the christian profession, is used on each side, to strike terror into the opposite enemy. How dare they, on this

In Erasmus, this paradox becomes nothing more than an immense blasphemy, often fed by those who are supposed to represent God on earth, namely, princes, emperors, and churchmen (priests, bishops, or even popes). The latter, who should counter the war by spreading the words of Christ and should avoid turning such a wicked act into something sacred, often find themselves to be the first ones to wage wars, as in the case of Julius II or the many bishops who take up their weapons and lead armies into battle, portraying the motives for these massacres as Christian. From the depths of his *fides viva*, Erasmus wonders how a soldier can recite the *Our Father* in the face of the wicked acts he commits by following these men who "non pudet tamen illos appellari Christianos, cum modis omnibus dissideant ab eo, quod Christo praecipuum est ac peculiar."[12] Even when churchmen are not engaged in such nefariousness, they find themselves unable to reach an agreement among themselves, as is the case with theologians when discussing the message of Christ:

> bonae literae reddunt homine, philosophia plusquam homines, theologia reddit divos. Apud hos certe dabitur conquiescere tot actae ambagibus. Verum proh dolor, en hic quoque bellorum aliud genus, minus quidem cruentum, sed tamen non minus insanum. Schola cum schola dissidet, [...] adeo ut ne in minutissimis quidem rebus inter hos conveniat ac saepenumero de lana caprima atrocissime digladientur.[13]

These words summarize how Erasmus felt about these men, the same ones who by their evil actions destroy peace and consequently make every aggregate of Christian life disappear.[14]

---

occasion, to attack what, on all others, they adore? Because they are unworthy to bear the true cross at all, and rather deserve to be themselves crucified." Author's translation.

12. Erasmus 1977: 68. These men who "are not ashamed to be called Christians, even though they differ in every way from what is essential and unique to Christ." Author's translation.
13. Erasmus 1977: 66. "It is said, learning makes the man; philosophy, something more than man; and theology exalts man to the divine nature. Harassed as I am with the research, I shall surely find among these a safe retreat to rest my head in undisturbed repose. Here also I find war of another kind, less bloody indeed, but not less furious. Scholar wages war with scholar [...] insomuch that they agree not in the minutest points, and often are at daggers drawing de lana caprina." Author's translation.
14. Erasmus 1977: 76.

Despite his fervid beliefs, at some point in his profound reflection Erasmus considers the possibility that maybe war is inevitable for human beings. If this is true, he states that it would be better to direct these efforts against those who do not belong to Christianity: "Quod si bellum vitari non potest, ita geratur, ut somma malorum in eorum capita recidat, qui belli dedere causas."[15] On this point the reflection becomes more articulated because, according to the humanist, the continuous disagreements that persist among Christians could lead the rivals, in this case the Turks, to attack and to defeat them, as an enemy who is divided is clearly weaker than one raising a single shield.[16] "Quod si hic fatalis est humani ingenii morbus, ut prorsus absque bellis durare nequeat, quin potius mallum hoc in Turcas effunditur, tametsi praestabat et hos doctrina, bene factis vitaeque innocentia ad Christi religionem allicere, quam armis adoriri."[17] It would be far more effective for Christianity to fight them with the weapons of Christ, raising in them the call to salvation. This can be achieved only by living in peace and showing them the true virtues of behaving by following the *religio*, even though Christians are more interested in fighting them with the sword in the name of Christ calling them infidels. But according to Erasmus, those who are called infidels are closer to Christianity than those who call themselves Christians.[18] To support this consideration we can find a short but powerful sentence in the last pages of the *Querela Pacis*: "Eia satis iam superque fusum est Christiani, si parum est humani sanguinis."[19]

These few words clearly describe the desire for cosmopolitanism. In this way peace becomes cosmopolitan, because it frees itself from qualitative barriers, elevating all victims as human victims.

This reflection combines the high ethical religious degree with the pragmatism of the advice of Erasmus on how to avoid war and make peace in a tangible way in the Europe in which he lived.

These ideas are traceable in the *Querela Pacis* from the very beginning, opening with praise for Philip III Duke of Burgundy, for his efforts

---

15. Erasmus 1977: 87.
16. Erasmus 1977: 96.
17. Erasmus 1977: 90.
18. Erasmus 1999: 40.
19. Erasmus 1977: 98.

to preserve peace.[20] Erasmus considers the last ten years of conflicts in the Europe of his day,[21] when wars were waged for frivolous causes by self-proclaimed Christian princes who were blinded by envy or thirst for power. He takes France as an example, a kingdom that was deemed as the uncontaminated flower of Christianity,[22] a beacon of superior prosperity, harmony between peoples and righteousness of those who administered it. France became the target of all foreign princes, who, instead of taking it as an example, preferred to succumb to envy and make war on it in the hope of toppling it from its position of superiority.

People never want war; if they did, they could be justified by their ignorance. Those who want war, as if caught up in an unjustifiable madness, are those who should avoid it: men of power.[23] If man were really interested in avoiding war, Erasmus provides us with the first piece of advice:

> Si ex animo tedet bellorum, dabo consiliu, quo concordiam tueri possitis. Solida pax haud constat affinitatibus haud foederibus hominum, ex quibus frequenter exoriri bella videmus. Repurgandi fontes ipsi, unde malum hoc scatet; pravae cupiditates tumultus istos pariunt. Et dum quisque suis inservit affectibus, interim affligitur respublica, nec tamen assequitur hoc ipsum quisque, quod malis rationibus affectat. Sapiant principes et populo sapiant, non sibi ac vere sapiant, ut maiestatem suam, ut felicitatem, ut opes, ut splendorem his rebus metiantur, quae vere magnos et excellentes faciunt. Sint eo animo erga rempublicam. Quo pater erga familiam.[24]

20. Erasmus 1977: 61.
21. Erasmus 1977: 77.
22. Erasmus 1977: 80.
23. Erasmus 1977: 84.
24. Erasmus 1977: 86. "If you are in your heart weary of war, I will tell you how you may avoid it, and preserve a cordial and general amity. Firm and permanent peace is not to be secured by marrying one royal family to another, nor by treaties and alliances made between such deceitful and imperfect creatures as men; for, from these very family connections, treaties, and alliances, we see wars chiefly originate. No; the fountains from which the streams of this evil flow, must be cleansed. It is from the corrupt passions of the human heart that the tumults of war arise. While each king obeys the impulse of his passions, the commonwealth, the community, suffers; and at the same time, the poor slave to his passions is frustrated in his private and selfish purposes. Let kings then grow wise; wise for the people, not for themselves only; and let them be truly wise, in the proper sense of the word, not merely cunning,

To this piece of advice we must add another one: the thrones of the world should not be mixed, but the kings should be kept in their own kingdoms. This would prevent borders from changing over time, which would damage countries. Even if parental ties may be used to create alliances, they are fictitious and not genuine.[25] In the same way, it would be good if the people of Europe no longer felt bound to their homeland but were united as a single nation. From these words it is evident how by the ending of the *Querela Pacis* Eramus shifts from the idea of a community united under the aegis of Christianity to a cosmopolitan one.

Our humanist also focuses on the value of peace in material and diplomatic terms. He claims that it is always better to accept an unjust peace than the most just war. Because when war is waged, even for an apparently just cause, it is necessary to consider the balance of violence, damage, and death that it generates; while accepting an unjust peace is already an immense victory, as universal peace, the most precious good that Christ has given us, has been gained without any bloodshed.[26]

What is hinted at frugally in the *Querela Pacis* ends up becoming an articulate and complete meditation in the *Istitutio principis christiani*,[27] where the discourse of Erasmus on peace inevitably ends up touching the political sphere. The book, dedicated to the young Charles of Burgundy, destined to become Emperor under the name of Charles V, was composed between 1514 and 1515, and first published in Basel in May 1516. This writing appears to be far from an occasional episode in the creative production of Erasmus. The political-pedagogical reflection constitutes an extemporaneous component linked to the circumstances that inspired his works, his essays and his epistles, certainly inspired by a strong reference to the ethical and religious content of the Christian message, oriented towards the pursuit of peace, harmony, and solidarity between men and nations. His work is not abstract, nor destined to remain closed to a restricted circle of scholars or erudite people, but directly addressed to

---

but really wise; so as to place their majesty, their felicity, their wealth, and their splendor in such things, and such only, as render them personally great, personally superior to those whom the fortune of birth has ranked, in a civil sense, below them." Author's translation.

25. Erasmus 1977: 88.
26. Erasmus 1977: 86, 90.
27. About the book see the Giosi's analysis (2016) and Quaglioni's article (1987).

sovereigns, princes, and both State and Church rulers. This work is far from the historical and political scenario of his time, which was marked by wars, ferocious religious struggles, and epoch-making events such as the Lutheran Reformation.

Alongside an interest in promoting, by means of the weapons of culture, a general reform of the European political conscience through a return to the spirit of the Gospel, there is a particular attention to the concrete political-institutional reality of his time. This can generate decisive effects on safeguarding peace, the well-being of peoples, the real rooting of emancipatory ethical-moral values proper to both a liberal and Christian education. In Erasmus we find a link between pedagogical-political meditation and history in its dramatic unfolding: on the one hand, a tension between the general vision of politics and history of a Christian matrix and, on the other, a new, incipient conception of the political, understood as a category of modern thought, autonomous and governed by rules and laws. However, we must not forget that the Dutch philosopher, in expressing publicly his thoughts on the political sphere, was referring to a long and illustrious philosophical and pedagogical tradition dating back to the Hellenistic, Latin, and Christian worlds, the *specula principis*.[28] These belong to a philosophical-literary tradition of great pedagogical value, in which were discussed the education of rulers and the elements necessary for the realization of a government based on virtue. In this framework Erasmus also launches his pacifist messages. It must be said that the humanistic *specula* were centered on the portrait of sovereigns orchestrating peace and justice, but Erasmus is the first one to broaden the speculative horizons. The prince described in the *Institutio* rejects war totally: he is not only capable of wanting peace for his people, but he is educated in order to establish universal peace.

But before we get to the crux of the matter, it is better to describe the main aspects of this ideal ruler, since these are the necessary precondition for the rejection of war and the achievement of its own dimension. Firstly, the prince must be a philosopher and must set an example to be reflected on the whole of society[29] according to the humanist organicist view.

---

28. About this topic see Tognon's work (1987) and Tateo's article (2006).
29. About the *princeps* as example and the organicist vision see Briguglia's work (2006) and Cappelli's articles (2012, 2016, 2020).

Before anything else the humanistic prince is characterized by his total and continuous visibility. The *imago principis*, continuously exposed to the eyes of the people, is the first form that modernity adopts to represent the exemplarity and therefore the legitimacy of political power. Moreover, thanks to this exemplarity linked to visibility, the humanists were also able to demonstrate the relationship between the head and the other components of the *corpus politicum*. The metaphor of sight is an unmistakable sign of collective control, of the actions of the sovereign being subjected to the scrutiny of his moral and civic qualities, in absolute transparency and with the responsibility of being *exemplar mundi*, in other words a mirror of the community. The prince fulfills his main task when he makes his own visibility politically useful, when he can set himself up as an *exemplum* or *exemplar*, an example and model for the entire socio-political body. As a virtuous and perennially visible leader, the sovereign is a model of the community and must therefore be constantly exposed to its view.[30]

The emphasis on the exemplary function is essential in the organicist conception, given the organic bond that ties together the parts of society, and is manifested with a refined rhetorical-ideological device. The sovereign, the image of the people and mirror of the community, must reflect his *virtus* on the entire social body: his legitimacy and his survival depend on his excellence. According to Erasmus, the dynastic factor is no longer sufficient to guarantee the legitimacy to govern.[31] At the same time, the structure of the absolute state requires a strong and unquestioned authority, but this cannot and must not be translated into indiscriminate arbitrariness. The sovereign represents the entire social organism, the "mystical body" of the community, following an organicist conception of *concordia ordinum* in the superior interest of the community. But the prince can be the guardian of the community only because he has firstly exerted control over himself. In Erasmus we can also see that the prince is placed in a *locus eminens*, which causes a dual effect: on the one hand it ensures that his actions are seen by everyone, as an example, but on the other his behavior is also censurable,[32] people can exert a form of control over the prince himself, by blaming him.

30. Erasmus 1974: 141–42.
31. Erasmus 1974: 139–40, 146.
32. Erasmus 1974: 210.

Erasmus has a very clear idea about the behavior of the prince and his relationship to the *corpus politicum*.[33] The government of the good prince must be based on love and not on fear. The question of setting limits to the power of the sovereign leads directly to the issue of the relationship between the prince and his subjects. Traditionally, this theme is approached with the binary alternative between love and fear, which leads us to the question of whether the prince should be more loved or more feared. The humanists answer the problem with the reciprocal relationship of trust and affection between prince and subjects, which is expressed in the concept of mutual *caritas*. According to this concept, love becomes nourishment and the connective tissue of the entire social body, an irreplaceable link between ruler and ruled. Here the analogy is based on the *De clementia* of Seneca and the *Naturalis historia* of Pliny.[34] The comparison, which serves to delineate the relationship between the king and the political body, is based on the non-violent nature of power; indeed, the queen bee is characterized by the lack of the sting, a strong self-control, and being armed only with *maiestas*. The fact that the queen bee, like the ruler, is devoid of the sting is very significant if we look at the historical context in which Erasmus lived. This need for reconciliation is even clearer to us if we look at Brancato's *Commendatio*,[35] where we can find a comparison with a very similar meaning to that of Erasmus but in this case the queen bee has the sting and so it is not necessarily the case that she cannot use it if in extreme need for the recovery of consensus: its employment depends on the will to use it or not. Moreover, the prince must be like the queen bee with no sting. He compares the monarchical political system with the social organization of bees. This parallelism is a widespread *tòpos* in legal and humanistic treatises and is also taken up by various intellectuals.

This idyllic vision is contrasted with the tyrant, who is diametrically opposed to the prince, because he does not pursue the common good. Erasmus shows us the tyrant as a lonely man who is not surrounded by others, an anti-political figure precisely because he is unable to experience

---

33. Erasmus 1974: 164.
34. Erasmus 1974: 156.
35. Cappelli 2016: 61–63.

sociality.[36] The good prince, in order to govern, must not be alone, but surrounded by intellectuals who guarantee the survival of the state according to the humanist point of view.[37] The previous explanation is necessary to understand how the prince should behave towards war. War must be avoided at all costs; even in the event of the loss of territories, the prince should give up the lost domains and not embark on a justified reconquest: in fact, the justification of war is seen as an absurdity. Erasmus does not admit justified wars; nothing can justify war, not even the war against the Turks, as already seen in the *Querela Pacis*, because war is against both human nature and the message of Christ.[38]

The thought of Thomas More is also fueled by cosmopolitan pacifist impulses, but he interprets them in a completely different manner from his friend Erasmus. Unlike Erasmus, More was a man of action. Like all politicians, his figure is marked by various contradictions. Although More preaches religious tolerance in *Utopia*, as Chancellor we see him forcefully suppressing Protestant movements.[39] However, without wanting to justify his repressive action, it should be remembered that he found himself passing from an age of relative intellectual freedom to an era marked by the tragic fracture of religious unity, which imposed peremptory choices without the possibility of seeking mediation or compromise.

Keeping in mind that More was a person with political power, helps us to delve into his most famous work: *Utopia*. Written between 1515 and 1516, it describes the evils of modern society, primarily in England. In More, power politics as a habitual practice of the rulers of the time (i.e., war) plays a major role. To end injustice, the whole structure of society must change, including the foreign policy of states. More condemns the expansionist aims of the rulers of his time. The institution of monarchy is primarily responsible for this state of affairs: the morality of the monarchs has transformed the international community, normally characterized by benevolence, into an arena in which treaties of alliance are concluded on the understanding that they will be violated shortly afterwards.[40]

36. Erasmus 1974: 68.
37. Erasmus 1974: 102, 104.
38. See p. 169.
39. About More's life see Petrilli 1972.
40. More 2002: 17–19.

All rulers are more interested in waging wars for conquest and riches rather than in wisely governing their own domains.[41] Itlodeus is upset with the mercenary armies that suffocate and paralyse European countries, particularly those in France and England. War is never a necessity, More observes:

> certe utcumque sese haec habet res, illud mihi nequaquam uidetur publicae rei conducere, in euentum belli, quod numquam habetis, nisi cum uultis, infinitam eius generis turbam alere, quod infestat pacem, cuius tanto maior haberi ratio, quam belli debeat. Neque haec tamen sola est furandi necessitas. Est alia magis quantum credo, peculiaris uobis.[42]

Therefore, according to More, peace should be the priority of European rulers, who on the other hand, seem to be interested only in extending their territories. According to Itlodeus, European rulers should consider as a model the wisdom of the Achorians who, after having militarily conquered a new territory over which their king had some hereditary right, realized that it was too burdensome to rule other people. So, they put their ruler in front of a choice: he must choose only one kingdom, because he would not be allowed to rule both. No one would have preferred a king halved in size. The King of the Achorians is essentially forced to "be satisfied" with his old kingdom. Another example can be taken from the Macarians, whose king, very wisely, on the very day of his investiture, solemnly swore to keep only 1000 pounds of gold in his treasury, because such a sum would be sufficient to defend the kingdom from possible aggression, but would not allow wars of conquest nor invasions.

More insists that Itlodeus, in the name of his experience and philosophical knowledge, should become a member of the council of some king. Faced with his being reluctant to become a councillor of some prince, because this would mean putting himself on the same level as those who

---

41. More 2002: 14.
42. More 2002: 16. "However that may be, though, I certainly cannot think it's in the public interest to maintain for the emergency of war such a vast multitude of people who trouble and disturb the peace: you never have war unless you choose it, and peace is always more to be considered than war. Yet this is not the only force driving men to thievery. There is another that, as I see it, applies more specially to you Englishmen." Author's translation.

make the world unjust and warlike, More points out that he, who knows the political and social reality of the time, should not abandon the State to itself, but should contribute by indirect means, to at least reduce the evil to a minimum, when it cannot be turned into good, since the best will only be achieved when everyone turns out to be good. According to Itlodeus it is necessary to change the register of discourse: war is a senseless thing, which depends on the calculations of short-sighted and miserly ruling elites. If the paradigm is not changed, the world will continue to get worse.

After this criticism, contained in the first book, we would expect that in the description of another world, the international community would be founded on bonds of mutual friendship between peoples and states. In the second book, in a chapter entitled "Military Practice," Itlodeus makes things clear from the outset: the Utopians are peaceful, they have achieved justice—which is a guarantee of peace—with the abolition of private property. They hate war as a truly brutal thing; they do not assign any value to military virtues, although they train themselves—men and women—in order to be prepared in event of war.[43] Despite the fundamental pacifism of Utopia's government, the citizens of the island often have to deal with war. In this case, More–Itlodeus, after arguing that the Utopians do not wage war for futile and ill-considered reasons, implying that they repudiate conquest and offensive wars, explains at least three instances of just war for Utopians: to defend their own borders, to repel enemies who have invaded friendly territories, or to free a people oppressed by a tyrannical form of government. Thus, Utopians, although pacifists, admit the existence of valid reasons for fighting. The war of self-defense is a case admitted by the medieval *bellum iustum*: the response to an *iniuria* is a just cause for war.[44]

At the time of these writings, the undisputed authority, even on the topic of war, was still St. Thomas Aquinas, for whom war was legitimate if it was declared by a legitimately constituted authority, if there was a just cause (i.e., a fault on the part of those against whom war was waged) and, finally, if the requirement of *recta intentio* was present (if the war had the aim of promoting good and preventing evil: revenge was not

---

43. More 2002: 85.
44. About just war in More see Cassi 2015.

allowed). Extending the possibility of war to cases where one's friends and allies are being harmed may seem a stretch, but it is understandable, because the conception of alliance and friendship in More is peculiar. Friends and allies are those states that have either benefited from Utopia or are governed by Utopian magistrates.[45] It is therefore understandable that an *iniuria* against them deserves the same kind of warlike sanction for More. It is clear, however, that such a position risks expanding disproportionately the possibilities of military intervention for a political community, especially in a context such as the international one, in which the interests that must be peacefully reconciled risk being too numerous.

The third just cause of war introduced by More constitutes an absolute novelty in internationalist thought: the Utopians can, out of pity, fight a war for people oppressed by tyranny with the aim of freeing them from their condition.[46] This way of justifying war is, compared to the times in which More writes, no less than revolutionary. In fact, the rulers of Utopia can promote the "liberalization" of the international system by breaking down tyrannies and despotisms. To what purpose? Again, our author's theory cannot be traced back to the paradigm of special interest. Utopians, in fact, wage such wars solely and exclusively out of "philanthropy," to free other peoples from political shackles.

Now, if we add to this justification of war also that passage, contained in the second book, in which More justifies the colonization of new lands as a function of Utopia's demographic balance, the picture is even clearer. At a time when the powers of the Iberian Peninsula and England itself threw themselves with conviction and impetus towards the conquest of the New World, More admitted that if on the island of Utopia there was an overabundance of young people, part of the population could emigrate to found a colony, which would have the same laws as the island. This could only be the case if there was a surplus of land and this was not cultivated. Indigenous people could join to create one people as long as they accepted the institutions and customs of the Utopians.

If the natives were to refuse to comply with the laws of the colony, they would be forcibly expelled from its borders, as the Utopians consider it a justifiable reason for waging war when a nation prevents others from

---

45. More 2002: 16–17.
46. More 2002: 19.

occupying a portion of land that they do not utilize but instead leave idle, since every man has, by the law of nature, a right to such a waste portion of the earth as is necessary for his subsistence.[47] The Utopian community trades with other peoples and gets rich. With this positive balance of trade, it either pays mercenaries or tries to incite riots and targeted killings in enemy kingdoms.[48]

The need for perfect political models, or those that can be considered such, to export their own model of society to others, supported by the conviction of a moral primacy that they tend to spread all over the earth, seems to rise to the role of the radiating center of civilization. After all, who could dispute the international role of a regime that constitutes the authentic model of freedom and equality. In this case, allies and friends are those who, respectively, are either governed or benefited by the Utopians, who have similar regimes. The search for international homogeneity, understood as respect for the same rules of the game, seems to be the main concern for the Utopians. In an attempt to seek this homogeneity, Utopia places itself at a higher level compared to the other actors, assuming the role of judge of international politics:[49] it orders the handing over of those guilty of wrongs, punishes them, and enslaves them.

The moral and political superiority of the Utopians over their neighbors is such that they claim the right to intervene in the political organization of their enemies, encouraging rebellions against the established power, promising great rewards to those who get rid of the abhorred rulers. If they cannot achieve the result by cunning, the Utopians prefer mercenaries to fight first. Once again, they show that the human life of soldiers is not of equal value. The life of a mercenary is worth far less than that of a Utopian. Indeed, the Utopians do not care so much if many soldiers of fortune die. Utopian warfare is quite civilized by the standards prevalent in the sixteenth century. In fact, they try not to hit civilians; they mercilessly kill only spies and fighters who resist surrender, while the other people are enslaved. The masses of the population, however, have nothing to fear except the payment of war expenses, which are of course paid by the losers.

47. More 2002: 48–54.
48. More 2002: 85–88.
49. More 2002: 91.

In this sense, the role of the clergy is also rather innovative in relation to the times. While in the wars of the early sixteenth century churchmen not only justified wars, but sometimes even placed themselves at the head of armies, the priests of Utopia place themselves in the middle of rival armies to prevent unnecessary slaughter. That is why Utopia must shape the world in its own image, conquer colonies, and increase the number of allied and friendly states. Only such a world will be a safe world for Utopia. Utopia's war is the war of the moralist politician who, far from concealing the demonic face of power, wants to impose on others his own moral and cultural superiority.

The Utopians seem to arrogate to themselves, by virtue of a presumed moral superiority, the right to impose their own political and cultural model on other entities. Christian education, evangelization, especially of princes, will make the world peaceful, because human nature stimulates humanity to peace, in particular because Jesus Christ is peace. More seems to think that war is motivated by the internal political organization of states, and that therefore the solution to the problem of conflict consists in changing radically the form of organization of society. In short, if the international system is homogeneous with the model of Utopia, if all states are governed like Utopia, or are friends or allies of Utopia, then the world will finally be directed towards peace. Only Utopia has the right to wage war according to the idea of the *bellum iustum*, which is absent from all the other states. The risk of the approach given by More is that of sliding into a fanaticism that generates a qualitative division between good and bad states. The final peace is imagined as the punishment of the bad states in favor of the good ones. In this way the foreign policy of Utopia degenerates into a power policy unable to avoid misdeeds.

So, both in the production of Erasmus and More, one can detect a cosmopolitan pacifist vision. Their thought can be defined as utopian-realistic because it tends toward Utopia, but without forgetting the political and social reality of the sixteenth century. This attitude leads Erasmus to hypothesize a sort of international law that should put an end to the disputes between the various rulers.[50] This conclusion was not trivial for his times and was the result not only of an accurate study of history and of his age, but also of another extraordinary intuition: to bring

---

50. Erasmus 1974: 216–17.

to a global scale the organicist vision of society. This idea generated from humanistic-renaissance political thought and was only eliminated from the history of political thought by Hobbes and his motto *homo homini lupus*.

More justifies war, but only until the model of the perfect *polis* prevails. Utopia must spread civilization around the world. It is not a closed ecosystem, but it increasingly takes the form of a supranational body that is a model of political, social, and moral perfection. Herein lies all of More's utopian realism, since he is aware that war is necessary for a fair civilization based on tolerance, *ratio*, and *logos*. War, of course, is always to be avoided, for the Utopians use cunning to defeat their enemies and impose their values. Only when the utopian ideal is taken as a model across the globe, can war be eradicated from humanity.

Author biographies

Antonello Mori is Junior Research Fellow at the Euronews Project of the University College Cork, Ireland. He obtained his first Master's degree in Historical Studies at the University of Naples Federico II cum laude and his second Master's degree in Digital and Public Humanities at the University of Venice Ca'Foscari. His research interests are related to digital and public humanities and the relationship between the religious and political power during the early modern period.

Antonio Senneca is Junior Research Fellow at the Euronews Project of the University College Cork, Ireland. He completed a Master's degree in Historical Studies at the University of Naples Federico II in July 2020 with a thesis titled "La riflessione sulla *maiestas* nel *De principe* di Giovanni Pontano e nel *De maiestate* di Giuniano Maio," focusing on Humanistic and Renaissance political thought. During his academic career, he trained himself in palaeography, diplomatics, digital humanities, and followed courses on Renaissance diplomacy, early modern politics and communication.

References

Primary sources

Erasmus, D. (1974), *Istitutio principis Christiani*, in O. Herding (ed.), *Opera Omnia Desiderii Erasmi Roterodami, Ordinis Quarti, Tomus primus*. Amsterdam: North-Holland Publishing Co.

Erasmus, D. (1977), *Querela Pacis*, in O. Herding (ed.), *Opera Omnia Desiderii Erasmi Roterodami, Ordinis Quarti, Tomus secundus*. Amsterdam and Oxford: North-Holland Publishing Co.

Erasmus, D. (1979), *Moriae Encomium*, in C. H. Miller (ed.), *Opera Omnia Desiderii Erasmi Roterodami, Ordinis Quarti, Tomus tertius*. Amsterdam and Oxford: North-Holland Publishing Co.

Erasmus, D. (1999), *Adagiorum Chilias Quarta*, in R. Hoven and C. Lauvergnat-Gagnière (eds.), *Opera Omnia Desiderii Erasmi Roterodami, Ordinis Secundi, Tomus septimus*. Amsterdam: Elsevier.

More, T. (2002), *Utopia*, edited by G. M. Logan and R. M. Adams. Cambridge: Cambridge University Press.

Secondary sources

Bainton, R. H. (2000), *La riforma protestante*. Torino: Einaudi.

Briguglia, G. (2006), *Il corpo vivente dello Stato. Una metafora politica*. Milan: Bruno Mondadori.

Cappelli, G. (2012), "'Corpus est res publica.' La struttura della comunità secondo l'umanesimo politico," in L. Geri (ed.), *Principi prima del principe*, 117–31. Rome: Bulzoni.

Cappelli, G. (2016), *Maiestas. Politica e pensiero politico nella Napoli aragonese (1443–1503)*. Rome: Carocci.

Cappelli, G. (2020), "Princeps vitae exemplar. Il principe umanistico come modello civico," in P. Borsa et al. (eds.), *Per Enrico Fenzi. Saggi di allievi e amici per i suoi ottant'anni*, 477–86. Firenze: Le Lettere.

Cassi, A. (2015), *Santa giusta umanitaria. La guerra nella civiltà occidentale*. Rome: Salerno editrice.

Giosi, M. (2016), "La tradizione degli specula principum e la Institutio principis christiani di Erasmo da Rotterdam," *Educazione: giornale di pedagogia critica* 2: 49–68.

Margolin, J. C. (1970), *Guerre et paix dans la pensée d'Erasme*. Paris: Aubier.

Pasini, E. (2013), "'Quae sunt Caesaris': l'oscillante rapporto di religione e politica in Erasmo da Rotterdam," in B. Centi and A. Siclari (eds.), *Religione e politica. Da Dante alle prospettive teoriche contemporanee*, 85–108. Rome: Edizioni di Storia e Letteratura.

Petrilli, G. (1972), *San Tommaso Moro*. Milan: Martello Editore.

Quaglioni, D. (1987), "Il modello del principe cristiano. Gli 'specula principum' fra Medio Evo e prima Età Moderna," in V. I. Comparato (ed.), *Modelli nella storia del pensiero politico*, I, 103–122. Firenze: Saggi.

Tognon, G. (1987), "Intellettuali ed educazione del principe nel Quattrocento italiano. Il formarsi di una nuova pedagogia politica," *Mélanges de l'école française de Rome. Moyen-Age, Temps modernes* 99/1: 405–33. https://doi.org/10.3406/mefr.1987.2915

Tateo, F. (2006), *La trattatistica sul principe. In Italia alla fine del Medioevo: i caratteri originali nel quadro europeo*, ed. F. Cengarle. Florence: Firenze University Press.

Chapter 7
Peace in the Material World: Objects as Meeting Points for Islamic and Christian Traditions in Late Sixteenth-Century Spain*

Francisco J. Moreno Díaz del Campo

Introduction

The Kingdom of Granada was the last Muslim bastion in Western Europe. In 1492, the Catholic monarchs entered its capital city and annexed its territories to the Crown of Castile. Founded in the thirteenth century, the Nasrid emirate had resisted the advance of the Christian armies for over two and a half centuries. At the time of the conquest, it covered approximately 25,000 square kilometres and was home to around 300,000 people.[1] It combined a rural agricultural population, particularly silkworm farmers, with a substantial urban sector whose economy was based on trade and manufacturing in a small number of cities such as Málaga, Almería, Ronda, Guadix, and Granada itself.[2]

---

* This chapter has been written as part of the research project *IMPI 2. Antes del orientalismo. Figuras de la alteridad en el Mediterráneo de la Edad Moderna: del enemigo interno a la amenaza turca* (Ref.: PID2019-105070GB-I00), supported by the Spanish Ministry of Science and Innovation [Ministerio de Ciencia e Innovación (Gobierno de España)].
1. Ladero 1972–1973: 486.
2. Literature on the history of the Kingdom of Granada is very extensive. General background works are Barrios 2000, and Barrios and Galán 2004. On the conquest and

The Christian conquest was formalized by the *capitulaciones*, a set of agreements whereby the conquerors committed themselves to respecting the religion and culture of the defeated people in exchange for the implementation of a fiscal and political system that acknowledged the sovereignty of the Castilian monarchs. At the same time, Ferdinand and Isabella implemented a colonization policy that resulted in the arrival of 35,000–40,000 Christians in the former Nasrid kingdom.[3]

Muslims and Christians coexisted under the auspices of this legal framework until the early sixteenth century. Between 1500 and 1502, however, the territory was plagued by outbursts of violence triggered by Muslim discontent at the aggressive evangelization policy imposed by Cardinal Cisneros, Archbishop of Toledo. His arrival in Granada in 1499 was due, to a large extent, to the poor results hitherto achieved by his predecessor, the Archbishop of Granada Hernando de Talavera. Once the riots were suppressed, Ferdinand and Isabella forced Granada's Muslims to either convert to Christianity or emigrate from Castile, an option chosen by very few. Thus began the singular history of the Moriscos: the Spanish Muslims and their descendants who became Christians by force.[4]

Between 1502 and 1568, coexistence between Moriscos and Old Christians moved through different stages. Both the Catholic monarchs and Emperor Charles V endorsed an assimilation policy, with mixed results. The Crown's ultimate goal was the sincere adoption of the Christian faith by the Moriscos, but its efforts to achieve this involved curbing the daily customs of former Muslims by law. Some of the new legislation introduced in the first quarter of the sixteenth century had a religious basis—such as the ban on Islamic slaughter of livestock or the transformation of mosques into churches—but was driven in other cases by purely cultural factors. As a result, traditional dances and festivals were curtailed, along with using the Arabic language, visiting public baths, and even wearing the traditional Granada dress. While these customs were not

    first few years of Christian domination, see Peinado 2011.
3. Ladero 1992: 57.
4. The Catholic monarchs' compulsory baptism decree was applied to all the territories ruled by the Castilian Crown. A different situation existed in the Crown of Aragon, where the *Mudejars*, as Muslims living in lands governed by Christians were known, were able to practice their religion freely until 1525. For an understanding of the forced conversion process of Aragon's Moriscos, see Benítez 2000.

religious manifestations per se, the Crown chose to restrict them because of their potential links to the religious heritage it was striving to stamp out.

The *Junta*, or Board, of the Royal Chapel of Granada—an assembly of political and ecclesiastical notables convened in 1526—collected these regulations in a single legal document, but the Moriscos managed to obtain a postponement, chiefly by offering large sums of money to the emperor, who was very short of funds on account of his wars in central Europe. By the mid-sixteenth century, the Crown's policy with regard to the Morisco minority was patchy, mixing evangelization programmes with repressive measures which were reinforced by inquisitorial activity.[5]

Philip II's rise to the throne marked a change in the Crown's policy. In 1566, the *Junta de Madrid* advised the king to enforce the prohibitions agreed forty years earlier. The resulting and foreseeable discontent among Granada's Moriscos triggered the uprising known as the War of the Alpujarras (1568–1570)—the last major conflict between Muslims and Christians in Western Europe. In the aftermath of Philip II's victory over his rebelling subjects, Granada's Moriscos were compulsorily deported, and resettled in Castile. From 1570 until their final expulsion from Spain in 1609–1614, this scattered Morisco population was closely monitored and forced to adopt the cultural habits of Old Christians. To achieve this, a variety of political, social, and religious control measures were deployed. Religious conversion was no longer enough: the Crown demanded full social and cultural assimilation.

On coexistence: theories, projects, and realities

Coexistence between Old Christians and Moriscos involved a peculiar combination of mistrust and forbearance, both before and after the war. Although no major conflicts erupted in the forty years the Granada Moriscos spent in Castile, the two collectives never achieved full integration. The war had left very little room for theorizing on the manner in which Moriscos and Old Christians should approach their relationship, let alone the possibility of consolidating an environment where they

---

5. On this matter, see Benítez 2001.

could live harmoniously together. Added to this, the social and ideological scenario that evolved in the wake of the Protestant reformation led the Catholic Church and the Hispanic monarchy to adopt increasingly uncompromising positions. Lastly, it should be noted that the Moriscos were a heterogeneous group and the degree of assimilation achieved was subject to geographical, chronological, and socio-cultural circumstances.

Against this multifaceted background, there were proposals to encourage harmony and peaceful coexistence between the two communities, but never a full discussion in which the arguments advanced by both sides were clearly formulated. The points in dispute were largely put forward by the Old Christian side, and on the whole the suggested solutions were confined to making demands on the Moriscos, rather than seeking mutual understanding.

Nevertheless, these approaches did encompass a variety of viewpoints. One set of proposals was led by individuals who advocated consensus under the aegis of Christianity. Their social origin was diverse, but several authors have suggested that they were—intellectually, if not biologically—linked to Islamic converts.[6] All of them took the religious conversion of Moriscos for granted, but they were open to compromise on cultural matters, an area in which the world of objects played a major role.

From a chronological point of view, this current is linked to maurophilia,[7] an asymmetrical minority movement that was clearly inspired by literature. The ideas of this short-lived phenomenon spread beyond the literary scene to take root in mid-sixteenth-century intellectual debate.[8] Maurophilia had a very clear time-span, peaking around the 1560s and fading away by the end of Philip II's reign. From a literary point of view, maurophilic authors wrote both in prose and in verse in highly convoluted language loaded with metaphors and rhetorical devices used as ornaments in a deliberately long-winded style. These skills were deployed for the benefit of a theme that looked back to the age-old ideal of chivalric

---

6. Márquez 1982: 522–24. On the possible Muslim origin of some members of this group, see Franco and Moreno 2019: 183.
7. On the emergence of this concept, see Cirot 1938–1944. For historiographic background, see Franco and Moreno 2019: 175–81.
8. On these ideas, including a critical review of the historical aspects of maurophilia, see García Cárcel 2014: 124–25.

coexistence between Moors and Christians, usually—but not always—set in the Middle Ages. The "Moors" described in these texts bore little or no relation to reality, but depicted instead an idealized image of their looks, dress, and behavior.

Morisco novels and romance poems offered writers a wide field of operation and ample opportunities to shine. They were very popular among the Spanish social and intellectual elite and were even enjoyed in certain courtly circles, but at no time did they amount to a mass movement.[9] Their true significance lies in the fact that, as well as a literary trend, these writings represented a political stance, a kind of statement of purpose which was used as a tool to address a very specific and urgent issue in mid-sixteenth-century Spain: the need to facilitate the smooth integration of former Muslims into mainstream society. From this point of view, maurophile literature could be described as a historical problem,[10] in the sense that it expressed the hopes of a generation of intellectuals who were certain that it was possible to reach an understanding under the umbrella of Christianity and proposed a model for coexistence that did not aim to annihilate the other.[11] In other words, they endorsed generosity, especially around issues directly relating to cultural manifestations and day-to-day behaviors.

Despite its short lifespan, maurophilia was not an "inert" movement.[12] The limited impact of maurophilic proposals can be explained by the context in which they were written. Their potential readership was very limited but influential; even if it could not directly intervene, it carried some weight in decision making with regard to the smooth integration of the Morisco minority. None of it had any effect. Their voices may have been heard, but they were seldom heeded.[13]

9. Anon. 1561; Pérez de Hita 1595; Alemán 1599. Juan de Timoneda and his sacramental compositions for the evangelization of Valencia's Moriscos, and the poetical works of Lucas Rodríguez and Pedro de Padilla, can also be included in this trend. On the emergence of the Moor in Spanish literature, see Carrasco 1989. For a detailed account of his representation as an individual in "Moorish style" dress, see Franco and Moreno 2019: 159–75.
10. Franco and Moreno 2019: 182; Vincent 2006: 132.
11. Guillén 1971: 178.
12. Fuchs 2009: 8.
13. Guillén 1971: 188.

The few voices that were raised from the Morisco side met a similar fate. Their arguments in favor of mutual understanding between the two sides found a powerful voice in Francisco Núñez Muley. Shortly before the War of the Alpujarras, this elderly Morisco nobleman tried to persuade Philip II that, to understand the Morisco issue, it was crucial to acknowledge the difference between religious practices and cultural traditions. His efforts were utterly unsuccessful and war soon broke out, giving way to a scenario that Muley had foreseen when he wrote his *Memorial* in 1566.[14]

After Muley, Morisco input in the debate was doomed to clandestinity. Their initial efforts to advocate syncretism eventually led to some fairly transparent attempts at historical fabrication. The most notorious bid to sway public opinion in favor of New Christians involved the discovery in late sixteenth-century Granada of certain relics and documents, first in the Turpiana Tower in 1588 and, a few years later, on Valparaíso hill—the famous Lead Books which were unearthed in 1595 and 1599.[15]

Today it is generally accepted that behind this attempt at historical deception stood the Morisco elite in Granada, with the possible addition of a pro-Morisco Old Christian or two. The most prominent members of this group tried to spread the notion that Granada's early Christianity originated in Arabic culture and that it was possible to merge Muslim and Christian practices in a single discourse.[16] The discovery of these objects shocked Granada, and some of the most illustrious people in the city, including the bishop himself, vouched for their authenticity. But it was all in vain. Initial commotion gave way to distrust, particularly when Rome made its misgivings known. Critical voices from large sectors of Spanish intelligentsia added their weight to the skeptics' camp and the ruling elite gradually accepted their disappointment, paving the way to a situation where suspicion and ideological radicalization held sway.[17]

---

14. On this figure and the *Memorial* he wrote, see Garrad (1954), and Bernard Vincent's detailed introductory study in the reprint of the minutes of the Guadix synod published by Gallego and Gámir 1996.
15. An overwhelming amount of literature on this subject exists, including exhaustive studies of every aspect of this affair. For a general contextualized account, see Barrios and García-Arenal 2006 and Barrios 2011; also Bernabé 1998.
16. García Cárcel 2014: 128.
17. Bernabé 2002: 480.

By then, however, the topic under debate had moved on. The last quarter of the sixteenth century was dominated by the proponents of assimilation and elimination of all cultural peculiarities. Most of these writers were clergymen whose contribution to the debate on the Moriscos dated from the period prior to their expulsion in 1609–1614. Rafael Benítez has drawn a detailed portrait of their ideology. Having examined over thirty memorials, treatises, and opuscules, Benítez concludes that there were two very clearly defined groups and clearly outlines the ideological boundaries of both trends. On one side were the "pessimists" or "excluders"—as labeled by Benítez—who resolutely endorsed the suppression of any Morisco cultural expression, expulsion from the kingdom, and some even harsher measures.[18] In other words, these authors openly advocated the wholesale dissolution of the Moriscos as a community. Their ideas achieved some success and were incorporated in the pro-expulsion literature, which replicated their arguments and exalted the figure of Philip III.[19]

On the other side were the "optimists." These authors were reluctant to accept that the Moriscos were universally guilty, but saw instead a sum total of responsibilities that needed to be examined collectively but atoned for individually. They were in favor of insisting on an evangelization policy that would do away with dissenters and enable full integration of the New Christians in the community of worshippers, but rarely contemplated the possibility of expulsion, which they opposed chiefly for political and economic reasons. Instead, they advocated the development of a wide range of solutions, from catechesis to geographical dispersion, through mixed marriages and the elimination of all cultural traits. As Benítez points out, suggestions to restrict, or even abolish, such idiosyncratic features as language or dress are easy to find among these authors.[20]

---

18. Benítez 2012: 69.
19. Moreno 2005.
20. Benítez 2012: 77–78. Overlapping views can also be found among these writers, some of whom were in favor of total acculturation. In this sense, their proposals cannot be detached from those of authors who supported collective punishment. Benítez himself (2012: 70) points out that some of these authors did not rule out the option of eventual expulsion and some of the measures they put forward were undoubtedly harsh, although they offered some respite by avoiding exile. García Cárcel (2014: 123) uses similar terms; in his view, opposing expulsion was not synonymous with tolerance.

The optimist group was inadvertently closer to everyday life than the other group. Their proposals failed, but they diagnosed the situation more accurately than their opponents. Their powers of observation allowed them to perceive regional differences within the Morisco collective as well as the internal changes that were taking place as one generation of Moriscos was replaced by a new one. They also noted that the group's economic recovery was aiding integration.

The material world as a stage for resistance and a mirror of assimilation

Theoretical analysis of religious disputes is a rewarding way to understand the degree of intellectual maturity of any society, but not always a useful tool to learn about everyday relations between the different communities that play a part in that society. Behind the great scholarly arguments, the recourse to the classics or the Scriptures and the more or less strict fundamentals lies the assumption that coexistence is only possible among people of the same creed or who share the same cultural values.

Moriscos and Old Christians played out their coexistence and developed relationships of a relatively friendly nature in the public—and even private—spaces where people socialized.[21] In those places where both groups shared the stage, everyday life was hardly ever contingent on creed. When all is said and done, Moriscos were, in fact, Christians, even if only in name—a fact that is often forgotten. While it is true that many used baptism as a blind to conceal their allegiance to Islam, others sincerely professed Christianity to a greater or lesser extent. Thus, behavior in public places is the context where the gradual socio-economic absorption of Moriscos by Old Christians can be most clearly observed.

What these individuals did in the privacy of their own homes is a different matter. Private activities are by their very nature difficult to apprehend and have left a barely detectable trace, virtually limited to inquisitorial and legal documents. It is easy to find in these sources records of Moriscos who were reported to the authorities for performing actions that contravened Christian orthodoxy or challenged the norms of social coexistence

---

21. Díez 2017: 53.

which had been imposed on them. Notarial documentation, being mainly concerned with financial affairs, complements the official image of this socio-religious conflict. These sources broaden our perspective to include the domestic and private spheres, opening a window on the environments where Moriscos were able to act out their dissension and develop cultural forms of resistance.

These notarial documents include dowry agreements recording the contributions pledged by the bride and groom and their families before marriage, which laid the financial foundations of the new home. They are therefore an eminently suitable tool to observe how people designed their families' future and arranged their private lives. Marriage contracts signed by Moriscos are relatively common. Researchers who have studied Granada's notarial archives prior to the War of the Alpujarras agree that these records accurately reflect the Morisco collective's gradual adaptation to Castilian legal customs. They also point out that the content of these deeds evolved towards material patterns that resembled more closely Old Christian habits, whilst retaining some of their Islamic cultural essence.[22] In certain respects, this evolution is a symptom of Morisco adaptability to the new reality which had been imposed on them through forced conversion.

The War of the Alpujarras marked a watershed in Old Christian–New Christian relations. After almost two years of all-out war, the defeated Moriscos were forced to relocate to areas that were completely alien to them. Their properties were confiscated and they were only allowed to travel with whatever possessions they could carry. As they settled in Castile, Granada's exiled Moriscos survived in appalling material conditions. Their arrival in the heart of the Iberian Peninsula caused uncertainty and fear on both sides.[23]

From 1571 onwards, the Spanish Crown adopted a strict monitoring policy. The Granadine Moriscos had their mobility restricted, were forbidden to carry weapons, and their linguistic and cultural manifestations were suppressed.[24] It fell to local authorities to implement the new regulations, helped by the Inquisition's deployment of its religious surveillance

---

22. Birriel 2002; Lecerf 2012; Mendiola 2012.
23. Vincent 1970.
24. Moreno 2009: 277–326; Moreno 2020.

and repression machine. The clergy also played a part at a later stage, when the catechization of Castile's Moriscos began to increase in the 1680s, although it does not seem to have yielded immediate or consistent results.[25] In these circumstances, everyday life was framed in a peculiar mix of coexistence and suspicion in which both communities influenced each other, shared spaces and daily practices, and handled a common material culture.

The study of "things" is vital in this context. In the past few years, Western historiographers have begun to explore this aspect. In a shift that has become known as the "material turn," researchers are focusing on the world of objects to deepen our knowledge of human beings.[26] Not only historians, but anthropologists, archaeologists, philologists, and even philosophers have sought to progress beyond economicist visions of the history of objects. As Marie-Pierre Julien and Céline Rosselin assert, it is not enough to study artefacts themselves. In fact, the object itself is less important than the social and cultural context in which it was manufactured and used.[27] Their position stems from the idea that artefacts are not inert but affect and reflect the actions of the people who use them.[28] The study of objects is therefore vital in environments dominated by cultural confrontation, by socio-religious opposition or, alternatively, by the search for ways to improve coexistence.[29]

This seems to apply to the topic in hand. Castile was the great stage on which what we could describe as a "peace through objects" was performed. In the years following their deportation from Granada, the Moriscos' lives were reduced to working for bare survival without any economic room for manoeuver. Notarial marriage deeds for Moriscos from this period are rare. No wonder: they owned nothing and had nothing to give their spouses. This applies to all areas of Castile and Andalusia

25. García Gómez 2002; Magán and Sánchez 1997.
26. On the material turn and its influence on subsequent historiography, see Bonnell and Hunt 1999; Hicks 2010; Green 2012; Bennet and Joyce 2013; Gerritsen and Riello 2015; and Roberts 2017, among others.
27. Julien and Rosselin 2005: 3–7.
28. Roberts 2017: 64–69.
29. For background reading on the case of the Moriscos, see Franco and Moreno 2018, and Pomara 2021, both of which offer comparative perspectives. On other scenarios, see Tagliaferri 2018 and the contributions included in Ivanič, Laven and Morrall 2019.

and is evidence of the huge responsibility that fell upon the shoulders of those expelled from Granada. Not only were they the direct victims of the conflict, but were forced into exile and to rebuild their communities, both socially and economically, hundreds of miles from their homeland. From the 1680s onwards, their role in the economic life of vast Castile gradually became more visible. Extant documentation accurately reflects that situation, offering a vantage point on the Moriscos' gradual adaptation to their new socio-economic reality. It fell to the young generation of men and women who had left Granada at a very early age and to those born in exile to lead the Morisco "rebirth." These were the people who signed marriage contracts, allowing us to study the material circumstances surrounding the Morisco collective as they adapted to the physical realities of Castile.

Dowry agreements are stereotypical documents. Most follow a common structure, facilitating geographical and chronological comparison. When a bride and groom registered a dowry, they focused on two very specific assets: estate and dwelling. Although this was a constant throughout the period, variations occurred across social groups.

Dwelling, land, and money were the main assets in which Castilians invested to boost their family economies in the early modern period. As may be expected, not everybody had the same capacity to meet their own needs. The size of an individual's patrimony depended on many factors, notably their family's inherited wealth and their personal solvency. This applied to both Old Christians and Moriscos, but the former were in a better position to build and make use of these assets. This trend is found throughout Castile and is comparable to Morisco behavior in Granada before the war.[30] Once the Granadines were forced to relocate, the sources show a radically different pattern.[31] A relatively high proportion of cash and jewelry dowries points to a tendency to save, but interest in property among this group dwindled to almost nothing. This is consistent with the subordinate social position Moriscos endured on a daily basis and the near-constant fear of another exile which might wipe out years of struggle and hard work. Consequently, those Granadines who had any financial means at their disposal chose to save rather than to purchase land.

30. Brumont 1993; García Fernández 2001; Zarandieta 2000.
31. Fernández and Pérez 2010: 141–42; Moreno 2017: 57–58.

Up to this point, the gap between Moriscos and Old Christians was confined to the economic realm. It may have been based on irrational criteria, but there is nothing to suggest that cultural—let alone religious or ideological—motivations played a part in it. The domestic scene, however, was a different matter. The bride's trousseau laid the foundations of the new household. All homes shared the same types of material resources, such as linen, furniture, household equipment, and clothing. The only variations detected relate to the distribution and value of those goods, which obviously hinged on the financial resources of each family, be they Moriscos or Old Christians. In this scenario, there was a good deal of mutual influence and cultural borrowing between the two communities which was particularly visible in two very specific areas: clothes and domestic interiors.

Dress is one of the best understood aspects of material culture in the early modern period. The sartorial peculiarities of Moriscos were one of the features visitors to Granada remarked upon in the first half of the sixteenth century. And while the male costume could be quickly and fairly accurately adapted to Castilian usage,[32] women's clothes posed a real problem. Travel narratives highlight some very specific garments worn by Morisco women, such as the *marlota* (a loose-fitting robe) or the *almalafa* (a mantle that covered the head and body leaving an opening for the eyes), as well as their penchant for bright colors and the use of silk as their fabric of choice.[33] Seen in perspective, and despite the subjective points of view displayed in some of these narratives, travelers' accounts suggest a certain resistance to change among the Moriscos. The latter insisted that their obduracy was merely due to cost considerations: if all their women were forced to replace their outfits, it would bankrupt some of their families.

One of the people who defended this stance was the above-mentioned Núñez Muley, who argued for changes to be introduced gradually, allowing garments to be replaced as they wore out. This would avoid Moriscos having to spend considerable sums to adapt their wives' and daughters' wardrobes to Castilian fashion.[34]

32. García Pedraza 2000: 58.
33. Díez 2017: 56–64; Franco and Moreno 2019: 255–63.
34. Garrad 1954: 209. Using this argument, Mudejars in Murcia in the early sixteenth century succeeded in obtaining a concession that would allow them to wear their

Núñez Muley also insisted that costume carried no religious connotations whatsoever, but Old Christians disagreed. Since the days of forced conversions, Castilian authorities were fully persuaded that items of clothing of Islamic origin carried huge cultural power. The Spanish Crown's main fear was that traditional Muslim dress might act as a catalyst for the survival of Islamic worship. Their misgivings explain why sartorial issues had such a prominent role in the legal provisions decreed in the first third of the sixteenth century with the aim of abolishing the Morisco minority's cultural peculiarities.[35]

These legal restrictions had a limited effect, partly because the Moriscos' generous covert tax payments persuaded the Crown to postpone their implementation.[36] But by the middle of the century, the issue of dress still took a great deal of space in the Church's discussions in Granada on the subject of speeding up Morisco evangelization.[37] Furthermore, the authorities' attempt to restrict the use of garments of Islamic origin was one of the issues that triggered the War of the Alpujarras.

The war itself and the hardship that followed exile proved to be the catalyst. No Morisco trousseau dated after 1570 consists primarily of traditional Granadine clothes. In fact, the presence of such garments in inventories is only residual.[38] In late sixteenth-century Castile, Old Christian and Morisco women wore similar outfits based on the Castilian-Christian standard. In contrast with other issues such as language, freedom of movement, dancing and social relations, dress was no longer a problem by this time, and after 1570 it ceased to be mentioned explicitly altogether in new Castilian legislation affecting the Moriscos.

Nevertheless, a tacit attempt was made to stop Moriscos using certain garments and fabrics. In the Spanish 1500s, wearing traditional Islamic clothes was closely associated with upward social mobility. Since the late fifteenth century, Iberian elites had enjoyed being seen wearing costumes inspired by Islamic dress. This attire was initially the prerogative of courtiers but eventually spread to aristocratic circles and local elites, to

> own clothes for as long as they were serviceable. See Pascual 2014: 129.

35. Gallego and Gámir 1996: 157–270; Domínguez and Vincent 1997: 21–23; Irigoyen-García 2017: 101–10.
36. Benítez 2001: 420–24.
37. Gallego and Gámir 1996.
38. Aranda 1984: 264; Franco and Moreno 2019: 259–60.

be worn at entertainments and festive occasions in particular, where only people in the highest echelons of society were allowed to wear this type of outfit.

Sumptuary laws had long played a part in medieval and early-modern Spain and evolved substantially in the course of the sixteenth century. They were conceived with the triple aim of setting boundaries on disproportionate expenditure on clothes and accessories, setting down some behavioral terms of reference for society as a whole, and drawing the boundaries for social stratification through dress.[39] This had a huge impact on Moriscos because a significant proportion of the fabrics and textile crafts banned by these laws were part of the costume worn in the Kingdom of Granada since time immemorial, including silk as well as needlework in gold and silver. These materials and techniques are generally associated in the sources with "Morisco-style" garments. The new rules also stipulated how certain items of clothing should be worn, with particular focus on headdress, which was henceforth regulated.

Javier Irigoyen has confirmed that sumptuary regulations went beyond strictly material considerations to become part of a wider symbolic, social, and cultural debate.[40] By banning certain articles of clothing, the Crown not only severed the link between Moriscos, their ancient sartorial customs and their cultural and religious tradition: it also enhanced the power of the Old Christian gentry. That specific form of dress worn by the elite is described in the sources as "Moorish style" (*a la mora*). Irigoyen contraposes this concept to a further two: "Morisco style"—as applied to tailoring and needlework, and "Morisco raiment." The latter refers to the clothes worn by New Christians across the Iberian Peninsula, while the former denotes sartorial fashions based on the heritage of these former Muslims, regardless of the socio-religious origin of the artificers who actually made each garment.[41] It could therefore be said that the Crown regulated the manufacture of "Morisco style" clothes to ensure New Christian dress was free from Islamic connotations and to indulge the Old Christian fancy of wearing "Moorish dress."

---

39. Puerta 2014: 220.
40. Irigoyen-García 2017: 36–56.
41. Irigoyen-García 2017: 21–23.

This legislation was only partly effective, both in the general Castilian context and in the particular case of the Moriscos. Although marriage inventories show the relative success of these laws in curbing the ownership and public exhibition of traditional Islamic dress, certain details reveal that the New Christians resisted such measures. It is in these details that Islamic cultural reminiscences emerge, offering a glimpse of a last stand by the former Muslims.

Morisco women living in Castile and Andalusia were no different from their Granadine counterparts in allocating a major part of their dowries to the acquisition of personal clothing.[42] This was common practice at the time and the content of their wardrobes did not vary substantially either. Morisco women adopted Castilian uses not only because their new material ecosystem forced them to do so but as a result of evolving fashion trends.[43] Their mutual borrowings and influences do not necessarily imply any degree of cultural hybridization.[44]

Against this background, Morisco resistance arose in two different but complementary spheres. First, the craftsmanship and materials that conformed "Morisco-style" sartorial culture continued to exist for a time. Although they still featured in household inventories, they became gradually rarer. However, the same inventories show that Morisco wardrobes kept their Islamic cultural traditions alive in the form of fringes and strips of fabric embroidered with geometrical patterns and plant motifs, and by using a wider range of colors than their Old Christian counterparts.[45] Their links to mid-sixteenth-century Granada are obvious.[46] Among other similarities, many of these decorations were worked onto garments made of silk, a quintessentially Granadine fabric. Despite the legal limitations on the use of this silk among the lower classes, it was habitually present in the wardrobes of Morisco women of Granadine origin. This does not mean, however, that Moriscos dispensed with cotton, linen, hemp, or wool fabrics, or that Old Christians were alien to the use of silk.

Silk was often made into smocks, shirts, caps, coifs, and so on. Less common, but not rare, were silken *almalafas*, *marlotas*, and bloomers.

42. Fernández and Pérez 2010: 142–43; Moreno 2017: 63–64.
43. Lecerf 2012: 138; Moreno 2015: 110–11; Fernández and Pérez 2010: 137.
44. Franco and Moreno 2019: 104–105.
45. Aranda 1984: 262; Prieto 1991: 72–79; Fernández and Pérez 2010: 136–37.
46. Martínez San Pedro 1997: 241–42; Fernández and Pérez 2010: 137.

The inventories usually describe garments in detail, sometimes profusely, leading us to the second scenario in which Moriscos manifested their distinctive dress choices. It is reasonable to think that these garments were not worn as everyday clothes, but had a symbolic purpose. They were "fetish" garments, worn in private on special occasions, and likely to be passed down the generations, thereby ensuring the survival of the cultural heritage they represented.

While the wardrobe reflects individual resistance, the home is a more appropriate environment to observe opposition and dissidence processes in a collective setting. Domestic interiors in the early modern period went beyond their purpose as dwellings to become meeting places, spaces for social interaction, and even workplaces. The social networks developed at home were more diverse and affected more individuals. Hence, they open a window on human behavior in a context of personal relationships where endogamy was rife and which were kept at all times within the boundaries drawn by the members of each household. From this point of view—and despite the fact that it was a far more open space at that time than it is today—the family home was a private place. Its internal arrangement, the use assigned to each room and the objects stored in it reflect the attitudes of its dwellers. This rigidity at times develops cracks and allows "system failures" to occur, opening gaps in the privacy that ensures family order. Examples of this type of rupture are the number of people who were reported to the Inquisition by family members or neighbors on the basis of experiences in which everyday domestic life was the main factor. But this was by no means common. The home is usually portrayed as a space for privacy and reflects the personal—and collective—microcosm of its inhabitants.

The political collapse of the Nasrid kingdom led to a rearrangement of the public spaces where social interaction took place, particularly in urban settings: mosques became churches, and cemeteries were eliminated. Public baths suffered the same fate. All were viewed as potential venues for the ongoing practice of the Moriscos' former religion. Mosque, cemetery, and baths were replaced with church, street, and square,[47] opening up the dense Muslim urban landscape to public use.

---

47. Vincent 1989: 715–18. Albeit with less political connotations, the phenomenon can also be seen in the Moorish quarters of Castile, Murcia, and Aragon. See Almagro

These measures had less impact on domestic architecture, although it should be noted that houses built in the final years of Islamic rule had already showed some degree of Christian influence. The most conspicuous aspect was the introduction of "Castilian-style" materials and ornamental techniques, but these changes were not radical enough to affect the essential privacy of Muslim homes.[48]

It is a well-known fact that Muslim homes were closed spaces designed for life to flow within their walls. Castilian authorities feared the potential of Morisco dwellings to become foci of religious dissidence which might then aggravate any nonconformity with catechesis and indoctrination. In the first half of the sixteenth century, Moriscos in Granada were repeatedly ordered by law to keep their doors open to enable the monitoring of daily activity within. This did not change substantially after the War of the Alpujarras, when Granadines were distributed in new neighborhoods using criteria aimed to maximize dispersion. Accounts of Old Christians unashamedly snooping on their most intimate acts are by no means unusual.[49] The goal was one and the same in both contexts: to prevent homes becoming "domestic mosques" of one sort or another.

Morisco dwellings in Granada had a unique identity. Despite growing Christian influence, they retained their original Al-Andalus essence, as is evident from the near—or total—absence of furniture.[50] Their interiors were all but diaphanous spaces furnished with mats, rugs, cushions, and pillows, and the social hierarchy is implicit in the expensive fabric wall-hangings. The value of these textile furnishings went beyond their mere monetary worth to become a cultural marker.[51] In the rest of the Iberian Peninsula, the continuity of customs inherited from the Mudejar period is indisputable. During the first half of the sixteenth century and even later, the interiors described in inventories maintained the open arrangements mentioned above and showed a preference for textile furnishings over wooden ones.[52]

    2015: 83–84; Pascual 2014: 135; Álvaro Zamora 2017: 212–13.
48. Orihuela 2007: 180–81.
49. Moreno 2009: 328–33.
50. Fernández and Pérez 2010: 138.
51. Serrano-Niza 2015: 327.
52. Conte 2009: 316–21; Álvaro Zamora 2017: 215; Reinaldos 2020: 275.

Having settled in Castile, Granadine Moriscos maintained some of their previous habits. Household equipment continued to be their main expense[53] and, within it, lower sums were invariably allocated to hard furniture than to the purchase and inventory of domestic fabrics.[54] A comparison with Old Christian inventories reveals some interesting facts: in the Morisco home, the most common items of hard furniture were limited to the strictly necessary for minimum comfort, such as beds and mattresses. Storage pieces were also present, but in a far smaller proportion than in the homes of Old Christians of a similar financial standing. The same applies to tables, chairs, benches, shelves, and so on. Indeed, as Manuel Fernández and Rafael Pérez point out, the sole fact that Granadine Moriscos used these objects at all is remarkable in itself.[55]

Whereas the use of wooden furniture was markedly different in both communities, "light, foldable, portable"[56] household linen had pride of place in inventories across the whole population—a likely legacy of Al-Andalus—from Castile to Aragón to Andalusia.[57] Indeed, both New and Old Christians attached great importance to items such as bedsheets, valances, blankets, and other textiles used for hygiene purposes and in the kitchen, but their behavior differed with regard to soft furnishings. Wall hangings continued to be popular among Moriscos, although their patterns became hybridized, mixing Castilian and Andalusí elements, and cushions, pillows, mats, and carpets covered their floors. These items were not unusual in Old Christian dwellings, but they were far more common among Moriscos.

A real novelty in Castilian settings was the appearance of Christian devotional objects in Morisco homes. These objects were present in Christian homes not only for spiritual reasons, but because of their strong social significance as symbols: they were a public display of their owners' piety, particularly in the case of sculptures and paintings which could be seen by third parties. Although not essential articles, many of these objects acquired a considerable significance in certain households. The items most commonly used for private prayer were medals, crosses,

53. Moreno 2017: 55.
54. Moreno 2014–2016: 93, 96.
55. Fernández and Pérez 2010: 138.
56. Álvaro Zamora 2017: 215.
57. Aranda 1984: 265; Magán and Sánchez 1993: 76.

agnusdei (a blessed wax disk, with the shape of a lamb on one side and a devotional figure on the other), and, above all, rosaries. Larger objects included pictorial representations and carvings of Jesus Christ, the Virgin Mary, and saints.

Merely having this type of item documented in Morisco homes indicates a turning point in the community's history. This assertion, however, needs to be qualified: very few New Christian families had any use for these objects, and those they did own displayed certain peculiarities. By and large, small devotional objects used in private prayer were favored over sculptures, prints and paintings. Moriscos were also highly selective in their choice of subjects. Besides the archetypical icons of "official" Christendom, Moriscos seem to have integrated their domestic devotions into the framework of their own cultural heritage, minimizing the use of figurative images or at least resorting to Eastern saints and religious figures with whose life history the Morisco minority could identify as individuals or as a group.[58]

Lastly, it should be mentioned that Christian domestic practices were adopted relatively late by Castile's Granadine Moriscos. Devotional objects began to be included in household inventories no earlier than 1600. Once again, the pioneers of this new behavior must have belonged to the generation of Moriscos who were born in exile or who had left Granada at a very early age.

Material peace, peaceful coexistence: work in progress

The Christian conquest of the last Islamic kingdom in the Iberian Peninsula by the Catholic monarchs was soon followed by a policy of integration and acculturation of its Muslim subjects. In the early sixteenth century, Ferdinand and Isabella forced Castilian Muslims to choose between conversion to Christianity and exile. Although some departures for North Africa did take place, the majority of the Mudejar population of Castile opted for conversion. This marked the beginning of the Morisco phenomenon, which was completed in 1525–26 with the compulsory baptism of all Muslims living in the Kingdom of Aragon.

---

58. Franco and Moreno 2018.

From that point onwards, the Morisco minority found itself at the center of various social, economic, religious, and political controversies. Despite their official status as Christians, their religious behavior was kept under constant surveillance. Doubts about their sincere conversion were certainly well-founded, particularly in some territories such as the Kingdom of Granada or the Valencia region. In Aragon and the inner areas of Castile, crypto-Islamic practices did not completely disappear, but the religious integration of former Muslims was smoother and even conspicuous at times. This state of affairs was overturned in the aftermath of the War of the Alpujarras, when thousands of Granadine Moriscos were banished from their homeland and forced to settle in Castile. From that time until 1609–14, when this minority was finally expelled from the peninsula, the so-called "Morisco problem" became ingrained in Spanish politics. Attempts to evangelize former Muslims were set in motion but seldom met with success, due either to tepid deployment strategies or to Morisco obduracy. Against this background, a lively intellectual debate evolved in a wide range of scenarios involving politicians, bureaucrats, clergymen, and literati. But the voices of the Moriscos themselves were virtually never heard. The arguments focused exclusively on how to remove the problem, rather than on finding solutions, and the word "expulsion" eventually eclipsed others like "integration" and "coexistence."

Reading the arguments on which the debate was based, it is easy to conjure an image of a society in which the two communities coexisted with barely any contact between them, and perhaps even isolated from each other. Nothing could be further from the truth. Moriscos and Old Christians went about their daily business in an environment defined by interaction. Coexistence was not always easy and was marred by episodes of intolerance, confrontation, and a fair amount of distrust. But there were also areas of mutual understanding. The two groups not only shared public spaces for collective social interaction, but also a common material reality. Old and New Christians used the same kind of tools, objects and utensils, adopted the same traditions and fashions, wore similar clothes, and used similar raw materials and fabrics to make their furniture, everyday objects, and clothes. This may not have removed all their differences, but it certainly made them similar. This change obviously did not happen overnight but, while in early sixteenth-century Granada or Valencia it was relatively easy to tell Old and New Christians apart on the basis of their looks, the arrangement of their domestic spaces, and their day-to-day routines, by the end of the century in Castile such an identification was a difficult, if not impossible, task.

The result was the apparent "material peace" that served as the foundation for a form of coexistence which was eventually frustrated by Philip III's expulsion decree. Civil laws, canonical prescriptions, diverging ideologies and surveillance enabled Moriscos and Old Christians to meet in the performance of their everyday activities. Those shared experiences were used by the Moriscos to integrate in public life and to slip into the most anonymous lifestyle possible.

What happened in the privacy of their own homes is a different story. Far from complying with the Old Christians' demands for uniformity, the Moriscos enjoyed their own spaces and tried to build their own distinct identity within them. To achieve this they made use of the meager resources allowed them by the required material homogeneity. It should be noted that the issue was not strictly speaking religious. Over and above their personal beliefs, the material behavior of New Christians was largely cultural and did not pursue the perpetuation of devotional practices that many of them had agreed to replace with Christianity. Or at least that was not their only concern. On the other hand, behaviors such as building a home with its own idiosyncratic features, keeping a wardrobe that preserved the sartorial heritage of their ancestors, and using garments, ornaments and fabrics that were linked to the proscribed habitus provide the clearest evidence that Moriscos refused to lose their essence. From this perspective, material reality was both a meeting point for the two communities and an instrument for differentiation and resistance. This was achieved not by confrontation, but by adaptation because, after all, peace can also be built through compromise.

Author biography

Francisco J. Moreno Díaz del Campo is Associate Professor in the UCLM Faculty of Arts in Ciudad Real, Spain. His main field of research is social history, principally in relation to the analysis of the Morisco minority in Castile. Currently, he focuses his work on subjects concerning the material culture and daily life of Morisco people. He is the author of *Los moriscos de La Mancha. Sociedad economía y modos de vida de una minoría en la Castilla* (Madrid, 2009). Recently (2019) he has written— in collaboration with Dr. Borja Franco—*Pintando al converso. La imagen del morisco en la península ibérica (1492–1609)*.

References

Alemán, M. (1599), "Historia de los enamorados Ozmin y Daraja," in *Primera parte de Guzmán de Alfarache*, Madrid (ed. M. García; Barcelona: Bruguera, 1983).

Almagro Vidal, C. (2015), "La comunidad mudéjar de Daimiel. Algunas noticias," in *III Jornadas de Historia de Daimiel*, 77–88. Daimiel: Ayuntamiento de Daimiel.

Álvaro Zamora, M. I. (2017), "La casa de los mudéjares y de los moriscos en Aragón. Localización, espacios, funcionalidad y ajuar," in M. M. Birriel Salcedo (ed.), *La(s) casa(s) en la Edad Moderna*, 193–230. Zaragoza: Institución "Fernando el Católico."

Anonymous (1561), *La Historia del Abencerraje y la hermosa Jarifa*, Toledo (ed. V. Lama and E. Peral; Madrid: Castalia, 2000).

Aranda Doncel, J. (1984), *Los moriscos en tierras de Córdoba*. Cordoba: Publicaciones del Monte de Piedad y Caja de Ahorros de Córdoba.

Barrios Aguilera, M., ed. (2000), *Historia del reino de Granada. Vol. II: La época morisca y la repoblación (1502–1630)*. Granada: Editorial Universidad de Granada-El Legado Andalusí.

Barrios Aguilera, M. (2011), *La invención de los libros plúmbeos. Fraude, historia y mito*. Granada: Editorial Universidad de Granada.

Barrios Aguilera, M., and Á. Galán Sánchez (2004), *La historia del reino de Granada a debate. Viejos y nuevos temas: perspectivas de estudio*. Malaga: Diputación Provincial de Málaga.

Barrios Aguilera, M., and M. García-Arenal, eds. (2006), *Los Plomos del Sacromonte. Invención y tesoro*. Valencia: Publicacions de la Universitat de València–Editorial Universidad de Granada–Prensas Universitarias de Zaragoza.

Benítez Sánchez-Blanco, R. (2000), "¿Cristianos o bautizados? La trayectoria inicial de los moriscos valencianos," *Estudis. Revista de Historia Moderna* 26: 11–36.

Benítez Sánchez-Blanco, R. (2001), "La política de Carlos V hacia los moriscos granadinos," in J. Martínez Millán and I. J. Ezquerra Revilla (eds.), *Carlos V y la quiebra del humanismo político en Europa (1530–1558)*, I: 415–46.

Madrid: Sociedad Estatal para la Conmemoración de los Centenarios de Felipe II y Carlos V.

Benítez Sánchez-Blanco, R. (2012), *Tríptico de la expulsión de los moriscos. El triunfo de la razón de Estado*. Montpellier: Presses Universitaires de la Méditerranée.

Bennet, T., and P. Joyce, eds. (2013), *Material Powers: Cultural Studies, History and the Material Turn*. London and New York: Routledge.

Bernabé Pons, L. F. (1998), *El texto morisco del Evangelio de San Bernabé*. Granada: Editorial Universidad de Granada.

Bernabé Pons, L. F. (2002), "Los mecanismos de una resistencia. Los libros plúmbeos del Sacromonte y el 'Evangelio de Bernabé,'" *Al-Qanṭara* 23/2: 477–98. https://doi.org/10.3989/alqantara.2002.v23.i2.192

Birriel Salcedo, M. M. (2002), "Entre una ley y otra: La transmisión del patrimonio entre los moriscos granadinos," in M.-C. Barbazza and C. Heusch (eds.), *Familles, Pouvoirs, Solidarités. Domaine méditerranéen et hispano-américain (XVe-XXe siècles)*, 227–36. Montpellier: Université de Montpellier III.

Bonnell, V., and L. Hunt, eds. (1999), *Beyond the Cultural Turn: New Directions in the Study of Society and Culture*. Berkeley and London: California University Press.

Brumont, F. (1993), "Le mariage, passeport pour l'ascension sociale: À Logroño au XVIe siècle," in J.-P. Amalric (ed.), *Pouvoirs et société dans l'Espagne moderne. Hommage à Bartolomé Bennassar*, 89–100. Toulouse: Presses Universitaires du Mirail.

Carrasco Urgoiti, M. S. (1989), *El moro de Granada en la Literatura*. Granada: Universidad de Granada (1st ed., Madrid: Revista de Occidente, 1956).

Cirot, G. (1938–1944), "La maurophilie littéraire en Espagne au XVIe siècle," *Bulletin Hispanique* 40/2: 150–57; 40/3: 281–96; 40/4: 433–47; 41/1: 65–85; 41/4: 345–51; 42/3: 213–27; 43/3–4: 265–89; 44/2–4: 62–102; 46/1: 5–25.

Conte Cazcarro, À. (2009), *Los moriscos de la ciudad de Huesca. Una convivencia rota*. Huesca: Instituto de Estudios Altoaragoneses.

Díez Jorge, M. E. (2017), "Under the Same Mantle: The Women of the 'Other' through Images of Moriscas," *Il Capitale Culturale*, Supplement 6: 49–86.

Domínguez Ortiz, A., and B. Vincent (1997), *Historia de los moriscos. Vida y tragedia de una minoría*. Madrid: Alianza Editorial.

Fernández Chaves, M. F., and R. M. Pérez García (2010), "Las dotes de las moriscas granadinas y sevillanas. Cambios y adaptaciones de una cultura material," in M. Lobo de Araujo and A. Esteves (eds.), *Tomar estado: Dotes e casamentos (séculos XVI–XIX)*, 121–45. Braga: Centro de Investigaçao Transdisciplinar "Cultura, Espaço e Memória."

Franco Llopis, B., and F. J. Moreno Díaz del Campo (2018), "The Moriscos' Artistic Domestic Devotions Viewed through Christian Eyes in Early Modern

Iberia," in M. Faini and A. Meneghin (eds.), *Domestic Devotions in the Early Modern World*, 107–25. Leiden and Boston: Brill.

Franco Llopis, B., and F. J. Moreno Díaz del Campo (2019), *Pintando al converso. La imagen del morisco en la península ibérica (1492–1614)*. Madrid: Cátedra.

Fuchs, B. (2009), *Exotic Nation: Maurophilia and the Construction of Early Modern Spain*. Philadelphia: University of Pennsylvania Press.

Gallego Burín, A., and A. Gámir Sandoval (1996), *Los moriscos del Reino de Granada, según el sínodo de Guadix de 1154*. Granada: Editorial Universidad de Granada.

García Cárcel, R. (2014), "La memoria histórica sobre la expulsión de los moriscos," *eHumanista/Conversos* 2: 120–32.

García Fernández, M. (2001), "Familia y cultura material en Valladolid a mediados del siglo XVI. Entre el matrimonio y la muerte," in J. L. Castellano Castellano and F. Sánchez-Montes González (eds.), *Congreso Internacional Carlos V. Europeísmo y universalidad*, IV: 275–96. Madrid: Sociedad Estatal para la Conmemoración de los Centenarios de Felipe II y Carlos V.

García Gómez, M. J. (2002), "Contribución de la Iglesia a un proyecto político de Felipe II: la integración de los moriscos granadinos deportados a Castilla (1570–1610)," in *Iglesia y religiosidad en España. Historia y archivos. Actas de las V Jornadas de Castilla-La Mancha sobre investigación en archivos. Guadalajara, 8–11 de mayo de 2001*, 1421–53. Castilla La-Mancha: ANABAD; Guadalajara: Asociación de Amigos del Archivo Histórico Provincial de Guadalajara.

García Pedraza, A. (2000), "Entre la media luna y la cruz: Las mujeres moriscas," in M. J. Osorio Pérez and M. E. Díez Jorge (eds.), *Las mujeres y la ciudad de Granada en el siglo XV*, 55–68. Granada: Ayuntamiento de Granada.

Garrad, K. (1954), "The Original 'Memorial' of Don Francisco Núñez Muley," *Atlante* 2: 199–226.

Gerritsen, A., and G. Riello (2015), *Writing Material Culture History*. London: Bloomsbury.

Green, H. (2012), "Cultural History and the Material(s) Turn," *Cultural History* 1/1: 61–82. https://doi.org/10.3366/cult.2012.0006

Guillén, C. (1971), *Literature as System: Essays toward the Theory of Literary History*. Princeton, NJ: Princeton University Press.

Hicks, D. (2010), "The Material-Cultural Turn: Event and Effect," in D. Hicks and M. C. Beaudry (eds.), *The Oxford Handbook of Material Culture Studies*, 25–98. Oxford: Oxford University Press.

Irigoyen-García, J. (2017), *"Moors Dressed as Moors": Clothing, Social Distinction, and Ethnicity in Early Modern Iberia*. Toronto: University of Toronto Press.

Ivanič, S., M. Laven, and A. Morrall, eds. (2019), *Religious Materiality in the Early Modern World*. Amsterdam: Amsterdam University Press.

Julien, M.-P., and C. Rosselin (2005), *La culture matérielle*. Paris: La Découverte.

Ladero Quesada, M. Á. (1972–1973), "Datos demográficos sobre los mudéjares de Granada y Castilla en el siglo XV," *Anuario de Estudios Medievales* 8: 481–90.

Ladero Quesada, M. Á. (1992), "Mudéjares y repobladores en el Reino de Granada (1485–1501)," *Cuadernos de Historia Moderna* 13: 47–71.

Lecerf, F. (2012), "La vie quotidienne des morisques entre 1502 et 1570 selon les protocoles notariés des archives de Grenade," PhD thesis, Universidad de Granada–Université de Caen-Basse-Normandie.

Magán Sánchez, J. M., and R. Sánchez González (1993), *Moriscos granadinos en La Sagra de Toledo, 1570–1610*. Toledo: Caja de Castilla-La Mancha.

Magán García, J. M., and R. Sánchez González (1997), "Los nuevos convertidos del reino de Granada en las sinodales de las diócesis castellanas," in A. Mestre Sanchís and E. Giménez López (eds.), *Disidencias y exilios en la España Moderna. Actas de la IV Reunión Científica de la Asociación Española de Historia Moderna*, 393–409. Alicante: Universidad de Alicante/Asociación Española de Historia Moderna.

Márquez Villanueva, F. (1982), "La criptohistoria morisca (los otros conversos)," *Cuadernos Hispanoamericanos* 390: 517–34.

Martínez San Pedro, M. D. (1997), "Algunos aspectos de la vida de las moriscas granadinas ante su matrimonio," in *Actes du VIIe Symposium International d'Etudes Morisques sur Famille morisque: Femmes et enfant*, 240–53. Zaghouan: Fundation Temimi pour la Recherche Scientifique et l'Information.

Mendiola Fernández, M. I. (2012), "Trayectoria y perfil de una minoría a través de las transmisiones patrimoniales por causa de matrimonio en Granada en el siglo XV," PhD thesis, Universidad Nacional de Educación a Distancia.

Moreno Díaz del Campo, F. J. (2005), "El espejo del rey. Felipe III, los apologistas y la expulsión de los moriscos," in P. Sanz (ed.), *La Monarquía Hispánica en tiempos del Quijote*, 231–46. Madrid: Sílex.

Moreno Díaz del Campo, F. J. (2009), *Los moriscos en La Mancha. Sociedad, economía y modos de vida de una minoría en la Castilla moderna*. Madrid: CSIC.

Moreno Díaz del Campo, F. J. (2014–2016), "Observando el hogar. Vida cotidiana y realidad material doméstica de os moriscos de Castilla. 1570–1610," *Sharq Al-Andalus. Estudios mudéjares y moriscos* 21: 79–113.

Moreno Díaz del Campo, F. J. (2015), "El hogar morisco: Familia, transmisión patrimonial y cauce de asimilación," *Al-Kurras. Cuadernos de estudios mudéjares y moriscos* I/1: 97–119.

Moreno Díaz del Campo, F. J. (2017), "Asimilación y diferencia a través de los patrimonios nupciales de los moriscos y los cristianos viejos (Ciudad Real, 1570–1610)," *Obradoiro de Historia Moderna* 26: 45–69.

Moreno Díaz del Campo, F. J. (2020), "Vigilar desde abajo. Las autoridades locales y el control de los moriscos granadinos de Castilla," *Mediterranea. Ricerche Storiche* 49: 275–304.

Orihuela Uzal, A. (2007), "The Andalusi House in Granada (Thirteenth to Sixteenth Centuries)," in G. D. Anderson and M. Rosser Owen (eds.), *Revisiting Al-Andalus: Perspectives on the Material Culture of Islamic Iberia and Beyond*, 169–91. Leiden and Boston: Brill.

Pascual Martínez, J. (2014), *Los moriscos mudéjares de Pliego: Origen y expulsión de una comunidad*. Murcia: Editum.

Peinado Santaella, R. G. (2011), *Cómo disfrutan los vencedores cuando se reparten el botín*. Granada: Comares.

Pérez de Hita, G. (1595), *Historia de los bandos de zegríes y abencerrajes (primera parte de las Guerras Civiles de Granada*, Zaragoza (ed. P. Blanchard-Demouge; Granada: Universidad de Granada, 1998).

Pomara, B. (2021), "Quand les objets de la foi fondent la réputation: Les morisques entre Espagne et Italie," in M. Lezowki and Y. Ligneureux (eds.), *Matière à discorde. Les objets chrétiens dans les conflits modernes*, 173–86. Rennes: Presses Universitaires de Rennes.

Prieto Bernabé, J. M. (1991), "Una minoría disidente en la Corte: Los moriscos de Madrid ante la expulsión (1610)," *Torre de los Lujanes. Boletín de la Real Sociedad Económica Matritense de Amigos del País* 17: 57–79.

Puerta Escribano, R. de la (2014), "Las leyes suntuarias y la restricción del lujo en el vestir," in J. L. Colomer and A. Descalzo Lorenzo, *Vestir a la española en las Cortes Europeas* (siglos XVI y XVII), vol. 1, 209–231. Madrid: Centro de Estudios Europa Hispánica.

Reinaldos Mirraño, D. A. (2020), "Cultura material de moriscos murcianos y granadinos del siglo XVI," in *XIV Simposio Internacional de Mudejarismo. La vida cotidiana, amor y muerte en el mundo mudéjar y morisco*, 271–86. Teruel: Centro de Estudios Mudéjares.

Roberts, J. L. (2017), "Things: Material Turn, Transnational Turn," *American Art* 31/2: 64–69. https://doi.org/10.1086/694067

Serrano-Niza, D. (2015), "Amueblar la casa con palabras. Fuentes lexicográficas árabes para el estudio del ámbito doméstico," in M. E. Díez Jorge and J. Navarro Palazón (eds.), *La casa medieval en la Península Ibérica*, 307–35. Madrid: Sílex.

Tagliaferri, F. V. (2018), *Tolerance Re-shaped in the Early-Modern Mediterranean Borderlands: Travellers, Missionaries and Proto-Journalists (1683–1724)*. New York: Routledge.

Vincent, B. (1970), "L'expulsion des Morisques du Royaume de Grenade et leur répartition en Castille (1570–1571)," *Mélanges de la Casa de Velázquez* 6: 211–46. https://doi.org/10.3406/casa.1970.1019

Vincent, B. (1989), "Espace public et espace privé dans les villes andalouses (XVe–XVIe siècles)," in J.-C. Maire-Vigueur (ed.), *D'une ville à l'autre: structures matérielles et organisation de l'espace dans les villes européennes (XIIIe–XVIe siècles)*, 711–24. Rome: École Française de Rome.

Vincent, B. (2006), *El río morisco*. Valencia: Universitat de València-Editorial Universidad de Granada-Prensas Universitarias de Zaragoza.

Zarandieta Arenas, F. (2000), "Riqueza y consumo en la Baja Extremadura en el siglo XVII. Análisis a través de las cartas de dote," *Historia Agraria* 21: 63–97.

Chapter 8

Political and Religious Moderates in the French Wars of Religion and the Revolt of the Netherlands: A Comparative Perspective

Alberto Hernández Pérez

Introduction

The aim of this chapter is to analyze the history of the discourses on peace and tolerance during the second half of the sixteenth and early seventeenth centuries in France and the Netherlands. It is necessary to make an in-depth review of these discourses during these modern centuries in order not to fall into a historical anachronism linked to the ongoing ideas of the nineteenth and twentieth centuries. However, it is also useful to investigate these discourses during these last convulsive times since in that moment, they referred to a situation of daily religious coexistence in various communities that can help us understand what we mean by tolerance in the Modern Age. Moreover, comparative history remains a fundamental tool to understand the theory on which these practices of coexistence were based and to contextualize these practices in a period of confessional wars that changed the social relations between religious communities.

Rethinking the concepts of peace and tolerance in mid-sixteenth-century political and religious discourses

One of the standards of today's Western societies is that of religious tolerance, understood as a right linked to religious freedom, not only of conscience but also of worship, whatever the professed religion. Going back to the origins of tolerance, closely linked to the discourses of peace, is a complicated task, as it is necessary to qualify and criticize the historiographic discourses that understood the Modern Age as a period of intolerance and religious persecution during the so-called "Age of Wars of Religion" between 1550 and 1650, in which the most dramatic episode was the slaughter of St. Bartholomew. During this phase, Catholic and Protestant armies clashed on the battlefield, while popular mobs committed atrocities in the name of God. Later, it was understood that, from 1650 to 1700, Europe had entered the "Age of the Enlightenment" and reason, tolerance, and religious peace prevailed in the face of bigoted fanaticism and confessional wars. According to this discourse, during the nineteenth century in Europe, principles of religious freedom were established as the political basis of the liberal system.

This metahistorical discourse originated in the mid-eighteenth century and developed during the nineteenth century as an unequivocal sign of European civilizational progress. While containing some true elements, it is a tautological discourse[1] that blurs the discourses of tolerance and peace that had already appeared in the sixteenth century during the confessional wars and, more importantly, its implementation and necessary explanation. As for religious violence, it continued to occur in the eighteenth century and has remained in multiple scenarios such as Northern Ireland, the Balkans, and India.

Furthermore, the history of tolerance is so complex and versatile that it cannot be understood as unidirectional but as a fluctuating process that, in the sixteenth century, did not yet cover values concerning religious freedom as they are understood today. The word "tolerance" itself was absent in all the edicts of pacification of the French Wars of Religion. When the verb *tolerér* or the word *tolérance* appeared in philosophical or political works, rather than to a principle that articulates society, these words

---

1. For an introduction on this topic: Kaplan 2002: 8–26; Kaplan 2019: 1–12.

referred to a temporary measure based on a momentary coexistence and ordered by a higher hierarchical power (the French Crown) towards its subjects. This was so to such an extent that the use of *permettre* or *permission* was more common thanks to the positive connotations it carried, as it emphasized the permission given by the Crown.[2] Therefore, it is a term full of ambiguities and that, if not qualified, can lead to a dangerous anachronism.

The very use of the term tolerance in the sixteenth century has been qualified by the Italian historian Mario Turchetti who claimed that tolerance, in the context of the French Wars of Religion, must be understood as a temporary measure until the subsequent religious concord under the Catholic Church. Since Poissy's colloquium in 1561, the French Crown tried to make concessions on religious matters to bring the Protestants closer together, something defended by the *Moyenneurs*. This same model was repeated in all edicts of pacification, beginning with the Edict of Amboise[3] and ending with the so-called toleration Edict of Nantes in 1598, as Protestant worship was limited to certain areas of France. The very appeal of "perpetual and irrevocable" was qualified by a contemporary of Henry IV, Pierre de Belloy, who defined it as a revocable measure when the Christian community reconciled.[4]

As for the United Provinces of the Netherlands, the term tolerance must also be qualified because, while freedom of conscience was a principle established in the Union of Utrecht (1579), it is also true that religious exercise, apart from the reformed one, was impossible in the public sphere, but not in the private. In this case, the religious policy of the republic was based on the harmony and social and civic coexistence where religious pluralism played a secondary role.[5] The situation in the Spanish Netherlands also allowed a timid civic tolerance with those reformed who were not involved in riots, for the sake of social reconciliation.[6]

In this case, as Olivier Christin has shown, neutral spaces were created where conflicts between the different interests of religious communities could be resolved. In other words, a progressive autonomy of the *raison*

2. Huseman 1984: 293–309.
3. Turchetti 1991: 22.
4. Turchetti 1993: 66–75.
5. Frijhoff 2002b: 28–31.
6. Junot 2017: 6–8.

politique and the growth of the *raison d'État* took place and were fomented beyond religious disputes.⁷ However, it should be remembered that the act of religious tolerance itself implies an intolerant act. That is because the dominant religious groups (Catholics in France and Calvinists in the United Provinces) were the ones defining the boundaries between normality and abnormality, which had to be regulated under a specific legislation. Dominant religious groups would also establish unequal forms of accommodation.⁸ Therefore, as Jo Spaans argues, it is believed that these well-defined borders make the United Provinces a less exceptional model than what historians had thought until then and contextualizes it better within the dynamics of the social and religious discipline of its time.⁹

Because of all this, historians cannot limit their attention to speeches of full tolerance, but it is also necessary to explore the confessional coexistence and religious pluralism that helped to forge the idealistic visions of tolerance, as well as the policies carried out by elites. It is necessary to study how this form of tolerance succeeded in some places and resulted in a stable coexistence between different religious groups. This did not necessarily mean the acceptance of that diversity or the elimination of any criticism or conflict, but it provided the tools to regulate these conflicts and maintain civic peace.¹⁰ Thus, in the sixteenth and first half of the seventeenth century, tolerance/intolerance, together with concord, were closely related to the daily evolution of these communities.

Genesis and evolution of the discourses of tolerance and peace of moderate politicians and religious people

Only by qualifying the concepts of tolerance and religious harmony can one understand the discourses that many magistrates, jurists, and religious people made about the need for religious peace that would bring coexistence to France and the Netherlands. Many historians have maintained the thesis that Dutch society was persuaded by the "tolerant spirit

---

7   Christin 1997: 201–205.
8   Kaplan 2002: 26.
9   About this renewing thesis: Spaans 2002: 72–86; Spaans 2003b: 1–18; Van Der Lem 1998: 121–25.
10. Kaplan 2007: 7–12.

of Erasmus" in the mid-sixteenth century. This spirit involved a total aversion to persecution based on religious grounds, as these persecutions were understood as spiritual errors that could be corrected by preaching. Erasmus's ideas were also very present in some French irenistic circles, from which Dutch thinkers also benefit.[11] These ideas were also incorporated by William of Orange to defend his cause against the religious persecution of Philip II.

But which were the ideas that Erasmus of Rotterdam (1466–1536) was defending? It has traditionally been suggested that the Dutch intellectual only alluded to a provisional tolerance, not a definitive one. However, at the same time, he was quite careful when developing his arguments against a policy of persecution and punishment for religious issues, which he described as a form of tyranny.[12] On the one hand, recent research has shown that Erasmus was already aware of the need for religious tolerance to maintain community coexistence and was very concerned about religious minorities in the Holy Roman Empire.[13] On the other hand, it should be qualified that Erasmus had a big influence on the irenistic circles in order to elaborate his theories in disparate religious communities. However, he did not change those societies or endow them with a "spirit" of his own; rather it was this context that lent itself to the formulation of these ideas.[14]

One of the forerunners of the idea of tolerance as a vertebrate concept of Christian societies was Sebastian Castellio (1515–1563). This poet and philosopher from Savoy, initially close to Calvin's reformed orthodoxy, led the protests against the execution of Miguel Servet and his treatise *Concerning Heretics: Whether They Are to Be Persecuted and How They Are to Be Treated* (1554) is the first where a full tolerance of conscience and religious worship is defended, turning to the Fathers of the Catholic Church such as St. Augustine or the Protestant reformers, including Luther or Melanchthon. Castellio even referred to Calvin's idea regarding the necessity to convert those punished with ex-communication to the Christian faith through "teaching, mercy, and appeasement."[15] However,

11. Mout 1997: 37–41.
12. Turchetti 1991: 18.
13. Tracy 1997: 50–54.
14. Tracy 1997: 62.
15. Robinson 2011: 47.

he never used the term tolerance in his writings, preferring peace, clemency, or lenity.

Following Erasmus's arguments, Castellio became critical of any ecclesiastical or political power that wanted to impose a discriminatory religious model and made clear his stance by defending that: "Killing a man is not defending a doctrine, it is only killing a man."[16] He was also inspired by his *Devotio Moderna* to affirm that imitating the life of Christ, his piety and "tolerance" with sinners was a model of Christian virtue. He considered it was only God's duty to determine who were the true heretics and punish them.[17] Therefore, he thought that confessional differences were based on how far believers were from finding the truth and therefore they misinterpreted it, but despite all that, they shared certain Christian doctrines and a common heritage.

This commitment to full tolerance was not shared by the moderate circles of the time, although they had to face a local reality founded on an evident religious pluralism, and their actions were more related to the impossibility of imposing religious uniformity. However, they did know the work of both intellectuals: evidence shows that the Prince of Orange and his followers used Castellio's ideas to defend peace and religious freedom.[18]

Before taking a closer look at the figure of the chancellor Michel de l'Hôpital, two religious moderates must be analyzed. Firstly, Georg Cassander (1513–1566), a Flemish Catholic scholar who, in his treatise *De officio pii viri in hoc religionis dissidio*, advocated a religious reconciliation based on the tradition of the Church and which led to the truth of Christ. He also emphasized the dogmas that Calvinists shared with Catholics. However, he defended a gentle coercion for those who were wrong, especially the Anabaptists, something that earned him Castellio's criticism.[19] Thus, the term tolerance was more blurred in his writings and he rather sought a religious concord based on the tradition shared from the early Christian Church, even if all this involved a religious reform within the present Church.

16. Kaplan 2007: 21.
17. Guggisberg 1997: 80–84. A more complete biography of Sebastian Castellio can be found at: Guggisberg and Gordon 2017.
18. Israel 1997: 4.
19. Van de Schoor 1997: 101–15.

This view was also shared by François Baudouin (1520–1573), a French jurist exiled from his homeland due to his approach to Protestantism. In his letters to Cassander, he also expressed the need for religious concord and religious reunification and even helped Cassander present his arguments at the Poissy colloquium in 1561 pursuing those same objectives. Both were named by the historian Hans Posthumus Meyjes as *irénistes étatiques*[20] since they developed a view linked to the duty of the State to reunify the Churches and pacify the kingdom. Both had a great influence on pacification policies in France during the 1560s and their ideas circulated throughout the Netherlands, especially among the Remonstrates circles.

The Edict of Saint Germain, also known as the Edict of January (1562), marked the first milestone in French history towards a religious tolerance to the Huguenots, both of conscience and worship, despite being provisional and limited. Such an idea was developed by Chancellor Michel de L'Hôpital in a very tense context due to the failure of the Poissy colloquium in 1561 when making concessions in confessional matters was proven to be extremely difficult.[21] However, irenistic voices were still emerging and advocating the freedom of reformed worship as the fastest way to achieve the pacification of the kingdom, as it had been defended in the anonymous *Exhortation to Princes*.[22] In a context of internal weakness within the Crown due to the progress of Calvinism among nobility and the tension in the kingdom, Catherine of Medici decided to introduce a new type of legislation that, drawn up by her chancellor, granted recognition to the Huguenots, although not tolerance in the current sense. They understood that repression had been ineffective and, to pacify the kingdom, it was necessary to apply authority more moderately.[23] In any case, religious issues and political issues were separated. Only on the latter did the edict of pacification legislate, despite leaving wide areas of uncertainty.

Similarly, L'Hôpital had also evolved since his entry into the chancellery in 1560. At first, he was closer to the ideas of Cassander or Baudouin,

20. Meyjes 1997: 67–68.
21. Wanegffelen 1997: 161–81.
22. Smith 1994: 37–38.
23. Christin 1999: 209–10.

who called for religious concord as a measure of pacification, but from an irenistic point of view he was closer to clemency towards heretics. All this changed in 1562 when the chancellor began to assume the impossibility of the religious unification ideal and the need to achieve peace and harmony of a civil nature, as he expressed clearly by noting: "It is not a question of the constitution of the religion but of the constitution of the republic [...] and some can be citizens who are not Christians."[24] This meant that Calvinists could have freedom of worship on the outskirts of cities, something that for many surpassed what was desirable. Negotiations with the Paris Parliament for publication reveal how unpopular these measures were.[25]

In line with the irenistic circles of his time, the chancellor also understood that only a king who had absolute sovereignty in his kingdom could bring religious pacification and, therefore, reforms were needed in bureaucracy and judicial structures. Hence, the struggle with parliaments was not only a religious one, but also of authority. L'Hôpital argued that it was the king who could implement laws, as he was the only one capable of acting in the interest of the majority, both legislatively and judicially, and parliaments should have only an advisory role. Therefore, the king was limited only by God and the fundamental laws of the kingdom, something that benefited the peace-making project of L'Hôpital.[26] However, the Paris Parliament indicated that this edict was a temporary measure until religious harmony was achieved and the Protestants themselves embraced this measure with the strategy of continuing to preach and demonstrate the truthfulness of their doctrine while calling for a council, as their Catholic congeners did.[27] Therefore, both confessions were far removed from being able to respect each other, and the outbreak of civil war took place only two months after the publication of the edict.

Again, the negotiating skills of the Queen and L'Hôpital succeeded in approving the second edict of pacification, promulgated in Amboise in 1563, which ended the war. For the first time, the principle of freedom of conscience was mentioned and recognized, but the exercise of worship

24. Turchetti 1999: 170.
25. Kim 1993a: 595–620.
26. Kim 1993b: 1–29; Kim 1997: 112–14.
27. Turchetti 1985: 342; Turchetti 1991: 19–20; Robinson 2011: 54–55.

had significant restrictions according to social origin. Nobles who held the rights of high justice enjoyed broad religious freedom and the right to preach among their subjects, while most reformed people had to be content with worship in a city by *bailliage* as the city was controlled by Protestants in March of that year, although temples had to be built on the outskirts.[28] Surely all this was due to the Crown's need to attract noble elites to enlarge their clientele and strengthen their authority, something that also explains the general amnesty that was granted and the use of language based on violence containment to live as "brothers, friends and co-citizens."[29]

In fact, the edict gave status to the Calvinist religion and, from there, in some cities bi-confessional councils were formed. This citizen status established a civil peace that was maintained until 1567. This strengthened royal authority as a guarantor of the common good thanks to the achievement of confessional coexistence which Michel de L'Hôpital had defended: through provisional tolerance for a future council that would bring the kingdom together.[30] The success of this route was also thanks to a collaborator of the Queen, Jean de Monluc (?–1579), Bishop of Valence, who believed that everything should be solved through the conviction and a general council of the Church, while he also defended the measures of religious tolerance prescribed in the edicts.[31]

The situation in the Netherlands was not so influenced since the beginning by confessional matters, but by a political struggle between, on the one hand, the noble factions along with the General and the Provincial States and, on the other hand, the Brussels government under King Philip II. The cause of the revolt was rather due to the attack on some long-held freedoms, rights and prerogatives. Those irenistics close to Orange as well as other nobles and magistrates believed that the solution was not to reinforce the *placards* against heresy but to obtain some religious freedom so that a civil war would not be triggered as in France.[32] All this led to the formation of a noble league that pushed the regent, Margaret of Parma, to sign a compromise guaranteeing religious freedom if the

28. Turchetti 1999: 172–73.
29. Christin 1997: 31, 44, 110.
30. Christin 1997: 189–97; Christin 1999: 212–14; Turchetti 1999: 173.
31. Smith 1994: 46–48.
32. Martínez Millán and de Carlos Morales 2011: 242; Woltjer 1999: 185.

people lay down their arms after the outbreak of the iconoclastic riot in August 1566. This allowed Calvinists to be able to preach freely.

Calvinists were convinced that the only religious truth was within their confession, but used the argument of religious freedom to expand and strengthen themselves. In addition, they attacked religious persecutions. In his *Brief Discourse Addressed to Philip II* (1566), the Calvinist minister Franciscus Junius (1545–1602) stated that these actions weakened foreign trade and that, if the king gave them religious freedom, of conscience and worship, they would help combat atheism and Anabaptism.[33] This reformer thought that only the Scriptures were essential to the faith and since they were shared by Catholics and Calvinists, there was no clear heresy.[34]

However, the consequence of this iconoclastic and political revolt was the decision of Philip II to send to the Low Countries the Duke of Alba, along with the *tercios*, so that all subjects would return to the royal and Catholic fold. Alba's repression managed to disarm all sorts of dissent, both among Calvinists and supporters of religious freedom, to the point that Orange himself had to go into exile to avoid being tried for treason and sentenced to be beheaded.[35] It seemed that the moderate cause had succumbed, but its strength, as well as that of Calvinism, would soon recover.

In the meantime, in France, attempts were made to reach mutual confessional concessions in 1566 at the Paris conference. The king, Charles IX, and his mother continued to surround themselves with the moderate circles that aimed to achieve religious harmony, even by reforming the Catholic Church. Apart from those mentioned above, we could also talk about the important role of Paul de Foix (1528–1584) in this conference. Paul was Archbishop of Toulouse and a friend of L'Hôpital who urged a more merciful treatment of heretics and the consideration of religious freedom if a council failed,[36] as happened with the above-mentioned one.

The outbreak of the Second War of Religion (1567–1568) ended with the Peace of Longjumeau, which restored the Edict of Amboise, but also

---

33. Pettegree 1996: 183–84.
34. Zijlstra 2002: 128–29.
35. Woltjer 1999: 190.
36. Smith 1994: 44–46.

brought the fall of Michel de L'Hôpital that same year.[37] His mark was no longer present in the Edict of Saint-Maur (1568), which recognized the freedom of conscience, but not of worship. The edict considered the moment had come to achieve the long-awaited religious concord, even if it was through the use of force, something that, since its retirement, L'Hôpital had rejected, continuing to maintain its tolerant idea to build a civic concord.[38] This was because the French Crown thought it was the ideal time to end the disloyalties of the Huguenots, as the Duke of Alba was doing in Flanders, and all this called France to a third religious war (1568–1570) which resulted in a more favorable edict to the Protestant cause.

The Edict of Saint Germain (1570) was the first to guarantee several security places for the Huguenots in the event of civil war. They were also guaranteed access to educational and charitable institutions, as well as to municipal and royal trades.[39] Civil rights equality was re-established, which demonstrated the conflicts in the Court among Catholics *zélés*, those followers of the chancellor's agenda, those moderates who continued to state that the solution passed through a council and legitimized a certain use of violence and Protestants. This is the only way the swings of the Crown can be explained. Their sole purpose was to keep their prerogatives intact, although they were already beginning to be attacked from different sectors of Calvinist Monarchomachs.[40]

This very indecisive royal policy was one of the main causes of St. Bartholomew's massacre against the Huguenots on the night of August 23rd in Paris, as well as of the aftershocks that accompanied him throughout France.[41] All this led to the Fourth War of Religion (1572–1573) which ended with another edict, Boulogne's, which restricted the cult to three Calvinist security squares: La Rochelle, Mountaban, and Nîmes.

However, everything changed thereafter. The Catholics *zélés* understood that it was impossible to exterminate the Huguenots and, surprisingly, the Protestants themselves began to embrace the discourse of tolerance and coexistence. One of the Calvinist intellectuals who

37. Kim 1993a: 619.
38. Turchetti 1999: 176–77.
39. Benedict 1996: 80.
40. Zagorin 1985: 84–93.
41. An excellent analysis on the subject can be found at: Diefendorf 1991.

developed these arguments the most was Innocent Gentillet (1535–1588), a French politician who, from exile, expressed the need for reconciliation to prevent the destruction of the kingdom. It was claimed again that both confessions shared essential points in common.[42] As for the Huguenots, prominent figures emerged, such as Philippe Duplessis-Mornay (1549–1623), who noted the need for "a good and sincere peace not a covert war, friendship not ill-will, frankness not dissimulation, a lasting repose not a four-day truce,"[43] and also François de la Noue (1531–1591), who defended religious coexistence in "Political and Military Discourses," as the enemy was the minority of Catholics *zélés*. However, François continued to defend the need for a council to make his positions clear.[44] It seemed that the Huguenot movement had accepted that it would be complicated to convert by force and that tolerance was the best way to perpetuate their confession and bring them closer to the Crown.

This change in the Huguenot ranks allowed some Catholics to emerge, who were referred to as *Malcontents* or *Associés* because of their moderate nature and tendency to partner with the Huguenots to fight the power of the Guise in the court of Henry III. This opportunistic and ambiguous union, which had a very important stately component, was headed, among others, by the king's brother, Francis, Duke of Alençon; Henry of Navarre (future Henry IV); Henry of Bourbon, Prince of Condé; and the Earl of Damville and 3rd Duke of Montmorency, Henry. The latter established a bi-confessional regime during the Fifth War of Religion (1574–1576) in those cities of Languedoc where Calvinism had been worshipped.[45] The moderate sector was granted a more benign peace, but its political pragmatism makes it very different when compared to the irenistic circles and the *Politiques* of the next decade.[46]

The Edict of Beaulieu (1576) maintained the spirit of Amboise and went further by allowing freedom of worship in any area of the kingdom, except in Paris and where the Court settled. The Huguenots were given equal civil status again by ordering the creation of *chambres mi-parties* that were courts divided between Catholics and Protestants who judged

---

42. Robinson 2011: 74–79.
43. Roberts 2007: 303, 309.
44. Robinson 2011: 82–86.
45. Le Roux 2014: 167–70; Holt 1985: 53.
46. Beame 1993: 357; Turchetti 1999: 178–80.

conflicts. This parity was also present in many municipalities,[47] but its application was difficult due to the pressure of Catholics, who formalized the creation of leagues to defend their religion as the only one allowed. The Sixth War of Religion (1576–1577) ended with the Edict of Poitiers (1577), which remained related to the spirit of Amboise, but restricted the cult to the suburbs.[48] These attempts to bring peace already seemed to prefigure the *Politiques* program that would gain more momentum and relevance over the next decade.

A few years before, in 1572, the anecdotal capture of the port of Brill by the "Beggars of the sea" triggered the outbreak of a rebellion that triumphed in the northern provinces and spread southwards, with the conquest of Antwerp in 1576. Orange's discourse on religious freedom continued to be widely supported, especially when compared to the support that Alba's actions had received and also because of the occupation of the territory by the *tercios*. Following this view, the Pacification of Ghent (1576) was reached to respect both confessions, despite the attacks against Catholics in those Calvinist-controlled municipalities. This effortless ban on Catholic worship was due to the Calvinist strengthening and the apparent cooperation provided by many magistrates who thought that the priority, following Orange's speech, was to combat the "Spanish invaders."[49]

All this led to a situation where any religion opposed to the reformed one had to settle for practicing its cults in a semi-clandestine way. Thus, the Utrecht Union itself (1579), among the northern provinces, guaranteed freedom of religious conscience and one of its principles stated that "nobody shall be persecuted or examined for religious reasons."[50] Religious pluralism was evident, but the public practice of divergent religions was not desirable because of the Calvinist consistories' need for stability, especially since it was believed that Catholics could help the royalist army. However, these radical actions turned the revolt into a confessional war between the Protestant north and the Calvinist south.

47. Christin 1999: 213; Holt 1985: 66–67.
48. Martínez Millán and de Carlos Morales 2011: 218.
49. Pettegree 1996: 186–87; Israel 1997: 4.
50. Mout 1997: 41.

In the 1580s, some magistrates began to emerge and, to a lesser extent, ministers of the Reformed Church called Libertines who spoke about the need to integrate all Christians into the Church and defended heterodox positions resulting from contact with their Huguenot co-religionists. One of them was Caspar Coolhaes (1536–1615), who believed in a society where religious divisions were something of the past and his defence of the Communion of Catholics in reformed churches earned him ex-communication.[51] All of which heralded future conflicts between orthodox and heterodox Calvinists in the United Provinces in the late sixteenth and early seventeenth centuries.

After a period of rapprochement with the Huguenots following the Seventh War of Religion (1579–1580), the League's strength kept Henry III bound to those intolerant principles between 1585–1588. Succeeding the assassination of the Guise in that last year, the king sought the support of his Calvinist successor, Henry of Navarre. Subsequently the tyrannicide of Henry III, Henry IV weakened the forces of the Catholic League during the Eighth War of Religion (1588–1598) by adopting a policy of tolerance, amnesty, and clemency, but under an absolutist program that reinforced the monarchical figure against the popular dismantling *ligueurs*.[52]

The *Politiques* were the architects of the Edict of Nantes (1598), which established a bi-confessional religious regime in the name of national unity under strong monarchical power. Many of the *Politiques* had already been in the surroundings of Henry III's court and continued to be faithful to a Henry IV converted to Catholicism to end the devastation that these civil wars were causing.[53] Michel de Montaigne (1533–1592) opposed any religious extremism and argued that the king was the only authority to maintain social order and allow religious tolerance as in Germany.[54] Jean Bodin (1529/30–1596) also shared this view, and he reformulated the absolutist theory of the king by divine right and the primacy of *raison d'Etat* above any religious division.[55]

51. Kooi 2002: 89; Robinson 2011: 126–27.
52. This neostoic program has been studied by Crouzet 1990: 566–74; Wanegffelen 1997: 397–406.
53. Bettinson 2003: 48–49.
54. Wanegffelen 1997: 395–96; Roberts 2013: 3.
55. Beame 1993: 377.

Among these religious moderates was also the Catholic Pierre de L'Estoile (1546–1611), who maintained the idea of the need for reform of the Catholic Church to unite the two confessions.[56] This line of thought was shared by Calvinists Jean de Serres (1540–1598)[57] and Jean Hotman de Villiers (1552–1636). The latter, in his work *Syllabus* (1607), was nourished by all the irenistic treatises and was in contact with his Dutch counterparts. He proposed returning to the origins of the Church in order to reach religious concord in the future.[58]

The Edict of Nantes[59] responded to this program of religious and political reform announced by the *Politiques*. The aim was to achieve, through a temporary religious tolerance, a political concord that would unite the French under royal sovereignty and to achieve a religious concord in the future. As expressed by the judge and jurist Pierre de Belloy (ca. 1540–1611/1613), tolerance would last "until the need [of Reformed Church] ceases and those who profess it are better instructed, or convinced in their consciences by the Holy Spirit of their error and heresy" and the idea of a council was something that was in the king's mind and heralded a project to control the Church to a greater extent, in a Gallican sense.[60] In any case, freedom of religious conscience and Calvinist worship were recognized in the nuclei where it was present in 1596 and August 1597, as well as in the suburbs of two villas by *bailliage* and in the houses of the lords of high justice. In addition, security seats were granted where their garrisons were placed. However, Protestant worship was forbidden in Paris and five leagues around, as well as in those places where the court resided. Moreover, the king granted the Huguenots the right to access royal offices, schools, and charitable institutions, and to be part of the edict *chambers* and *mi-parties chambres* to ensure their proper compliance.[61]

This regime of civil and confessional tolerance established a social peace that, despite the fact that religious conflicts did not completely

56. Wanegffelen 1997: 465–67, 471–72.
57. Wanegffelen 1997: 451–56.
58. Meyjes 1997: 67–70.
59. A version of this and other pacification edicts can be found digitized at: http://www.religionsfrieden.de/index.php_article_id=5.html.
60. Turchetti 1989: 277–97; Turchetti 1993: 61–71; Turchetti 1998: 109–14.
61. Le Roux 2014: 348–52.

disappear and that the Huguenots were a religious minority who took time to settle down, but where no one was discussing the actual option of religious pluralism anymore.

At the end of the sixteenth century, a debate on regime tolerance began to be forged in the United Provinces of the Netherlands. The vast majority of Dutch magistrates approached the stance advocated by the Catholic Flemish Justus Lipsius (1547–1606), who considered freedom of worship to be private and did not consider freedom of religion to be a value in its own right. He thought that a strong state power should give social and political uniformity and saw full tolerance as a dividing element. Surprisingly, although Lipsius referred to the regime imposed in the Catholic Netherlands, his ideas were supported in the Dutch republic.[62]

The Libertine Calvinist minister of Haarlem, Dirck Coornhert (1522–1590) attacked these ideas, as he was opposed to any idea that forced religious uniformity and believed that religious coexistence was about accepting all confessions, which would be the civic and religious concord. He also argued that only the religious debate would lead to the understanding of what confession had the truth, and the State should not only allow the existence of the Reformed Church, as truth would not be achieved that way.[63] Statements such as "what each Church holds to be true doctrine is not the Scripture itself but its interpretation of Scripture," along with the help he provided to Haarlem Catholics, earned him the condemnation of the States of the Holland for being a "disturber of the public peace."[64] Coornhert seemed to approach Castellio's ideas as he defended complete religious freedom, but, ultimately, the objective remained to be religious concord once the truth was attained, following the thought of Erasmus.[65]

The debate on tolerance became very important since the Twelve Years' Truce (1609–1621) due to political and religious struggle within political assemblies and the Reformed Church. The struggle between the Arminians or Remonstrants (Heterodox Calvinists) and the Gomarists or Counter-Remonstrants (Orthodox Calvinists) generated a crisis in the Dutch state. The former maintained more sympathetic attitudes towards

62. Israel 1997: 6; Israel 1995: 372–74; Frijhoff 2002b: 30, 46.
63. Israel 1995: 372–74; Kaplan 2019: 74.
64. Israel 1997: 7; Tracy 1997: 57.
65. Van Nierop 2002: 104.

the other confessions and their founder, James Arminius (1560–1609). Other Arminians such as Johannes Wtenbogaert (1557–1644), Johan van Oldenbarnevelt (1547–1619), and Hugo Grotius (1589–1645) thought that the Reformed Church should accommodate other ways of living the faith, although they were intolerant with the Gomarists as they rejected any political dissent in the institutions.[66] After condemning the Arminian doctrines in the synod of Utrecht (1618–19) and their departure from the institutions, the movement began to defend a full tolerance, especially in the work of Simon Episcopius (1583–1643) who turned the argument around and believed that states remained strong if any religious or intellectual practice was free.[67]

By the end of the Eighty Years' War (1568–1648), the debate on tolerance had gone a long way and society was more tolerant regarding religious practices outside the Reformed Church. This context created a very peculiar patriotic civility that maintained peace in the country. All this brought the situation of the United Provinces closer to France before the revocation of Nantes in 1685. The debate on tolerance and its related works, which circulated through the intellectual networks of these two countries, had a great influence on the political power and responded to the reality of religious coexistence on which we now proceed to comment in a general way.

An overview of religious coexistence at the time of the Wars of Religion (1550–1650)

The confessional coexistence and religious pluralism that determined the day-to-day life of many communities in France and the Netherlands have attracted less attention from historians, but it is worth mentioning that much of the tolerant theory previously presented was based on these everyday realities. However, it is necessary to remember the enormous importance of religion as the vertebrate axis of the communities' social and political life, as their identities were also based on its principles. The cases on which we are going to comment, and which took place in France, were a kind of "islets of full tolerance." In other areas, the migration or

66. Israel 1997: 10–12.
67. Israel 1997: 18–20; Israel 1995: 503–505.

displacement of the Huguenot cult to the outskirts of towns served to maintain these minority religious practices in a space where their practice was tolerated and this involved the acceptance of this religious group and the proliferation of churches in those spaces.[68]

The Edict of Amboise (1563) regulated in several articles what urban life should be like in that situation and the local differences were very diverse—from those towns where religious minorities could only exercise freedom of conscience, to those where both confessions practiced their cults in the public space, in addition to those where religious and political parity had been established.[69] The latter case took place in the towns of Lyon, Orleans, Caen, Nyons, or Montélimar (in the latter, parity municipal charges were established) where the Protestants were able to co-manage municipal issues and the exercise of worship did not involve any problems, as it strengthened the spirit of civil concord.[70] However, all this led to difficulties. Municipal and royal authorities had to intervene when verbal violence occurred in the processions or when Protestants did not close on Catholic holidays.[71] Even so, this solidarity across communities could be maintained, in most cases, until 1568 and, for example, in the case of Limoges, a massacre in 1572 could have been avoided.[72]

Facing the threat of the outbreak of another civil war in 1568, the inhabitants of a dozen towns such as Caen, Montélimar, Annonay, Nyons, Orange, and Saint-Laurent-des-Arbres concluded solemn friendship pacts so as not to be swept away by conflict. These pacts were reached by consensus from almost the entire citizen community gathered in assemblies or general councils and agreed on how public order would be maintained in the town.[73] All this was stated in strict clauses prohibiting any form of controversy or partisan mobilization and was justified based on royal edicts and the need to live in peace under royal authority. However, for the French historian Olivier Christin, these pacts were ambiguous because of their inability to restrict certain disputes. He also considered them to be

68. Kaplan 2007: 167–68, 186.
69. Christin 1997: 80.
70. Christin 1997: 87–93.
71. Christin 1997: 108–17.
72. Christin 1997: 95–102.
73. Kaplan 2007: 218–19.

marginal as they eventually failed in contrast with the rise of the Wars of Religion.

A decade later, on the territory of the Languedoc, controlled by the Duke of Montmorency-Damville, this tolerance for both faiths was established. This was the case in the Huguenot-controlled city of Montpellier between 1574 and 1577, and then it continued after 1582. This tolerance was also established in the small town of Saillans in the Dauphiné.[74] Of course, Henry IV's arrival on the throne stabilized a long-running bi-confessional regime until 1685, even though the Protestants remained a weakened religious minority during the royal absolutism process that led to greater confessionalization and social discipline among the French.

During this time, this bi-confessional regime involved protecting and assisting in the maintenance of Catholicism and Protestantism that had churches in or outside towns, and the entire community had to collaborate with these tasks. The issue was difficult in those rural towns in which both religions had to share the sacred space and there were situations of harassment and confrontation, but so limited that they managed to maintain those regimes that were based on royal legality.[75]

It was common for Catholics and Protestants to do business together, to visit doctors or notaries of another confession, to be godparents to the child of parents from a different confession, or to teach children to be apprentices or servants in houses of other confessions. Protestants also took their children to Jesuit schools.[76] Facts such as the existence of mixed cemeteries and marriages also serve to indicate the level of religious coexistence. Although religious inbreeding was the rule, in the Protestant-majority city of Nîmes, 24 percent of marriages were mixed, while in Layrac they reached 12 percent.[77] In addition, in the public space, there were also lay festivities and it was normal for neighbors to help each other because charity was valued.

In France, the success of religious pluralism was also due to the role played by municipal elites in maintaining this status quo, the good work of royal commissioners,[78] and the rigidity and detail of successive edict

74. Benedict 1996: 78–79.
75. Kaplan 2007: 216–17.
76. Kaplan 2007: 255–56.
77. Benedict 1996: 89–90.
78. Roberts 2013: 56–75.

rules. This seemingly impartial justice also strengthened this type of regime and the king had to intervene on certain occasions to standardize the dictates of the various legal entities.[79] In conclusion, all this benefited royal power as the only one capable of ensuring peace and the common good by institutionalizing religious differences for nearly a century.

In the case of the United Provinces of the Netherlands, the only religion accepted was Calvinism and the Reformed Church was dominant, although this did not mean that the entire civic community had to be part of it. Rather, being a member of the Reformed Church involved a rigor in behavior and morality that not everyone was willing to accept and this explains why, at the end of the sixteenth century, only between 10 and 20 percent of the population belonged to it.[80] Since the time of Charles V's rule in the Netherlands, the role of religious practices and doctrines was diffuse and with the emergence of Calvinism, conversions of faith were natural even without total conviction in the postulates of the Reformation.[81]

Later, *de facto*, the Dutch Republic was constituted as a regime that tended towards tolerance of other religions to maintain civic coexistence and concord in a situation of intermittent warfare. For this reason, there was a "civil religion" that occupied the social and cultural life of Dutch citizens and defined public space as totally alien to religious differences since a common Christian tradition was emphasized.[82]

However, non-Calvinist religions had only the right of freedom of conscience, proclaimed in the Union of Utrecht (1579), and Catholic worship was not allowed, even though it did take place in the private sphere of houses. It is therefore known that Catholic or Anabaptist congregations operating semi-clandestinely in *schuilkerken* (clandestine churches that looked like houses) were formed with the complicity of some magistrates, in exchange for money or other favors so as not to face the consequences of breaking the law.[83] These *schuilkerken* were known

---

79. Roberts 2013: 232–33; Christin 1997: 164–67.
80. Spaans 2003a: 3; Spaans 2003b: 12.
81. Frijhoff 1997: 214–15.
82. Spaans 2003a: 14; Frijhoff 2002a: 39–65.
83. Kaplan 2019: 255.

to magistrates and other citizens as they were richly decorated, even with Baroque altarpieces.[84]

Consequently, this made these religions fit into Dutch society and violence and religious persecutions were absent. Additionally, local coexistence between people of different religions was normal and civil rights were the same without relying on professed religion. There were mixed marriages as there were no legal provisions against it[85] and professions and schools were shared. However, this coexistence was unequal and discriminatory because, for example, there were laws that banned entry into public offices to citizens of other confessions.[86]

Thus, in the United Provinces, there was a complex situation between a society that was strictly regulated, while tolerance was evident in day-to-day life. Even so, this cannot obviate the fact that Catholics had to constantly readjust and renegotiate a situation of absolute uncertainty and precarious accommodation. Payment to sheriffs or bailiffs was a constant pecuniary service to maintain their cult.[87] The patronage or protection given by magistrates to clerics was also related to the need for no riots in those cities where Catholics were a not-so-minority contingent and creating a system of their own was needed to continue organizing their religious life.

Apart from this everyday reality, persecutions did take place when it was thought these groups could betray the state. This explains why, in Amsterdam, Jews and Lutherans could build spaces of worship from 1630.[88] These differences in accommodating the different religious groups are also explained by the political decentralization that dominated the Dutch Republic and also by the power disputes between the magistrates and Calvinist ministers in each area. Exceptionally, in Maastricht, the lands of Overmaas and the Upper Gelderland, Catholics could practice their cults in public spaces, indicating a persistence of the old bi-confessional project.[89] That is why, in the northern part of Amsterdam, it was common

84. Kaplan 2019: 123. An overview of this phenomenon in: Kaplan 2019: 164–203; Kaplan 2007: 172–97.
85. Kaplan 2019: 298–315.
86. Kaplan 2007: 122–23.
87. Kooi 2002: 87–101.
88. Spaans 2002: 81; Israel 1995: 374–77.
89. Kaplan 2019: 21.

for magistrates to meet before large assemblies of Catholics who celebrated Mass and went on pilgrimages outside the territory. Taking all this into consideration, it was very difficult for magistrates to act.[90] At the same time, it was not strange to find Catholics and Mennonites in some local government bodies or public institutions and, in Haarlem, the existence of Catholic priests was officially accepted.[91]

The case of the Mennonites was similar to that of the Catholics as there were areas such as Friesland where they accounted for a quarter of the population. However, their situation was more stable as they were not perceived as a "fifth column" and they managed to maintain their own identity by contributing to taxes and commercial activities.[92] For the Jews, the fact that they were perceived as immigrants and had their own organization made it easier for them to maintain their worship while being socially segregated.[93]

It is also necessary to point out the situation in which the Spanish Netherlands were located. The objective of Alexander Farnese's government, from 1585, supported civic reconciliation and amnesty. All those who wished to return to Catholic territory should profess that faith, expiate their faults, and swear allegiance to Philip II. At the same time, those who had caused riots in previous years were granted the right to leave and take their property.[94] Punishment for heresy became rare during those years, unless conflicts were caused. For economic reasons, the magistrates acted with leniency towards those working in Calvinist areas and Calvinists entering the Netherlands. However, it is clear that there was no trace of religious freedom of conscience and if there was, it was only part of the strict family sphere, as was the case of four or five Calvinists in Valenciennes who, when discovered, had to go into exile for a few years to another city, but were not subjected to any greater penalty.[95]

90. Van Nierop 2002: 102–11.
91. Woltjer 1999: 200; Van Der Lem 1998: 122.
92. Zijlstra 2002: 112–21.
93. Van Rooden 2002: 132–47.
94. Junot 2017: 3–4.
95. Soen and Junot 2019: 93–96.

Conclusion

Comparative history has served to show that, since the mid-sixteenth century, there was a flow of ideas and treaties among those moderate intellectuals seeking an end to religious wars and also looking for social coexistence, which they considered possible in many territories. This work has shown that Protestant and Catholic figures shared an irenistic cultural background based on Erasmus's ideas and almost all, with the exception of Sebastian Castellio, Michel de L'Hôpital, the environment of the Prince of Orange and the Remonstrantes from 1619, defended tolerance as a temporary measure to stabilize their regimes and to achieve a civil-style concord that would restrain religious disputes. Under no circumstances was it an easy path since they faced a context of violence and religious disputes that ran through their societies. However, in the long run, they cemented a political discourse that paved the way for the end of the Wars of Religion. Moreover, they witnessed religious coexistence and that became a source of inspiration to conceive their ideas, even though tolerance had not yet been forged as a vertebrate principle of European societies. Still, their efforts built more tolerant regimes if we look back to their recent history. In France, the advances and setbacks in the edicts culminated in a bi-confessional regime that promoted Catholic coexistence with a Protestant minority, within an absolutist regime that was tending towards uniformity. As for the United Provinces, they were strengthened by the fact that, *de facto*, a non-Protestant cult was allowed in a semi-clandestine way and the new civic and political values got the rest, but it was not an oasis of full tolerance either. Although it seems contradictory, these situations eventually resulted in societies where confessional identity and social discipline were key elements in strengthening seventeen-century states.

Author biography

Alberto Hernández Pérez is currently undertaking a research initiation scholarship at the Department of Modern and American History at the University of Granada, Spain. A forthcoming article that was presented at a scientific seminar deals with the management and construction of memory by members of the Catholic militias at the end of the sixteenth century.

References

Beame, E. M. (1993), "The Politiques and the Historians," *Journal of the History of Ideas* 54/3: 355–79. Online at: https://www.jstor.org/stable/pdf/2710018.pdf?refreqid=excelsior%3A2bfb0742241a896326bb6a8e7120be31.
Benedict, P. (1996), "Un Roi, une Loi, deux Fois: Parameters for the History of Catholic-Reformed Co-existence in France, 1555–1685," in B. Scribner and O. P. Grell (eds.), *Tolerance and Intolerance in the European Reformation*, 65–93. Cambridge: Cambridge University Press.
Bettinson, C. (2003), "The Politiques and the Politique Party: A Reppraisal," in K. Cameron (ed.), *From Valois to Bourbon: Dynasty, State and Society in Early Modern France*, 35–49. Exeter: University of Exeter.
Christin, O. (1997), *La paix de religion: l'autonomisation de la raison politique au XVI siècle*. Paris: Éditions du Seuil.
Christin, O. (1999), "From Repression to Pacification: French Royal Policy in the Face of Protestantism," in P. Benedict et al. (eds.), *Reformation, Revolt and Civil War in France and the Netherlands 1555–1585*, 201–214. Amsterdam: Royal Netherlands Academy of Arts and Sciences.
Crouzet, D. (1990), *Les guerriers de Dieu: la violence au temps des troubles de religion (vers 1525—vers 1610 vol. 2)*. Seyssel: Champ Vallon.
Diefendorf, B. B. (1991), *Beneath the Cross: Catholics and Huguenots in Sixteenth-Century Paris*. New York: Oxford University Press.
Frijhoff, W. (1997), "Dimensions de la coexistence confessionnelle," in C. Berkvens-Stevelinck et al. (eds.), *The Emergence of Tolerance in the Dutch Republic*, 213–37. Leiden: Brill.
Frijhoff, W. (2002a), *Embodied Belief: Ten Essays on Religious Culture in Dutch History*. Hilversum: Uitgeverij Verloren.
Frijhoff, W. (2002b), "Religious Toleration in the United Provinces: From 'Case' to 'Model'," in R. P.-C. Hsia and H. van Nierop (eds.), *Calvinism and Religious Toleration in the Dutch Golden Age*, 27–52. Cambridge: Cambridge University Press.
Guggisberg, H. R. (1997), "Castellio: Problems of Writing a New Biography," in C. Berkvens-Stevelinck et al. (eds.), *The Emergence of Tolerance in the Dutch Republic*, 75–89. Leiden: Brill.
Guggisberg, H. R., and B. Gordon (2017), *Sebastian Castellio, 1515–1563: Humanist and Defender of Religious Toleration in a Confessional Age*. Abingdon: Routledge.

Holt, M. P. (1985), *The Duke of Anjou and the Politique Struggle during the Wars of Religion*. Cambridge: Cambridge University Press.

Huseman, W. H. (1984), "The Expression of the Idea of Toleration in French during the Sixteenth Century," *Sixteenth Century Journal* 15/3: 293–310. Online at: https://www.jstor.org/stable/pdf/2540765.pdf?refreqid=excelsior%3Ae06c1de7f6cb8c1b55c38611c449ec4e.

Israel, J. (1995), *The Dutch Republic: Its Rise, Greatness, and Fall 1477–1806*. Oxford: Clarendon Press.

Israel, J. (1997), "The Intellectual Debate about Toleration in the Dutch Republic," in C. Berkvens-Stevelinck et al. (eds.), *The Emergence of Tolerance in the Dutch Republic*, 3–36. Leiden: Brill.

Junot, Y. (2017), "Exiles-Migrants and Reconciliation in the Spanish Low Countries after the Peace of Arras (1579)," *Culture & History Digital Journal* 6/1: 1–9. https://doi.org/10.3989/chdj.2017.003

Kaplan, B. J. (2002), "'Dutch' Religious Tolerance: Celebration and Revision," in R. P-C. Hsia and H. van Nierop (eds.), *Calvinism and Religious Toleration in the Dutch Golden Age*, 8–26. Cambridge: Cambridge University Press.

Kaplan, B. J. (2007), *Divided by Faith: Religious Conflict and the Practice of Toleration*. London: Harvard University Press.

Kaplan, B. J. (2019), *Reformation and the Practice of Toleration: Dutch Religious History in the Early Modern Era*. Leiden: Brill.

Kim, S.-H. (1993a), "'Dieu nous garde de la messe du chancelier': The Religious Belief and Political Opinion of Michel de L'Hopital," *Sixteenth Century Journal* 24/3: 595–620. https://doi.org/10.2307/2542111

Kim, S.-H. (1993b), "The Chancellor's Crusade: Michel de L'Hôpital and the *Parlement* of Paris," *French History* 7/1: 1–29. https://doi.org/10.1093/fh/7.1.1

Kim, S.-H. (1997), *Michel de L'Hôpital: The Vision of a Reformist Chancellor during the French Religious Wars*. Kirksville, MO: Sixteenth Century Journal Publishers.

Kooi, C. (2002), "Paying Off the Sheriff: Strategies of Catholic Toleration in Golden Age Holland," in R. P.-C. Hsia and H. van Nierop (eds.), *Calvinism and Religious Toleration in the Dutch Golden Age*, 87–101. Cambridge: Cambridge University Press.

Le Roux, N. (2014), *Les Guerres de Religion, 1559–1629*. Paris: Belin.

Martínez Millán, J., and C. J. De Carlos Morales (2011), *Religión, política y tolerancia en la Europa Moderna*. Madrid: Ediciones Polifemo.

Meyjes, H. P. (1997), "Tolérance et irénisme," in C. Berkvens-Stevelinck et al. (eds.), *The Emergence of Tolerance in the Dutch Republic*, 63–73. Leiden: Brill.

Mout, M. E. H. N. (1997), "Limits and Debates: A Comparative View of Dutch Toleration in the Sixteenth and Early Seventeenth Century," in

C. Berkvens-Stevelinck et al. (eds.), *The Emergence of Tolerance in the Dutch Republic*, 37–47. Leiden: Brill.

Pettegree, A. (1996), "The Politics of Toleration in the Free Netherlands, 1572–1620," in B. Scribner and O. P. Grell (eds.), *Tolerance and Intolerance in the European Reformation*, 182–98. Cambridge: Cambridge University Press.

Roberts, P. (2007), "The Languages of Peace during the French Religious Wars," *Cultural and Social History* 4/3: 297–315. https://doi.org/10.2752/147800407X219223

Roberts, P. (2013), *Peace and Authority during the French Religious Wars 1560–1600*. Basingstoke: Palgrave Macmillan.

Robinson, D. L. (2011), "Calvinism and Religious Toleration in France and the Netherlands, 1555–1609," PhD thesis, University of New Brunswick.

Smith, M. C. (1994), "Early French Advocates of Religious Freedom," *Sixteenth Century Journal* 25/1: 29–51. https://doi.org/10.2307/2542551

Soen, V., and Y. Junot (2019), "Changing Strategies of State and Urban Authorities in the Spanish Netherlands towards Exiles and Returnees during the Dutch Revolt," *Journal of Early Modern Christianity* 6/1: 69–98. https://doi.org/10.1515/jemc-2019-2003

Spaans, J. (2002), "Religious Policies in the Seventeenth-century Dutch Republic," in R. P.-C. Hsia and H. van Nierop (eds.), *Calvinism and Religious Toleration in the Dutch Golden Age*, 72–86. Cambridge: Cambridge University Press.

Spaans, J. (2003a), "Reform in the Low Countries," in R. P.-C. Hsia (ed.), *A Companion to the Reformation World*, 1–17. Oxford: Blackwell.

Spaans, J. (2003b), "Violent Dreams, Peaceful Coexistence: On the Absence of Religious Violence in the Dutch Republic," *De Zeventiende Eeuw* 18: 1–18. Online at: http://dspace.library.uu.nl/handle/1874/26642.

Tracy, J. D. (1997), "Erasmus, Coornhert and the Acceptance of Religious Disunity in the Body Politic: A Low Countries Tradition?," in C. Berkvens-Stevelinck et al. (eds.), *The Emergence of Tolerance in the Dutch Republic*, 49–62. Leiden: Brill.

Turchetti, M. (1985), "'Concorde ou tolérance?' de 1562 à 1598," *Revue Historique* 274/2: 341–55. Online at: https://www.jstor.org/stable/pdf/40954309.pdf?refreqid=excelsior%3Ae29502184e00d3a9933278ccaac21685.

Turchetti, M. (1989), "Henri IV entre la concorde et la tolérance," in Colloque de Pau-Nerac (ed.), *Advenement d'Henri IV. Quattrieme Centenaire*, 277–99. Pau: J&D Editions. Online at: https://core.ac.uk/download/pdf/43663835.pdf.

Turchetti, M. (1991), "Religious Concord and Political Tolerance in Sixteenth- and Seventeenth- Century France," *Sixteenth Century Journal* 22/1: 15–25. Online at: https://www.jstor.org/stable/pdf/2542013.pdf?refreqid=excelsior%3A3c891f88ff75c77bc15da00af4129218.

Turchetti, M. (1993), "Une question mal posée: La qualification de 'perpétuel et irrévocable' appliquée à l'Édit de Nantes (1598)," *Bulletin de la Société de l'Histoire du Protestantisme Français (1903–2015)* 139: 41–78. Online at: https://www.jstor.org/stable/pdf/24297156.pdf?refreqid=excelsior%3A70c5cc4884fe3713d763dda504f17de8.

Turchetti, M. (1998), "L'arrière-plan politique de l'édit de Nantes, avec un aperçu de l'anonyme De la concorde de l'Estat. Par l'observation des Edicts de Pacification (1599)," *Bulletin de la Société de l'Histoire du Protestantisme Français (1903–2015)* 144: 93–114. Online at: https://www.jstor.org/stable/pdf/43498916.pdf?refreqid=excelsior%3A72bf6fa978fed2eca60d0bfc227df05e.

Turchetti, M. (1999), "Middle Parties in France during the War of Religions," in Philip Benedict et al. (eds.), *Reformation, Revolt and Civil War in France and the Netherlands 1555–1585*, 165–83. Amsterdam: Royal Netherlands Academy of Arts and Sciences.

Van der Lem, A. (1998), "Concordia et pax civium. La valeur de la tolérance aux Provinces-Unies: qualité positive ou négative?," in G. Saupin et al. (eds.), *La tolérance: colloque international de Nantes (mai 1998): quatrième centenaire*, 121–25. Rennes: Presses Universitaires de Rennes.

Van Nierop, H. (2002), "Sewing the Bailiff in a Blanket: Catholics and the Law in Holland," in R. P.-C. Hsia and H. van Nierop (eds.), *Calvinism and Religious Toleration in the Dutch Golden Age*, 102–111. Cambridge: Cambridge University Press.

Van Rooden, P. (2002), "Jews and Religious Toleration in the Dutch Republic," in R. P.-C. Hsia and H. van Nierop (eds.), *Calvinism and Religious Toleration in the Dutch Golden Age*, 132–47. Cambridge: Cambridge University Press.

Van de Schoor, R. (1997), "The Reception of Cassander in the Republic in the Seventeenth Century," in C. Berkvens-Stevelinck et al. (eds.), *The Emergence of Tolerance in the Dutch Republic*, 101–15. Leiden: Brill.

Wanegffelen, T. (1997), *Ni Rome, ni Genève. Des fidèles entre deux chaires en France au xvie siècle*. Paris: Honoré Champion.

Woltjer, J. (1999), "Political Moderates and Religious Moderates in the Revolt of the Netherlands," in Philip Benedict et al. (eds.), *Reformation, Revolt and Civil War in France and the Netherlands 1555–1585*, 185–200. Amsterdam: Royal Netherlands Academy of Arts and Sciences.

Zagorin, P. (1985), *Revueltas y revoluciones en la Edad Moderna*. Madrid: Cátedra.

Zijlstra, S. (2002), "Anabaptism and Tolerance: Possibilities and Limitations," in R. P.-C. Hsia and H. van Nierop (eds.), *Calvinism and Religious Toleration in the Dutch Golden Age*, 112–31. Cambridge: Cambridge University Press.

Chapter 9
Religious Co-Existence in Malta, 1530–1798

Frans Ciappara

Introduction

Confessionalization studies generally concentrate on the processes of differentiation—religious, social, and cultural—underlying thereby the strengthening of the barriers among different confessional groups. Samuel P. Huntington describes the encounter between Christianity and Islam as a "clash of civilizations."[1] This dichotomy is also apparent, among others, in Norman Daniel, *Islam and the West*, Paolo Preto, *Venezia e i Turchi*, and Dorothy Vaughan, *Europe and the Turk*.[2] However, scholars have largely abandoned this discourse under the influence of the new cultural history.[3] Molly Greene, for one, discarding this bipartite vision of the early modern Mediterranean, argues for a "shared world" and describes the peaceful coexistence of Muslims and Christians on Crete after the Ottomans had conquered the island from the Venetians in 1669.[4] Richard Bulliet concurs; far from being diametrically opposed, the histories of Christianity and Islam are so closely intertwined that the Mediterranean should be envisioned in terms of a shared Islamo-Christian civilization.[5] Eric Dursteler, writing about the Venetians in Constantinople, puts it even

1. Huntington 1993: 22–49.
2. Daniel 2000; Preto 1975; Vaughan 1976.
3. See, for instance, Burke 1997: 191–206 and Hunt 1989.
4. Greene 2000.
5. Bulliet 2004: 1–43.

more bluntly. We should not perceive the Mediterranean world in simple binary divisions that assume an inherent collision between civilizations. Only then, he states, can the striking evidences of peace and co-existence between peoples of diverse religious and cultural backgrounds be more readily understood.[6] This rapprochement is especially striking in frontier areas where, Jonathan Riley-Smith reminds us, acculturation is a recurring theme; frontiers not only separate but even unite people.[7]

This topic is particularly concerned with the island of Malta in the center of the Mediterranean, a busy thoroughfare with Christians, Muslims, and Jews crossing paths. Like Venice, it was "uniquely situated to function as both boundary and cultural middle ground, a place of transition in which people from throughout the Mediterranean and from every corner of Europe came together."[8] This chapter aims to examine the nature of these cultural contacts and asks whether the Hospitaller frontiersmen and the Maltese Church, especially the inquisitors, were hostile to any form of cultural ambiguity in consonant with the moral strictness of a triumphant Roman Catholicism. Did they respect the other cultures and follow a policy of peaceful coexistence and mutual toleration? The research is based mainly on the rich archives of the Roman inquisition in Malta housed at the cathedral museum at Mdina and the deposits at the National Library at Valletta.[9]

"An open and closed door"

Significantly, the Augustinian friar Anguisciola, who preached the sermon when the first stone of Valletta was laid in March 1566, referred to Malta not only as a "secure fortress" and a "reliable seat" of the Hospitaller Order of St John but, just as importantly, as "a shield to Sicily, a bulwark to Italy, and a hindrance to the infidels."[10] His comments tell us a great

---

6. Dursteler 2008: 185.
7. Riley-Smith 2012: 121–31.
8. Dursteler 2008: 2–3.
9. For details of how these rich deposits escaped being fed to the fire during the French invasion of Malta in 1798, see Ciappara 2000: 24.
10. Abela 1647: 12. He had made the same remarks a month earlier when he delivered an oration to the chapter general of the Order. See Zammit-Ciantar 2008: 16–26.

deal about the island's strategic importance. If it were to be conquered it would serve as an ideal place for the conquest of the Christian West, "a disaster for Christendom."[11] Malta, like Poland[12] and other frontier areas,[13] was a gate or a door to Christendom.

This image is pregnant with meaning because it includes the concepts of both exclusion and inclusion, an open and a closed door, a rampart and a fluid frontier. It must be established first whether Malta and the Muslim world, especially North Africa, could be identified as two irreconcilable enemies. The answer is definitely no, the most cogent reason being their essential economic interdependence.[14] Far from being a barrier, the Maltese frontier played the role of a "living membrane," a "trading frontier." Its bastions, as Michel Balard has said of medieval Caffa, were only a symbolic boundary; they were formidable and awe-inspiring but porous to every influence.[15]

Commercial imperatives oblige the various ethnic groups to maintain constant relations in border areas.[16] Malta was no exception since it carried a considerable trade with the regencies.[17] Maltese merchants went to trade at Sfax, Tunis, and Tripoli,[18] thereby going against the wishes of Inquisitor Mgr Giacomo Cantelmo who in 1680 recommended to Grand Master Gregorio Carafa to issue passports with greater attention to prevent people from going to Barbary.[19] In return, Muslims and Jews came

---

11. Braudel 1973: 1014, 1017.
12. For the emergence of the concept of Poland as one of the bulwarks of Europe, see Knoll 1974: 381–401.
13. Berend 2002: 208–15; Berend 2003: 1012.
14. These commercial encounters were further enhanced by diplomatic relations. Take the case of the Bey of Tunis who in 1737 asked the help of the Order to regain his throne. Inquisitor Carlo Francesco Durini sought the advice of the cardinal inquisitors, who assented on the condition that the war armaments would not be used against Christians. See Vatican City, ACDF, St St HH4-d, unnumbered, Gualtieri to the cardinal inquisitors, October 25, 1748.
15. Balard 2002: 147–50.
16. Audisio 1996: 317, 326.
17. For the case of Genoa and the Franco-Genoese Salt Company which operated from Zarzis, Tunis, see Boubaker 1990: 123–39.
18. For the two tailors Gaspare Calleja and Francesco Refalo at Alexandria in 1742, see AIM, Proc. 121B, f. 866r.
19. AIM, Corr. 14, f. 24r, Card. Cybo to Mgr Cantelmi, June 8, 1680.

244 *Narratives of Peace in Religious Discourses*

to Malta with their wares.[20] A good example of how infidel merchants were welcomed in Malta and went wherever they pleased is provided by the Jew Judas Sitbon. On June 27, 1768 he imported from Tunis on board the Ragusan ship *La Madonna del Rosario, S. Biagio e S. Nicola* (Captain Luca Sargotta) a merchandise of oil, soap, sallow, butter, cuscus, and tanned leather.[21] He lived with his servant in two rooms at the far end of the *barriera* or quarantine post and though he was not supposed to go abroad at nighttime he attended the theatre several times and went to see the fireworks at Valletta.[22] More remarkable is the case of the Jew, Samuele Farfara. In 1728 Mgr Serbelloni complained to Grand Master de Vilhena that Farfara had been in Malta already for five years without his permission.[23] The grand master, who let Farfara stay in a room at his palace, even keeping its key,[24] opposed the inquisitor's sole right to issue safe conducts to infidels. The Maltese ambassador reminded Pope Benedict XIII that that right belonged exclusively to the government. De Vilhena was only imitating other Christian princes in this endeavor and, besides, the presence of these traders in Malta could be profitable both to the treasury and the inhabitants, Farfara having been instrumental in the redemption of several Christian slaves.[25]

"The enemy within"

The above information makes the theory of a sharply divided Christian and Muslim world untenable and must be discarded. This chapter, though,

20. The Maltese government rarely issued passports to "Turkish" captains but made them use European vessels to subject their economy to the merchant navies of the Christian states. See Valensi 1963: 82.
21. NLM, Arch. 6529, f. 383v. That year he also imported calves, beans, canary seed, spelt, dates, camel skins, tobacco, barley and maize. See Ciappara 2003: 451.
22. AIM, Proc. 129, ff. 335r–338r.
23. NLM, Libr. 703, f. 21r; AIM, Corr. 95, f. 2v, Card. Ottoboni to Mgr Stoppani, May 31, 1732. On August 1, 1716, the cardinal inquisitors left it to the pro-inquisitor's discretion whether to let the Jew Sabatai Gignati come to Malta from Venice with his son and servant to attend to his business matters. See AIM, Corr. 21, f. 61r, Card. Spada to Pro-Inquisitor Napulone, August 1, 1716.
24. ACDF, St St HH4-b (1729), unnumbered.
25. AIM, Corr. 94, ff. 216v–217v, Mgr Serbelloni to Card. Otthoboni, November 6, 1728. See also ibid., ff. 226r–227r, Serbelloni to Otthoboni, February 12, 1729.

is concerned more with captives than with free men[26] because, if Malta and North Africa cultivated friendly relations,[27] they still preyed on each other's shipping and hordes of slaves oiled their economy. How this feature of society arose must now be explained. The Mediterranean enjoyed relative peace after the battle of Lepanto (1571) until the first half of the seventeenth century.[28] The two empires of Spain and Turkey, which had up until then dominated the Mediterranean and fought each other for a century, turned their attention elsewhere. Spain was engaged in a long series of wars while the Ottoman Empire likewise experienced a long political, economic, and military crisis. The death of the Sultan Selīm II (1566–1574) signified the suspension of Ottoman military activity in the Mediterranean. Wars in the east against Persia were followed with others on the European front. The length of these conflicts, together with a massive mobilization of men, had a disastrous effect on the finances of the empire. At the same time, the Barbary regencies in North Africa declared their independence from the sultan. Unable to fight on several fronts, the two empires concluded peace in 1581.[29]

The vacuum created by the withdrawal of Spain and Turkey allocated a free space to the dynamic Protestant states from the north of Europe, especially the Dutch and the British.[30] Besides, the resulting insecurity, with no state strong enough to impose order, was succeeded by another kind of war—the "long sordid war" of corsairing. The "tired giants," as Fernand Braudel calls Spain and Turkey, were replaced by upstarts such as Malta, whose economy, like Leghorn's, experienced a boom without precedence. As well as representing an answer to the regencies' increasing danger, this informal kind of war was also a vital means with which Malta justified its existence. Lying in the bottleneck between Sicily and North Africa, it was perfectly placed to act the part of what Peter Earle

---

26. These amounted to only a handful. In 1729, for instance, the Jews totalled only three. See AIM, Corr. 94, f. 226r, Mgr Serbelloni to Card. Otthoboni, February 12, 1729.
27. Brogini 2006: 358–70. See also Ciappara 2001: 223–25; Ciappara 2004: 165–87; Ciappara 2008: 23–35.
28. For how Lepanto fits into the history of the Mediterranean, see Benzoni 1974. For the historical impact of the holy league's victory, see Hess 1972: 53–73.
29. Bigelow Merriman 1962: 78–156.
30. Greene 2002: 42–71.

called "the capital of Christian piracy" or, as Pierre Boyer put it, "the great Mediterranean market of Muslim slaves."[31]

Captives constituted a significant number in Malta. A papal official reported in 1582 that more than 600 belonged to the Order of St John and 200 to private owners.[32] Of a population of about 35,000 this equated to 2.3 percent. This was a smaller percentage than, say, Seville's, where the proportion was 3.3 percent in 1565 but higher than in Sicily, where it was only 1 percent for the same period.[33] By 1630 the number of slaves in Malta had increased to 3,000 (5.9 percent of the population)[34] but by the end of the eighteenth century it had fallen to 1,000 or 1.0 percent[35] as a result of the decline of the importance of corsairing.[36]

The problem now is: how was this "enemy within" treated? Did the slaves and the local Catholic population on the island enjoy peaceful co-existence? What is beyond doubt is that the presence of these infidels among Christians could be a source of corruption. The challenge that they posed to the Catholic identity of the island of Malta was real enough, as the following incident vividly illustrates. "Do you believe that Jesus Christ is the Son of God?," a Jew asked in 1613 Giacoba, the widow of Oliveri Formosa. "This is not true because there is only one God." He denied that Jesus ever made miracles, least of all having resuscitated himself from death. And, besides, if he were the Son of God could he not have redeemed humankind without suffering and dying? "Moreover, we Jews why did we kill him if he was not an evil doer?"[37]

Lest the infidels, therefore, contaminated the inhabitants with their beliefs, the divide between them and Christians had to be marked in a number of ways. Slaves were "forced into a sort of internal exile," confined within "prisons" or *bagnos*.[38] And since "one should know with whom one is talking" they wore distinctive marks to be distinguished

---

31. Earle 1970; Boyer 1969: 53–74. See also Fontenay 2001: 391–414 and Gauci 2016.
32. NLM, Libr. 1306, f. 8r.
33. Bono 1993: 194–95.
34. Bonnici 1974: 315, n. 46.
35. Wettinger 2002: 553–62.
36. Cavaliero 1959: 224–38.
37. AIM, Proc. 32B, ff. 635r–640v.
38. *Decreta Melivetanae* 1647: 17–18. See also NLM, Libr. 5: 236–37. For the various possible origins of the term *bagno*, see Audisio 1957: 363–80. For a detailed description of these *bagnos*, see Wettinger 2002: 85–125.

from Christians.[39] A law of 1593 ordered iron rings for all of them, worn visibly on the foot and weighing twelve ounces,[40] while from 1663 onwards they all had their hair cut short except for a *bisbusa* (tuft).[41] The legal restrictions imposed on Jews were likewise meant to humiliate them in order to bring them to convert, make them feel their inferiority and realize that they were a race apart. Cardinal Ruffo ordered Inquisitor Passionei in 1753 to keep them under his watchful eye and, in accordance with Pius IV's Bull *Cum Nimis absurdum* of 1555, to see that they wore a distinctive headgear, a yellow, finger-wide ribbon around their hat to differentiate them from Christians.[42]

It is small wonder that a great deal of attention was dedicated to matters of sexual purity. In a document from 1658 we read that Grand Master de Redin issued a proclamation against sexual relations between Christians and infidels. It decreed the stiffest penalties against "mixing the blood of dogs with that of Christians which has been redeemed by the blood of Jesus Christ." Slaves who were caught with women could be whipped and have their ears and nose cut off.[43] These laws must have proved largely ineffectual because in 1667 Grand Master Nicholas Cottoner prohibited the slaves from hawking their wares around the streets of Valletta in order "to prevent as much as possible giving offence to His Divine Majesty."[44] By 1691 the slaves were again "entering without any fear the houses of scandalous and dishonest women at all hours of the day." The comment that needs to be made here is that the boundaries between the faiths were not always well defined or rigidly enforced. It is clear that the harshest laws could not keep all the slaves chaste all the time and, to cite one more instance, in 1742 a Muslim slave was arrested and condemned to row for two years on the galleys on being found inside the door of a Christian woman's house while buying an old dress from her.[45]

---

39. AIM, Memorie 3, f. 7v.
40. NLM, Libr. 704, f. 101v.
41. NLM, Libr. 738: 299–300.
42. NLM, Libr. 703, f. 21v; AIM, Corr. 91, f. 226r, Card. Ruffo to Mgr Passionei, April 30, 1753; Skippon 1732: 621. On the marking and restriction of the Jews, see Hughes 1986: 3–59.
43. NLM, Libr. 738: 234–39.
44. NLM, Libr. 740, part C, ff. 91r-v.
45. NLM, Libr. 666, entries dated October 25, 26 and 31, 1742.

As a response to the crossing of one another's thresholds the Maltese Church sought to construct the parameters of Christian–Muslim relations, too. Sexual intercourse of Christians with non-Christians was a reserved sin, forgiveness for which needed the consent of a higher authority than that of the parish clergy.[46] In addition, the diocesan synod of 1620 legislated to mark the social distance between the infidels and the rest of civil society. Christians were not to go to their festivities, receive medicines from them, or take their sick to them to be cured. Nor were they to hold anything in common with them but as much as possible keep away from all feasting or commerce with them.[47]

The Inquisition

Inquisitor Lazzaro Pallavicini (1718–1719) recorded in his memoirs that Malta was so near to Africa; it was exposed to the "violent whirlwind of the wicked opinions of the Muslims," and he warned his successors to guard against the "tiring tempests sustained by the great quantity of infidel slaves."[48] In "so small and lazy a place like Malta" they could easily undermine Christianity, making it seem fragile. This comment points to a very real problem because if captives were separated from the indigenous population by their religion, in the case of the Muslims, their language meant that they could mix freely with the Maltese, who spoke a form of Maghribī (North African) Arabic.

Archival material sheds much light on the efforts of the inquisitors to safeguard the inhabitants from the threatened perversion of the people.[49] The Roman Inquisition was set up in 1542 to defend Catholicism against the northern reformers as much as to reactivate Catholic life.[50] Inquisitors were instructed to maintain the purity of holy faith and see that the souls of Christians "were not infected with false opinions."[51] Slaves, therefore, were prosecuted if they offended Christian sensibility, for instance

46. NLM, Libr. 6, f. 107v.
47. Wettinger 2002: 451.
48. AIM, Memorie 3, f. 2r.
49. On this point, see Clancy-Smith 2011: 76.
50. To cite two general works, Del Col 2006 and Black 2009.
51. AIM, Microfilm 6530, f. 1v.

when they blasphemed against God and the saints,[52] ill-treated sacred images, slapping[53] or spitting at them,[54] or further, when they referred to Catholicism as "the religion of dogs and thieves"[55] or as another form of idolatry and a "dirty religion full of inventions," which labels mysterious anything that cannot be explained by reason.[56]

Reports on the activities of slaves reveal a disrespectful attitude towards the things of the Church, disparaging the practices admired and celebrated by the faithful. Vincenzo Czarin reported in 1642 that Giacchi d'Elia refused to doff his cap as the host passed by in procession and instead pulled it down his eyes as much as he could, saying, "It isn't God."[57] The strongest theme that comes out of looking at these instances is the threat that slaves offered to the "vulnerable" Maltese and to good Christian living. Homosexuality, of course, was intimately related to this discourse.[58] It was the worst of all sexual sins, and was regarded with so much horror that in 1744 the capuchin *padre* Andrea could not bring himself to name it directly but referred to it as *il peccato nefando* (the nefarious sin).[59] There is no easy way to gauge the frequency of these perceived deviances but a few examples do flesh them out, making it possible to obtain a brief glimpse into these most personal experiences. The grand master, announcing in 1691 that he wanted to prevent the "execrable

52. AIM, Proc. 121A, ff. 283r–303v.
53. On Friday, April 1, 1757, the feast of Our Lady of Sorrows, Claudio Azzupardo, the *procuratore* of the *sodalità della Beatissima Vergine dei Dolori*, was collecting alms at the entrance of the convent of the Friars Minor, Valletta. Towards 4.30 pm, while the faithful were gathering at the oratory nearby to assist at vespers, a six-year-old Jewish boy slapped an *Ecce Homo* of papier mâché exhibited on a small table. See AIM, Proc. 124B, ff. 665r–667r.
54. The case refers to Moyse Buynac, a Jew who wore a large wig and a dark blue jerkin. On September 1749, towards 3.00 pm, he entered the church of the minims and went round the altars. As he looked fixedly at the paintings, he spat each time on the ground. See AIM, Proc. 121C, ff. 1540r–1543v.
55. AIM, Proc. 133A, ff. 328r–329v.
56. AIM, Proc. 132B, ff. 943r–952v.
57. He was tied to a column in the main square of Vittoriosa and lashed. AIM, Proc. 55A, ff. 488r–505v.
58. For the proverbial addiction of the Muslims to such practices, see Cervantes's *Don Quixote*: "among those barbarous Turks a handsome boy or youth is more highly prized than the most beautiful woman" (1970: 884).
59. AIM, Proc. 120B, ff. 840r–841v.

crimes" that were wont to be committed through the friendships that infidels had with beardless youths, prohibited them from entering the slaves' prisons.[60] He would not have issued such a decree if no such practices existed, and in fact there are references to slaves caught red-handed alone with a lad in a cellar, a shop, in a small room (*gorboċ*) in the vicinity of the mosque, or near the tunnel beneath the convent of the capuchins at Floriana.[61]

Nonetheless, these challenges to the moral ordering of Malta were minimal when compared to the number of witchcraft cases with which slaves were charged. In Malta witchcraft has little or nothing to do with the Sabbat[62] or with witches riding brooms.[63] The Maltese sought slaves' services to retrieve lost objects, win the hand of a lover, identify thieves, make a husband impotent, cast a spell *ad mortem* on an enemy, become wise and virtuous and, since slaves claimed to undo as well as to cast spells, to be cured from a curse or malefice.[64]

Needless to say, all these practices were a threat to the Church and inquisitors campaigned virulently against them, even when they brought relief from illness. In the middle of the seventeenth century Mgr Federico Borromeo (1653–1654) expressed his preoccupation with the Muslim slaves who spread "vanities" among the women and the simple-minded while they went about the town "selling their wretched goods."[65] Like other inquisitors he was particularly troubled by their fumigations, incense, candles, magical circles and numbers, which were a real threat to correct Christian practice and true doctrine. This was the time when the Church authorities were seeking to define and regulate access to the power of the sacred and opposed such attempts. Can the host, for instance, be used for witchcraft purposes? Are not sacramentals to be used only to worship God?[66] Did not their use in such experiments, therefore, imply, as

---

60. NLM, Libr. 740, part C, ff. 131 et seq.
61. NAM, Libro dei Carcerati (1781–88), ff. 6r, 52r, 142r, 129r.
62. For a solitary instance describing how the Discalced Carmelite nun Caterina, having anointed herself with some white and stinking ointment, flew in 1741 on a cow to meet the devil, see AIM, Proc. 118B, ff. 855r–863r.
63. Cassar 2004: 25–41.
64. On this topic, see Ciappara 2001: 261–320.
65. NLM, Libr. 23, f. 258v.
66. For the way sacramentals could become magical, see Scribner 1993: 480.

Aquinas explains in *Summa Contra Gentiles*, reverence towards another power other than God Himself?[67]

This is a crucial point for the ceremonies were acts of worship. By attributing to the devil powers that are God's alone, for instance to foresee the future, meant placing the devil on a par with God. Is not divination a sacrilegious wish to take mastery from God over time? Can the devil force the free will of men into love or hate? Is it not unworthy to ask God for such base and selfish ends to receive stolen goods and capture thieves or to further adultery, theft, and murder? Were not such invocations, therefore, directed to the devil? And did not "unknown characters" written on pieces of paper to make people rich or invisible if placed on the head and wise and virtuous when tied round the arm represent the names of demons? Finally, were not the salt, alum, and blood used in these practices payment for the devil for his services?[68]

Inquisitors were deeply concerned to prevent the Maltese from falling into these heresies and lashed out against the demonic inspiration behind these activities. In 1756, therefore, Tuppan, the lame slave from Jerusalem of the *gran visconte* (commissioner of police) had his hands tied and put on a donkey, wearing a miter on his head and a placard denoting his crime on his breast. Heralded by the secular court's trumpeter, he was whipped through the streets of Vittoriosa, Senglea, and Cospicua.[69]

"The *Giornata*"

Jews were a "perverse nation," who, according to Gregory X (1271–1276), "prefer to persist in their stubbornness rather than to recognize

---

67. Aquinas 1914, Book 3, Part II: 67–75.
68. The literature on this topic is vast. See, among others, Martin 1989; Ruggiero 1993; Duni 2008; Decker 2008: 185–93; O'Neil 1987: 88–114; Watt 2010: 675–89.
69. According to Giuseppe Pace, a chair maker from Valletta, the experiment consisted in trying to find a golden cow and a silver calf which he had dreamed were in the catacombs of Rabat. He lighted eight lamps and stopped at the place where the treasure possibly was, while praising God and cursing the devil. Next, he fumigated the place with benzoin three or four times daily; and on the ninth day, having heard several noises, he started reading from a book to quieten the demon. Then he cut the throat of a hedgehog, a white hen and a black cock and poured their blood in a hole where the treasure was supposedly hidden. See AIM, Proc. 125B, ff. 595r–608v.

the words of their prophets and the mysteries of the Scriptures, and thus to arrive at a knowledge of Christian faith and salvation." For their part, Muslims were "dogs" and "enemies of the Christian name," followers of the "sect of the wicked and damned Muhammad."[70] These are revealing words which show how sharp could be the feeling of the boundary between the Maltese Catholics and the infidels. The extraordinary expression of violence that accompanied the slaves' uprising in 1749, the executioner tearing bits of flesh from the rebels' limbs with red-hot pliers and pouring boiling pitch on the open wounds before being hanged or quartered, underlined the deep cultural division between the two civilizations. Only long-repressed anger mixed with a hatred of an alien religion and a social system can explain the vicious behavior that accompanied the revolt's collapse.[71]

Slaves were captives, chattels to be bought, sold, or exchanged at will. In 1553 Mahamete Jubel, a slave of Grand Master Homedes, was sent as a present to the wife of the viceroy of Sardinia[72] while in 1637 two well-dressed slave-girls were given to the wife of the viceroy of Naples.[73] Those of them found roaming in the countryside unaccompanied at night were arrested.[74] They were punished for fighting, robbery, stealing, drunkenness, opium smoking, homicide, and for ill behavior in general. According to one attentive historian of slavery,

> They were far from being always the cowed and submissive victims of circumstances one might imagine, and their frequent acts of brigandage and their general lawlessness were a continual worry to the law-abiding public and a well-nigh insoluble problem to the government.[75]

There is no doubting the abject status of the slaves, but one must be careful not to present too gloomy a picture of the life of the slaves as

70. For perceptions of Muslims in Maltese literature, see Vella Gauci 2010 and Galea 2006: 29–34.
71. Testa 1989: 119–27. There are several contemporary accounts of the revolt but see especially Acciard 1751.
72. NLM, Arch. 423, ff. 229r-v.
73. NLM, Arch. 218, ff. 222r-v.
74. AIM, Proc. 110B, ff. 775r-v; AIM, Proc. 113B, ff. 506r-v.
75. Wettinger 2002: 532.

being unduly ill-treated. As Salvatore Bono has observed for Italy,[76] so too for Malta: if Muslim slaves were harassed, the same fate would befall Maltese captives held in Turkish lands.[77] Accordingly, in July 1720 Grand Master Zondadari assured the apostolic prefect of Tunis that he would not fail to ask the Bey to deal in a charitable manner with the Christian slaves in Tunis in the way he himself dealt with the Muslim slaves in Malta.[78] In confirmation of this good treatment, the slaves owned by the Order were issued with a complete outfit of winter and summer clothes[79] as well as a daily ration of bread[80] and a plateful of *minestra* (soup).[81] When sick they were taken to the infirmary at their prison in Valletta. Here they did not sleep on hard boards as otherwise they would never regain their health, and they were well provided with food, too: mutton, chicken, pullet, eggs, soup and bread. The doctor, who had to be available both day and night for urgent calls, made two daily visits of the sick in the company of one of the *prodomi* (the prison heads) and wrote prescriptions for them.[82]

And, as has been observed for other Catholic countries like Genoa,[83] slaves carried on their own private enterprise during slack periods of work and on feast-days. They had only to pay a fee for leave of absence, known as the *giornata* to the *agozzino* (the official responsible for the security of the *bagnos*). They were shoemakers and shoe-repairers, woodcarvers, butchers, blacksmiths, tailors, greengrocers, and coopers. Hairdressing and shaving were two of their main tasks, which they exercised inside the slave prison at Valletta, in a room at fort St Elmo, or near the statue of Neptune at the Valletta wharf.[84]

Most slaves preferred, though, to hawk their wares around the streets of the towns and villages. In 1656 Rimeli, a slave of the Order, sold second-hand objects[85] and a proclamation of 1574 referred to the fact that

76. Bono 1983: 85–102; Bono 1994: 331–51; Bono 1999: 89–93.
77. NLM, Arch. 452, ff. 277v–284v.
78. NLM, Arch. 1481, letter dated July 31, 1720.
79. NLM, Arch. 296, ff. 165 seq.
80. NLM, Arch. 636, f. 102v.
81. NLM, Arch. 296, ff. 166r-v.
82. Wettinger 2002: 509.
83. Bono 1999: 90.
84. They also erected their booths around the palace but on February 27, 1741 the grand master had them removed to behind the Jesuits' church. See NLM, Libr. 9: 430.
85. NLM, Arch. 666, ff. 281r-v.

most of the meat of animals and most of the hens and other poultry as well as eggs were bought and sold by way of retail throughout Malta by the Muslim and Jewish slaves.[86] They sold all kind of wares, from tobacco, carob beans, oil, chickpeas and spoons, to hairpins, water, bread, dates and slippers, as well as candles, soap, ox-hides, indigo, cloth, and iron-ware, to leather goods, fans, brooms, baskets, garlic and honey. Some of them were porters and scavengers while others repaired *capotti* or went round with an axe on their shoulder breaking logs for firewood. They ran errands and washed linen for whoever asked for their services. And it was to the slaves, too, especially Jewish captives, that the Maltese went to pawn their belongings like a hat or a skirt, and more generally when they were ill.[87]

Religious acculturation?

But was there any mechanism for their assimilation in the religious culture of their masters? The legacy of the forced baptisms of Jews and Muslims in Spain and Portugal, many of whom continued to practice their former religion, weighed heavily on the conscience of the Church authorities. Paul III (1534–1549) questioned the legitimacy of involuntary baptisms and in 1543, by means of the bull *Illius in articulos fidei*, he founded the *Casa dei Catecumeni* at Rome, a hospice where catechumens, adults born outside the Christian religion who asked to be baptized, would be housed, fed, and educated in the basic tenets of Christianity.[88] The 1584 edition of the Roman ritual instructed bishops to open such hospices in every diocese, which flourished throughout Italy.[89]

No such institution was ever set up in Malta, even though Inquisitor Gregorio Salviati (1754–1759) did harbor the idea of setting one up.[90] Be that as it may, there is solid evidence to indicate that significant numbers of Muslim captives actually converted: 239 infidel adults and 136 infants were baptized in the two Valletta parishes of Porto Salvo and St

86. NLM, Libr. 149: 168–69.
87. Ciappara 2001: 212–14.
88. Mazur 2016: 18–42; Pagano 1998: 313–90; Raunio 2009.
89. *Rituale Romanum iussu Gregorii XIII papae*.
90. ASPF 1, Fondo Scritture Riferite nei Congressi, ff. 103r–110v.

Paul's between 1595 and 1605;[91] and it has been calculated that 2,278 infidels were baptized at the church of Our Lady of Victories also at Valletta between 1617 and 1798.[92] These significant statistics compare very favorably with the 3,044 baptisms at the house of catechumens in Rome between 1614 and 1797.[93]

But we must now turn to the question of whether these Muslims and Jews recanted their faith freely. Did Anna, the Bosnian slave of Giovanni Vassallo of St Philip's, perhaps commit suicide for having been forced to receive baptism? She was first sent to the inquisitor's prisons when she started doubting her new faith and then in 1700 to the *conservatorio delle zitelle* at Valletta where she threw herself into the well.[94] Again, how much did Abraham, the slave of Catarina Abela, accept baptism willingly? He told the inquisitor in 1606 that he knew how to recite the Ave Maria and much of the Credo and wanted to "dedicate himself entirely to Jesus Christ our Lord and the true Messiah." Was he, like other children, as Barrio Gozalo says, led to be baptized by his mistress, which was relatively easy in his case, having not yet assimilated his own religion?[95] Perhaps we may never know but the conversion of infidels represented the triumph of true faith over heresy. Recorded cases indicate that their baptism was a special occasion, characterized by solemnities and rejoicing. Not infrequently they were baptized on Easter Sunday and perhaps in the chapel of the Holy Office, with the inquisitor acting as godfather. In the case of Abraham, Mgr Diotallevi came down from his dais and gave his godchild "a Christian embrace."[96]

Forced baptisms were against the catechism of the council of Trent, which laid down that "as in baptism we all die to sin and resolve to live a new life so it is fit that it be administered only to those who receive it of their own free will and accord."[97] The conciliar fathers were only repeating the teaching of theologians like Aquinas. St Thomas considered Muslims to be unbelievers and castigated Muhammad for seducing the

---

91. Ciappara 2013: 261.
92. On this topic, see Zammit 2019: 160–71.
93. Mazur 2016: 31.
94. AIM, Proc. 95A, ff. 160r–89v.
95. Barrio Gozalo 2008: 141.
96. AIM, Proc. 25A, ff. 36r–37v.
97. McHugh and Callan 1982: 180.

people with promises of carnal pleasure, for his fables and false doctrines[98] but still he prohibited the baptism of infants and young children against the wishes of their parents (*invitis parentibus*):

> It would be contrary to natural justice if children who have not yet the use of free will were to be baptized against their parents' will; just as it would be if one having the use of reason were baptized against his will. Moreover, under the circumstances it would be dangerous to baptize the children of unbelievers for they would be liable to lapse into unbelief, by reason of their natural affection for their parents.[99]

Having said this, is it not a good thing to win a soul for God? Both the synods of 1591 and 1620 decreed that infants born to infidel slaves should be baptized and brought up separately from their parents, to be given a Catholic education.[100] This was also the professed aim of the government of the Order of St John. A proclamation of September 28, 1661 declared that no child born or conceived in captivity could be sold to infidels; nor could it be ransomed, set free, or allowed to return to its parents' country before it reached the age of ten. The proclamation ended with an exhortation to all owners of such children to provide them with an education in Catholic doctrine, "to instruct them in all charity in our Holy Faith so that they might be illuminated by the Holy Spirit to embrace it and receive Holy Baptism."[101]

But it is Benedict XIV's bull *Postremo mense* (1747) which must be especially mentioned in this instance. He admitted that it is not licit to baptize infidel infants without their parents' consent. In case, however, they were in danger of death or else abandoned by their parents it is "without doubt a praiseworthy and meritorious thing."[102] What this meant in practice is that the principle of *favor fidei* (in faith's favor) prevailed over any other consideration and if the perpetrator was punished, the sacrament

---

98. Aquinas 1923, Book 1, chap. 6, art. 4: 13. Aquinas explains the essential points where the Catholic faith differs from and transcends Islam in *De rationibus fidei*. For its translation in English, see Kenny 1996: 31–52. For an appraisal of this work, see Ellul 2003: 177–200.
99. Aquinas 1914, Book 3: 159–61. On this topic, see Tapie 2018: 289–329.
100. NLM, Libr. 6, ff. 2v, 17r.
101. NLM, Libr. 740, ff. 48r-v.
102. Benedict XIV 1747: 9.

was still valid.[103] One such case from the proceedings of the inquisition of Malta refers to nine-year-old Ibraimo. Don Salvatore Mangion of St Nicholas', fearing that he "would die of an epileptic stroke," baptized him in 1768 in a shoemaker's shop.[104] Another case concerns a 15-month-old Muslim girl, the slave of one Francesco of Valletta. In 1784 Pulcra Bonnici took pity on her as she did not want to see her a slave all her life. Moved by Christian zeal, believing it to be a "piece of meritorious work," she baptized her, giving her the name of Fortunata. Inquisitor Mgr Gallarati Scotti scolded Pulcra sharply but the child was separated from her mother, even though she was allowed to see Fortunata twice a month on the promise of never talking about religion in her presence.[105] These are sporadic examples, though, which cannot be compared to the forced baptisms at Rome, about which Marina Caffiero has written so well.[106]

It is hardly surprising that pressure was exerted, too, on slaves awaiting execution to secure their last-minute conversion.[107] And likewise chaplains in their daily round of the hospital lovingly exhorted sick infidels to be baptized. They explained to them that they would either enjoy eternal life in heaven if they embraced the Christian religion or eternal damnation in hell if they continued in their infidelity. The chaplains commended them to God and asked his divine goodness for ardent words to enable them to gain the soul on the point of eternal loss through its own fault.[108]

But aside from this terror of the afterlife, there were various benefits which accrued to baptized slaves.[109] They were not only under any obligation to wear Muslim clothes but they obtained their Christian clothes free from the government so that they were dressed in a Christian manner "to the greater glory of the Order."[110] They were entitled to white bread[111] and

---

103. Caffiero 2004: 81. See also Greco 2011: 163–78.
104. This is an example, among many others, of an owner who gave no thought to "winning him [the slave] over to Christ" and instead looked upon the matter as injurious to his financial well-being. He had been offered 405 scudi for the boy and demanded to be compensated. AIM, Proc. 129, ff. 51r–52v.
105. AIM, Proc. 133A, ff. 365r–367v.
106. Caffiero 2000: 306–28; Caffiero 2003: 503–37. For the nineteenth century, see Kertzer 2003: 539–56.
107. For one such conversion in 1654, see AIM, Proc. 69A, ff. 86r–91v.
108. NLM, Arch. 1927, ff. 136r–137v.
109. Azzopardi-Ljubibratic 2018: 152–57.
110. NLM, Arch. 666, ff. 262r-v.
111. NLM, Libr. 143/1, f. 94r.

money allowances to supplement their rations by buying cheese, cured ham, olives and fruit.[112] They could ransom themselves for much less than the current market price and (which slaves appreciated the most) they were allowed to marry and live with their families in their own homes.[113] Following the example of the reforming Archbishop Burali d'Arezzo of Naples (1576–1578), freedom may have been held out as an enticement towards conversion[114] but baptism did not necessarily break the bond of slavery.[115] Converts were rarely freed and generally extraneous factors were involved, such as infirmity or length of service. In fact, years might have to pass before a convert could obtain his freedom. Michele Centeno was converted in 1611 but freed only in 1618.[116] It needs to be said, though, that inquisitors like Angelo Durini, who considered piracy to be "so odious to God's and man's laws,"[117] could pay for the slaves' ransom[118] and would offer them help whenever their masters ill-treated them—though there was little for inquisitors to do against their cruel masters except to appeal to the latter's Christian charity.[119] For some, baptism availed them nothing, not even to escape a sentence of death,[120] and they could remain marginalized. For instance, Paolo, a 60-year-old baptized slave, led a most miserable life; his master hired him to a pig-breeder, who sent him to collect refuse from the streets of Valletta.[121]

112. NLM, Arch. 1939, f. 104r.
113. Wettinger 2002: 464–70. In 1606 Giovanni Simone Spilletta, a Jewish neophyte, lived with the parish priest of St Paul's, Valletta. See AIM, Proc. 20A, ff. 162r–168v.
114. Lopez 1984: 107–109.
115. AIM, Corr. 96, f. 163r, Mgr Durini to Card. Corsini, February 8, 1763. For the juridical status of baptized slaves, see Ciappara 2000: 57–58 and Rostagno 1983: 19–20.
116. NLM, Arch. 663, f. 170v.
117. AIM, Memorie 16, f. 11v.
118. For the case of Eiza, for whose redemption Inquisitor Zondadari disbursed 25 Roman scudi, see AIM, Corr. 66, ff. 104r-v, Card. Pallavicino to Mgr Zondadari, February 16, 1779.
119. Maria, the slave of Teresa Manduca, twice sought the help of Mgr Paolo Passionei in 1756. She was always called by her former Muslim name, Ifgi, and was told that it would have been better if the water with which she had been baptized had been thrown on the floor instead. She was beaten with a bridle and when her mistress went to the country in a carriage she was made to follow on foot. See AIM, Atti Civili 508, ff. 81r–98v.
120. NLM, Arch. 1482, letter to the apostolic prefect in Tunis, August 26, 1721.
121. AIM, Proc. 130, ff. 55r–75r.

"Dhimmi people"

What is beyond doubt is that in the overwhelming majority of cases most slaves preferred to cling to their faith.[122] They enjoyed a *dhimmi* (people of the Holy Book) status and could exercise their religion without any hindrance. They were not made to attend, as in Spain, appropriate sermons for their conversion[123] but were guaranteed security and protection in the exercise of their religion. As at Leghorn, Civitavecchia, and Genoa, the Muslims in Malta had a mosque in which to worship. Patrick Brydone, a Scot on the Grand Tour, was surprised to find in 1770 one in each of the three *bagnos*—"notwithstanding the supposed bigotry of the Maltese."[124] These must have been at first simple rooms furnished for the purpose. However, not later than 1738, the Muslims had a much better building, specially built as a mosque, just outside the town bastions and adjoining their cemetery at Marsa. Here, led by the *imam* (prayer-leader), they met to perform their evening prayer during the holy month of Ramadan and to celebrate *laylatu l-gumgha* (Friday night). The government helped them keep these places in good condition, providing the beams and other timber, as, for example, in 1702.[125] It supplied them with oil for the night lights "as their Lent is approaching, during which they are obliged to stay awake throughout the night."[126] Slaves also had the right to go out of the prison and celebrate their Easter or *id al-fitr* (the three days following Ramadan). If it fell when the galley squadron happened to be away, they commemorated it on their return to harbor.[127]

Besides a mosque, the Muslims had a cemetery at Marsa from 1675 onwards. The site had been obtained in exchange for another one nearby which had been incorporated into the outlying fortifications of Floriana.[128] The corpse first received the customary ablutions consisting mainly of

122. For this incident, see Carasi 2010: 158–59.
123. Greco 2011: 165–66. St Vincent Ferrer disapproved of forced conversions but demanded that Jews and Moors attended sermons. See Losada 2015: 206–27. For the sermons delivered by the Jesuit Tirso Gonzáles in seventeenth-century Spain, see Colombo 2007.
124. Wettinger 2002: 442–50; Ciappara 2003: 455; Brydone 1773, vol. 1: 331.
125. NLM, Arch. 647, f. 205v.
126. NLM, Università 338, October 30, 1741.
127. NLM, Arch. 672: 33–37.
128. NLM, Arch. 484, f. 267v.

pouring hot water over it. It was then borne to the burial place by four slaves accompanied by the imam, who observed whether it showed any bruises or other signs of ill treatment for an inquiry to be made.[129]

The same can be said for the Jews, who by no means were a persecuted minority. They had their *hacham* or spiritual leader[130] as well as their synagogue at the *bagno* at Birgu.[131] The synagogue was used at first only on festivals, then on Sabbaths as well. The prison *agozzino* took care of it, for which he was paid presumably by the Jewish slaves or their co-religionists abroad. It was furnished with the scrolls of the law adorned with bells, the Ark behind a curtain, the perpetually burning lamp, and a reading desk.[132] Here the Jews celebrated *Kol Nidre*, "singing so that I could hear them from the street," as Martino Vella, the inquisitor's captain, reported in 1620.[133] They commemorated their festivals,[134] such as the *sukkot* (feast of the tabernacles), and baked and distributed *matzot* (unleavened bread) for Passover.[135] As the Muslims refused them burial in their cemetery,[136] they had their own burial ground, where they were buried with decorum; whoever pelted the graves with stones or insulted them were sentenced to five years on the galleys.[137] Their first graveyard was situated on a plot of ground outside Vittoriosa, which was purchased for seventy-five ducats in the name of the Jewish community of Venice by Garsin, their agent in Malta.[138] By the late eighteenth century they had another one at Kalkara, paid for by the *Cassa degli Ebrei* of Leghorn.[139]

129. NLM, Arch. 6570, ff. 3r–4r.
130. AIM, Proc. 32, f. 456v.
131. AIM, Proc. 78A, f. 119r.
132. Roth 1929: 227–29.
133. AIM, Proc. 20, f. 163r.
134. AIM, Proc. 59A, ff. 115r-v.
135. AIM, Proc. 30, f. 335v.
136. AIM, Corr. 94, f. 226v. Mgr Serbelloni to Card. Otthoboni, February 12, 1729.
137. *Del Dritto Municipale di Malta* 1784: 260.
138. Roth 1931: 234–35.
139. NLM, Libr. 429/7: 178. See also Davis 1984: 145–70. Its origins are recorded in a Latin inscription on a tablet over the door: *Recondendis Gentis suae Exuviis Hebrhaeorum Mancipiorum Redemptio Liburniensis Coemeterium Hoc Aere Proprio Comparavit Anno MDCCLXXXIV* (This cemetery was established in 1784 by the Leghorn Fund for ransoming Hebrew slaves, at its own expense, for the burial of the dead of its race).

Conclusion

Moving beyond the "clash of civilizations" model, and focusing on a localized microcosm such as the Maltese islands, this chapter illuminated the complex ways in which Christians, Muslims, and Jews interacted and coexisted. Malta safeguarded the frontier between Islam and Christendom but this religious cleavage was elastic and followed conflicting lines. Dissonance and strife certainly existed but coexistence was more common. The conventional representation of a rigid dividing-line was unreal in actual fact since it ignored existing conditions. In border territories, where historical and geographical circumstances brought different religions together, cultural contact was not impossible. Put differently, the constant religious and ideological confrontation between the three religions did not necessarily mean that they lived in continuous dissension.[140]

Author biography

Frans Ciappara is an Associate Professor at the International Institute of Baroque Studies of the University of Malta. His specialist field of study is the eighteenth century. His articles and books deal with the Roman inquisition, the council of Trent, the professionalization of the Maltese clergy, the eccesiastical court, the enlightenment, marriage and the family, death, the place of the parish priest and the people in the parish, confraternities, ecclesiastical immunity and religion, kinship and godparenthood as elements of social cohesion. His latest book is *Church-State Relations in Late-Eighteenth-Century Malta: Gio. Nicolo Muscat (1735–1803)* (Malta: Malta University Press, 2018). He is the editor of the *Journal of Baroque Studies*.

Abbreviations

ACDF   Archivio della Congregazione per la Dottrina della Fede
AIM   Archives of the Inquisition Malta

140. Audisio 1996: 317.

Arch. Archives of the Order of Malta
ASPF Archivio Storico di Propaganda Fide
Corr. Correspondence
Libr. Library
NAM National Archives Malta
NLM National Library Malta
Proc. Proceedings

References

Primary sources

Vatican archives
   ACDF   St St HH4 – b, d.
   ASPF   1: Fondo Scritture Riferite nei Congressi
Maltese archives
   AIM   AC 508
              Corr. 14, 21, 66, 91, 94, 95, 96
              Memorie 3, 16
              Microfilm 6530
              Proc. 20, 20A, 30, 25A, 32, 32B, 55A, 59A, 69A, 78A, 95A, 110B, 113B, 118B, 121A, 121C, 120B, 121B, 122C, 124B, 125B, 128B, 129, 130, 132B, 133A.
   NAM   Libro dei Carcerati (1781–1788)
   NLM   Arch. 218, 296, 423, 452, 484, 566, 647, 663, 666, 672, 1481, 1482, 1927, 1939, 6529, 6570.
              Libr. 5, 6, 9, 23, 143 (i), 429 (vii), 149, 666, 703,704, 738, 740, 1306.
              Università: 338.

Secondary sources

Abela, G. F. (1647), *Della descrittione di Malta Isola nel mare siciliano*. Malta: Paolo Bonacota.

Acciard, M. (1751), *Mustafà Bassà di Rodi schiavo in Malta, o sia la di lui congiura all'occupazione di Malta*. Naples: Benedetto ed Ignazio Gessari.

Aquinas, T. (1914), *Summa Theologica*, Book 3, trans. English Dominican Fathers. London: Burns Oates and Washbourne.

Aquinas, T. (1923), *Summa Contra Gentiles*, Book 1, trans. English Dominican Fathers. London: Burns Oates and Washbourne.

Audisio, G. (1957), "Recherches sur l'origine et la signification du mot bagne," *Revue Africaine* 101: 363–80.
Audisio, G. (1996), "Renégats Marseillais (1591–1595)," *Provence Historique* 185: 305–331.
Azzopardi-Ljubibratic, S. (2018), "Conversions religieuses des juifs à malte (XVIe–XVIIIe siècles): une approche compare du marranisme," PhD thesis, University of Lausanne.
Balard, M. (2002), "Genuensis civitas in extremo Europae: Caffa from the Fourteenth to the Fifteenth Century," in D. Abulafia and N. Berend (eds.), *Medieval Frontiers*, 143–51. Aldershot: Ashgate.
Barrio Gozalo, M. (2008), "Conversione o semplice cambio di religione degli schiavi musulmani e cristiani nel XVIII secolo," in G. Fiume (ed.), *Schiavitù, religione e libertà nel Mediterraneo tra Medioevo e età moderna*, 129–62. Cosenza: Luigi Pellegrini Editore.
Benedict XIV (1747), *Lettera della Santità di Nostro Signore Benedetto XIV a Monsignor Arcivescovo di Tarso Vicegerente sopra il Battesimo degli Ebrei o infanti o adulti*. Rome.
Benzoni, G., ed. (1974), *Il Mediterraneo nella seconda metà del 500 alla Luce di Lepanto*. Florence: Olschki.
Berend, N. (2002), "Hungary, 'the Gate of Christendom'," in D. Abulafia and N. Berend (eds.), *Medieval Frontiers: Concepts and Practices*, 195–215. Aldershot: Ashgate.
Berend, N. (2003), "Défense de la chrétienté et naissance d'une identité. Hongrie, Pologne et Péninsule Ibérique au Moyen Âge," *Annales: Histoire, Sciences Sociales* 5: 1009–1027. https://doi.org/10.1017/S0395264900018102
Bigelow Merriman, R. (1962), *The Rise of the Spanish Empire in the Old World and in the New*, vol. 4. New York: Cooper Square.
Black, C. (2009), *The Italian Inquisition*. New Haven, CT: Yale University Press.
Bonnici, A. (1974), "Aspetti della vita Cristiana nell'isola di Malta verso la metà del seicento," *Maltese Folklore Review* 1/4: 305–35.
Bono, S. (1983), "Schiavi Musulmani a Genova (Secoli XVI–XVIII)," in R. Belvederi (ed.), *Rapporti Genova-Mediterraneo-Atlantico nell'Età Moderna. Atti del IV Congresso Internazionale di Studi Storici*, 85–102. Genoa: University of Genoa.
Bono, S. (1993), *Corsari nel Mediterraneo. Cristiani e musulmani fra Guerra, schiavitù e commercio*. Milan: Mondadori.
Bono, S. (1994), "Schiavi maghrebini in Italia e cristiani nel Maghreb. Proteste e attestazioni per la 'reciprocità' di trattamento," *Africa* 49: 331–51.
Bono, S. (1999), "Schiavi musulmani a Malta nei secoli xvii–xviii: connessioni fra Maghreb e Italia," in P. Xuereb (ed.), *Karissime Gotifride: Historical*

Essys Presented to Godfrey Wettinger on His Seventieth Birthday, 89–96. Malta: Malta University Press.

Boubaker, S. (1990), "Les relations économiques entre Gênes et la régence de Tunis au début du XVIIIeme siècle: La compagnie du Sel Gergis, 1714–1724," in R. Belvederi (ed.), *Rapporti Genova-Mediterraneo-Atlantico nell'Età Moderna. Atti del IV Congresso Internazionale di Studi Storici*, 123–39. Genova: Istituto di scienze storiche.

Boyer, P. (1969), "La chiourme turque des galères de France de 1685 à 1687," *Revue de l'Occident Musulman et de la Méditerrané* 6: 53–74. https://doi.org/10.3406/remmm.1969.1005

Braudel, F. (1973), *The Mediterranean and the Mediterranean World in the Age of Philip II*, vol. 2. London: Collins.

Brogini, A. (2006), *Malte, frontière de chrétienté, 1530–1670*. Rome: École Française de Rome.

Brydone, P. (1773), *A Tour through Sicily and Malta in a Series of Letters to William Beckford*, 2 vols. London.

Bulliet, R. W. (2004), *The Case for Islamo-Christian Civilization*. New York: Columbia University Press.

Burke, P. (1997), *Varieties of Cultural History*. Ithaca, NY: Cornell University Press.

Caffiero, M. (2000), "'Il Pianto di Rachele'. Ebrei, Neofiti e Giudaizzanti a Roma in età moderna," in *L'Inquisizione e gli storici: Un cantiere aperto. Tavola rotonda (Roma, 24–25 giugno 1999)*, 306–328. Rome: Accademia nazionale dei Linceia.

Caffiero, M. (2003), "'La caccia agli ebrei'. Inquisizione, casa dei catecumeni e battesimi forzati nella Roma moderna," in *Le inquisizioni cristiane e gli ebrei. Tavola rotonda nell'ambito della Conferenza annuale della ricerca (Roma, 20–21 dicembre 2001)*, 503–37. Rome: Accademia nazionale dei Lincei.

Caffiero, M. (2004), *Battesimi forzati. Storie di ebrei, cristiani e convertiti nella Roma dei papi*. Rome: Viella.

Carasi, M. (2010), *The Order of Malta Exposed or a Voyage to Malta*, translated by T. Freller. Malta: Gutenberg Press.

Cassar, C. (2004), "Magic, Heresy and the Broom Riding Midwife Witch: The Inquisition Trial of Isabetta Caruana," in *Proceedings of History Week 2003*, 25–41. Malta: The Malta Historical Society.

Cavaliero, R. (1959), "The Decline of the Maltese Corso in the XVIIIth Century: A Study in Maritime History," *Melita Historica* 2/4: 224–38.

Cervantes, de Saavedra, M. (1970), *The Adventures of Don Quixote*, translated by J. M. Cohen. Harmondsworth: Penguin.

Ciappara, F. (2000), *The Roman Inquisition in Enlightened Malta*. Malta: Pubblikazzjonijiet Indipendenza.

Ciappara, F. (2001), *Society and the Inquisition in Early Modern Malta*. Malta: Publishers Enterprises Group (PEG).
Ciappara, F. (2003), "The Roman Inquisition and the Jews in Seventeenth- and Eighteenth-Century Malta," in *Le Inquisizioni Cristiane e gli Ebrei*, 449–70. Rome: Accademia Nazionale dei Lincei.
Ciappara, F. (2004), "Christendom and Islam: A Fluid Frontier," *Mediterranean Studies* 13: 165–87.
Ciappara, F. (2008), "La Chrétienté et l'Islam au XVIIIe Siècle: Une Frontière Encore Floue," in François Moureau (ed.), *Captifs en Méditerranée XVIe–XVIIIe siècles*, 23–35. Paris: PUPS.
Ciappara, F. (2013), "The Date Palm and the Olive Tree: Safeguarding the Catholic Frontier of Malta (c. 1595–c.1605)," in D. A. Agius (ed.), *Giorgio Scala and the Moorish Slaves: The Inquisition—Malta 1598*, 253–79. Malta: Midsea Books.
Clancy-Smith, J. A. (2011), *Mediterraneans: North Africa and Europe in an Age of Migration c. 1800–1900*. Berkeley, CA: University of California Press.
Colombo, E. (2007), *Convertire i musulmani. L'eperienza di un gesuita spagnolo del seicento*. Milan: Mondadori.
Daniel, N. (2000), *Islam and the West: The Making of an Image*. Oxford: Oneworld Publications.
Davis, D. (1984), "The Jewish Cemetery at Kalkara, Malta," *Jewish Historical Studies* 28: 145–70.
Decker, R. (2008), *Witchcraft and the Papacy: An Account Drawn from the Formerly Secret Archives of the Roman Inquisition*. Charlottesville: University of Virginia Press.
Decreta Melivetanae Synodi Actae in Cathedrali Melitensi (1647), Rome.
Del Col, A. (2006), *L'Inquisizione in Italia dal XII al XXI Secolo*. Milan: Oscar Mondadori.
Del Dritto Municipale di Malta (1784), Malta.
Duni, M. (2008), *Under the Devil's Spell: Witches, Sorcerers and the Inquisition in Renaissance Italy*. Florence: Syracuse University.
Dursteler, E. R. (2008), *Venetians in Constantinople: Nation, Identity, and Coexistence in the Early Modern Mediterranean*. Baltimore, MD: Johns Hopkins University Press.
Earle, P. (1970), *Corsairs of Malta and Barbary*. London: Sidgwick and Jackson.
Ellul, J. (2003), "Thomas Aquinas and Muslim-Christian Dialogue: An Appraisal of *De rationibus fidei*," *Angelicum* 1: 177–200.
Fontenay, M. (2001), "Il mercato maltese degli schiavi al tempo dei Cavalieri di San Giovanni (1530–1798)," *Quaderni Storici* 2: 391–414.
Galea, M. (2006), "Renewing an Enemy Ship: Turk Sightings in Nineteenth-Century Maltese Literature," *Sacra Militia* 5: 29–34.

Gauci, L. (2016), *In the Name of the Prince: Maltese Corsairs 1760–1798*. Malta: Heritage Malta.

Greco, G. (2011), *BenedettoXIV. Riforme e conservazione, rigore e compromessi: il governo e il magistero di un "sovrano pontefice" alle soglie della secolarizzazione della società europea*. Rome: Salerno Editrice.

Greene, M. (2000), *A Shared World: Christians and Muslims in the Early Modern Mediterranean*. Princeton, NJ: Princeton University Press.

Greene, M. (2002), "Beyond the Northern Invasion: The Mediterranean in the Seventeenth Century," *Past and Present* 174: 42–71. https://doi.org/10.1093/past/174.1.42

Hess, A. C., ed. (1972), "The Battle of Lepanto and Its Place in Mediterranean History," *Past and Present* 57: 53–73. https://doi.org/10.1093/past/57.1.53

Hughes, O. (1986), "Distinguishing Signs: Ear-rings, Jews and Franciscan Rhetoric in the Italian Renaissance City," *Past and Present* 112: 3–59. https://doi.org/10.1093/past/112.1.3

Hunt, L., ed. (1989), *The New Cultural History*. Berkeley and Los Angeles: University of California Press.

Huntington, S. P. (1993), "The Clash of Civilizations?" *Foreign Affairs* 72: 22–49. https://doi.org/10.2307/20045621

Kenny, J. (1996), "Saint Thomas Aquinas: Reasons for the Faith against Muslim Objections (and one Object of the Greeks and Armenians) to the Cantor of Antioch," *Islamochristiana* 22: 31–52.

Kertzer, D. I. (2003), "Inquisizione e ebrei negli Stati pontifici, 1823–1846," in A. Prosperi (ed.), *Le inquisizioni cristiane e gli ebrei*, 539–56. Rome: Accademia Nazionale dei Lincei.

Knoll, P. W. (1974), "Poland as antemurale christianitatis in the Late Middle Ages," *Catholic Historical Review* 60/3: 381–401.

Lopez, P. (1984), *Clero, Eresia, e Magia nella Napoli del Viceregno*. Naples: Adriano Gallina.

Losada, C. (2015), "Powerful Words: St Vincent Ferrer's Preaching and the Jews in Medieval Castile," in T. V. Cohen and L. K. Twomey (eds.), *Spoken Word and Social Practice: Orality in Europe*, 206–27. Leiden and Boston: Brill.

Martin, R. (1989), *Witchcraft and the Inquisition in Venice, 1550–1650*. Oxford and New York: Blackwell.

Mazur, P. A. (2016), *Conversion to Catholicism in Early Modern Italy*. London and New York: Routledge.

McHugh, J. A., and Charles J. Callan, trans. (1982), *The Catechism of the Council of Trent*. Rockford, IL: TAN Books.

O'Neil, M. (1987), "Magical Healing, Love Magic and the Inquisition in Late Sixteenth-century Modena," in S. Haliczer (ed.), *Inquisition and Society in Early Modern Europe*, 88–114. London and Sydney: Croom Helm.

Pagano, S. (1998), "L'Ospizio dei Convertendi di Roma fra charisma missionario e regolamentazione ecclesiastica (1673–1700)," *Ricerche per la Storia religiosa di Roma* 10: 313–90.

Preto, P. (1975), *Venezia e i Turchi*. Firenze: Sansoni.

Raunio, A. (2009), *Conversioni al Cattolicesimo a Roma tra Sei e Settecento. La presenza degli scandinavi nell'Ospizio dei Convertendi*. Turku: University of Turku.

Riley-Smith, J. (2012), "Government and the Indigenous in the Latin Kingdom of Jerusalem," in David Abulafia and Nora Berend (eds.), *Medieval Frontiers: Concepts and Practices*, 121–31. Aldershot: Ashgate.

Rituale Romanum iussu Gregorii XIII papae (1584), Rome.

Rostagno, L. (1983), *Mi faccio Turco. Esperienze ed immagini dell'Islam nell'Italia moderna*. Rome: Istituto per l'Oriente Carlo Alfonso Nallino.

Roth, C. (1929), "The Slave Community of Malta," *The Menorah Journal*, 219–33.

Roth, C. (1931), "The Jews of Malta," *Transactions of the Jewish Historical Society* 12: 212–42.

Ruggiero, G. (1993), *Binding Passions: Tales of Magic, Marriage and Power at the End of the Renaissance*. Oxford: Oxford University Press.

Scribner, R. W. (1993), "The Reformation, Popular Magic, and the 'Disenchantment of the World'," *Journal of Interdisciplinary History* 23/3: 475–94. https://doi.org/10.2307/206099

Skippon, P. (1732), *A Journey Thro' Part of the Low-Countries, Germany, Italy and France*, edited by A. Churchill. London.

Tapie, M. A. (2018), "*Spiritualis Uterus*: The Question of Forced Baptisms and Thomas Aquinas's Defense of Jewish Parental Rights," *Bulletin of Medieval Canon Law* 35: 289–329. https://doi.org/10.1353/bmc.2018.0006

Testa, C. (1989), *The Life and Times of Grand Master Pinto, 1741–1773*. Malta: Midsea Books.

Valensi, L. (1963), "Les relations commerciales entre la régence de Tunis et Malte au XVIIIème siècle," *Cahiers de Tunisie* 43: 71–83.

Vaughan, D. M. (1976), *Europe and the Turk: A Pattern of Alliances, 1350–1700*. Liverpool: Liverpool University Press.

Vella Gauci, J. (2010), *Christian-Muslim Relations as a Topos in Maltese Historiography and Literature*. Malta: author.

Watt, J. R. (2010), "Love Magic and the Inquisition: A Case from Seventeenth-Century Italy," *Sixteenth Century Journal* 41/3: 675–89.

Wettinger, G. (2002), *Slavery in the Islands of Malta and Gozo ca. 1000–1812*. Malta: Publishers Enterprises Group (PEG).

Zammit, W. (2019), "The Faith Triumphant: Muslim Converts to Catholicism and the Order of St John, 1530–1798," in Nicholas Morton (ed.), *The Military Orders*, vol. 7, *Piety, Pugnacity and Property*, 160–71. Abingdon: Routledge.

Zammit-Ciantar, J. (2008), "Orations on the Victory of the Order of St John over the Turks in 1565 and on the Occasion of the Laying of the Foundation Stone of Valletta in 1566," *Symposia Melitensia* 5: 1–30.

Chapter 10

Tolerance, Peace, and Otherness in Spanish Jesuit Thought of the Baroque Period*

David Martín López

Introduction

As the spearhead of the Roman Catholic Church, the Society of Jesus undertook a substantial effort to expand the reform that issued from the Council of Trent, both in the countries that espoused the defence of Catholicism and in those that implemented their own parallel reforms (Lutherans, Anglicans, Calvinists, Huguenots). In the performance of their missionary activities across Europe, they engaged in theological disputes with these groups. Additionally, as part of their endeavour to normalize religious orthodoxy in Catholic states they became immersed in connections with members of the other two major monotheistic religions—Jews and Muslims—who were classified as infidels by the Catholic church. The Jesuits also took their missionary efforts to the rest of the known world, and in the process they encountered many other cultures which they approached to pursue their evangelical aims. As an aid to their missionary

---

* This chapter has been written as part of the national research project "La República política entre Clío y Caliope. Representaciones y prácticas políticas en la Monarquía Universal Hispánica en la Alta Edad Moderna" (reference PGC2018-093833-B-I00) and the consolidated research group "DeReHis (De Re Hispanica)" based at the Universidad de Castilla-La Mancha (reference 2021-GRIN-31050) and supported by a FEDER grant. Thanks to María Fernández for the translation.

work, they used the existing knowledge of the newly discovered population to inform and explain Catholicism. This was a very useful and successful means to attract souls, but it gave rise to two problems: misinterpretation of Catholic dogma and mysteries, and hostile reactions from political and religious authorities which led to the persecution and eventual expulsion of the Jesuits from their territories, as was the case in Japan.

The rapport between Jesuits and other societies left a record of cross-cultural relationships over time. In this chapter, we shall review several accounts dating from the decades surrounding the turn of the seventeenth century which illustrate how Jesuits perceived those cultures. These texts, together with chronicles of contemporary events, open a window onto the relationship developed by the Ignatians with other world religions, such as Japanese Buddhism, Judaism, Islam, and American indigenous creeds.

The approach I have adopted includes theory and practice. The theoretical component explores Jesuit views of alien communities through the writings of Juan Azor, Francisco Suárez, and others. The practical side examines certain historical events, such as the 1580 Tenshō embassy, in which a group of Japanese men journeyed across the world to visit several European Catholic countries and pay their respects to Pope Gregory XIII. This two-pronged approach will reveal how Jesuit attitudes to other civilizations varied, not only according to their own knowledge of those cultures, but also in proportion to the degree of development they attributed to each of them, and always from a position of perceived superiority. The Nippon case is particularly eloquent because it highlights the contrast in the Jesuits' view of Japanese people on one hand, and the members of the non-Christian monotheistic faiths on the other. This will in turn shed light on the meaning of tolerance in contemporary Ignatian thought, a concept that, as we shall see, was closer to forbearance than to respect. Through the overwhelmingly Catholic Jesuit lens, other civilizations were judged as more or less wrong or worthy of tolerance, but always from the moral high ground on which these men firmly stood.

Along with the issues surrounding the development of tolerance and rapport between Jesuits and the "other," I will discuss the notions of peace and war as they appear in the works of these authors. Their position on these matters is significant not only on account of the Society of Jesus's strong involvement in politics, but also because these clergymen became acquainted with other cultures while they were embedded in armies and military units. In their view, the challenge was not so much how to bring peace to a place, but how to avoid war and, above all, how to justify military intervention. Where peace is not possible, let war, at least, be "just."

Religious tolerance and the exercise of government

The coexistence of several creeds in one territory had a strong presence in the advice that political authors conveyed to the king and in their contributions to the training of princes. The reasons for this strong presence are rooted in the European political environment since the rise of Protestantism. The use of Luther's maxims for political ends had led on many occasions to military conflict and clashes between supporters of different branches of Christianity. Confrontations took place even in countries with a majority official religion and rivers of blood flowed over large swathes of the continent as a result. Heterodoxy was hounded and its followers publicly executed. Catholics, including some Jesuits, were persecuted in England. In Catholic Spain, Protestants and *alumbrados* fell into the hands of the Inquisition and "atoned for their sins" in *autos-da-fé* (acts of faith). In 1609, the Moriscos were expelled from Spain.

The main issues highlighted by Jesuit treatise writers in their advice to princes and monarchs were the standardization of all aspects of the population's lives and the defence of Catholic orthodoxy. Not every author writing on political matters addressed these matters directly or indirectly,[1] but they were present in the works of the most influential Jesuits of that

---

1. Political writers belong to one of two types. On the one hand, authors whose works were specifically intended for the training of princes. On the other, those whose works had a political overtone and a practical purpose related to the exercise of power, but also a wider scope and a broader readership that went beyond government circles. Among the latter, such writers as Luis de la Puente, Gaspar de Astete, and Luis de la Palma wrote moral works and cases of conscience intended to be read by the general population. These books exhorted readers to lead a virtuous life and, although they included political teachings among other things this was not their main purpose.

period, such as Juan de Mariana, Francisco Suárez, Pedro de Ribadeneyra, and Juan Azor.

Following parallel lines of argument, these Jesuit authors concurred on the need for a single religion among the population. Faith was conceived as the only possible means to unite all individuals for the common good because "nothing binds people's souls better than one Lord, one faith, one baptism."[2] In a similar vein, Juan de Mariana wrote that "neither blood, nor similarity of habits, nor lifestyle, nor even a shared motherland bind men's goodwill as religious difference drives them apart."[3]

The words of Azor and Mariana, like Suárez's and Ribadeneyra's, were not only applicable to one territory or even to a single civilization. For instance, they used a similar argument in response to the persecution of Catholics in early seventeenth-century Japan by the *daimyos*—elite landowners—who saw the evangelization efforts of Franciscans and Jesuits as foreign interference. The Ignatians themselves saw the spread of a new religion within a community with concern because it challenged the social uniformity that was achieved through faith and that cleared the way for government action. Naturally, from these authors' perspective, Catholicism was the only faith an individual could identify with without falling into error. As we shall see below, the Jesuits' perception of other faiths and modes of worship was based on the assumption that they were wrong, since the only possible Church to join was the Roman Catholic one.

Unity of action, behaviour, and worship were the key to avoiding social conflict—including armed confrontation, paving the way for political action.[4] State and religion were seen as a single, inseparable entity and any dissociation between them arising from the existence of subjects who did not share the king's creed was considered harmful. The 1578 engraving by the Flemish artist Pieter van der Borcht (Figure 10.1) on the difficulties that beset any government in a plural, diverse nation embodies the image these thinkers had in mind.

2. Azor 1608: 1686.
3. Mariana 1981: 441.
4. Azor 1608: 1686; Ribadeneyra 1595: 103.

Figure 10.1. *The Difficulty of Ruling over a Diverse Nation* (1578). Rijksmuseum.

In his well-known book *De Rege et Regis Institutione* (Toledo, 1599) Juan de Mariana wrote the most thorough analysis of this question of the religious unit within a state to facilitate its government. In this mirror of princes, he described the different situations a monarch would have to face if several creeds were to coexist in his territory, and the potential challenges that would ensue. Although he resolutely denied any possible benefits to a multi-confessional state and refused to recommend it, in a certain sense Mariana accepted that such a state could exist along the lines of the Holy Roman Empire after the Peace of Augsburg (1555).[5] Nevertheless, he firmly underscored the problems that would result from a heterogeneous population. Confrontations would be provoked by "love of religion [...] the most powerful of all devotions";[6] multiple religious authorities might be required, along with multiple legal systems; this would cause divisions among the population, followed by distrust and

---

5. Mariana supported his arguments with several examples from the history of the Roman empire and even mentioned the German peasant revolt of 1524–1525.
6. Mariana 1981: 442.

loss of loyalty should one sector be seen as enjoying special treatment;[7] and finally, pressures and threats could arise from those who felt powerful enough to impose their own goals.[8] The outcome would be a weak sovereign who lacked the support of his subjects and would reign under the twin menaces of internal rebellion and external threat.

Azor and Ribadeneyra largely agreed with Mariana, but dismissed the possibility of multiple creeds under one ruler. They argued for a hard, strict monarch who would ensure compliance with the precepts of a single religion and obviated listing the challenges a king would have to face in a multi-confessional state. In their view, one of the key features of a sovereign was the defense of Catholicism. As part of this role, the king would impose severe penalties on heretics, ensuring that "people who thus gave themselves [to heresy or disloyalty] be arrested and punished."[9] The aim would be to achieve peace in the Republic, preventing dissension and hatred through conversion to Christianity. Yet Azor shows a slight inconsistency when he states, in the first volume of his work, that Christian princes may punish Muslims within their jurisdiction if they committed offenses such as theft, adultery, parricide, or murder,[10] thereby implicitly admitting such a possibility.

Conversely, Luis de Molina, who had studied the circumstances of American indigenous people in the wake of the Spanish conquest, argued that overseas subjects under the sovereignty of a Catholic king should not be forced to convert. Should "men be forced to embrace it, it would be considered tyrannical, a device of the devil and contrary to natural light, because no more means appropriate than force had been found to introduce it to the world."[11] It follows from his argument that more than one religion could exist under the same ruler and, in contrast to the other Jesuit authors, Molina did not see this as a hindrance to good government practice. Indeed, he claimed that neither the king nor the pope had any power whatsoever over people who had not converted to Catholicism,

7. Mariana 1981: 445.
8. Mariana 1981: 444.
9. Azor 1608: 1686; see also Ribadeneyra 1595: 103.
10. Azor 1600: 1024.
11. Calafate and Mandado 2014: 268.

and therefore indigenous monarchs should legitimately retain control of their territories.[12]

The search for peace and the exercise of "just war"

Both strictly political treatises and those of a moral nature engaged with the issue of "just war." Their authors' positions ranged from idealistically rejecting violence in all its forms to advocating its use for the sake of the state's advancement regardless of moral or natural laws.[13] Peace was commonly presented as the ideal state a population should aspire to. What this discourse described, however, was not so much peace but the means to avoid war and, should this prove impossible, to ensure it was justified. This is important to our inquiry because the Jesuit clergymen in question had traveled to America as army chaplains and therefore their encounters with indigenous people came about in the aftermath of a war. It is in this context that José de Acosta, Luis de Molina, and Francisco Suárez wrote their remarks about American Indians and about the possibility of Christian military intervention in conflicts between rival populations. Also relevant are Juan Azor's views on pagans and the militaristic vision of Muslim relations that pervades his *Institutionum moralium*, as we shall see below.

Azor sustained that any declaration of war must be soundly justified because, should it be launched "without regard to the other's law" and without valid reasons, it would be the sovereign's duty to restore any damage caused.[14] Nevertheless, he left the matter of reparations loosely up to the offender's judgment and failed to suggest a prior assessment of losses, expecting the ruler instead to pay whatever his conscience dictated.

Juan de Mariana elaborated on this subject further. Added to the need to consider whether war was an appropriate course of action, it was essential to examine the potential economic fallout and its likely repercussions. Thus, he claimed that "war is only waged justly when the goal is peace, and war is not to be sought in peace, but peace in war."[15] Together with

12. Calafate and Mandado 2014: 269–70; Molina 1611: 102–106.
13. Macedo 2013: 188.
14. Azor 1608: 1680.
15. Mariana 1981: 310–11.

Alonso de Andrade, Mariana is the most categorical of these writers in his assertion that warfare is a monarch's last resort, that it should only ever be defensive, and that the overarching principle should be to seek alliances and the "tranquillity of the Republic," only taking up arms when forced to, that is, to defend oneself from war waged by another or to "avenge vicious affronts."[16] To drive the point home, in the closing statements of *De Rege* he wrote: "Everybody wants peace and enjoys it as the source of all goodness and detests war as the worst of all evils."[17]

Some years later, Andrade expressed a similar view when he pointed out some issues surrounding the declaration of war, should it prove impossible to maintain peace, which Andrade described as "a very necessary thing for kingdoms to preserve and increase their vassals."[18] The arguments for war must be clear, powerful, and decided after discussion with experts.[19] Additionally, it was imperative to make an accurate appraisal of the forces at the king's disposal. Failure to do this would render the action "rash and reckless," because not only would the war be lost but also the lives and possessions of the king's vassals, "causing universal sorrow and grief to his own people."[20] As a moralist, Andrade's discourse was based on the principle that "God fights for justice and helps those who have it and harms those who attempt to overrun it and breaks them asunder and contradicts them,"[21] not forgetting the many sins committed in war.[22] He addressed his arguments not only to rulers but also to the soldiers themselves, who were advised to obey their superiors' orders, ignoring any ethical issues arising from their actions in battle "because the body dies [...] temporarily and the soul dies eternally in hell's torments. But when a war is just [...] the individual's soul lives on because it dwells in heaven."[23]

In a similar vein, Suárez declared that defensive war was legitimate and even mandatory in the face of an external threat. Consequently, the

16. Mariana 1981: 310.
17. Mariana 1981: 439.
18. Andrade 1642: 461.
19. Andrade 1642: 454.
20. Andrade 1642: 462.
21. Andrade 1642: 53.
22. Andrade 1642: 462.
23. Andrade 1642: 41.

state should claim the right to resort to force if it found itself at risk.²⁴ He elaborated this topic at length in his works *De bello* and *Principatus politicus*,²⁵ but I shall confine this discussion to the area that is directly relevant to the subject at hand. The Granadan Suárez argued that a just war had an impact on the conquered land and their people, who by being deprived of freedom got what they deserved, whereas the victor "acquired true rights and dominion over that realm, because that is fair punishment according to the justice of war."²⁶ He added that faith did not change the situation when the conqueror was a pagan ruler and the vanquished a Christian monarch, because "in this case common law applies, which is derived from natural law and not annulled by faith."²⁷ This rationale justified most of the armed conflicts the Hispanic kingdom was engaged in, particularly those against the Ottoman empire and Protestant heretics in the sixteenth century²⁸ and it legitimized the American conquest. In this case Suárez sanctioned both the military process and the subsequent colonization on the grounds that, since waging war against indigenous American people was justified and lawful, so was the occupation and exploitation of their land and the takeover of civil power from the conquered communities.²⁹

Despite these justifications, Suárez noted, kingdoms were frequently occupied by means of unjust wars. This was, after all, how the most famous empires on earth expanded.³⁰ Ribadeneyra took a very similar position. Although he did not refer directly to this matter in his *Príncipe Christiano*, he touched upon it when he criticized the inordinate effort exerted by those who strove for possessions and wealth, using any means at their disposal to achieve their goal, including "open warfare against

24. Mantovani 2017: 245.
25. Macedo 2013: 197–201.
26. Suárez 1965: 32.
27. Suárez 1965: 51.
28. A case in point with regard to the Jesuits' justification of wars with religious undercurrents is the so-called "Reconquest," a term established by traditional Spanish historiography which refers to the process of conquest and repopulation carried out by Christian kingdoms in the Iberian Peninsula between the eighth and fifteenth centuries. I draw attention to this phenomenon because it was conceived by historiographers in the early modern period and eventually acquired epic dimensions on account of its significance as part of the fight against Islam (Ríos 2011).
29. Calafate 2014: 82.
30. Suárez 1965: 32.

those who can or try to hinder them," or appealing to human corruption through bribes.³¹

Nevertheless, Jesuits differed in their views of America. A case in point is the above-mentioned Luis de Molina, who said that "it was not legitimate to force any of these infidels to embrace the faith or receive baptism, or to wage war against them for that reason or to subject them."³² In his view, it was licit to evangelize and convert indigenous people, but always voluntarily and never by force. He also rejected the claim that a society's incivility justified assault and slavery.³³ Despite certain differences and nuances, José de Acosta's position was very close to de Molina's. While he argued that idolatry, homosexuality, incest, contumacy, and delinquency ought to be punished even by death, he was aware of the sheer weight of dissension and conflict that would derive from violent intervention. It was legitimate to wage a just war as long as it was helpful, but its potential consequences needed to be assessed because "there are innumerable testimonies to the fact that many more Indians have lost their lives in the wars we have engaged them in, than they ever suffered under the tyranny of barbarians. The sacrifice and slaughter of Indians caused by the Spanish sword are beyond reckoning."³⁴

"The other" through the eyes of Juan Azor in his *Institutionum moralium*

The Jesuit writer Juan Azor has passed almost unnoticed in recent research on early-modern moral theology. Despite his far-reaching influence in the seventeenth century, when several editions of his *Institutionum moralium* were printed, studies of his work have been limited to a few initial approaches.³⁵ The sheer size of this work—three volumes including over

---

31. Ribadeneyra 1595: 273–75.
32. Calafate and Mandado 2014: 268.
33. Calafate and Mandado 2014: 271.
34. Calafate and Mandado 2014: 372.
35. Such as Pelster (1943), Dziuba (1988 and 1996) and a few recent works in Spanish and Italian: Sarmiento, Molina, and Trigo 2013: 314–21; Prodi 2000: 325–89; Martín 2022.

2,500 pages—and the fact that it was written in Latin may have played a part in the relative neglect of this author compared with other theologians.

Juan Azor's significance lies in his connection with teaching. He held several high-level college posts in Rome and in the Jesuit province of Toledo, among them reader in philosophy (1566) and theology (1568–1571) at Alcalá de Henares, and reader in theology and rector in Plasencia (1571). By the time he was called to the Roman Curia in 1580, he had also been rector of the Ocaña and Alcalá colleges. At the Eternal City he taught scholastic and positive theology at the Jesuit college (1580–1595), where he was prefect of studies (1586–1589 and 1592–1594). He was chosen by General Acquaviva as Spanish representative to collaborate in the draft of the *Ratio Studiorum* (1599)—the educational plan which, after several amends, revisions, and redactions, drove the modernization of Jesuit teaching plans.[36]

Azor's role in that project is a key aspect of his pinnacle work, which was essentially a moral theology textbook to be used in the two-year course on cases of conscience prescribed in the *Ratio*. Initially following the structure of the Ten Commandments, Azor addressed a broad range of themes relating to the family, the law, the economy, politics, and warfare, among others, from a Catholic moral perspective. Its question-and-answer structure around each of the commandments made it easy to use by teachers, pupils, confessors, and so on. Furthermore, the book was based on teaching materials he used in his lessons, which enabled two of the three volumes to be published posthumously (1608 and 1612). Some of those materials may be seen today at the *Archivio della Pontificia Università Gregoriana* in Rome.[37]

These particulars explain the reasons for including an extended discussion of Juan Azor's work in this chapter. As well as conveying the Jesuit image of non-Catholic communities worldwide, his *opus magnum* played a key role in the development of moral theology in the seventeenth

---

36. The biographical data have been compiled from a variety of sources, such as the yearbooks kept in the *Archivum Romanum Societatis Iesu* (ARSI), the *Archivo de España de la Compañía de Jesús* (AESI-A), Bartolomé de Alcázar's *Chrono-Historia*, Monzón's *Menologio*, and the bio-bibliographic repertories of Pedro de Ribadeneyra, Felipe Alegambe, and Nicolás Antonio among others.
37. Martín 2022.

century. Besides, having been written in Rome, it allows us to observe certain differences between his approach and those of other Spanish authors.

I will discuss only the first volume of this work, where he mentions other religions and cultures. As the only volume Azor was able to see in print (he died in 1603), it is the most likely to reflect his actual thinking. Although volumes two and three were based on his manuscripts, they were out of his control and the possibility of editorial interference cannot be dismissed.

Azor devotes several chapters of his first volume to other world religions and their relationship to Catholicism, including apostates, schismatics, pagans, Saracens, and the "perfidious" Jews. We shall focus on the latter two and on the varied casuistry he compiled around them.

Azor's references to Jews are striking. Beginning at the chapter heading, he describes them as perfidious, obstinate, and nefarious. In the course of eighteen questions and answers, we can observe the image he projected of the Hebrew nation, focusing on the economy and on Jewish-Catholic relations, both individual and institutional—including the Church and the Inquisition. His approach is understandably broader than those of his co-religionists in his native Spain. It emerges from his writing that the book was composed in Rome for a far wider readership than if it had been written in Spain and intended to be applied only in Spanish territories. Azor's potential readers and users might have been based anywhere in the world and their interests could have related to any aspect of daily life.

It is surprising to find day-to-day contact between Catholics and Jews discussed during Philip II's reign, or at any rate as openly as Azor does in some of the questions. When the Catholic monarchs Ferdinand and Isabella ordered the expulsion of all Jews from Spain in 1492, the latter were given two options: exile or conversion to Catholicism. As it was discovered that many converts continued practising their former religion, these false converts were henceforth known as *judaizantes* (Judaizers). This topic is linked to the issue of "purity of blood" and the situation of so-called New Christians, which are beyond the scope of this chapter. It also relates to the role of the Inquisition in the search and identification of such Judaizers, which Azor does address in his works.

Azor's general advice regarding contact between Catholics and Jews was to avoid familiarity and proximity as dangerous and prone to treachery. In question three, he explains that this kind of familiarity might lead a Christian, for instance, to deliver food to a Jew, a scenario in which the latter might appear as having a higher status than the former.[38] He listed several situations which he considered punishable with excommunication for laymen and with dismissal for members of the clergy: cohabiting with Jews; celebrating their holidays and sharing food with them; sharing baths; caring for sick Jews; receiving or making Jewish medicines; looking after their children; serving them; and sharing unleavened bread with them.[39] He also mentioned certain contexts in which this might be justified.[40] For instance, the fifth question asked whether it was legitimate to buy medicines for a sick Jew, to which he replied that it was forbidden to purchase such remedies, but not to donate them, as this should be considered a token of goodwill between individuals.

Once he had made it clear that contact with Jews should be minimized, Azor tackled other topics, including financial matters such as trade and contracts, whether it was permissible to serve Jews, and the governance of secular and religious institutions. He addresses the first of these topics over several answers in which he seems to perpetuate the stereotype of the Jew as a usurer and a miser who takes advantage of other people's needs through loans. Except, however, on Jewish holidays, when they devoted themselves to their own celebrations.[41] Azor's proposed solution is therefore to avoid any financial dealings with Jews. He illustrates this advice with a simile: buying a sword or a bottle of poison is not in itself reprehensible, but the potential destruction and loss of life that might ensue certainly are.

On the matter of servants, Azor presented an interesting set of scenarios exploring whether it was legitimate or not and in what circumstances. Despite ruling out closeness and familiarity, as we saw above, the seventh, eighth, and ninth questions posed situations that escaped such a categorical assertion. Accordingly, Christian women were allowed to look after Jews, as long as they did not do so in their own homes, in public, or outside the Jews' dwellings.[42] This is an interesting detail because it dovetails with the advice of contemporary moralists to Catholics regarding their

38. Azor 1600: 1009.
39. Ibid.
40. Azor 1600: 1010.
41. Ibid.
42. Azor 1600: 1011.

appearance in public settings: Alonso Rodríguez, Nicolás de Arnaya, Luis de la Puente, and others insisted that the virtuous image one projected abroad reflected his inner Christian quality.[43]

Concerning their relationship with Catholic political and religious institutions, Jewish people were barred from holding honorific titles, dignities, or administrative posts[44] but as subjects of the Christian sovereign they were liable to prosecution for civil offences. Therefore, although Azor put spiritual transgressions in a separate category to rule out excommunication as a penalty for civil offences, he stipulated that in certain cases Jews could be punished with exile or expropriation for actions of a religious nature, such as circumcision of a Christian—whether voluntary or forced—or inducing a Christian to convert to Judaism and renounce their faith in Christ. The latter case appeared in question twelve, in connection with the areas ecclesiastical judges and inquisitors could legitimately investigate, namely blasphemy, preventing the christening of catechumens, holding heretical and Talmudic literature, invoking the devil and performing Satanic sacrifices and offerings.[45] Finally, he encouraged inquisitors to investigate and prosecute heretics and any Christians who shielded, protected, and abetted them in their efforts to convert others to observance of the Talmud.[46]

Azor's thoughts about Muslims are the subject of chapter 23 of *Institutionum moralium*, where he discusses various related matters such as the meaning of the term "Saracen", the locations where Saracens lived, their relationship to Christians, and the war against Islam. His approach to Muslims differs from his treatment of Jews in some respects. As mentioned above, his pronouncements on the latter would have been applicable in other parts of Europe, but not in Spanish territories, where Judaism was persecuted by the Inquisition. Conversely, Azor's prescriptions in relation to Islam would have been relevant in Spain, which still had a substantial Morisco population by 1600, but not to most of Europe, where Muslim presence was limited to south-eastern areas of the continent which had been under Ottoman rule.

43. Martín 2013: 104–108.
44. Azor 1600: 1011.
45. Azor 1600: 1012.
46. Azor 1600: 1018.

Azor designated Muslims as the "impious and heinous Mohammedan sect," be they "Turks, Tartars, Persians, Arabs, Egyptians, Africans or Moors,"[47] and including every person who lived in Christian lands and helped Muslims perpetrate attacks against Christians—occasionally Jews and far more often Protestant heretics.

As in the case of Jews, he claimed that bishops and inquisitors were legitimately empowered to investigate Christian converts to Islam and to punish all those who sheltered and helped any person who was involved in such conversions.[48] To support this, he quoted papal bull *Coena Domini* in which Gregory XIII decreed that any Christian who facilitated Muslim conversions should be excommunicated.

Warfare and the weapons Muslims used against Christians were vital matters to Azor. No doubt this was partly due to the religious conflict that was raging at the time across the Mediterranean and Eastern Europe, but the Spanish context should not be ignored. The atmosphere of uncertainty and suspicion towards Moriscos in the aftermath of the Alpujarras rebellion (1568–1571) came to a head in 1609 with the expulsion decree. Although it may have been slightly ahead of its time, Azor's view runs parallel to the discourse developed during the seventeenth century in the fields of historiography, literature and art, which justified the expulsion by associating the Moriscos with the Turkish enemy.[49]

Azor's wide-ranging casuistry on the subject of warfare established, among other things, the excommunication of Christians who gave or traded in weapons or horses with Muslims, be it in Saracen or Christian lands, on the grounds that such items would be used against the name of Christ. Conversely, Greek, Armenian, Venetian, or even Saracen people who contributed to the fight against other Muslims would be exempted.[50] Furthermore, in question nine he addressed the issue of quality in the weapons trade and denounced the sale of untameable, worthless horses to Christians and robust, valuable ones to Muslims.

The theme of war in association with the image of Muslims was developed further in Azor's treatise with the addition of two other topics—armament and the complex matter of the Christian captives who served

47. Azor 1600: 1018–19.
48. Azor 1600: 1018.
49. Franco and Moreno 2019.
50. Azor 1600: 1020, 1022.

in Saracen galleys. Over several sections, Azor describes the variety of weapons used by Muslims to attack and defend; their war machines, such as wooden galleys and "those [devices] that hurl stone and iron balls"; their shields, helmets, coats of mail, swords, spears, arrows; domestic tools such as knives, axes, sickles, hoes, sticks, needles, pins; and other instruments, like tubas and horns, "which are habitually used in the art of war."[51]

On the circumstances of prisoners of war who plied the oars in Saracen galleys, Azor pointed out different scenarios that should be considered in cases of potential excommunication of these Catholics. In his view, captives aboard merchant vessels would be exempted, but not those who, having been captured by Saracens, contributed to the war against Christians by "rowing, bearing or supplying weapons, giving aid or offering counsel."[52] Nevertheless, quoting the Navarra Jesuit Martín de Azpilcueta, he proposed that the beatings, torment, and death threats captive men might suffer if they refused to cooperate with the Saracens should be seen as mitigating factors that would save them from excommunication. Not, however, from "mortal sin."

Japanese culture in the eyes of Spanish Jesuits

We finally turn to how Jesuit clergymen perceived Japanese people. The Society of Jesus first made contact with Japan in the late 1540s, when Francis Xavier arrived on its shores after spending several years in India, where he carried out most of his evangelical mission. In Japan the Jesuits conducted an intense campaign to spread Catholicism among the population. To achieve their aim, they adapted Christian dogma, liturgy, and sources of knowledge to Japanese imagery and cult patterns, particularly Buddhism.

This form of acculturation hinged on the translation into Japanese of catechisms and moral treatises originally written in Spanish and Portuguese.[53] Grammatical works were also translated to help preachers prepare their sermons and to support the composition of catechisms and

51. Azor 1600: 1020–21, 1023.
52. Azor 1600: 1023.
53. Sobczyk 2020: 159–77; Hoyos and Gavirati 2017: 13–32.

doctrinal tracts in the local language.[54] As part of the process to make this new Western religion understandable to Japanese people, the Jesuits reworked the images conveyed by the Holy Scriptures, as can be seen in Nanban art, a popular current in that country until the mid-seventeenth century.[55] The Jesuits applied similar missionary strategies in Asia and America, although their artistic adaptations were more pronounced in China and Japan, as the orientalization of European features in Nanban paintings demonstrates. In other areas, however, their procedures were practically identical in both regions. In America, catechisms, vocabularies, and grammars were translated into various indigenous languages such as Nahuatl, Aymara, Guarani, and Mapuche.[56]

Despite the success of these campaigns in terms of souls acquired for the Catholic church, Rome had reservations as to whether the newly converted really believed and followed correctly the Catholic way of life. Covert worship of former deities, whether conscious or unconscious, was the subject of several warnings from the Order's general, particularly during Claudio Acquaviva's tenure between 1581 and 1615.[57] The image of Japan which the Society of Jesus circulated in those early years is revealed in the following quote where Xavier, the "Apostle of the Indies," makes a positive assessment of Asian people. Despite their condition as infidels, he placed them almost on an equal level with Catholics and suggested that this would make their conversion to Christianity easier:

> As for Japan, from the experience we have of this land, let me tell you what we have achieved so far. First, the people we have conversed with to date are the best ever discovered, and it seems to me that among infidels no other people are likely to surpass the Japanese. They eat soberly, although they are a little fond of drink. Many of them can read and write, which is a great advantage for learning prayers and God's things quickly [...] this island of Japan is quite ready for our holy faith to grow greatly in it and I have no doubt that many of them would become Christians if we could speak their tongue.[58]

54. Toyoshima 2020: 149–58; Kishimoto 2020: 179–99.
55. García 1971: 31–37; Curvelo 2001: 59–69; Arimura 2011: 93–106.
56. Gaune 2013: 13–36.
57. St. Clair 2002: 109–40.
58. García-Villoslada 1940: 154.

We shall return to these words later, when we explore the story of the Tenshō embassy and the descriptions of Japanese people recorded by fathers Jerónimo Román de la Higuera and Luis de Guzmán after the legation's visit to Toledo and Belmonte respectively. Their accounts show that, while displaying the usual Jesuit—and generally Catholic—sense of superiority toward every other religion, in the case of Japan these authors went beyond their comfort zone and came to appreciate Japanese culture. As reported in a number of studies, confrontations between religious leaders of either faith took place in Japan, especially in the seventeenth century, including attacks on Buddhist temples and persecutions of Catholics.[59] But it is remarkable that, while religious conflict was rife in the far-eastern archipelago, on the other side of the planet people had nothing but kind and welcoming words for its culture. The key to this apparent contradiction, as I understand it, lies in the divide between religion, on one hand, and the rest of culture and daily life on the other. The embassy's Jesuit hosts accepted and admired Japanese difference, but only as long as they saw it in people who had converted to Catholicism, as opposed to those who remained loyal to their own faith.

Throughout the second half of the sixteenth century, the Society of Jesus flourished in Japan and broadened its influence in the political sphere, becoming close to some of its main players, such as Oda Nobunaga (1534–1582). This had two important consequences. First, the eventual persecution of Jesuits under Toyotomi Hideyoshi's rule; and second, the organization of what became known as the Tenshō embassy. The Italian Jesuit Alessandro Valignano played a very significant part in this project, having secured the conversion of some of the most prominent individuals in Japanese society among the 150,000 conversions achieved by 1582.[60]

In such auspicious circumstances, the Jesuit missionaries and their allies decided to undertake a journey from Japan to Europe, where they would appear before the two pillars of Christendom: King Philip II and, above all, Pope Gregory XIII. Added to this, Valignano intended to promote Francis Xavier's beatification—which eventually took place in 1619—and to obtain more support for Jesuit missions in Asia, a goal that

59. Tramon 2006: 46; Míguez 2014: 91–92. Thanks to Sara Arias Gómez for her help in understanding the Japanese background to the Jesuit evangelization effort and their conflict with Buddhist monks.
60. García Villoslada and Llorca 1987: 1.000–1.001.

also met with success when Pope Gregory granted the Order exclusive missionary rights in Japan.[61]

The legation included representatives of the kings of Bungo and Arima, and of the prince of Oruma. The chosen delegates were Mancio Ito, a cousin of the prince of Hyuga selected by the first monarch, and Miguel de Chijiwa, a nephew of the prince of Oruma and cousin of the king of Arima who represented the latter two personages. On account of their youth, they were accompanied by two laymen (Julián de Nakaura and Martín de Hara) and several Jesuits (the Portuguese Diego de Mesquita, the Japanese Jorge Loyola and Constantino Dourado, and Alessandro Valignano himself[62]). The embassy set sail from Nagasaki in February 1582 and endured a harrowing journey across the Indian Ocean and around the Cape of Good Hope, finally arriving on the Portuguese coast in August 1584.[63] After two and a half years at sea, they were welcomed by the authorities in Lisbon to the thunder of artillery salvoes. As gunpowder was a common element in both religious and secular festivals, this kind of performance was repeated at every stop along the route. These gestures bear witness to the high esteem and warm welcome extended to the travelers.

From Lisbon, the Japanese legation wended its way to Rome via Madrid, covering a wide strip across the center of the Iberian Peninsula. Their itinerary was determined by the locations of the different Jesuit establishments scattered between Lisbon and the royal palace at El Escorial, and between Madrid and Alicante, where they boarded the ship that conveyed them to Rome. Before crossing the border into Castile they visited Évora, where the Society of Jesus had one of its oldest colleges, with close links to the town's renowned university. Their next stop, in the heart of the Spanish kingdom, was the Talavera college—founded in 1582—followed by the city of Toledo, where the Jesuits had founded St Eugene's College in 1583, although their presence in the city dated back to 1558.[64]

61. Bangert 1981: 196–97.
62. Archivo de España de la Compañía de Jesús (AESI-A), M-114, *Relación de la Embaxada que embiaron al Papa algunos Principes del Japón...*, p. 1.
63. Ibid., 3. The dificulties encountered along this journey were the likely reason for the 1613–1617 Keichō embassy's decision to travel to Spain by the opposite route, sailing across the Pacific and Atlantic oceans and crossing Central America on foot.
64. Martín 2015: 213, 243–74.

The travelers were forced to extend their stay at the Toledo college by a month when Miguel de Chijiwa fell ill with smallpox. As Father Jerónimo de la Higuera reports in his *Historia eclesiástica de la imperial ciudad de Toledo*, the embassy's sojourn in the town proved beneficial to all parties. The Japanese visitors explored the city guided by Juan de Mendoza, prebendary of the cathedral and brother of the Duque del Infantado—one of the most prominent Spanish aristocrats—who showed them the relics, ornaments, and treasures stored in the Cathedral sacristy.[65] The Spanish clergymen, on their part, acquired first-hand knowledge of various aspects of Japanese culture, as we glean from the chronicle written by Higuera, who lived in the professed house and taught at the Jesuit college. His words help us understand the contrasts experienced by all concerned in those few weeks and the people of Toledo's amazement at the Nippon men's physical features and the clothes they wore at different events:

> They were the colour of cooked quince, with small eyes and great intelligence, very modest and well spoken. They entered the city in a carriage lent by Doña Guiomar Pardo and were escorted by several students on horseback. They came to the Professed House in this town, where they were welcomed with many tokens of love and charity.
> [...] they were invited to the Cardinal's College, which belongs to the Society, where they were welcomed with much music, apposite Latin verse which they understood well, and enjoyed seeing such fine skills [...] They chose to be registered as brothers of the Anunciata Congregation and signed the book with their names in the hieroglyphic writing they use. They dressed in their Japanese knights' garb for the fathers to see, which is very majestic and gives men a handsome appearance because they wear a kind of bonnet, taller than the usual ones, and over their shirts they wear some rather large and wide doublets in white satin. Then a purple fitted taffeta robe, similar to a surplice, and over it and below another garment with a pattern of greenery and foliage and a kind of drape half a yard tall. Their clothing rather resembles German dress, save that it has sleeves. Both men and women wear these clothes around the house and when they go outdoors they wear very wide pantaloons resembling those worn by Walloons, large enough for the two long robes

---

65. Guzmán 1601: 235.

to be tucked inside, and their purpose is like that of Spanish capes or cloaks, and when they return home they take off these pantaloons. They carry golden daggers and swords at their navels. All in all this is the finest costume I have ever seen.[66]

As soon as Chijiwa recovered from his illness, the embassy resumed their journey to El Escorial, where the Japanese ambassadors arrived in November 1584, a short time before Philip III was sworn in as heir to the throne. In their audience with Philip II on November 14th,[67] they acknowledged him as the "great monarch of Christianity [...] who favoured and promoted Christendom in Japan," and begged him "to continue this celebrated act of benevolence."[68] At El Escorial they also met the Holy Roman Empress, the French ambassador, and some members of the Spanish nobility.[69] A month later they continued on their journey across the Peninsula stopping at other Jesuit centers in Spain: the novitiate at Villarejo de Fuentes and the colleges at Alcalá de Henares, Belmonte, Murcia, Elche, Orihuela and, finally Alicante, where they set sail for Italy in March 1585.[70]

Another extant account of the Japanese embassy's tour of the Toledo Jesuit province can be found in Luis de Guzmán's *History* of the Jesuit missions in China, India, and Japan. Like Higuera, Guzmán witnessed the splendid welcome celebrations in their honor as rector of Belmonte college. This is his description of the Japanese visitors on their arrival in Madrid:

> Their fabric was a fine taffeta-like silk in white, intertwined with other colours and decorated with figures of birds and flowers which gave it great beauty. The Japanese usually wear three garments made from this material, one over the other, open at the front and so long they almost touch the ground. The sleeves were wide, elbow length, and although other Japanese people usually show their bare forearms, these gentlemen wore white satin doublets underneath for decency's

66. Biblioteca Nacional de España (BNE), Mss. 1293: Higuera, Jerónimo Román de la: *Historia eclesiástica de la imperial ciudad de Toledo*, ff. 216r-v.
67. Guzmán 1601: 236.
68. AESI-A, C-187,1: Alcázar, Bartolomé de, *Chrono-Historia de la Provincia de Toledo...*, 1710–1712, p. 396.
69. Ibid.
70. Guzmán 1601: 239–43.

sake. Their pantaloons were of the same weave, silk and colour, but long, like the ones worn by sailors. Their outfits also included a piece of the same material but more finely made than the rest of their garments, whose sole purpose was to look handsome. It was two spans wide and three long, and at either end a tape or ribbon two fingers wide was wrapped across the chest, around the back and again to the front, holding that strip of fabric in place and girding the body.

They usually gobareheaded because when they go outdoors they protect themselves from the sun and the rain with certain parasols, although these gentlemen consented to wear hats or bonnets to abide by our customs. They do not usually wear hose, save for some linen stockings for the sake of cleanliness, which they do not take off even to sleep. Over these stockings they wore some boots just over a span high, made of very delicate tanned leather. The foot was divided like a glove because the big toe was on its own and the rest together. Over these boots they wore some sandal-like shoes, open at the top and attached with a ribbon, with fine palm soles woven like our espadrilles.

All Japanese men carry a sword and a dagger from the age of twelve and these are made of such fine steel that they can cut any weapon, however strong. The scabbards in which noble folks carry them are very rich and beautiful, like the ones these gentlemen brought with them because one was made of a certain black glossy mixture and scattered with pieces of mother-of-pearl in several colours, so well set and close together that whoever stroked the sheath with his fingers found it smooth like very finely polished paper. The other scabbard was covered all over in ormolu, but as smooth and beautiful as the first.[71]

These texts show that the cultural contrasts perceived throughout their journey must have been so astonishing that Fathers Higuera and Guzmán could not help but write a full account of what they saw. It is interesting to note that both chroniclers were particularly impressed by the visitors' outfits and peculiar customs, and that both drew parallels between Japanese sartorial habits and those that were more familiar to them and their readers, in order to make their descriptions easier to understand.

The cultural differences between the visitors and their hosts are conspicuous throughout these texts, contrary to what we observe in Figure 10.2. This is a very well-known engraving printed in Augsburg in

71. Guzmán 1601: 236–37.

1586 showing the four Japanese men (Julián and Mancio above, Martín and Miguel below) surrounding Father Mesquita. In a reversal of the images of Europeans in Nanban art, in which figures such as St. Francis Xavier were given oriental features, in the Augsburg print the Japanese gentlemen's appearance is westernized—albeit not completely. Were it not for their cropped hair, they could easily be taken for Europeans. In a similar vein, the ruffs worn by the laymen are at odds with the eyewitness descriptions of their attire written by Higuera and Guzmán. On the other hand, the coloring of their garments and the leafy decorations on the edges of their doublets suggest an East-West mixture which is totally unlike the images of noble personages in contemporary prints and paintings. This imagery can be seen today in the sculpture erected in remembrance of the Tenshō embassy in the city of Omura (Nagasaki Prefecture) representing four young men with oriental features wearing European-style dress instead of the clothes described in contemporary accounts of the event (Figure 10.3).

Figure 10.2. *News sheet with a report and image of the Japanese ambassadors.* Augsburg, 1586. Kyoto University Library. Source: Catalogue of the exhibition "En busca del sol naciente. Las embajadas Tenshō (1582–1588) y Keichō (1613–1617)," p. 9.

292 *Narratives of Peace in Religious Discourses*

Figure 10.3. Detail of the sculpture in memory of the Tenshō embassy in Omura, Japan. Source: Wikimedia.

Conclusion

In this chapter we have explored the concept of tolerance in the early modern period through the relationships developed by the Society of Jesus with other cultures and the way they set them down in their works. Generally speaking, these authors wrote from the Catholics' assumed position of cultural superiority, with some subtle variants. First, the Jesuits Molina and Acosta rose in defense of American indigenous people, whose sovereignty, in their view, should not be questioned. Second, Jesuits projected an image of Japanese people which reflected the high esteem in which this culture was held from their first contact, in contrast with other societies. At the other end of the scale, Juan Azor's depictions of Jews and Muslims in his wide-ranging casuistry were packed with negative stereotypes from the realms of economy and warfare.

The Jesuit relationship with "the other" was the subject not only of historical accounts, anthropological descriptions, and legislative arguments, but left its mark in the area of governance too. Jesuit authors also wrote extensively about the need to seek peace, the justification of war and its potential drawbacks.

Author biography

David Martín López is a Lecturer in the History department at the Universidad de Castilla-La Mancha, Spain. His research interests are the Toledo province of the Society of Jesus, its territorial expansion and consolidation during the sixteenth century and its heritage after Jesuits were expelled from Spain in 1767; the University of Toledo in the early modern period; Hispanic political thinking and its relationship to ethics in the Baroque period.

References

Primary sources

Andrade, A. de (1642), *El buen soldado católico y sus obligaciones*. Madrid: Francisco Maroto.
Azor, J. (1600), *Institutiones morales. Pars prima*. Rome: Apud Aloysium Zannettum.
Azor, J. (1608), *Institutiones morales. Tomus secundus*. Coloniae Agrippinae: Apud Antonium Hierat.
Guzmán, L. de (1601), *Historia de las missiones que han hecho los religiosos de la Compañía de Jesús para predicar el sancto Evangelio en los Reynos de Japón. Segunda parte*. Alcalá: por la viuda de Juan Gracián.
Ribadeneyra, P. de (1595), *Tratado de la religión y virtudes que deve tener el Príncipe Christiano para gobernar y conservar sus Estados*. Madrid: P. Madrigal.

Secondary sources

Arimura, R. (2011), "Las misiones católicas en Japón (1549–1639): análisis de las fuentes y tendencias historiográficas," *Anales del Instituto de Investigaciones Estéticas* XXXIII/98: 55–106. https://doi.org/10.22201/iie.18703062e.2011.98.2362
Bangert, W. V. (1981), *Historia de la Compañía de Jesús*. Santander: Sal Terrae.
Calafate, P. (2014), "A Escola Ibérica da Paz nas Universidades de Coimbra e Évora (Século XVI)," *Teocomunicação* 44/1: 78–96. https://doi.org/10.15448/1980-6736.2014.1.18283
Calafate, P., and R. E. Mandado Gutiérrez (2014), *Escola Ibérica da Paz: A Consciência Crítica da Conquista e Colonização da América*: 1511–1694. Santander: Editorial Universidad Cantabria.
Curvelo, A. (2001), "Arte 'kirishitan': la práctica artística en la acción misional de los jesuitas en el Japón," *Reales Sitios: Revista del Patrimonio Nacional* 149: 59–69.

Dziuba, A. (1988), *Jan Azor teolog-moralista*. Warsaw: Wydawnictwo Archidiecezji Warszawskiej.

Dziuba, A. (1996), "Juan Azor S.J., teólogo moralista del siglo XVI–XVII," *Archivo Teológico Granadino* 59: 145–55.

Franco Llopis, B., and F. J. Moreno Díaz del Campo (2019), *Pintando al converso. La imagen del morisco en la península ibérica (1492–1614)*. Madrid: Cátedra.

García Gutiérrez, F. (1971), "El arte del 'Siglo Cristiano' en Japón ('Namban Geijutsu')," *Boletín de la Asociación Española de Orientalistas* 7: 31–37.

García Villoslada, R. (1940), *Manual de Historia de la Compañía de Jesús*. Madrid: Compañía Bibliográfica Española.

García Villoslada, R., and B. Llorca (1987), *Historia de la Iglesia Católica. Tomo 3: Edad Nueva. La Iglesia en la época del Renacimiento y de la Reforma Católica (1303–1648)*. Madrid: Biblioteca de Autores Cristianos.

Gaune, R. (2013), "El jesuita como traductor. Organización, circulación y dinámicas de la Compañía de Jesús en Santiago de Chile, 1593–1598," *Historia Crítica* 50: 13–36. https://doi.org/10.7440/histcrit50.2013.01

Hoyos Hattori, P., and P. Gavirati Miyashiro (2017), "Traducir, editar, evangelizar: el discurso jesuita del 'siglo cristiano en Japón' desde la perspectiva de la modernidad-colonialidad (siglo XVI)," *Historia Crítica* 63: 13–32. https://doi.org/10.7440/histcrit63.2017.01

Kishimoto, E. (2020), "Lexicografía latina en Japón: Dictionarium Latino Lusitanicum, ac Iaponicum (1595)," in Y. Orii and M. J. Zamora Calvo (eds.), *Cruces y áncoras. La influencia de Japón y España en un Siglo de Oro global*, 179–99. Madrid: Abada editores.

Macedo, P. E. V. B. (2013), "El derecho de la guerra en Francisco Suárez: o proyecto civilizador de la España escolástica," *Revista de la Secretaría del Tribunal Permanente de Revisión* 1: 185–211. https://doi.org/10.16890/rstpr.a1.n1.185

Mantovani, M. (2017), "Algunas notas sobre la teoría de la 'guerra justa' en Francisco Suárez," *Sophia: colección de Filosofía de la Educación* 23(2): 239–63. https://doi.org/10.17163/soph.n23.2017.09

Mariana, J. de (1981), *La dignidad real y la educación del rey*. Madrid: CEPC.

Martín López, D. (2013), "'Escaleras hacia el cielo.' La búsqueda de la virtud en la tratadística moral jesuítica entre los siglos XVI y XVII," in E. Serrano Martín (ed.), *De la tierra al cielo. Líneas recientes de investigación en Historia Moderna*, 101–16. Zaragoza: Institución "Fernando el Católico".

Martín López, D. (2015), "Religión, poder y pensamiento politico. Los jesuitas de la Provincia de Toledo (1540–1621)," PhD thesis, Universidad de Castilla-La Mancha.

Martín López, D. (2022), "Entre la tradición y la modernidad: los manuales de Teología moral de la Compañía de Jesús y la obra de Juan Azor," *Edad de Oro* 41. https://doi.org/10.15366/edadoro2021.41.013

Míguez Santa Cruz, A. (2014), "Referencias histórico-culturales en los escritos de los jesuitas en el Japón del siglo XVI," *Hispania Sacra* 66: 75–107. https://doi.org/10.3989/hs.2013.047

Molina, L. de (1611), *De Iustitia et Iure*. Venice: Sessas.

Pelster, F. (1943), "Zwei Verträge über Druck und Verlag der 'Institutiones morales,' des J. Azor," *Archivum Historicum Societatis Iesu* 12: 134–44.

Prodi, P. (2000), "La norma: il diritto della morale," in P. Prodi, *Una storia della giustizia*, 325–89. Bologna: Il Mulino.

Ríos Saloma, M. F. (2011), *La Reconquista. Una construcción historiográfica (siglos XVI–XIX)*. Madrid: Marcial Pons.

Sarmiento, A., E. Molina, and T. Trigo (2013), *Teología moral fundamental*. Pamplona: EUNSA.

Sobczyk, M. (2020), "Estrategias de domesticación y extranjerización en la traducción al japonés de Tratado de la oración y meditación," in Y. Orii and M. J. Zamora Calvo (eds.), *Cruces y áncoras. La influencia de Japón y España en un Siglo de Oro global*, 159–77. Madrid: Abada editores.

St. Clair Segurado, E. M. (2002), "La cuestión de los ritos chinos y malabares: desobediencia e idolatría en la Compañía de Jesús," *Hispania Sacra* 54: 109–140. https://doi.org/10.3989/hs.2002.v54.i109.190

Suárez, F. (1965), *Defensio Fidei III. Principatus Politicus o La soberanía popular*. Madrid: CSIC.

Toyoshima, M. (2020), "Gramáticas normativas y descriptivas, adaptación de la influencia ibérica por los jesuitas en Japón," in Y. Orii and M. J. Zamora Calvo (eds.), *Cruces y áncoras. La influencia de Japón y España en un Siglo de Oro global*, 149–58. Madrid: Abada editores.

Tramon Castillo, J. (2006), "El catolicismo en Japón. Testimonio del encuentro de dos culturas," *Pharos* 13(1): 41–57.

Chapter 11
"Tiered Tolerance": Protestants and the "Other" after 1685

Nora Baker

Introduction

The most prominent of Huguenot thinkers on tolerance is undoubtedly Pierre Bayle (1647–1706). Bayle's religious convictions were less dogmatic than those of his erstwhile friend Pierre Jurieu,[1] and he is often considered an early Enlightenment figure, known for his *Commentaire philosophique* and the *Dictionnaire historique et critique*, which condemned religious persecution and the use of violence to compel conversions. Differences of conscience, claimed Bayle, should be tolerated, at least in the majority of circumstances.[2] The philosopher argued against compelling particular worship, and also against violence.[3] Though his work has often been credited with providing inspiration for the likes of Voltaire, Diderot, and Rousseau, many other scholars have sought to revise this reading, arguing that Bayle must be understood in his own contemporary, Calvinist context, and that he should not be confused with the later *encyclopédistes*.[4] Even prior to the 1598 Edict of Nantes, amid the sixteenth-century Wars of Religion, a number of thinkers had made

---

1. See van der Lugt 2016: 2.
2. Bayle did allow for "intolerance" in the case of beliefs which had the potential to disrupt the stability of society. See, for example, Bayle 1740: 190.
3. Bayle 1740: xvii.
4. See, for example, Labrousse 1964; Rex 1965; Serrurier 1912; Solé 1971.

the case for toleration of religious differences, from the Catholic Jean Bodin to the Protestant Sebastian Castellio.[5]

However, the Revocation of the Edict of Nantes in 1685 saw the carefully-brokered peace in France—already fractured by the onslaught of the *dragonnades*—dissipate as refugees sought to leave the kingdom, and millenarist theories such as those espoused by Bayle's rival Jurieu took hold.[6] The early years of the eighteenth century saw many bloody scenes of rebellion take place during the Wars of the Cévennes (1702–1704), as Camisards—poor, mainly illiterate Protestants living in the Languedoc region—took up arms against those whom they saw as state oppressors. After the Revocation, Huguenot thinkers such as Pierre Jurieu and Jean Claude "snatched up the banners of popular sovereignty and the rights of a people to resist tyranny with force."[7] However, Bayle opposed Huguenot resistance to the French Crown after 1685, due to the threat this posed to order. Indeed, we know that the Camisard uprising was a slight anomaly among France's Protestant population, as many Huguenots preferred a pacifist approach. Jeanne Terrasson, who was among those Protestant prisoners detained in the *Hôpital de Valence* in 1687, recorded herself as telling soldiers who threatened to burn her: "if your religion was the true one, you would not use violence to bring to your Communion those who do not adhere to it. […] Never have those of our religion done such things."[8]

It is the goal of the present chapter not to engage in a reassessment of the output of Bayle, but to consider whether aspects of his theories on tolerance can be seen in the writings of some less well-known Huguenot figures in the years following his death. It is often argued that the connection

---

5. Cashmere 1969: 14.
6. For more on the impact of the Revocation on the Huguenot community, see Stanwood 2020.
7. Cashmere 1969: 29.
8. Terrasson 1880: 237–38. This is of course far from the truth—there were many instances of Protestant violence against Catholics in France's early modern period, with perhaps the best known being the instance of the *Michelade*. However, the history with which Terrasson would have been familiar would likely have emphasized the horrors of such events as the St. Bartholomew's Day Massacre and downplayed aggression from her own side: see van der Linden 2016: 348–70. All translations of excerpts from Huguenot memoirs in this chapter are my own.

between Bayle and the later Enlightenment writers is overemphasized.[9] Why, then, should we consider his impact on Jean-François Bion and Jean Marteilhe, whose mid-eighteenth-century writing is explored in this chapter? There are two reasons: firstly, and most importantly, both of these men were themselves firmly situated within the "Calvinist context," having fled France for the sake of their religion before putting pen to paper to denounce the horrors they had witnessed in their home country. They make frequent use of the *langue du Canaan*[10] and allude to the Huguenot commonplace of martyrdom.[11] It is probable that they would have been familiar with the contents of many of the same texts that Bayle would have grown up with, such as the Geneva Bible, the Psalter of Beza and Marot, and Jean Crespin and Simon Goulart's *Histoire des Martyrs*.[12] In addition to this, it is worth examining the articulation of tolerance in these men's writings precisely because they were *not* themselves typical "philosophers." This chapter will refute some of the arguments made in Séverine Collignon-Ward's thesis for the consideration of Marteilhe in an Enlightenment context. By comparing Bayle's ideas to those espoused in the writings of more "ordinary" people like Marteilhe and Bion, we can develop our appreciation of how widespread theories of various forms of tolerance were in the early modern world.

Rather than focusing solely on tensions related to the Protestant/Catholic dichotomy in early modern France, the present chapter considers representations of Turkish slaves and Camisards in accounts set among the melting pot of creeds that was the French galley ship. Protestant men found attempting to leave France in the aftermath of the Revocation risked being condemned to perpetual toil on these vessels, known as *galères*, under the command of officers known as *comites*. The visual spectacle associated with the rowers aboard the ships, known as *galériens*, served as a symbol of the might of France's rule: as Ruth Whelan terms it, "a baroque theatre of power."[13]

---

9. Cashmere 1969: 8.
10. See Whelan 2007: 141.
11. See van der Linden 2016.
12. Indeed, Bayle includes entries on these texts in his *Dictionnaire Historique et Critique* (see 5th edn).
13. Whelan 2010: 3. See also Zysberg 1983: 130, and Vigié 1985: 14.

It is to this fate that Jean Marteilhe was resigned when apprehended trying to cross the French border, having left his home in Bergerac in October 1700, at the age of just sixteen. It was not until the year 1713 that he was released, during an amnesty negotiated by Queen Anne in the Treaty of Utrecht. Marteilhe writes that Jesuit missionaries in Marseille continued to cause difficulties for him and for other former *galériens* following their release, but he eventually succeeded in leaving the country, and settled in the Netherlands. Marteilhe's *Mémoires* recounting his experience on board the galleys did not appear in print until 1757, but it is thought that he commenced writing his story prior to the death of his friend and publisher Daniel de Superville in 1728.[14]

Jean-François Bion, on the other hand, went to the galley ships willingly, to work as a Catholic chaplain. However, Bion was so moved by the suffering he witnessed on board the *galères*—and so horrified at the corruption that appeared to permeate all levels of their bureaucratic structure—that he eventually renounced his original faith and converted to Protestantism. Following a stint in Geneva, Bion moved to London, where he worked as a minister in the French Refugee Church. It was there that he published, in 1708, his *Relation des Tourments qu'on fait souffrir aux protestants qui sont sur les galères de France*, which was then released in English as *An account of the sufferings the French Protestants endure aboard the galleys*. As Bion was a learned minister, with a review of his work even appearing in the *Nouvelles de la République des Lettres*,[15] it does not seem beyond the bounds of possibility that he may have been familiar with some of Bayle's work.

Marteilhe and Bion originated from different theological backgrounds, and occupied different positions in the hierarchy at sea. They did not serve upon the same ships, and there is no evidence to suggest that the two men ever met. However, they describe several similar events in similar terms, drawing upon the common Huguenot vocabulary of the *langage du Canaan*. It is of course possible that Marteilhe had the opportunity to read Bion's work before completing his own, which is far longer, and which incorporates a number of anecdotes and side stories that at times

---

14. Collignon-Ward 2007: 11.
15. Bion and Conlon 1966: 30, n. 31. See the October 1708 volume of the *Nouvelles*: 468–69.

appear to deflect from the author's own role in his tale.[16] I argue that the central aim of Marteilhe's text is nonetheless to affirm the righteousness of the Protestant detainees and particularly that of his own person. Paul Bamford notes that Marteilhe and the other Huguenots received some preferential treatment, but he attributes this to the Protestants' shrewd utilization of monies they had available.[17] Pierre-Oliver Léchot writes that Marteilhe was moved by the Turkish men's non-monetary interest in helping the Protestants,[18] but Marteilhe does not express this in so many words himself—rather, he seems somewhat to expect it.

Collignon-Ward has argued that Marteilhe's sympathetic portrayal of Ottoman detainees indicates that the author can be linked to mid-eighteenth-century Enlightenment writers such as Voltaire and Diderot.[19] However, as this chapter illustrates, the positive aspects of the depictions of Turks in Marteilhe and Bion's works were far from radical: their words have antecedents in a wealth of literature from previous centuries. Indeed, in spite of their praise for the zeal with which the Ottomans practiced their religion, both men give rather reductive descriptions of the non-French individuals whom they encounter. Clarence Dana Rouillard, looking at representations of Turkish culture in French written production from the mid-sixteenth to the mid-seventeenth centuries, notes that the early modern period saw both "tolerant" and "intolerant" portryals of Turks—though he does not define what exactly he means by "tolerant."[20] The picture that emerges is rather too complex to be considered a straightforward "stepping stone" on the path to open-minded acceptance. The sort of tolerance Marteilhe and Bion appear to offer their Muslim interlocutors falls under the branch of what Rainier Forst terms *"permission conception"* of toleration: non-conforming groups are accommodated to the extent that they recognize the superiority of a primary group.[21] Forst argues that the brand of toleration that Bayle articulated ranged from permission conception to respect conception.[22]

16. Collignon-Ward 2007: 8.
17. Bamford 1973: 194: 201–202, 229.
18. Léchot 2021: 233.
19. Collignon-Ward 2007: 2.
20. Rouillard 1938: 37.
21. Forst 2008: 79–80.
22. Forst 2008: 81.

The philosophies of Bion and Marteilhe, however, as this chapter will show, were located firmly within the first of those two approaches, with the Protestants in the position of the superior elect. I have termed this "tiered tolerance," for the Turkish slaves in these narratives only appear to be accepted when they show themselves to be docile and loyal to the authors' interests.

Following an exploration of the articulation of Huguenot pre-eminence in the depiction of Muslims in Bion and Marteilhe's accounts, this chapter will consider moments in these men's narratives which appear to condone violence in certain contexts, and compare and contrast these with the ethical stances voiced by Bayle.

The figure of the "Turk"

Léchot writes that the punitive galley ships were one of the most common places for Protestants and Muslims to come into contact with each other, particularly as roughly one fifth of all captives on board these ships were adherents of Islam.[23] For Bamford, the galleys of Louis XIV were intrinsically linked to an agenda of Christianization, having been designed in the image of the vessels of the Knights of Saint John.[24] Certainly during the Sun King's reign, there was a great deal of tension evident between the Catholic powers of Western Europe and the "infidels" of the Ottoman Empire. The early modern French conception of the Orient was flavored by the historical legacy of the Crusades,[25] and the use of Muslims and other non-Christians as galley slaves was generally societally accepted.[26] The Turks' physical strength was also seen as a justification for slavery, particularly, according to Bamford, as the Christianizing argument behind their detention later began to wane in the eighteenth century.[27] In her introduction to *Littérature et exotisme, XVI–XVIIIe siècles*, Dominique Courcelles writes that the figure of the Turk or of the Moor was often used in literature as a means for occidental authors to reflect on their own

---

23. Léchot 2021: 233, and Dakhlia and Vincent 2011: loc. 7108.
24. Bamford 1973: 5–8.
25. Longino 1997: 38–39.
26. Bamford 1973: 138–39. See also Weiss 2011.
27. Bamford 1973: 142–43.

customs and characteristics.²⁸ This figure "remained the chief symbol of the Orient in French eyes during the fifteenth, sixteenth, and seventeenth centuries."²⁹ As Gaston Tournier suggests and Collignon-Ward notes, "It is certainly from [the Turks] that our Protestant *galériens* found the most help, sympathy, and comfort."³⁰

The term "Turk" in this period was a nebulous one. As Jean-Baptiste Xambo notes, not all Turks were Muslim, nor did all those who were designated as Turks actually come from the Ottoman Empire.³¹ *Turc* in Bion and Marteilhe's accounts tended to refer to all Muslim prisoners.³² In Pierre Corneille's *Le Cid*, the Moorish characters appear "all the same, interchangeable, difficult to distinguish from one another."³³ A similar pattern appears to arise when we consider the depiction of the galley slave bodies in general on board ships in Bion and Marteilhe, but the Turkish slaves in particular seem interchangeable, with fewer references to individual names giving rise to a perception of these men as a homogenous group.

Michele Longino writes that the association of the Moors with Africa suggests that they are an ever more "foreign" phenomenon, belonging to a different continent.³⁴ Such a claim may seem strange, considering the atmosphere of cultural exchange inherent in the Mediterranean area, but it does appear that Marteilhe bears some prejudices against "Turks" from the Maghreb which do not apply to his description of Turks from the area around Asia Minor. Longino considers the exoticism evident in Corneille's *Le Cid* to seek to consolidate a sense of French "supériorité,"³⁵ but, in Marteilhe and Bion's case, the aim is to infer the superiority of the Protestant religion.

On several occasions, the Turkish slaves are used by Marteilhe to desecrate Catholic rituals, such as in the case of Galafas,³⁶ or as a means to

28. Courcelles 1997: 3–4.
29. Rouillard 1938: 8.
30. Tournier, cited in Collignon-Ward 2007: 70.
31. Xambo 2017: 158.
32. Bion and Conlon 1966: 72, n. 9.
33. Longino 1997: 55.
34. Courcelles 1997: 58.
35. Courcelles 1997: 38.
36. Collignon-Ward 2007: 130.

highlight Protestant charity.[37] Collignon-Ward notes that Marteilhe distinguishes himself from "Enlightenment" writers due to his concern with crafting "a subtle accolade for Protestants."[38] I argue, however, that the praise Marteilhe awards himself and his Huguenot brethren is far from subtle; it is the primary goal of his text.

Moreover, use of a "foreign" figure to criticize European establishment, though often associated primarily with eighteenth-century writing such as Montesquieu's *Lettres Persanes*, was not a revolutionary concept. As Rouillard's appraisal of sixteenth- and seventeenth-century works shows, "travelers frequently indulged in or frankly expressed approval of the merits of the Turk in an attempt to satirize or correct the shortcomings of Frenchmen, or of Christians in general. [...] It may be too early to speak of the beginnings of the *esprit philosophique* so long before the eighteenth century, but at least the[se works] demonstrate [a sort of] early growth of that phenomenon."[39]

Rouillard notes that, while some medieval preconceptions of Turkish peoples remained present throughout the early modern period, in general, criticism tended to be directed more often at their religion than at other characteristics, "and even [this is] somewhat nuanced by the oft-praised zeal of their religious practices."[40] Bion and Marteilhe's writing certainly falls within this tradition.

Collignon-Ward notes that the way in which Marteilhe's text features non-Protestant protagonists alongside those "of the religion" marks him out from other Huguenot authors.[41] This is true, but we must consider that the only unreformed individual to really be awarded the role of a "protagonist" in the narrative sense in the story is Goujon, a Catholic and close personal friend of the author. That Marteilhe and Goujon were able to overcome religious divides and strike up an understanding is commendable, though perhaps not entirely unusual in a world where pragmatic concerns often required doctrinally opposed peoples to work alongside each other. Collignon-Ward moves from remarking on Goujon's substantial treatment in the narrative to mentioning that the author "also speaks

37. Collignon-Ward 2007: 131.
38. Collignon-Ward 2007: 10.
39. Rouillard 1938: 289–90.
40. Rouillard 1938: 291.
41. Collignon-Ward 2007: 139.

to us of his many Turkish friends."[42] Indeed, Marteilhe does make several references to so-called "Turks," and often praises the ways in which they conduct themselves. But they are always spoken of in a top-down, patronizing manner. Turkish suffering can, at times, be considered a metaphor for the Protestants, but Huguenots always appear to have the upper hand in their exchanges with the Muslim men.

One of the earliest mentions of a Turkish slave in Marteilhe's writing comes during his description of a battle his galley is involved in on the Thames in London. The ship is bombarded and the author awakes to find himself surrounded by the unconscious bodies of his fellow *galériens*. Amid this scene of horror and shocking *enargeia*, Isouf, one of the Ottoman detainees, is introduced, in a fragmented state:

> The Turk from my row, who had been a janissary, and who boasted of never feeling fear, lying down like the others, made me take a jovial tone: "What," I said, "Isouf, here then is the first time that you are scared; come on, get up"; and at the same time, I tried to take his arm, to help him. But, oh horror, which makes me tremble still, when I think of it! In my hand was his arm, detached from his body. Horrified, I flung this arm back to the body of this poor miserable creature, and I soon realised that he, like the four others, were chopped up like mincemeat; for all the shrapnel of the cannon had fallen on them.[43]

It is clear that Marteilhe has a sympathetic relationship with Isouf, and his loss is a tragic moment in the narrative. However, the description of the Turkish man's body in this abject manner reinforces the perception of him as "Other," as something to be rejected. The only impression the reader has in this passage of Isouf's character prior to his demise comes from Marteilhe's assertion that he "boasted of never being afraid," itself a rather unrealistic claim. Naturally, Marteilhe cannot be expected to give suppositions on the thoughts of the other characters in this scene, particularly as they are all revealed to be dead. However, even the most charitable reading of this passage would have to consider that its rather graphic description of Isouf's demise seeks to inspire sympathy for Marteilhe himself, rather than for the fate of his deceased companion.

42. Collignon-Ward 2007: 8.
43. Marteilhe 1865: 189.

We do not see Isouf described as he was when he was alive until over 50 pages[44] after the scene of his death, and then, as before, he is initially introduced just as "a Turk" before any detail on his individual identity is revealed. The Huguenot *galériens* are in receipt of alms from co-religionists stationed outside of France. Marteilhe is tasked with doling out this monetary assistance to his fellow Protestant detainees, but there is a high risk involved with this role. Luckily for him, the Turkish slaves appear to have been only too happy to put themselves in danger for the Huguenots by clandestinely distributing the allowances for them.

> This Turk knew well, that if he was caught in the act of performing this service for us, he would have been subjected to the *bastonnade* until he was dead. [...] This Turk therefore, who was named Isouf, served me very loyally in this affair for some years. [...] This good Turk was killed during the battle on the Thames. It was he whose arm came away in my hand, as I recounted. I was very upset by his death, and I did not know how I might go about finding another to serve me in such a perilous undertaking.[45]

It is not until Marteilhe has made extended reference to the peril involved with the dealing out of the Huguenots' secret rations that he confirms that Isouf is the same man who featured in the earlier episode. It is of course possible that Marteilhe was so moved by the loss of his friend that he did not wish to relive the emotions he experienced by describing them in detail. However, noting his difficulties finding another man to help him with money matters in the same sentence as his comment on Isouf's death seems to cheapen somewhat the impact of the latter. We also see Isouf aligned with a lack of agency: he is unable to keep the secret Marteilhe entrusts him with, a fault that the author associates with his religion:

> Even though I had frequently begged Isouf not to tell anyone of the service he was performing for me, he could not help himself, as a principle of religion, from saying it to his *papas*, as I realised after his death.[46]

44. In the 1865 edition. In the Zysberg edition, there are 40 pages between the initial horror-filled introduction to Isouf and his next appearance in the story.
45. Marteilhe 1865: 254.
46. Marteilhe 1865: 255.

In the end Isouf's inability to keep quiet is shown to have worked to Marteilhe's advantage. The *papas* to whom Isouf opens up are depicted as eager to assist the author in selecting another man to help him in his task. That Muslims are shown in Marteilhe's account to care for the maintenance of the Protestants is heartening, but such magnanimity was not without precedent: the *topos* of the "Charitable Turk" was a common one in early modern France, often used to highlight Christian shortcomings.[47] Indeed, in Marteilhe's account, the Turks' supposed belief that helping the Huguenots will assist them in making their way to heaven could be seen as justification of the Protestant position even by those who are not members of their religious community.

> These good people then, seeing that I was concerned that I did not know whom to trust, came all, one after the other, to beg me to make use of them, showing me such pious sentiments and such affection for those of our religion, whom they called their brothers in God, that I was moved to tears. I accepted one named Aly, who jumped with joy at having obtained such a dangerous task. [...] This Turk was poor, and I tried several times to have him accept an *écu* or two [...]. He always refused this insistently, saying, in his figurative manner, that that money would burn his hands; and when I said to him that, if he did not take it, I would use another [in his place], this poor Turk appeared desperate, begging me with joined hands not to close the road to Heaven for him.[48]

Similarly, Bion contrasts the Muslim men's actions with those of his own religion: "One can say, to the shame of Christians, that charity among them is without contradiction greater than among the faithful. [...] In fact, one can say that in the galleys, the Turks are Turks in name and Christians in effect, and the Christians have the name of Christian and the barbarity of infidels."[49]

As Pierre Conlon, Bion's editor, has noted, this quotation can be compared with a very similar passage in Marteilhe: "It is these people whom

---

47. See Rouillard 1938: 348, 350, etc.
48. Marteilhe 1865: 255–56.
49. Bion and Conlon 1966: 48, 90.

the Christians call 'barbaric', and who, in their morals, so little resemble this word that they shame those who call them thus."[50]

We see this praise of Islamic practice again in Bion when he speaks of Ramadan: "I have never known a more religious observer of his faith."[51] However, we should note that use of the figure of the fasting Muslim to exhort Christians to better observe their own faith was far from unique to the eighteenth century. Rouillard describes many an early modern author praising the Turk's willingness to forego the delicacies to which Christians were accustomed.[52] There is a long list of earlier authors who take interest in "the reverence of the Turks at worship."[53] As Rouillard notes, "The intention of those who [praised Islamic practices] was, of course, not to exalt the Turk, but to shame the bad Christian."[54] We should acknowledge, however, that Bion and Marteilhe are not concerned with "sap[ping] the foundations of Christian pride" in a broad sense,[55] but rather with criticizing particular Catholic misdemeanors. Those who remain good Protestants—like the beaten man Sabatier, whose story is told by both Bion and Marteilhe—are not associated with fault; quite the opposite.

What of the conception of the Turk in the foundations of the reformed religion? John Calvin's attitude towards the Ottoman Empire was generally negative, though he did recognize that Muslim worship did not have evil intentions.[56] Pierre Viret was more positive, noting instances of Turkish tolerance.[57] Rouillard notes that "Catholic and Protestants [...] hurled in each other's faces references to either Turkish cruelty or Turkish tolerance, as convenience suggested them."[58]

We could read Marteilhe and Bion's defences of such practices as Ramadan as reponses to this, but it is more likely that they were concerned with more contemporary discourses. It would seem that, when

50. Marteilhe 1865: 256 (Bion and Conlon 1966: 91).
51. Bion and Conlon 1966: 90.
52. Rouillard 1938: 298–99.
53. Rouillard 1938: 340.
54. Rouillard 1938: 337.
55. Rouillard 1938: 344.
56. Slomp 2009: 56.
57. Rouillard 1938: 413.
58. Rouillard 1938: 397.

defending non-hegemonic religious practices in France, Protestant writers were also keen to show their aptitude for tolerance, to contrast and highlight Catholic mistreatment and misunderstanding of both Turks and Huguenots themselves.

Léchot writes that Marteilhe's cooperation with Turks is evidence that interreligious relations improved greatly since the time of Luther, who barely saw Muslims as human, but I would argue that, while the barrier between Christianity and Islam had perhaps begun to crack at this stage, as Léchot suggests, it was still far from crumbling entirely.[59] The *topos* of Turkish cruelty transformed into the *topos* of "even the Turk," contrasted with a lack of tolerance on the Christian's part.[60] Even Guillaume Postel, in spite of his belief in the Crusades, awards a degree of respect to the Muslim religion, acknowledging that it was "one not to be conquered by ridicule, nor by authority alone, but by reason."[61] Apart from Bion's attempt to convert the Turk on his deathbed, our galley ship narrators profess little interest in "conquering" Islam, but they also perpetuate a hierarchy.

Léchot writes that Marteilhe eventually comes to see Isouf and Aly as "brothers," rather than as "Turks,"[62] but the only time when the term "brother" appears in Marteilhe's narrative in relation to the Turkish slaves is in the quote above. I would argue that it is the Muslims whom Marteilhe cites who are depicted as projecting a fraternal love onto the Huguenots, not vice versa, and there is little to indicate that the respect conferred upon the Protestants by the "Turks" is reciprocated in any meaningful sense.

Collignon-Ward argues that Marteilhe associates "good" Turks from the near East with Protestants, and "bad" Turks from North Africa with Catholics, based on a lexical similarity between a word he uses to describe the North Africans ("moraille") and a derogatory term to describe a priest ("prétraille"[63]). Marteilhe, at times, does link the downtrodden fate of oppressed Turks with that of his Protestant brothers, when such a tactic appears effective as a means to highlight the martyrdom of the latter men.

59. Léchot 2021: 234.
60. Rouillard 1938: 326.
61. Rouillard 1938: 336–37.
62. Léchot 2021: 456.
63. Collignon-Ward 2007: 131–32.

However, the contrast the author makes between "Moors" and "Turks" is not a clear-cut analogy for the Catholic versus Protestant situation in France, as it is laced with a racialized edge, as we shall see in the quote below. It would appear that the true goal of this passage in Marteilhe, which he writes that he "believed [...] was owed to the reader of th[e] memoir,"[64] is to reaffirm the author's value as an authority on persons exotic. Not only this, but the diversion also perpetuates a hierarchy in which the Protestant slaves are to be deferred to. The "Asian Turks" who are loyal to them are lauded, whereas the "Africans" are condemned.

> One must however distinguish these Turks from those who, though of the same religion, do not have the same customs. The latter are the Turks of Africa, [...] who are in general a villainous people, mischevious, cruel, disloyal, traitors and scoundrels of the highest degree. Therefore we need to refrain from trusting them. But the Turks of Asia and of Europe [...] are in general very well-built, white and fair of face, wise in their conduct, zealous in the practice of their religion [...]. As for the Turks of Africa, whom I have described above, and generally referred to as *Moors*, notwithstanding their religion, they become drunk like beasts, and commit, when they can, the most horrible of crimes. Therefore the Asian Turks, who are known as *Turqué fino* or *Turcs fins*, abhor the Africans and never speak with them.[65]

Marteilhe puts emphasis here on the fact that the Africans are supposedly not to be trusted, in contrast with their fairer counterparts. Of course, as Collignon-Ward notes, the author makes several disparaging references to Jesuits, as well, but the latter are never linked together with Protestants under the one heading, as the "Turks" are here, nor are their physical attributes discussed in a racialized manner. It would seem that, in the hierarchical conception of the world according to Marteilhe, the "Asian" Turks are the loyal lapdogs of the Huguenot elect, but the "Africans" are boisterous beings who do not even deserve a place in the service of the upper échelons.

64. Marteilhe 1865: 258.
65. Ibid.

Servitude appears to be inescapable for the Turks whom Marteilhe describes: even when they are free from chains, they apparently do not pose any flight risk, on account of their physical nature:

> Every evening they came back to the galley, there being hardly any example of one attempting to escape. Indeed they would not have an easy time trying to do so, free though they may be; for they are so recognizable on account of their generally burnt complexion, and by their frank manner of speaking, which is complete gibberish, that they would not be able to get more than a half-league from the town before being brought back to the ship.[66]

In fact, Jocelyne Dakhlia and Bernard Vincent observe, a number of Turks did succeed in escaping, and in learning Romance languages to an advanced degree, as one might expect of those who spent a prolonged period of time abroad.[67] It would seem that Marteilhe's reporting on this occasion, like on so many others, is founded on presumption rather than fact.

When Marteilhe speaks of how his difficulties in distributing alms were solved by Isouf, he takes the opportunity not only to describe the actions of his interlocutor, but also to explain the meaning behind them:

> However, I opened up to the Turk on my bank, who joyfully agreed to assist me in my task, putting his hand on his turban (which is their way of indicating their heart pouring out towards God).[68]

Not only do we have here an example of a sort of innocent "Turk" for whom danger appears to be no concern, he only too happy to assist, but we also have an example of Marteilhe revealing some of his knowledge of the Turks' customs to the reader. Both Marteilhe and Bion assert their value as witnesses to the general conditions of the ship,[69] but also foreground their knowledge when it comes to "foreign" traditions. The emphasis on the expertise of one who has been a visual witness to exotic phenomena is nothing new: there is a long tradition of occidental authors

---

66. Marteilhe 1865: 481–82.
67. Dakhlia and Vincent 2011: loc. 7478.
68. Marteilhe 1865: 254.
69. Marteilhe 1865: 430; Bion and Conlon 1966: 77.

claiming authority over others when recounting their experiences of the Orient.[70]

In the case of the majority of the earlier Orientalist/exotic narratives to feature Turks, however, "Turkish" customs are described as they take place within the context of the Ottoman Empire: the author-traveler is an outsider to their culture, a visitor to Constantinople. Longino describes how these French writers are able to adopt Turkish "symbols of identity" in order to fit in, and pass under the radar, to gain access to parts of foreign society that would otherwise be off-limits to them.[71] Aboard the galleys, the Turkish slaves' practices are evidently not taking place in a "home turf" context, and Marteilhe and Bion have no need to adapt linguistically or culturally when engaging with these men.

As witnesses, Marteilhe and Bion are also in control of the narratives they present, and thus have the ability to influence how their readers view other individuals depicted therein. One of the most harrowing punishments in use on the galley ships was the *bastonnade*, a brutal whipping which Turkish slaves were ordered to deliver upon those hapless *galériens* who incurred the wrath of the *comites*. Bion appears to associate more responsibility with the Turks involved in the action:

> He is then placed in the hands of four Moors or Turks, who strip him, put him naked and without a shirt [...] The Turk destined to function as the executioner [...] believes that he is honouring Mohammed by beating this poor creature.[72]

Why Bion thought that the Turkish slave would associate these brutal actions with Muslim religious practice is unclear. Marteilhe, in contrast, writes that the Turks themselves were beaten at the same time as the recipient of the *bastonnade*; they risked harsher blows themselves if they appeared to show mercy to their victim.[73]

---

70. See, for example, Alcoba 1997: 23, as well as on Pedro de Urdemalas (ibid.: 22).
71. Longino 1997: 39, especially note 8, referring to Grelot's *Relation nouvelle d'un voyage de Constantinople*, 1680.
72. Bion and Conlon 1966: 110.
73. Marteilhe 1865: 123. Pierre Conlon also notes this in his edition of Bion's *Relation*: Bion and Conlon 1966: 110, n. 163.

Though Bion does not condone coercion in attempts to win Muslims over to the Christian faith, he does reflect on the fact that he tried to convert one "Turk"—as usual, unnamed—on his deathbed.

> I embraced him, I told him that I would answer for his salvation, if he wished to renounce Mohammed who was but an imposter, and believe in Jesus Christ, our Redeemer [...]. I explained to him in a few words the nature of the sacrament of Baptism. He consented to all that I wanted of him. [...] But one of his Turkish friends who also understood French, and who had observed all my holy undertakings, took my place, and having said in his language some words to my proselyte, when I returned, I could obtain nothing from him.[74]

In spite of his admiration for the Turks' constancy during the period of Ramadan, Bion still feels compelled to wrest the dying man away from his faith in his final moments. It is true that the author does not appear to support the use of force in his plan to interfere with the Turkish man's faith, though he does record the ship's *comite* as threatening the man in question with being whipped if he continued to refuse the sacrament of baptism. Even when faced with flogging, the Muslim remains firm in his resolution after being spoken to by his friend. Can we read this episode as a parallel for the circumstances and the determination of the Protestants on board ship? Perhaps, were it not for the fact that the dying man's friend is not depicted in especially positive terms, having "taken the place" of Bion at the Muslim doubter's side. However, when we turn the page, the real reason Bion has included this event in his narrative becomes clear: he wishes to call attention to his rejection of his previous life as a Catholic:

> If I had known my religion as I have the fortune to know it now, [...] I would have exhorted him to repent for his faults without harassing him with the absolute necessity of Baptism. I beg the reader here to forgive me for the error in which I acted at that time. I was there myself in good faith, and therefore in winning his soul, I would have much worked for my own.[75]

---

74. Bion and Conlon 1966: 91.
75. Bion and Conlon 1966: 92.

It seems that this anecdote was never really about the Turkish man at all; what we are invited to focus on in the end is Bion's repentance for his Catholic considerations. Moreover, what are we to make of his insistence that he acted "in good faith," keeping in mind Bayle's stipulations that those who truly believe in their heresy cannot truly be thought of as sinners?[76] Did not the Turk and his friend also act in "good faith," albeit of a different shade?

We may contrast Bion's attempt to convert the "Turk" on his deathbed with his reaction to the Camisards who are incarcerated on board his *galère* in 1703. The author writes that he was shocked at his *comite*'s insistence that those Protestants who refused to kneel or remove their cap during the presentation of the Eucharist should be subjected to the *bastonnade*. He claims to have been acting out of sympathy for his fellow human beings when he offers to convince the men to show respect during the Mass, in order to spare them the suffering of this cruel punishment. Like in the case of the "Turk," Bion is asking forgiveness and understanding for actions taken during his previous life as a Catholic. However, in contrast to the Muslim men, the Camisards' constancy is praised:

> God [...] preserved his servants from the dangerous traps that I had, albeit unintentionally, lain for them. But I found magnanimous adversaries, [...] with the sweet nature of the predestined, [...] with the constancy of the Maccabees.[77]

After these Protestants are subjected to the *bastonnade*, Bion writes that he was moved to tears by the sight of "the wounds of these martyrs."[78] The Huguenots, to him, are "holy victims,"[79] whom God had equipped with a "constancy and a patience [which were] truly Christian."[80] Use of this language of martyrdom simultaneously affirms Bion's familiarity with the shibboleths of the Huguenot community and perpetuates the conception of this community as "chosen." He also grounds his description of the *bastonnade* in an intention to indicate to Queen Anne the extent of the cruelties which took place on board the galleys, which

76. See Kilcullen 1988: 67–69.
77. Bion and Conlon 1966: 109.
78. Bion and Conlon 1966: 111.
79. Bion and Conlon 1966: 98.
80. Bion and Conlon 1966: 111.

would soften the heart [...] of those who are born in the most barbarous of nations, if they were to see the torments that Christians make other Christians endure, when their crime is but to have prayed to God and walked beneath the standard of the pure Gospel of Jesus Christ.

That the *comite*'s threat to beat the dying Turk does not provoke such an emotional reaction in Bion's narrative is surely indicative of the author's predisposition to see the Protestant path as the ideal.

Bion and Marteilhe's intentions may have been pure and their words largely positive, but do such infantile depictions of Turks not serve to perpetuate, rather than critique, Leibniz's 1672 reference to Ottoman "servile souls"?[81] It would seem, therefore, that though neither author examined here advocates for compulsion or interference with the practices of the Muslims in the galleys, both see the latter men as tools fit for rhetorical purposes and little else. The role of the practicants of Islam here is to defer to the Protestants; they are not considered as individuals in their own right.

Excusing violence

Another marginalized group in early modern France were the *Camisards*, Protestants of the southern Languedoc region, whose nickname was supposedly derived from the simple shirts they wore, called "camisa" in Occitan. The first few years of the eighteenth century saw the outbreak of a series of bloody uprisings in the region which became known as the Wars of the Cévennes (1702–1704). The Camisards were often seen as the illiterate, poorer cousins of the Huguenots of northern and eastern France, their brand of reformed Christianity more deeply associated with mysticism and prophecy. Tensions were known to arise between Camisard and other Huguenot refugees when both groups had settled abroad.

Lionel Laborie describes Protestant nobles in the Languedoc as attempting to distance themselves from "embarrassing peasant prophetism."[82] Laborie also notes that Camisard and Huguenot refugees generally

---

81. Cited by Longino 1997: 42 who references the 1864 edition, p. i.
82. Laborie 2013: 126, n. 11.

remained distanced from each other on arrival in England.[83] That Bion should wish to cross this divide and embrace the Camisard cause by defending its more violent actions is surprising. This was a man who, we can assume, was looking to assimilate into the Huguenot community in London, coming not just from France, but from a former association with the Catholic oppressor. Why would he wish to link himself with a controversial faction, particularly when we consider that both the London consistory and the general public were quite strong in their condemnation of the "French Prophets"[84]—a scandal that took place only a year before Bion published his pamphlet? Laborie writes that the Huguenot rejection of the Prophets in London was indicative of French refugees' loyalty to the British Crown,[85] and we know that Bion was also dedicated to Queen Anne, from his address to her in the preface to his *Relation*.[86]

Bion, however, speaks in glowing terms of the Camisard galériens whom he encounters on the galleys. He also gives a highly sympathetic account of the breakout of the Wars of the Cévennes (1702–1704). He considers the event that triggered the wars, the murder of the Abbot Du Chaila, to have been a necessary evil:

> He would make them come, on some pretext, to his house, and, be they man, woman, or girl, he would have them attached to a tree, after having them searched by his valets and stripped naked from the shoulders to the belt. Then, he would whip them with a horse whip until they bled. Even the Papists of France admit this, who themselves recognise that this Duchélas [Du Chaila] was a scoundrel. However, his behaviour was recompensed by the bishops. But finally, *because it is permitted to fight force with force*, the Protestants of his neighbourhood, seeing that they could neither by sweetness nor by submission escape the cruelty of this priest, broke into his house at night. He jumped from the window to his garden, but was not able to save himself; he asked for mercy, but, *as he had never showed any*, they refused it to him on this occasion, and killed him.[87]

---

83. Laborie 2013: 127, n. 13.
84. Laborie 2013: 128–29.
85. Laborie 2013: 129.
86. Bion and Conlon 1966: 29.
87. Bion and Conlon 1966: 103–104. Emphasis mine.

It is clear that there is a performative aspect to Bion's description of events. Aside from the fact that he openly despairs at the inaction of those whom he calls "papistes de France"—amongst whom he himself still numbered until only a short while prior to writing this tract—he excuses the violence on the Camisards' part as an act of necessity. We can contrast the pitiful images of Protestant suffering at Du Chaila's hands with the absence of detail of the circumstances of the priest's death. Bion merely indicates that Du Chaila tried a cowardly escape from jumping from the window, and received his just reward for past cruelties. Pierre Conlon adds in a footnote to the 1966 edition that it was reported that Du Chaila broke his leg during his fall from the window, his house having been set on fire by the fifty-odd men who had descended upon his living quarters.[88] He was then pierced by "fifty-two thrusts of the knife."[89] Bion also refrains from giving a description of what happened to Du Chaila's murderers in the aftermath of the event. We know that Esprit Séguier, the leader of the band of Camisards who hunted down Du Chaila, was sentenced to be executed for his part in the crime. Accounts of Séguier's behavior on the scaffold portray his deeds in a manner sufficiently miraculous to impress the likes of Crespin and Goulart: it was said that the hangman was ordered to chop off the hand that had struck Du Chaila before burning Séguier alive, but the removal of the extremity proved difficult. The rebel thus bit it off himself, before breaking into Psalm 69.[90] That Bion declines to give detail on this event or on the alleged prediction of Du Chaila's death by the shepherd girl Françoise Brès while she herself was on the scaffold would seem to imply that the author had little time for "fanaticism," or the "passions" Bayle speaks of, yet he aligns himself with Jurieu's belief in the righteousness of the Camisard uprising nonetheless.

As François-Maximilien Misson's *Théâtre Sacré des Cévennes* (1707) engendered a great deal of discussion when it was published in London a few months prior to Bion settling there, it seems plausible that he would have had some degree of familiarity with its contents. But Bion's description of Du Chaila's death is in some ways more reminiscent of that of Jean-Baptiste Louvreleuil (1704) that than published by Misson—Élie Marion,

88. Bion and Conlon 1966: 104.
89. Tournier, cited in Collignon-Ward 2007: 207.
90. Monahan 2014: 71.

when citing Abraham Mazel in his *Théâtre Sacré* account, implies that Du Chaila died when jumping out of the window of his house.[91] Louvreleuil does specify that it was those who broke into the Abbot's house who killed him, though, in contrast to Bion, he demonizes the Camisards' role, particularly that of Séguier, who, he says, was a rapist with no upper set of teeth.[92]

Furthermore, who were these "Papists of France" who themselves admitted Du Chaila's wrongdoing? As Bion had been formed in the Catholic tradition, it is possible to conjecture that he may have been familiar with popular Catholic accounts of the same murder, such as that of Louvreleuil. However, as one might expect, these versions of the story downplay violence on Du Chaila's part: he is a victim to be pitied, merely trying to fulfill his role as *convertisseur* among the wild Camisards.[93] Apologists for the uprising, on the other hand, tended to emphasize the Cévenols' poverty and generally miserable condition, just as Bion has done in the account above.[94]

Though Claude Brousson,[95] Bayle, and others advocated for pacifism even in the case of the Cévennes, Bion was poised to condone violence on the Camisards' part in this instance due to a determination to overshadow his link to the Catholic structures in France. However, he refrained from indulging in the mystical speculation so often associated with this faction of Protestantism. It is also worth noting that Bion refers to the Camisards he encounters at sea as "Maccabees."[96] He was the only Protestant of the time to make mention of these Apocryphal brothers: Jurieu uses their example as evidence that violence could, at times, be an appropriate response to persecution, such as in the case of the Dutch Revolt.[97] Jacques-Bénigne Bossuet, Bishop of Meaux, refuted the comparison of Protestants to Maccabees, and declared that it was hypocritical of Jurieu

91. Misson 1707: 87. Admittedly Mazel's own account does depict a showdown where Du Chaila is judged and murdered: see Mazel 1965: 36–37.
92. Louvreleuil 1868: 28. One wonders how this might have affected his supposed ability to bite off his own hand.
93. For more on conflicting accounts of Du Chaila's death, see Monahan 2014: 64–89.
94. See Joutard 1977: 89.
95. Admittedly, Brousson's leanings as a pacifist have been implied to have been overstated. See Utt and Strayer 2003.
96. Bion and Conlon 1966: 104, 109.
97. Jurieu 1688: 200–201.

to reference Apocrypha.[98] As Bion refers to Bossuet and his "cruel jealousy" in his later volume *L'origine [...] des quiétistes de Bourgogne*,[99] we may conjecture that he would have been familiar with the Bishop's writing and thoughts on the matter. However, like Jurieu, Bion's aim here is to frame a contemporary rebellion—in his case, that of the Camisards—in the style of a well-known precedent, and there is no discussion of source criticism in the *Relation*.

Though he does not make mention of Camisards, Marteilhe also appears to condone violence in some specific circumstances. Marteilhe's reflection on violence is, of course, situated in a completely different context to that in which Bion was writing: he is reasserting the right of the state to punish those who seek to undermine it. The individual whose punishment is described is Captain Thomas Smith, of the ship *The Nightingale*. Smith is set up by Marteilhe as a typical, almost pantomime-like, villain: "burning with hatred against his country, [he] was always conniving to harm the English."[100] He then joined the French forces due to his Catholic beliefs. Following the description of the battle faced by the *galère* in which Isouf died, Marteilhe continues his story by discussing other events. However, just prior to the close of his account, the author revisits the fate of Captain Smith, in part responsible for the tragedy on the Thames in which the Turkish slave lost his life.

Smith may have been acting according to his conscience, but his actions upset the stability of society. Moreover, Smith is also shown to not have upheld the integrity of his own morals: Marteilhe tells us that the man offered to become Protestant in return for his life. Naturally, Marteilhe rejects the possibility that a scoundrel such as Smith could ever be accepted into the Reformed community's fold, qualifying his attempt at conversion as "cowardly." The reader is encouraged to marvel at Smith's audacity one last time before Marteilhe gives a description of the Englishman's death that is so graphic that it was omitted from later English translations of the text.[101]

98. Bossuet 1710: 176, 274–76.
99. Bion and Conlon 1966: 21, 27.
100. Marteilhe 1865: 170.
101. Compare, for example, the 1758 edition, 1765 edition, etc.

> Though he cowardly offered to become Protestant in order to be pardoned, he was condemned to be quartered alive, which was carried out in the way that they deal with traitors in England, by striking their face with their still-beating heart. And I saw, in the year 1713, when I was in London, the quarters of his body exposed along the Thames. A solemn lesson for those who, like him, give in to their passion to the extent of betraying their own country![102]

Not only does Marteilhe affirm the right of the English to stamp out Smith's treachery by violently executing him, his reference to "giving into 'passions'" recalls Bayle's condemnation of the same.[103]

We could read this incident as merely indicating that the English took matters of abjurations and conversions more seriously than the Catholics in France.[104] However, I believe that we must also consider the fact that Marteilhe's judgment of the man, in addition to its allusion to religious matters, references treason. That Marteilhe, who has left his own country, should feel so strongly about Smith's betrayal of England could be explained purely on account of his religious beliefs: the actions of Smith, as a "Papist," were not approved of in the way that those of a Huguenot fighting for the English might have been. However, we may note that, in Marteilhe's case, he did not cause offense to the general "order" in France in a manner that Smith supposedly aspired to in regard to his former *Patrie*. The former galley slave even makes what appears to be charitable reference to the reign of Louis XV.[105] In comparison, Marteilhe's sympathetic portrayal of his Catholic friend Goujon, who is revealed to be a highly disruptive character, seems harder to justify. However, we may note that Goujon's actions bear no relation to religious tensions in France; he is merely unruly, and the description of his reckless escape plans appear primarily to be included to entertain, rather than edify, the reader, as Collignon-Ward's reading would suggest.[106]

---

102. Marteilhe 1865: 534–35.
103. Bayle 1740: 139–40.
104. Trivisani-Moreau 2005: 80.
105. Marteilhe 1865: 527.
106. Collignon-Ward 2017: 142.

Conclusion

Though Bion and Marteilhe's narratives strongly resemble each other in their depictions of Turks, and the particular brand of approval given to the latter men's practices, their descriptions of violent occurrences differ. Bion refrains from condoning mysticism but carries the flag for the Camisards in his writing, whereas Marteilhe's piece more closely resembles Bayle's condemnation of bloodshed except in the case of a state aiming to eradicate uncertainty. In these men's writings, we see a nuanced tolerance, flavored by their close encounters with "the Other" but also by their convictions regarding the righteousness of Calvinism.

There is certainly some degree of value in a patronizing form of tolerance, and it is not the intention of this chapter to suggest otherwise. Base-level acceptance of difference is commendable in many ways for its rejection of violence and promotion of peace, but we might question whether using figures of "the Other" solely for the profit of one's own agenda constitutes the ideal that a truly progressive society should strive towards. Using "Others" in this manner seems to strip them, in a sense, of their humanity, and instead cloak them in the guise of the "Noble Savage"—a trope from which, according to Frank Lestringant's reading of the *Histoire d'un voyage faict en la terre du Brésil*, Protestant writer Jean de Léry attempted to distance himself back in the sixteenth century.[107] Again, while the hierarchical tolerance we see in Bion and Marteilhe is preferable to persecution, it remains imperfect.

Author biography

Nora Baker is a postdoctoral fellow at the University of Tokyo, having completed a PhD in Early Modern French at the University of Oxford. Her research focuses on the writing of Huguenot refugees following the Revocation of the Edict of Nantes, and she is also interested in migration studies, minority cultures, and religious history more broadly.

---

107. Lestringant 1997: 14.

References

Primary sources

Bayle, P. (1740), *Dictionnaire historique et critique, cinquième edition*. Amsterdam: Chez P. Brunel.

Bayle, P., J. Kilcullen, and C. Kukathas (2005), *A Philosophical Commentary on these Words of the Gospel, Luke 14:23, Compel them to Come in, that my House May Be Full*. Indianapolis: Liberty Fund Incorporated.

Bion, J., and P. Conlon (1966), *Jean-François Bion et sa relation des tourments soufferts par les forçats protestants*. Geneva: Droz.

Bossuet, J.-B. (1710), *Avertissements aux protestans sur les lettres du Ministre Jurieu contre L'histoire des variations*. Liège: Chez Françoise Houyoux.

Jurieu, P. (1688), *Lettres pastorales adressées aux fideles de France qui gemissent sous la captivité de Babylone. Troisieme année*. Rotterdam: Chez Abraham Acher.

Louvreleuil, J.-B. (1868), *Le fanatisme renouvelé, ou histoire des sacrilèges, des incendies, des meurtres et des autres attentats que les calvinistes révoltés ont commis dans les Cévennes, et des châtiments qu'on en a faits*. Avignon: Seguin Ainé [1704].

Marteilhe, J. (1865), *Mémoires d'un protestant condamné aux galères de France pour cause de religion*. Paris: Société des Écoles du Dimanche.

Marteilhe, J., and A. Zysberg (1989), *Mémoires d'un galérien du Roi-Soleil, par Jean Marteilhe*. Paris: Mercure de France.

Mazel, A. (1965), "Relation d'Abraham Mazel," in P. Joutard (ed.), *Journaux Camisards (1700–1715)*, 29–73. Paris: Union générale d'éditions.

Misson, F. (1707), *Le théâtre sacré des Cévennes; ou récit de diverses merveilles nouvellement opérées dans cette partie de la province de Languedoc. Première partie*. London: Chez Robert Roger.

Terrasson, J. (1880), "Recueil des choses les plus remarquables qui me sont arrivées en France et des maux qu'on m'y a fait souffrir, à moi la veuve Reymond, née Jeanne Terrasson, une des confesseurs de Jésus-Christ, y reconnoissant les graces que j'ai receu de lui dans la même pérsecution," in T. Claparède, *Deux héroïnes de la foi: Blanche Gamond et Jeanne Terrasson, récits du XVIIe siècle*, 217–375. Paris: Librairie Sandoz et Fischbacher.

Secondary sources

Alcoba, L. (1997), "La question du pouvoir au miroir ottoman: le Viaje de Turquía," in D. Courcelles (ed.), *Littérature et exotisme, XVIe–XVIIIe siècle*, 17–33. Paris: École national des chartes.

Bamford, P. (1973), *Fighting Ships and Prisons: The Mediterranean Galleys of France in the Age of Louis XIV*. Minneapolis: University of Minneapolis Press.
Cashmere, J. (1969), "Pierre Bayle, Tolerance and History: A Study of the Influence of Bayle's Defence of Toleration on the Idea of History Expressed in the *Dictionnaire Historique et Critique*," MA thesis, University of Tasmania.
Collignon-Ward, S. (2007), "Les Lumières de Marteilhe," PhD thesis, Michigan State University.
Courcelles, D., ed. (1997), *Littérature et exotisme, XVIe–XVIIIe siècle*. Paris: École nationale des chartes. https://doi.org/10.4000/books.enc.1034
Dakhlia, J., and B. Vincent (2011), *Les Musulmans dans l'histoire de l'Europe. I. Une intégration invisible*. Paris: Albin Michel.
Forst, R. (2008), "Pierre Bayle's Reflexive Theory of Toleration," *Nomos* 48: 78–113. https://www.jstor.org/stable/24220050
Joutard, P. (1977), *La légende des Camisards: une sensibilité au passé*. Paris: Gallimard.
Kilcullen, J. (1988), *Sincerity and Truth: Essays on Arnauld, Bayle, and Toleration*. New York: Oxford University Press.
Laborie, L. (2013), "The Huguenot Offensive against the Camisard Prophets in the English Refuge," in J. McKee and R. Vigne (eds.), *The Huguenots: France, Exile, Diaspora*, 125–33. Brighton: Sussex Academic Press.
Labrousse, E. (1964), *Pierre Bayle tome II: hétérodoxie et rigorisme*. The Hague: Martinus Nijhoff.
Léchot, P.-O. (2021), *Luther et Mahomet: Le protestantisme d'Europe occidentale devant l'islam, XVIe–XVIIIe siècle*. Paris: Les éditions du cerf.
Lestringant, F. (1997), "L'exotisme en France à la Renaissance, de Rabelais à Léry," in D. Courcelles (ed.), *Littérature et exotisme, XVIe–XVIIIe siècle*, 5–16. Paris: École national des chartes.
Longino, M. (1997), "Politique et théâtre au XVIIe siècle : les Français en Orient et l'exotisme du *Cid*," in D. Courcelles (ed.), *Littérature et exotisme, XVIe–XVIIIe siècle*, 35–59. Paris: École national des chartes.
Monahan, W. G. (2014), *Let God Arise: The War and Rebellion of the Camisards*. Oxford: Oxford University Press.
Rex, W. (1965), *Essays on Pierre Bayle and Religious Controversy*. The Hague: Martinus Nijhoff.
Rouillard, C. (1938), *The Turk in French History, Thought, and Literature (1520–1660)*. Paris: Boivin & Co.
Serrurier, C. (1912), *Pierre Bayle en Hollande*. Lausanne: Imprimerie coopérative la Concorde.
Slomp, J. (2009), "Calvin and the Turks," *Studies in Interreligious Dialogue* 19/1: 50–65. https://doi.org/10.2143/SID.19.1.2036228

Solé, J. (1971), "Religion et conception du monde dans le dictionnaire de Bayle," *Bulletin historique et de la société de l'histoire du protestantisme français* 117: 545–81.

Stanwood, O. (2020), *The Global Refuge: Huguenots in an Age of Empire*. New York: Oxford University Press.

Trivisani-Moreau, I. (2005), "Un protestant entre limiers et barbets. Choix et nuances du mémorialiste Jean Marteilhe," in M.-P. de Weerdt-Pilorge (ed.), *L'idée d'opposition dans les mémoires d'Ancien Régime*, 75–85. Tours: Presses Universitaires François-Rabelais.

Utt, W., and B. E. Strayer (2003), *The Bellicose Dove: Claude Brousson and Protestant Resistance to Louis XIV, 1647–1698*. Brighton: Sussex Academic Press.

Van der Linden, D. (2016), "Histories of Martyrdom and Suffering in the Huguenot Diaspora," in R. A. Mentzer and B. van Ruymbeke (eds.), *A Companion to the Huguenots*, 348–70. Leiden: Brill.

Van der Lugt, M. (2016), *Bayle, Jurieu, and the* Dictionnaire historique et critique. Oxford: Oxford University Press.

Vigié, M. (1985), *Les galériens du roi*. Paris: Fayard.

Weiss, G. (2011), "Infidels at the Oar: A Mediterranean Exception to France's Free Soil Principle," *Slavery & Abolition* 32/3: 397–412. https://doi.org/10.1080/0144039X.2011.588477

Whelan, R. (2007), "From the Other Side of Silence: Huguenot Life-Writing, a Dialogic Art of Writing the Self," in B. Tribout and R. Whelan (eds.), *Narrating the Self in Early Modern Europe*, 139–60. Bern: Peter Lang.

Whelan, R. (2010), "Turning to Gold: The Role of the Witness in French Protestant Galley Slave Narratives," *Seventeenth-Century French Studies* 32/1: 3–18. https://doi.org/10.1179/026510610X12713438444558

Xambo, J.-B. (2017), "Servitude et droits de transmission. La condition des galériens de Louis XIV," *Revue d'histoire moderne et contemporaine* 64/2: 157–83. https://doi.org/10.3917/rhmc.642.0157

Zysberg, A. (1983), "Convertir et punir sous le règne de Louis XIV: l'exemple des galériens protestants," in L. Godard de Donville (ed.), *La conversion au XVIIe siècle. Actes du XIIe colloque du Centre méridional de rencontres sur le XVIIe siècle*, 127–60. Paris: Centre National des Lettres.

Chapter 12

Religious Freedom and History of Religions in Benjamin Constant

Roberto Celada Ballanti

> Tout est libre entre la terre et le ciel.
> Au contraire dans les religions sacerdotales
> le ciel se ferme; un triple rempart entoure
> les immortels. Toutes les issues sont gardées
> par des intermédiaires jaloux.
> (Benjamin Constant,
> *De la Religion*, I, 9)

"De la Religion": a missed *Wirkungsgeschichte*

"Alas, dear friend, this scene is over."[1] Thus Gotthold Ephraim Lessing wrote on December 19, 1780 to his friend Moses Mendelssohn, complaining of his loneliness and the deterioration of his health, almost expressing a sense of the imminent end that would eventually reach him on the evening of February 15, 1781 in Braunschweig. But, at the same time, if this year marks Lessing's departure—sealed at the peak of the *Fragmentenstreit* by the dramatic poem *Nathan the Wise* (1779) and by the expanded version of the *Education of the Human Race* (1780)—it also heralds the dawn of a new age of thought. Naturally, I am alluding to the appearance in 1781 of the Kantian *Critique of Pure Reason*. This work was intended to fix that "turning point of time" to which, in the reading

---

1. See Lessing 1968: 362.

that Karl Barth makes of it in his *Protestant Theology in the Nineteenth Century*,[2] also belong Lessing and Rousseau. This is the turning point, for Barth, between *Aufklärung* and *Romantik*, which Kant had embodied, in his own way, interpreting the eighteenth century "in itself within its limits." Kant therefore remains anchored to *Grenze* and renounces to force it in the direction of the absolute.

The reference to the Barthian text—which ends up being an authentic history of the philosophy of modern religion coming, paradoxically, from the most tenacious opponent of "religion"—is naturally not accidental. There is no doubt that Benjamin Constant would have figured well within it, at least as regards the theory of religion, alongside Rousseau, the neologists, Lessing, Kant, Herder, Schleiermacher, and Hegel. Constant represents that humanization of Christianity which marks, in Barth's perspective, the liberal age of Protestant theology, but he also represents that epochal turning point and, in it, the crucial *metaxu* between the late Enlightenment, the *Frühromantik*, and the *Klassik*. Constant is in fact the author of a vast work on religion—*De la Religion, considérée dans sa source, ses formes et ses développements*—dedicated to the forms of ancient polytheisms, published between 1824 and 1831. Its long gestation brings it back to the last two decades of the eighteenth century and the innovations that occurred in the domain of religious studies.

The marginalization of Constant's work, which is repeated in the classic *Geschichte der neuern evangelischen Theologie* by Emmanuel Hirsch,[3] is due to the oblivion in which the work fell in the aftermath of the appearance of the first tome, in 1824. If, as Barth writes, the nineteenth century was Schleiermacher's century on a religious level, the same could not be said of Constant, despite their affinity in many respects. The absence of debate about his work hoped for by Constant cannot only be explained by the long duration of its publication (his work was banned by the Catholic Church and it took seven years for the five volumes to be published), and not only by his anthropology and the theory of religion, too ahead

2. Barth 1960.
3. Hirsch 1960. Naturally, the list of exclusions and silences that accompanied Constant's work, exemplified here through two classic works of the history of Protestant thought, in an equally if not even more symptomatic way, could continue. For a history of the effects of Constantian's work, see Kloocke 2013; Violi 1984; Kloocke 1988.

of its time, which it contains. There is another reason, which marks the fate of thinkers who, like Constant, have followed the path of thought in the wake of that *religious-liberal tradition*—the same as Lessing, Kant, Schleiermacher, Herder, to indicate some of its inspirers—who, in order to honor the value of freedom in the search for *de vera religione* and *de vera ecclesia*, pay with solitude for their desituation from confessional orthodoxies as from immanentistic secularisms.

Constant, moreover, was well aware that his theory of religion was in contrast with the rigid orthodoxy of the "dévots" as well as with the incredulity of the "philosophes," programmatically posing as a "third way" capable of tying religion to the principle of freedom: he affirmed a free search for Transcendence against confessionalism and atheism of his time. In this, the Lausanne thinker, while linking religion, freedom, and nascent historicism in an original union, placed himself in the wake of an ancient and venerable tradition of thought, that is, the religious-liberal one. In the *Aufklärung* of Lessing, of Kant, of Schleiermacher, this tradition receives its highest determination, but it has its origins much further away: in that humanistic season in which Tzvetan Todorov places, not surprisingly, Constant.[4]

Constant's project of a history of religions

In a letter dated September 20, 1821 to Philipp Albert Stapfer, Constant defines the meaning of his work on religion, declaring himself almost ready to undertake its publication:

> This work, which is in some way a history of religious sentiment from its crudest to its purest form, is now, in the light of the investigation I am making of it, after six years of interruption which followed three years of constant work in Göttingen, in a much more advanced condition than I thought, and, except for the events that the

---

4. Cf. Todorov 2009. See also *De la religion*'s introduction: Todorov 1999. On the tradition of religious liberalism, I refer to my book Celada Ballanti 2009, and my introduction in Celada Ballanti 2019: 1–86.

Holy Alliance prepares for us, I will be able to publish the first two parts next summer.[5]

A "history of religious sentiment": for Constant, in reality, what primarily in the domain of religions deserves the attribute of "religious" in an axiological sense, is certainly the sentiment.[6] That is the name assumed by the omnipervasive religiosity present *a priori* in the conscience, the constitutive and transcendental religious determination which, due to its breadth, includes all the specific human domains.

In this sense, Denis Thouard appropriately recalls the "demonstrative character of Constant's book" and its logic: it is the story which takes the form of a comparative history of religions, "in which the protagonist encounters obstacles before being able to assert itself, matured through trials, in its purity, at the end of the adventure."[7] The comparative history of religions—carried out in the five books of the work from fetishism to polytheism followed up to the moment of maximum perfection—becomes a gigantic probe of man as a *naturaliter* religious being through the historical process. It is an analysis of religious sentiment and its progressive liberation and amendment through forms, aimed at documenting its universality and the link with the principle of freedom, even though this connection is obscured and betrayed in the majority of historical experiences. As Kurt Kloocke pointed out,[8] the *Religion* is not a history of religions except as filtered by a theory of religion. It is a theory of religion that makes use of a great historical erudition: within which (this is the qualifying point), instead of reabsorbing the philosophy of religion into the metaphysics of history, as does the Hegelian idealistic line, Constant, faithful to Schleiermacher, poses the philosophical problem within the history of religions. In this way he supports the other historicism: that which, distinct and opposite to the Hegelian one, remains close to Kant and prolongs his philosophy of limit in a historical

5. I quote from Deguise 1966: 187. On the religious theme, I also remember the fundamental volume Thompson 1978. An essential tool for understanding the evolution of Constant's religious thought is the analysis contained in Thompson 1998.
6. Kurt Kloocke traces an essential genealogy of the notion of sentiment in Kloocke 2012: 117–23.
7. Cf. *Introduction*, in OCBC 2015: 48.
8. Cf. Kloocke 2008, and Kloocke 2014.

perspective. Instead of the new evolutionary-progressive historicist apologetics which, through the philosophy of history, recover the philosophy of religion from metaphysics or theology, Constantian religious theory is linked to the history of religions, offering philosophical, anthropological, and transcendental bases to scholarly, ethnological, sociological, and philological research. This is what separates Constant from the nascent historicistic idealism of Fichte, Schelling, and Hegel, but soon he fell into oblivion or, we can say, his novelty was not appropriately measured.

Furthermore, Constant's belonging to this incipient critical and problematic Historismus can be grasped by a further trait that his work shows: the renunciation of embracing the pan-historical totality in favor of an ideal-typical, selective Weberian method,[9] which preserves within itself the consciousness of incompleteness, of the powerlessness to embrace the whole of events as from above, panoptically. Constant's comparative history of religions is also from this point of view, crossed transversely by the Kantian sense of the limit, of the renunciation of historical holisms.

The "broken" dialectic between religious sentiment and forms

What are the essential contradictions in the unfolding of the "vicissitudes of religious sentiment," a *Bildungsroman* that, in its competitive nature and struggle for freedom, reveals its inherent political essence? Man is born marked by a need to communicate with invisible powers: a need that cannot be produced or explained afterwards, starting from fear or ignorance of the causes,[10] but rooted in the "depth of the soul." In this sense Constant writes with a language that is mindful of the mystical tradition, which, in his unavoidable historical disposition—from the crudest or fetishistic forms to the most amended, typical of theism, passing through polytheism—finds himself having to struggle not only with the limits that belong to every historical form, but also with that specific typology of forms constituted by the priestly religions, in their establishing an essential dichotomy with religions free or independent of priests.

Religious sentiment, therefore, in Constant, is always concrete existence, experience, and it does not live except within a historical-existential

9. Cf. Kloocke 2000: esp. 128.
10. Cf. the first chapter of Book I of the *De la Religion*, in OCBC 2013: 90ff.

process, nor does it coincide with an abstract or disembodied essence waiting for a form. The result is a tension between sentiment and form. A structural dissymmetry marks this relationship: between the supernatural naturalness of the sentiment, which is a movement of transcendence, thirst for infinity, desire, cry of the soul, freedom and furtherity, and the historicity of the form, which, arising from the urgency to order, stabilize, and preserve the revelation that occurs in the sentiment, carries within itself a stationary principle of inertia, which contrasts with the dynamism of sentiment. If the sentiment molds religious forms by modeling itself on them, it does not cease to frenzy inside them, almost pressing against the walls of a cell, to free itself from them. Religion—such is the principle that neither theologians or believers in the confessional sense nor atheists could understand—is always beyond its historical incarnation. A constitutive surplus inhabits it and pushes it beyond the concretion in which it occurs. The Kantian transcendental nature of religious sentiment, as a space and condition for possible religious experience, is all here. Like the Kantian *Vernunft*, with its ideas, with its vertigo in front of the infinite, with its dizziness on the threshold of the eternal, on the edge of the abyss, religious sentiment also protrudes over an abyss that cannot be defined. There are no categories to define it, and their use, even if practiced, would be inadequate and a source of illusions.

To fix an image of religious sentiment independent of forms, says Constant, it is necessary to think of the most indefinable, more frayed, less circumscribable experiences, such as being in the silence of the night, on the seashore, in the solitude of the countryside, prey to an ineffable nostalgia and abandonment. It is a question of shifts, transits, "ecstatic" fractures towards transcendent worlds, which open faults of Transcendence. In a way, it is as if the space of interests and calculation, of instrumental rationality, apparently so compact, cohesive, was actually full of hatches, cavities, cracks, interstices, ready to deal with whoever looks at it, in a dimension where, in its cogency and peremptoriness, it appears suspended.

Recalling the Kantian image of the two circles used in the second Preface of his *Religion within the Bounds of Bare Reason*, the relationship between sentiment and form in Constant extends this metaphor, somewhat exasperating it: if, as in Kant, historical religions (the outer circle) are not deducible from the *a priori* principle (the inner circle), in

De la religion the concentric relationship of "independent dependence" between the two circles is accentuated, in the sense that between the first and the second there is a conflictual link, of permanent disproportion, as between a force that becomes form to get rid of the form at the end. That is, as in Kant, an open dialectic between *a priori* and *a posteriori*, a crossing of the two domains viable in a double sense: from historical experience to its conditions of possibility and vice versa, without a relationship of deducibility. Religious sentiment, which contains the idea of divinity and of a "permanent, universal revelation" which "has its source in the human heart," is in itself ahistorical and complete, so to speak, in every moment, but it can only be communicated through a historical translation, that is, a finite form in which it contracts itself, thus immersing in the impurities and limits of time, as well as relativizing and partializing itself. The transit from sentiment to form, its historical contamination, that is, the temporalization and spatialization of feeling, mediated by the "spirit" (*esprit*), brings with it a phenomenon of contraction. This reduction is the reason that moves the sentiment to progressively free itself from the form in view of new and more perfect incarnations.

In this sense, sentiment is doomed not to be exhausted in the form, and therefore the value of a religion is measured by their ability of not becoming totally absorbed in the historical form: it is necessary, writes Constant in the *Principles of Politics*, that religion "does not cease to be a feeling, to become a simple form."[11]

The *polemos* between the two polarities is therefore called to be permanent, so that religious sentiment is not tamed, bent, subservient to power or to the habitual mechanism of social conventions. Like the Socratic demon, sentiment says "no" to every form, it contains a principle of negation. Keeping open the dissymmetry between sentiment and form is, for Constant, the trait of free religions compared to those dominated by priestly power. Freedom in religion is preserved where the form never completely saturates the religious space but preserves within itself a free zone, an area of silence, of the unspeakable, an ungovernable point.

The "good" form, free and progressive, for Constant, is the one that knows how to keep freedom, generativity, and stability in balance.

---

11. I quote from the 1815 edition of the *Principes de politique*, OCBC 2001: 829–30.

Free and progressive religions and priestly and stationary religions: Politics of *De la religion*

Every religion, for Constant, is *ab origine* both *revelatio* and hermeneutic act, a luminous synolon of revelation and interpretation. Therefore, freedom belongs to the religious act in its original institution. Schleiermacher in the fifth of his *Reden* says that heresy is "a word that should again be brought to honour."[12] Heresy (*hairesis*) is at the heart of religious *Erlebnis*: it is the center of every intuition. Every religious act is heresy in the sense that it implies a choice, a deviation from what has been acquired. There is cooriginarity and no succession between revelation and freedom. Religion and freedom are united at the germinal point of the religious. The priestly power breaks precisely this synolon of sentiment, form, freedom, making us believe that revelation in its absoluteness has spoken in unique places and in qualitatively exceptional experiences, and that it is necessary to submit to them one's inner independence. Priestly authority therefore breaks that synolon, in favor of a subjugation of revelation to a theological-political power.

Corruption, error, and the violence that follows are found precisely in this unhinging of the unity of the original religious act. Freedom is replaced by obedience to authority, by Scripture or the institution. As Constant claims, it is possible that different beliefs do not contrast, but only by conceiving revelation as a religious sentiment present in the soul of every man, only by thinking of it in the human-divine, divine-human *metaxu*, without hypostasizing it as an absolute that descends from above. Constant opposes the absoluteness of revelation to the theandric plexus, Goethian demonic, neither totally divine nor totally human, as the original space of the religious. Absoluteness is replaced by the free hermeneutic act, *naturaliter* "heretical," as "the imperative" which, according to the sociologist of religions Peter L. Berger, dominates modernity.[13] The "voice of God" is audible only through religious sentiment, and is always the end of a daily, tiring reading, liable to error, impurity.

---

12. Cf. Schleiermacher 1958: 216.
13. Cf. Berger 1980. On the illustrious sociologist of religion, I refer to my essay in Celada Ballanti 2014.

This synolon of revelation, sentiment, freedom, interpretation, is therefore more primitive than the priestly deviations that distort it, shattering its unity in favor of a power. The history of religions is the history of the struggle between what is at the origin and the deviations induced by religious power, between the religions that have managed, in some way, to preserve their purity intact and those who have become corrupted by the priestly power. But that story is also the tension of a pluralism of forms, Weberian and Troeltschian, of individual totalities in dialogue. These individual totalities and their perennial transformation make up a story as a conflictual field of struggling forces, innervated by eruptive peaks, leaps, rises and falls, stasis and accelerations, oscillating and wavering in continuities and discontinuities, in developments and outcomes, but always marked by a conflicting and competitive vision.

Of this conflict, Constant describes a peculiar figure in the history of religions, the one that appears to him to be decisive: the dichotomy, already underlined, between priestly religions and religions free or independent of priestly power. According to Constant, sentiment has to make its way through the suffocating meshes of power held by priestly orthodoxies, which, despite their efforts to block their intimate freedom and unavoidable change, can only postpone it, but not prevent it. A greater force eventually makes its way and reaffirms freedom over the constricting power of forms.

History of religions represents for Constant the privileged observatory for looking at political history, in its being a history of liberation from the constraints of power. There is no space here to dwell on this point, but it is important to point out that Constant's religious anthropology is political anthropology: Constant's liberalism rests on religious sentiment, on its disinterested nature, and not on "well understood interest"[14] and on calculating rationality. From religion and not from utilitarianism emerges the liberal foundation of the political and civil subject and of its struggle against the impediments to its own expressive space. Religion mirrors the essence of modern freedom, even in a political sense. At the same time, it reflects the restless soul of Constant's liberalism.

---

14. For a criticism of the "well understood interest," see the *Préface* in *De la Religion*, in OCBC 2013: 71–83. For a lucid examination of this point see Thouard 2000: 271ff. Cf. also the recent book Thouard 2020.

History as an infinite refinement

The Jaspersian conflict, translatable in terms of *Liberalität* and *Orthodoxie*[15] that innervates the history of religions, and history *tout court*, has in itself an essential force that guides its oscillating motions, accelerations, stasis, eruptive peaks, dead zones: the principle of perfectibility. This is the third pillar of Constantian religious theory, after the dialectic between sentiment and forms and the dichotomy between free and priestly religions, to form a complex, problematic plan on several levels.

Religion contains in itself, in its origin from the religious, natural and universal sentiment, the idea of perfection. Denying itself in the historical figure, the sentiment re-emerges in terms of the desire for perfection that no form can contain, therefore as a tendency towards perfectibility that leaves no quiet, inoculating in it a sense of restlessness that only priests' stationary cults can temporarily atrophy.

What is the nature of this *a priori* law of perfection which is intrinsic to the history of religions? Ultimately, is this a return to a metaphysical view of religion, despite the initial leanings we observed, which were anti-ontological, anti-metaphysical, and against a naturalistic perspective? Would Constant's *Bildungsroman* thus end up in close proximity to the Hegelian one? In the end, would Constant's *Religion* be a *Phenomenology of Spirit* carried out by other means?

We cannot argue that. This assumption is prevented by the transcendental (therefore non-metaphysical) principle that governs Constant's idea of religion, of which the law of perfectibility, inevitable and based on fixed laws, reflects nature. Just as the transcendental is a law of necessity that opens up to the possible, the same is true for the law of perfectibility: a *desse* inscribed in the *esse* of conscience and religious sentiment which, as a necessary tendency, opens up to the possible. As the transcendental, the principle of perfection is a necessary law of the possible. It does not define the triumphalistic direction of unstoppable progress, but a tendency included in human consciousness that appears to be a barrier,

---

15. Here I am referring to the thesis argued by Jaspers in the dispute with Bultmann on the problem of demythization. Cf. Jaspers and Bultmann 1954. I refer in particular to my introduction to this work: Celada Ballanti 2018. Cf. also Kloocke 1989 and Kloocke 2014.

a point of resistance placed against the despair and death that mark historical fortune.

The law of perfection is resistance against death, therefore openness to hope and the capacity for sacrifice within history. This law in Constant has no origin as *Ursprung*, as an ontological foundation, and is expert only in *Anfänge*, in always provisional beginnings, and also in destinies and eschatologies. In Constant there are neither dowsing traces of the *archai* to the discovery of primitive religions, nor prophetic preconceptions of the "kommender Gott." If the origin is subtracted—to the point that not even primitive religions, fetishisms, can represent such an *Ursprung* in the history of religions—and the *eschaton* is equally unfathomable, history is the realm of an open, possible progress, and the place of ethical commitment in favor of freedom. No historical teleologism dominates here, but rather a teleology without absolute religion.

"Reform the Reformation"

All of this ends up translating into an acute, enlightening reinterpretation of religious modernity. We know that the two works of Constant dedicated to religion—*De la Religion* and *Du Polythéisme romain*, published posthumously in 1833[16]—concern the historical evolution from primitive religious practices to the mature phase of Greek polytheism, and then the decline of polytheism, leading to the emergence of theism. If Constant had written, as a third, a history of theism, on which he left a few brief essays and fragments, he would certainly have given a peculiar importance to the turning point of the Reformation, as can be seen from the observations dedicated to it.

In accordance with the "marche des idées," the transition from polytheism to theism was historically inevitable. Theism is axiologically superior, both because it reveals the idea of infinity that resides in religious sentiment and because it is more propitious to morality as it is less willing to fixate itself on dogmas and doctrines. Despite this, it too is subject to the law of progression and perfectibility that dominates the history of man and religions. But it remains that theism is not, for Constant, even in

---

16. Constant 1833.

its eminent form, Christianity, the true, definitive, revealed religion, but a possible form, itself transitory, destined to change, as it actually happened, in the course of its historical story.

Certainly, in the historical parable of Christianity, the Reformation represented for Constant a crucial moment, inaugural of modernity, in which sentiment cracked the form, recalling to its truth. Therefore, this is a paradigmatic moment of purification and amendment of a religion that has fallen victim to the clergy and institutional atrophy for centuries. But even the Reformation, which arose in the name of freedom of conscience, had quickly subjected itself to priestly power, betraying its inspiration. Thus was now the time for a "reform of the Reform."

> The Reformation—writes Constant in a fragment—marked an era.
> The time has come today for a second Reformation.[17]

It was the Germany of the time that, according to Constant, heralded a new phase of Protestantism. A new phase in social practice, as a religion of the heart more than participation in worship, and in philosophical and theological thought, outlining the traits of a neo-Protestantism, to quote Troeltsch, which was opposed to the early Old Protestantism, recovering to itself those humanistic, spiritualistic, mystical currents, expelled by the Reformation since the early years. Constant appears to be an eminent representative of this liberal neo-Protestantism alongside Lessing, Kant, and Schleiermacher. And in the name of this liberal Protestantism, Constant stands as an acute interpreter of modern religious processes, from religious freedom to secularization and pluralism of faiths.

The hermeneutic key to this interpretation is, of course, the distinction of religion on two levels, sentiment and forms, and the broken dialectic that marks its relationship. Precisely this *religio duplex* allows Constant to interpret modern secularization as a set of processes of erosion of literalism, of metamorphosis, of exodus or migration of religious demand from traditional institutions, and finally as a pluralism of faiths. The two positions opposed to Constant, namely the "devotees" and the "atheists," are instead united by the idea of religion on a single level, that of doctrine, worship, dogma, institution. Religion therefore coincided for them with

---

17. Cf. Constant 1966.

only one level, accepted in an exclusive possession by the "devotees," and denied by the "atheists."

Distinguishing the *a priori* source of the religious sphere from historical forms, on the other hand, allows a hermeneutic operation capable of intercepting the changes induced by secularization, recognizing the religious space in its transformations, in its distancing from institutions. The phenomenon of religious pluralism, defined as beneficial by Constant, as a source of a call to religious authenticity, is in line with this thought. Pluralism does not exhaust or cancel religious sentiment. In the process of de-institutionalization that pluralism brings, religious sentiment is rather exalted, renewed in its primacy over forms. This process also offers religious sentiment the possibility of regaining consciousness of its own truth. Secularization is not in contrast with religion; it does not mark its decline but favors it, provided, however, that it is not imposed by the authorities and that it does not become Rousseau's *religio civilis*.

Where the discredited forms are subjected to processes of disintegration or liquefaction, religious sentiment can rise again purified. The modern age is, in this regard, propitious to religious sentiment, and allows us to elaborate the grammar of a religious "third way," which has been crushed in the confessional clashes between the Churches and between believers and atheists. What those conflicts had obscured was now praised, in the resumption of that universalistic program that Humanism and the Renaissance had glimpsed but which remained like an unfinished dawn.

This is Constant's qualifying reading in a liberal sense of modern religious experience, which ideally links to the Schleiermacherian *Reden*: two works united by a hermeneutic effort to rehabilitate religion starting from the Enlightenment. In the conscience of the individual there is an interior instance of truth, an intimate and personal voice—the voice of religious sentiment—aimed at the principles of conscience, where freedom and Transcendence come together and the church-dogmatic stiffenings disappear. Such a *lumen*, which is at the same time darkness, represents the source of religious life. It is not only a natural resource of desire (*Desiderium naturale videndi Deum*), even if it shows the instinctual nature of desire. Rather, the structural connaturality between nature and enlightenment that, in a transcendental perspective, is established here, should be thought as a synolon of activity and passivity, receptivity and creativity, as *locus revelationis*, and universalized to the point of excluding the need for specific charisms or privileged channels. There is no *intuitus mysticus* in Constant: transcendental nature involves not the intuitive grasp of the origin, but rather its perpetual dislocation. "Religious sentiment" is therefore not the name of the origin, but of its constant cancellation. After the original source is no longer known, what persists is the diverse range of ways in which this origin is presented, never in a final or conclusive manner.

Never recurring in its pure state, in every moment religious sentiment requires a process of *emendatio* that dissolves concretions, freed from authoritative burdens, separating the authentic from the inauthentic. Modernity in its Enlightenment phase, and in the figure of liberal Protestantism, appears to Constant as a process of essentialization capable of bringing theism back to its purity, in the form of a minimal theism, freed from literal and institutional burdens. Constant believes that religion, along with the structural need for it, is present in every individual, transcending specific religious affiliations. With the syntagm of Marcel Gauchet, an acute interpreter of Constant, we could conclude: the Constantian hermeneutics of the modern age allows us to read "le religieux après la religion,"[18] that is, the religious Copernican revolution which modernity has brought with it, increasing its repercussions till our time.

Author biography

Roberto Celada Ballanti is Full Professor of Philosophy of Religion and Philosophy of Interreligious Dialogue at the Department of Antiquity, Philosophy and History of the University of Genoa, Italy. His research interests include the philosophy of modern religion, spanning from Humanism to the Enlightenment, as well as the religious challenges in the contemporary era, particularly in relation to nihilism. He also investigates the history of interreligious dialogue, considering various aspects, including significant developments in the twentieth century. Among his recent works are *Religione, storia, libertà. Studi di filosofia della religione* (Naples: Liguori, 2014) and *La parabola dei tre anelli. Migrazioni*

---

18. Cf. Ferry and Gauchet 2004. See also Gauchet 1997.

e metamorfosi di un racconto tra Oriente e Occidente (Rome: Storia e Letteratura, 2017).

References

Primary sources

Constant, B. (1833), *Du Polythéisme romain, considéré dans ses rapports avec la philosophie grecque et la religion chrétienne*, introduction by M. J. Matter, 2 vols. Paris: Béchet aîné.

Constant, B. (1966), *Nouveau système du Théisme*, in *Benjamin Constant méconnu. Le Livre "De la Religion," avec des documents inédits*, 273–75. Geneva: Droz.

Constant, B. (2001), *De la Religion, considerée dans sa source, ses formes et ses développements*, in idem, *Œuvres complètes, Série Œuvres*, vol. IX, edited by O. Devaux and K. Kloocke. Berlin and Boston: De Gruyter [cited as OCBC 2001].

Constant, B. (2013), *De la Religion, considerée dans sa source, ses formes et ses développements*, in idem, *Œuvres complètes, Série Œuvres*, vol. XVII, edited by M. Winkler and K. Kloocke. Berlin and Boston: De Gruyter [cited as OCBC 2013].

Constant, B. (2015), *De la Religion, considerée dans sa source, ses formes et ses développements*, in idem, *Œuvres complètes, Série Œuvres*, vol. XIX, edited by D. Thouard and K. Kloocke. Berlin and Boston: De Gruyter [cited as OCBC 2015].

Constant, B. (2017), *On Religion, Considered in Its Source, Its Forms, and Its Development*, translated by P. P. Seaton Jr., with an Introduction by P. Manent. Carmel, IN: Liberty Fund.

Lessing, G. E. (1968), *Sämtliche Schriften*, edited by Karl Lachmann, text revised by Franz Muncker, vol. XVIII. Stuttgart: Göschen, 1886–1924; Berlin: De Gruyter, 1968.

Schleiermacher, F. D. E. (1958), *On Religion: Speeches to its Cultured Despisers*, translated by J. Oman. New York: Harper & Row.

Secondary sources

Barth, K. (1960), *Die protestantische Theologie im 19. Jahrhundert: ihre Vorgeschichte und ihre Geschichte*. Zürich: Evangelischer Verlag.

Berger, P. L. (1980), *The Heretical Imperative: Contemporary Possibilities of Religious Affirmation*. London: Collins.

Celada Ballanti, R. (2009), *Pensiero religioso liberale. Lineamenti, figure, prospettive*. Brescia: Morcelliana.
Celada Ballanti, R. (2014), "Dalla 'sacra volta' all' 'imperativo eretico.' Fenomenologia e sociologia della religione in Peter L. Berger," in idem, *Religione, Storia, Libertà. Studi di filosofia della religione*, 215–33. Naples: Liguori.
Celada Ballanti, R. (2018), "Introduzione," in K. Jaspers and R. Bultmann, *Il problema della demitizzazione*, curated by R. Celada Ballanti. Brescia: Morcelliana.
Celada Ballanti, R. (2019), "Benjamin Constant tra pensiero religioso liberale e storicismo critico," in B. Constant, *Della religione, considerata nella sua sorgente, nelle sue forme e nei suoi sviluppi*, 1–86. Rome: Edizioni di Storia e Letteratura.
Deguise, P. (1966), *Benjamin Constant méconnu. Le Livre "De la Religion," avec des documents inédits*. Geneva: Droz.
Ferry, L., and M. Gauchet (2004), *Le religieux après la religion*. Paris: B. Grasset.
Gauchet, M. (1997), "Préface," in B. Constant, *Écrits politiques*, 9–110. Paris: Gallimard.
Hirsch, E. (1960), *Geschichte der neuern evangelischen Theologie im Zusammenhang mit den allgemeinen Bewegungen des europäischen Denkens*, 5 vols. Gütersloh: Gerd Mohn.
Jaspers, K., and R. Bultmann (1954), *Die Frage der Entmythologisierung*. München: Piper.
Kloocke, K. (1988), "Échos de l'œuvre de Benjamin Constant en Italie. La réception de l'ouvrage sur la religion," in M. Matucci (ed.), *Il gruppo di Coppet e l'Italia, Atti del Colloquio Internazionale (Pescia 24–27 settembre 1986)*, 147–61. Pisa: Pacini.
Kloocke, K. (1989), "Le concept de la liberté religieuse chez Benjamin Constant," *Annales Benjamin Constant* 10: 25–39.
Kloocke, K. (2000), "Religion et societé chez Benjamin Constant," in L. Jaume (ed.), *Coppet, creuset de l'esprit libéral. Les idées politiques et constitutionelles du groupe de Madame de Staël*, 121–33. Aix-en-Provence and Paris: Presse Universitaires d'Aix-Marseille/Economica.
Kloocke, K. (2008), "Benjamin Constant et l'Allemagne," *Œuvres & Critiques* XXXIII: 19–38.
Kloocke, K. (2012), "Le sentiment religieux chez Jean-Jacques Rousseau et Benjamin Constant," in F. Lotterie and G. Poisson (eds.), *Jean-Jacques Rousseau devant Coppet*, 105–23. Geneva: Slatkine.
Kloocke, K. (2013), "Introduction," in B. Constant, *Œuvres complètes, Série Œuvres*, vol. XVII, 53–59. Berlin and Boston: De Gruyter.

Kloocke, K. (2014), "La théorie de la religion chez Benjamin Constant," *Annales Benjamin Constant* 39: 53–67.
Thompson, P. (1978), *La religion de Benjamin Constant. Le pouvoir de l'image*. Pisa: Pacini Editore.
Thompson, P. (1998), *Les Écrits de Benjamin Constant sur la religion. Essai de liste chronologique. Préface et révision par P. Deguise avec la collaboration de B. Anelli*. Paris: Honoré Champion.
Thouard, D. (2000), "Religione e soggettività in Schleiermacher e in Benjamin Constant," in *Religione e religioni*, 261–94, curated by S. Sorrentino. Assisi: Cittadella.
Thouard, D. (2020), *Liberté et religion. Relire Benjamin Constant*. Paris: CNRS Éditions.
Todorov, T. (1999), "Un chef-d'œuvre oublié," in B. Constant, *De la Religion*, ed. T. Todorov and E. Hofmann, 9–19. Arles: Actes Sud.
Todorov, T. (2009), "Constant, politique et religion," in idem, *La signature humaine: essais 1983–2008*, 357–71. Paris: Edition du Seuil.
Violi, C. (1984), *Benjamin Constant. Per una storia della riscoperta. Politica e religione*. Rome: Gangemi.

Index

Aaron 138, 139n, 156
Abbias 96
Abela, Catarina 255
Abela, Giovanni Francesco 242n
Abellán, José Luis 64n
Abiram 138, 138n, 139n, 140, 140n, 143n, 156
Abraham 49
Abraham (slave of Catarina Abela) 255
Abulafia, Abraham 69
Acciard, Michele 252n
Acosta, José de 275, 278, 292
Acquaviva, Claudio 279, 285
Adrian VI (Pope) 78, 79
Ahab 140n
Aikin, Scott F. 48n, 51n
Alba, Fernando Álvarez de Toledo, Duke of 223–224
Alberigo, Giuseppe 140n
Albert III (Margrave of Brandenburg) 46, 52
Albert of Hohenzollern (Archbishop of Mainz) 150
Alcázar, Bartolomé de 279n, 289n
Alcoba, Laura 311n
Aleander, Hieronymus 152, 152n
Alegambe, Felipe 279n
Alejandro Lueiro, José María de 74n
Aleksander, Jason 48n, 51n
Alemán, Mateo 191n
Alençon, Francis, Duke of 225
Alexander VI (Pope) 68, 93, 119
Alfarabi 72

Alfonso V (King of Aragon) 63n
Alfsvåg, Knut 27
Alighieri, Dante 62n, 93n
Allen, Percy Stafford 152n, 153n
Almagro Vidal, Clara 202n
Álvaro Zamora, María Isabel 203n, 204n
Aly (character in Marteilhe's *Mémoires*) 306, 308
Amadeus, Beatus 96n
Andrade, Alonso de 276, 276n
Andrés, Juan 65
Andretta, Stefano 3n
Anguisciola, Spiritus Pelo 242
Anna (slave of Giovanni Vassallo) 7–8, 255
Anne (Queen of England), 299, 313, 315
Antonio, Nicolás 279n
Aquinas, Thomas 72, 75, 180, 251, 251n, 255, 256n
Aranda Doncel, Juan 199n, 201n, 204n
Arimura, Rie 285n
Aristotle 64, 68, 71, 75
Arminius, James 230
Arnaya, Nicolás de 282
Arsaces (King of Parthia) 38, 39n
Asaph 142
Asclepius 71
Astete, Gaspar de 271n
Athanasius of Alexandria 144
Audisio, Gabriél 243n, 246n, 261n
Augustine of Hippo 5, 72, 75, 82, 120n, 142, 218
Avempace 72

Averroes 67, 72
Avicenna 72
Azor, Juan 270, 272, 272n, 274, 274n, 275, 275n, 278–281, 281n, 282, 282n, 283, 283n, 284, 284n, 292
Azpilcueta, Martín de 284
Azzopardi-Ljubibratic, Sarah 257n
Azzupardo, Claudio 249n

Babinger, Franz 35n
Baglioni, Malatesta 111
Bainton, Roland H. 168n
Baker, Nora 2–3, 296, 320
Balard, Michel 243, 243n
Bamford, Paul 300, 300n, 301, 301n
Bandello, Matteo 62
Bangert, William V. 293n
Barral-Baron, Marie 135n
Barrio Gozalo, Maximiliano 255, 255n
Barrios Aguilera, Manuel 187n, 192n
Barth, Karl 325, 325n
Bartholomew (Saint), 215, 224
Bataillon, Marcel 78n
Battista, Ludovico 1, 3n, 7, 134
Baudouin, François 220
Bayle, Pierre 296–299, 301, 313, 316, 317, 319, 320
Bayona Aznar, Bernardo 75n
Beame, Edmund M. 225n, 227n
Beccaria, Antonio 105
Belloy, Pierre de 216, 228
Bembo, Pietro 94n
Benedict XIII (Pope) 60, 244
Benedict XIV 256, 256n
Benedict, Philip 224n, 232n
Benítez Sánchez-Blanco, Rafael 188n, 189n, 193, 193n, 199n
Benivieni, Antonio (father of Girolamo) 92, 92n
Benivieni, Antonio (nephew of Girolamo) 98, 98n
Benivieni, Domenico 92, 92n, 105n, 107, 109, 123n
Benivieni, Girolamo 2, 90, 90n, 92–94, 94n, 95, 95n, 96, 96n, 97, 97n, 99–100, 100n, 101–102, 102n, 103, 103n, 104, 104n, 105, 105n, 106, 106n, 107, 107n, 108, 108n, 109, 109n, 110, 110n, 111, 111n, 112, 112n, 113, 114, 114n, 115, 115n, 117, 117n, 122–123, 123n, 124, 126, 126n
Benivieni, Lorenzo 94n
Benivieni, Paolo 92
Benjamin, Walter 9, 9n
Bennet, Tony 196n
Benzoni, Gino 245n
Berend, Nora 243n
Bermúdez Vázquez, Manuel Ignacio 83n
Bernabé Pons, Luis F. 192n
Berger, Peter L. 9, 331, 331n
Bernardino, Pietro 96
Bertini, Giovanni 67n
Bettinson, Christopher 227n
Beza, Theodore 298
Bidese, Ermenegildo 27
Biechler, James E. 48n
Bigelow Merriman, Roger 245n
Bion, Jean-François 298–303, 306–308, 310–318, 320
Birriel Salcedo, Margarita María 195n
Bisaha, Nancy 13n, 36n, 43n
Black, Christopher F. 48n
Boccaccio, Giovanni 62
Bodin, Jean 227, 297
Boeckler, Johann Heinrich 65
Bond, H. Lawrence 48n
Bonnell, Victoria 196n
Bonner, Michael 52n
Bonnici, Alessandro 246n
Bonnici, Pulcra 257
Bono, Salvatore 246n, 253, 253n
Borghesi, Francesco 72n
Borgia, Giovanni (Duke of Gandia) 119
Borromeo, Federico 250
Bossuet, Jacques-Bénigne 317, 318, 318n

Botticelli, Sandro 103, 140
Boubaker, Sadok 243*n*
Boyer, Pierre 246, 246*n*
Bramante, Donato 84*n*
Bramanti, Vanni 124*n*
Brancato, Giovanni 177
Braudel, Fernand 243*n*, 245
Brès, Françoise 316
Briguglia, Gianluca 175*n*
Brogini, Anne 245*n*
Brousson, Claude 317, 317*n*
Brumont, Francis 197*n*
Bruni, Leonardo 63
Brydone, Patrick 259, 259*n*
Buber, Martin 116*n*
Bucer, Martin 150
Budé, Guillaume 63, 154, 154*n*
Bulliet, Richard 241, 241*n*
Bultmann, Rudolf 333*n*
Burckhardt, Jacob 61
Buriali d'Arezzo, Paolo 258
Burke, Peter 241*n*
Burton, Simon J. G. 48*n*
Buynac, Moyse 249*n*
Byrne, Susan 61*n*, 64–67

Cacciari, Massimo 32*n*, 125*n*
Caesar, Gaius Julius 42
Caffiero, Marina 257, 257*n*
Cajetan, Thomas (or Thomas de Vio) 152, 152*n*, 153, 153*n*
Calafate, Pedro 274*n*, 275*n*, 277*n*, 278*n*
Calixtus III (Pope) 35
Callan, Charles J. 255*n*
Calleja, Gaspare 243*n*
Calvin, John 218, 307
Cantelmo, Giacomo 243, 243*n*
Capistran, John 35, 35*n*, 47
Capito, Wolfgang 150, 150*n*
Cappelli, Guido 175*n*, 177*n*
Carafa, Gregorio 243
Carasi, M. 259*n*
Caravale, Giorgio 99, 99*n*, 100*n*

Carlos Morales, Carlos Javier de 222*n*, 226*n*
Carnesecchi Pietro 151
Carrasco Urgoiti, María Soledad 191*n*
Cashmere, John 297*n*, 298*n*
Cassander, Georg 219–220
Cassar, Carmel 250*n*
Cassi, Aldo 180*n*
Cassirer, Ernst 16, 16*n*, 29*n*
Castellio, Sebastian 218–219, 229, 236, 297
Catherine of Aragon 78
Cavaliero, Roderic 246*n*
Celada Ballanti, Roberto 2, 2*n*, 9, 324, 326*n*, 331*n*, 333*n*
Celestine V (Pope) 97*n*
Centeno, Michele 258
Cervantes, Miguel de 62, 65, 65*n*, 70, 249*n*
Charlemagne (Emperor) 97
Charles V (Emperor) 59, 60*n*, 72, 78, 81, 92, 117*n*, 136, 174, 188, 233
Charles VIII (King of France) 110, 115, 118, 120
Charles IX (King of France) 223
Chigi Zondadari, Antonio Felice 258*n*
Chijiwa, Miguel de 287–289, 291
Christin, Olivier 216, 217*n*, 220*n*, 222*n*, 231, 231*n*, 233*n*
Churchill, Buntzie Ellis 52*n*
Ciappara, Frans 2, 7, 241, 242*n*, 244*n*, 245*n*, 250*n*, 254*n*, 255*n*, 258*n*, 259*n*, 261
Cirot, Georges 190*n*
Cisneros, Francisco Jiménez de 69*n*, 188
Clancy-Smith, Julia A. 248*n*
Clareno, Angelo 97, 97*n*
Claude, Jean 297
Clement of Alexandria 24
Cochlaeus, Johannes 3*n*, 7, 151*n*, 152, 152*n*, 154–157

Collignon-Ward, Séverine 298–300, 302–304, 308, 308n, 309, 316n, 319, 319n
Colón, Cristóbal 65
Colón, Hernando 65
Colombo, Emanuele 259n
Coluccio Salutati, Lino 62, 83
Columbus, Christopher 68
Commynes, Philippe de 105n
Condé, Henry of Bourbon, Prince of 225
Conlon, Pierre 299n, 306, 306n, 310n, 311n, 312n, 315n, 316, 316n, 318n
Constant, Benjamin 2, 324–337
Conte Cazcarro, Ánchel 203n
Coolhaes, Caspar 227
Coornhert, Dirck 229
Corneille, Pierre 302
Corsini, Neri Maria 258n
Corvinus, Antonius 160, 160n, 161n, 162n
Cotta-Schønberg, Michael 37n, 38n, 39n, 40n, 41n, 47n, 140n
Cottoner, Nicholas 247
Courcelles, Dominique 301, 302n
Crespin, Jean 298, 316
Cronicus, Antonius (Antonio Vinciguerra) 69
Crouzet, Denis 227
Crucitti, Angela 94n
Cuozzo, Gianluca 20n, 24n
Curvelo, Alexandra 285n
Cusanus, Nicholas (or Nicholas of Cusa) 1, 5–6, 12–32, 35, 44–53, 72–79, 81, 84
Cybo, Alderano 243n
Czarin, Vincenzo 249

Dakhlia, Jocelyne 301n, 310, 310n
Dall'Aglio, Stefano 97n, 100n, 113n
Damasus I (Pope) 151n
Daniel, Norman 49, 50n, 52, 52n, 241, 241n

Danielis, John (Giovanni Danieli) 152, 152n
Daniels, Tobias 140n
Dathan 138, 138n, 139n, 140, 140n, 143n
David (King of Israel) 109–110, 124–125, 141
Davis, Derek 260n
Decker, Rainer 251n
Deguise, Pierre 327n
Del Col, Andrea 248n
Del Lungo, Isidoro 92n
Del Medigo, Elia 68
De Redin, Martin 247
Di Benedetto, Sergio 93n, 94n
Di Camillo, Ottavio 60, 60n, 61n, 62, 62n, 69n, 77n, 83, 83n
Diderot, Denis 296, 300
Diefendorf, Barbara 224n
Diéz Jorge, María Elena 194n, 198n
Dionisotti, Carlo 93, 93n, 94n, 99, 99n
Dionysius the Carthusian 48, 48n
Diotallevi, Ettore 255
Domínguez Ortiz, Antonio 199n
Dourado, Constantino 287
Duclow, Donald F. 48n
Duni, Matteo 251n
Dunn, James 113n
Duns Scotus, John 72
Duplessis-Mornay, Philippe 225
Durini, Angelo Maria 258, 258n
Durini, Carlo Francesco 243n
Dursteler, Eric 241, 242n
Dust, Philip C. 134n
Dziuba, Andrzej 278n

Earle, Peter 245, 246n
Eckhart, Meister 18, 23, 24
Egidio da Viterbo 117n
Eliab 138n
Ellul, Joseph 256n
Episcopius, Nikolaus 136n
Episcopius, Simon 230

Erasmus, Desiderius 1, 4, 6–7, 42, 43, 43n, 44, 53, 54, 78, 134–162, 167–178, 183, 218–219, 229, 236
Esmorís Galán, Lorena 70n
Ettlinger, Leopold 140n
Eugene IV (Pope) 47, 140
Eusebius of Caesarea 24, 141n
Ezekias 38, 39n

Faldi, Luca 100n
Fallica, Maria 2, 90, 144n
Farfara, Samuele 244
Farnese, Alexander 235
Feijoo de Montenegro, Benito Jerónimo 66
Ferdinand (King of Aragón) 68, 188, 205, 280
Ferdinand I (Emperor) 136, 151
Fernández Chaves, Manuel Francisco 197n, 201n, 203n, 204, 204n
Ferrer, Vincent 259n
Ferry, Luc 337n
Fichte, Johann Gottlieb 328
Ficino, Marsilio 60, 63–69, 71, 76n, 84, 93
Filipepi, Simone 94n
Filtner, Andreas 157n
Firpo, Massimo 100, 100n
Flavius Josephus 140n
Foix, Paul de 223
Fontán, Antonio 62n, 69n, 83, 84n
Fontenay, Michel 246n
Forcilloni, Antonino 35n
Fortunata (slave of Francesco of Valletta) 257
Forst, Rainier 300, 300n
Fortunati, Francesco 102
Fournel, Jean-Louis 121, 121n
Francesco of Valletta 257
Francis I, King of France 136
Franco Llopis, Borja 190n, 191n, 196n, 198n, 199n, 201n, 205n, 283n
Frederick III (Emperor) 375

Friedensburg, Walter 152n
Frijhoff, Willem 216n, 229n, 233n
Froben, Hieronymus 136n
Fuchs, Barbara 191n

Gaia, Pio 14n
Galea, Marco 252n
Gallarati Scotti, Giovanni Filippo 257
Gallego Burín, Antonio 192n, 199n
Galli, Carlo 125n
Galán Sánchez, Ángel 187n
Gamaliel 98
Gámir Sandoval, Alfonso 192n, 199n
García, Pedro 70, 70n
García-Arenal, Mercedes 192n
García Cárcel, Ricardo 190n, 192n, 193n
García Fernández, Máximo 197n
García Gibert, Javier 63n
García Gómez, María J. 196n
García Gómez, Mercedes C. 74n
García Gutiérrez, Fernando 285n
García Pedraza, Amalia 198n
García Villoslada, Ricardo 285n, 286n
Garfagnini, Gian Carlo 123n
Garin, Eugenio 70, 71
Garrad, Kenneth 192n, 198n
Garsin 260
Gauchet, Marcel 5, 5n, 337, 337n
Gauci, Liam 246n
Gaune, Rafael 285n
Gavirati Miyashiro, Pablo 284n
Geraldini, Antonio 62n
Gerbhardt, Georg 153n
Gerritsen, Anne 196n
Giacchi d'Elia 249
Gignati, Sabatai 244n
Ginzburg, Carlo 8, 8n
Giosi, Marco 174n
Giustiniani, Paolo 97
Godfrey of Bouillon (Duke of Lower Lorraine) 40
Godin, André 144n

Goliath 109
Gómez Moreno, Ángel 61, 61n, 62n
Góngora, Luis de 65
Goñi Zubieta, Carlos 68n, 69n, 70, 70n
Gonzaga, Ercole 155
González de la Calle, Urbano 65
González Vega, Felipe 69n
Gordon, Bruce 219n
Goujon (friend of Marteilhe) 303, 319
Goulart, Simon 298, 316
Gouwens, Kenneth 117n
Greco, Gaetano 257n, 259n
Green, Harvey 196n
Greene, Molly 241, 241n, 245n
Gregory of Nyssa 18
Gregory X (Pope) 251
Gregory XIII (Pope) 270, 283, 286–287
Grelot, Guillaume Joseph 311n
Grotius, Hugo 230
Gualtieri, Ludovico 243n
Guggisberg, Hans R. 219n
Guicciardini, Francesco 114, 115n
Guillén, Claudio 191n
Guy, Alain 71, 71n
Guzmán, Luis de 9, 286, 288n, 289, 289n, 290, 290n, 291

Habermas, Jürgen 6–7, 6n
Haggai 122
Halff, Maarten 47n
Halkin, Leo H. 136n
Hallauer, Hermann 44n
Hankins, James 36, 36n, 42n, 50n
Hara, Martín de 287, 291
Hatfield, Rab 103n
Hegel, Georg Wilhelm Friedrich 325, 328
Helmrath, Johannes 44n, 47n
Henry III (King of France) 225, 227
Henry IV (Henry of Navarre, then King of France) 216, 225, 227, 232
Henry VIII (King of England) 78–80, 136

Hentze, Wilhelm 145n
Herder, Johann Gottfried 325, 326
Hernández Pérez, Alberto 2, 7, 214
Hess, Andrew C. 245n
Hicks, Dan 196n
Hideyoshi, Toyotomi 286
Higuera, Jerónimo Román de la 286, 288, 289n, 290
Hilary of Poitiers 141n
Himelick, Raymond 136n, 137n, 139n, 141n, 142n, 144–149n, 158n
Hirsch, Emmanuel 325, 325n
Hobbes, Thomas 184
Hoeppner Moran Cruz, Jo Ann 50n
Hoffmann, Martin 147n, 148n, 149n
Hollmann, Joshua 46n
Holt, Mack P. 225n, 226n
Homedes, Juan de 252
Honée, Eugène 136n
Hopkins, Jasper 14n, 45n, 48n, 49n, 51n
Horace (Quintus Horatius Flaccus) 102
Hosea 150
Hotman, Jean de Villiers 228
Housley, Norman 35n, 36, 36n, 37n, 42n, 44, 44n, 46, 46n, 47n
Hoyos Hattori, Paula 284n
Hughes, Diane Owen 247n
Huizinga, Johan 135n
Hunt, Laura 150n, 151, 151n
Hunt, Lynn 196n, 241n
Huntington, Samuel P. 241, 241n
Hunyadi, Janos 35
Hurtado de Mendoza, Diego 65
Huseman, William H. 216n

Iamblichus 72
Ibraimo 257
Inalcik, Halil 35n
Innocent VIII (Pope) 110
Irigoyen-García, Javier 199n, 200, 200n
Isabel (Queen of Castilla) 68, 188, 205, 280
Isaiah 119, 170

Isouf (character in Marteilhe's *Mémoires*) 304–306, 308
Israel, Jonathan 219n, 226n, 229n, 230n, 234n
Itlodeus (character in More's *Utopia*) 179, 180
Ito, Mancio 287, 291
Ivanič, Suzanna 196n
Izbicki, Thomas M. 35n, 43, 44n, 46n, 48n, 49n, 53
Izhar 138n

Jacobsen, Anders-Christian 144n
Jaspers, Karl 333n
Jerome of Stridon 141, 141n
Jesus Christ 17, 23, 27, 28, 37, 41, 49, 50, 73, 76, 83, 106, 111, 116, 116n, 120–121, 121n, 123, 125n, 137, 142, 146, 158, 161, 162, 167, 168, 170–172, 174, 178, 183, 205, 219, 246, 247, 255, 257n, 312
Joachim of Flora 120
Job 73, 119
John VIII Palaeologus (Byzantine emperor) 47
Joutard, Philippe 317n
Joyce, Patrick 196n
Juan de la Cruz (John of the Cross) 65, 67, 67n
Juana Inés de la Cruz 65
Jubel, Mahamete 252
Julian (Emperor) 122
Julien, Marie-Pierre 196, 196n
Julius II (Pope) 171n
Jungić, Josephine 96, 96n
Junius, Franciscus 223
Juno 71
Junot, Yves 216n, 235n
Jupiter 71
Jurieu, Pierre 296, 297, 316, 317, 317n, 318

Kagay, Donald 64n

Kaiser, Ronny 4n
Kant, Immanuel 2, 6, 8, 8n, 325, 326, 327, 329, 330, 335
Kantzenbach, Friedrich W. 136n, 147n, 150, 150n, 160n
Kaplan, Benjamin J. 215n, 217n, 219n, 229n, 231n, 232n, 233n, 234n
Kenny, Joseph 256n
Kent, Dale 101n, 106, 106n
Kertzer, David I. 257n
Kilcullen, John 313n
Kim, Seong-Hak 221n, 224n
Kishimoto, Emi 285n
Kloocke, Kurt 325n, 327, 327n, 333n
Knoll, Paul W. 243n
Kohath 138n
Konrad III (Emperor) 40, 41n
Kooi, Christine 227n, 234n
Korah 136, 138, 138n, 139, 140, 140n, 141, 142, 142n, 143, 143n, 156
Koselleck, Reinhart 6, 6n

Laborie, Lionel 314, 314n, 315, 315n
Labrousse, Elizabeth 296n
Ladero Quesada, Miguel Ángel 187n, 188n
Laguna, Andrés de 3–4, 4n, 72, 72n, 81
Langlande du Chaila, François (Abbot du Chaila) 315–317, 317n
La Noue, François de, 225
Latomus, Bartholomaeus 151n
Laven, Mary 196n
Lawrance, Jeremy N. H. 62n
Lazzerini, Luigi 100n
Leaños, Jamie 75n
Lecerf, Florence 195n, 201n
Léchot, Pierre-Oliver 300, 300n, 301, 301n, 308, 308n
Leftley, Sharon 96, 96n
Leibniz, Gottfried Wilhelm 68, 314
Lentzen, Manfred 83n
León, Luis de 64, 67, 76n
Leporatti, Roberto 93n, 95, 95n

Lerner, Robert E. 112*n*
Le Roux, Nicolas 225*n*, 228*n*
Léry, Jean de 320
Lessing, Gotthold Ephraim 324, 324*n*, 325, 326, 335
Lestrigant, Frank 320, 320*n*
Lettieri, Gaetano 5*n*, 18*n*, 24*n*, 34, 116*n*, 117*n*, 125*n*, 139*n*, 144*n*
Levi 138*n*
Levy, Ian Christopher 33, 48*n*
L'Estoile, Pierre de 228
Lewis, Bernard 52*n*
L'Hôpital, Michel de 219–222, 224, 236
Liberato (friar) 97
Lipsius, Justus 229
Llorca, Bernardino 286*n*
Lodone, Michele 91*n*, 92*n*, 96*n*, 126*n*
Longino, Michele 301*n*, 302, 302*n*, 311, 311*n*, 314*n*
Lopez, Pasquale 258*n*
López Forjas, Manuel 2, 3*n*, 4, 59, 85
Lo Re, Salvatore 115*n*
Losada, Carolina 259*n*
Louis XI (King of France) 41
Louis XIV (King of France) 301
Louis XV (King of France) 319
Louvreleuil, Jean-Baptiste 316, 317, 317*n*
Loyola, Jorge 287
Luther, Martin 43, 80, 99–100, 100*n*, 135, 136, 141, 144, 150*n*, 151, 152, 155, 156, 157*n*, 159–162, 218, 271, 308

Macedo, Paulo Emílio Borges de 275*n*, 277*n*
Machiavelli, Niccolò 91, 91*n*, 120, 120*n*, 125, 125*n*, 126*n*
Magán Sánchez, Juan Manuel 196*n*, 204*n*
Maimonides 66
Malón de Chaide, Pedro 64

Mandado Gutiérrez, Ramón 274*n*, 275*n*, 278*n*
Manduca, Teresa 258*n*
Manent, Pierre 38
Mangion, Salvatore 257
Mann Philips, Margaret 135*n*
Mantovani, Mauro 277*n*
Margaret of Parma 222
Margolin Jean-Claude 169*n*
Maria (slave of Teresa Manduca) 258*n*
Mariana, Juan de 272, 272*n*, 273, 273*n*, 274, 274*n*, 275, 275*n*, 276, 276*n*
Mariano da Genazzano (friar) 109
Marion, Élie 316
Marot, Clément 298
Márquez Villanueva, Francisco 190*n*
Marsilius of Padua 75
Marteilhe, Jean 298–311, 314, 318–321
Martin, Ruth 251*n*
Martín López, David 2, 9, 269, 278*n*, 279*n*, 282*n*, 287*n*
Martin V (Pope) 60
Martínez, Emilio 67*n*
Martínez Arancón, Ana 64*n*
Martínez Gómez, Luis 67, 72, 72*n*, 73, 73*n*
Martínez Millán, José 60*n*, 222*n*, 226*n*
Martínez San Pedro, Manuel D. 201*n*
Mary (mother of Jesus) 102, 118, 205
Masson, Jacques 151
Maurizi, Marco 14*n*, 17*n*, 23*n*
Mazel, Abraham 317, 317*n*
Mazur, Peter A. 254*n*, 255*n*
McHugh, John A. 255*n*
Medici, Alessandro de' 124
Medici, Catherine of 220
Medici, Cosimo de' (the Elder) 64, 106, 126*n*
Medici, Cosimo de', I (the Duke) 93*n*
Medici, Giovanni de' (Giovanni dalle Bande Nere) 93*n*, 102

Medici, Giovanni di Lorenzo de' (Leo X, Pope) 42, 80, 94–96, 96n, 100, 115, 125n, 126
Medici, Giovanni di Pierfrancesco de' 92
Medici, Giuliano de' 93
Medici, Giulio de' (Clement VII, Pope) 92, 136, 153, 153n, 93n, 94, 96–100, 102, 104, 104n, 106–107, 115, 123, 123n, 126
Medici, Lorenzo di Pierfrancesco de' 92n
Medici, Lorenzo di Piero (the Magnificent) 64, 68, 93, 109–110, 140n
Medici, Lucrezia de 93n
Medici, Piero de' 111, 118
Mehmed II (Sultan) 12, 14
Melanchthon, Philip 218
Mendelssohn, Moses 324
Mendiola Fernández, María Isabel 195n
Mendoza, Juan de 288
Menedemus (character in Terentius' comedy) 4
Menéndez Pelayo, Marcelino 65
Menéndez Pidal, Ramón 66
Mercury 71, 122
Mesquita, Diego de 287, 291
Meuthen, Erich 44n, 47n, 52n
Micah 122
Míguez Santa Cruz, Antonio 286
Milanesi, Gaetano 104, 106
Miller, Clarence H. 152n
Misson, François-Maximilien 316, 317n
Mithridate, Flavio (Guglielmo Raimondo di Moncada) 69, 69n
Mohammed (the Prophet of Islam) *see* Muhammad
Molina, Enrique 278n
Molina, Luis de 274–275, 275n, 278, 278n, 292
Monaco, Davide 15n, 19n
Monahan, W. Gregory 316n, 317n
Monfasani, John 36n, 52, 52n

Monluc, Jean de 222
Montaigne, Michel de 227
Montepulciano, Francesco da 91n
Montesquieu (Charles-Louis de Secondat) 303
Montmorency, Henry de, Earl of Damville 225, 232
Monzón, Bernardo 279n
More, Thomas 63, 78, 167, 178–184
Moreno Díaz del Campo, Francisco J. 2, 8, 187, 190n, 191n, 193n, 195n, 196n, 197n, 198n, 199n, 201n, 203n, 204n, 205n, 283n
Mori, Antonello 1–2, 167
Morrall, Andrew 196n
Moses 124–125, 125n, 126n, 138, 138n, 139, 139n, 140, 140n, 142, 142n, 143, 143n, 156
Mougel, D. Ambroise 49n
Mout, Nicolette M. E. H. 218n, 226n
Muhammad (prophet) 7, 41, 48–52, 252, 255, 311, 312
Muley, Francisco Núñez 192, 198–199
Mussolin, Mauro 101n

Najemy, John M. 126n
Nakaura, Julián de 287, 291
Napulone, Giovanni Battista 244n
Nardi, Jacopo 97, 97n, 98, 98n, 104, 104n
Nausea, Friedrich 158, 158n, 159n
Nebrija, Antonio de 69, 69n, 83
Niccoli, Ottavia 90n
Nicholas V (Pope) 13, 37
Nicolini, Iacopo 123n
Nieto Ivarra, Juan Gonzalo 80n
Nimrod 140n
Nobunaga, Oda 286

Obehut 96
O'Brien, Emily 42n
Ocker, Christopher 49n
Olin, John C. 134n

Oliveri Formosa, Giacoba 246
Olivetti, Marco Maria 5, 5n, 32, 32n
O'Malley, John W. 50n
On 138n, 143n
O'Neil, Mary 251n
Origen of Alexandria 18, 24, 30, 120n, 141n, 144n
Orihuela Uzal, Antonio 203n
Ortega y Gasset, José 63n
Ottoboni, Pietro 244n, 260n

Pace, Giuseppe 251n
Padberg, Rudolf 134n
Padilla, Pedro de 191n
Pagano, Sergio 254n
Pallavicini, Lazzaro (inquisitor of Malta) 248
Pallavicini, Lazzaro Opizio (cardinale) 258n
Palma, Luis de la 271n
Palumbo, Matteo 123n
Paolo (baptized slave) 258
Papirius (Roman consul) 126n
Pardo, Guiomar 288
Pascual Martínez, José 199n, 203n
Pasini, Enrico 168n
Passionei, Paolo 247, 247n, 258n
Paul III (Pope) 258
Paulus of Tarsus 14, 72, 113, 118, 157
Pedro de Rúa 69n
Peinado Santaella, Rafael G. 188n
Pelazza, Maria Assunta 67n
Peleth 138n
Pellegrini, Marco 109n, 118
Pelster, Franz 278n
Pérez de Hita, Ginés 191n
Pérez de Oliva, Hernán 71, 71n
Pérez Garcia, Rafael M. 197n, 201n, 203n, 204, 204n
Peroli, Enrico 12n, 27n
Perugino 141
Peter (apostle) 14
Petrarca, Francesco 62, 71n, 84

Petrilli, Giuseppe 178n
Pettegree, Andrew 223n, 226n
Pflug, Julius von 136, 136n
Philip II (King of Spain) 60n, 64, 65, 189–190, 192, 280, 286, 289
Philip III (King of Spain) 193, 207, 218, 222–223, 235, 289
Philip III (Duke of Burgundy) 172
Philo of Alexandria 24
Pico della Mirandola, Gianfrancesco 69n, 104, 123, 123n
Pico della Mirandola, Giovanni 3n, 59, 60, 63, 65–74, 78–82, 84, 93, 95n, 107, 109
Pierozzi, Antonino (Bishop of Florence) 101, 101n
Pietro (apostle) 72, 141
Pio di Carpi, Alberto 152
Pitti, Jacopo 98, 99n
Pius II (Pope, or Aeneas Silvius Piccolomini) 35–42, 46, 47, 52–53, 75, 75n, 140
Pius IV (Pope) 247
Platina 140n
Plato 24, 63n, 64, 65, 71, 81, 84
Pliny the Elder 177
Plotinus 72
Politi, Lancillotto (Ambrogio Catarino) 99, 99n, 100
Poliziano, Angelo 92n, 93
Polizzotto, Lorenzo 96n, 99n, 104n
Pollet, Jacques V. 136n
Pomara, Bruno 196n
Postel, Guillaume 308
Posthumus Meyjes, Hans 220, 220n
Preston, Patrick 99n
Preto, Paolo 241, 241n
Prieto Bernabé, José Manuel 201n
Proclus 72
Prodi, Paolo 116n, 278n
Pseudo-Dionysus the Areopagite 18, 23–25, 25n, 65
Puente, Luis de 271n, 282

Pugliese, Olga Zorzi 93n, 94n, 96, 96n, 97n, 100, 100n, 101n, 104, 104n, 105, 105n, 106n

Quaglioni, Diego 174n
Quirini, Vincenzo 97

Ramusio, Girolamo 68
Raphael 67
Raunio, Anu 254n
Re, Caterina 94n, 95, 100n, 102n, 104n, 123, 123n
Reeves, Marjorie 91, 91n, 97n, 120n
Refalo, Francesco 243n
Reinaldos Miñarro, Diego Antonio 203n
Remer, Gary 135n
Rensi, Giuseppe 66
Reventlow, Henning G. 63n, 66
Rex, Walter 296n
Ribadeneyra, Pedro de 272, 272n, 274, 274n, 279n
Ricci, Francesco de' 104n
Rico, Francisco 63n, 64n
Ridolfi, Roberto 94n, 105, 105n
Riello, Giorgio 196n
Riley-Smith, Jonathan 242, 242n
Rimeli 254
Ríos Saloma, Martín Federico 277n
Roberts, Jennifer L. 196n
Roberts, Penny 225n, 227n, 232n, 233n
Robinson, David L. 218n, 221n, 225n, 227n
Rodríguez, Alonso 282
Rodríguez, Lucas 191n
Rodríguez de Pisa, Juan 69n
Ron, Nathan 1, 7, 35, 43n, 134n
Rosselin, Céline 196, 196n
Rossi, Paolo 34
Rostagno, Lucia 258n
Roth, Cecil 260n
Rouillard, Clarence Dana 300, 300n, 302n, 303, 303n, 306n, 307, 307n, 308n

Roush, Sherry 93n, 98n, 99n
Rousseau, Jean-Jacques 296, 325, 336
Ruggero, Guido 251n
Ruffo, Antonio 247, 247n
Rummel, Erika 150n, 151, 151n, 160n
Rupescissa, John of 92n
Rusconi, Roberto 96n

Sadoleto, Jacopo 154, 154n
Salviati, Giorgio Benigno 96
Salviati, Gregorio 254
Salviati, Jacopo 93n, 123
Sánchez González, Ramón 196n, 204n
Santillana, Marquis de (Íñigo López de Mendoza) 62
Sargotta, Luca 244
Sarmiento, Augusto 278n
Satan 49, 50, 144, 144n, 146, 146n
Saul 140n
Savonarola, Girolamo 2, 91, 91n, 92–94, 100n, 103, 103n, 104, 104n, 105, 105n, 107, 107n, 108, 109, 109n, 110, 110n, 111, 111n, 112, 112n, 115–117, 117n, 118, 118n, 119, 119n, 120, 120n, 121, 121n, 122, 122n, 123, 123n, 125, 125n, 126, 126n
Schätti, Karl 153n
Schelling, Friedrich Wilhelm Joseph 328
Schleiermacher, Friedrich Daniel Ernst 325–327, 331, 331n, 335, 338
Schwoebel, Robert 43n
Scotus Eriugena, John 18
Scribner, Robert W. 250n
Segovia, Juan de 77, 77n
Séguier, Esprit (Pierre Séguier) 316, 317
Selīm II (Sultan) 245
Seneca, Lucio Anneo 82, 177
Senneca, Antonio 1–2, 167
Serbelloni, Fabrizio 244, 244n, 245n, 260n
Serrano-Niza, Dolores 203n

Serres, Jean de 228
Serrurier, Cornelia 296n
Servet, Miguel 64, 66, 218
Setton, Kenneth Meyer 35n, 36n, 41n, 42n
Sforza, Caterina 92, 92n
Siculo Marineo 62n
Simoncelli, Paolo 115n
Simonetta, Marcello 123n
Simonetti, Manlio 120n
Simplicius 72
Sitbon, Judas 244
Sixtus IV (Pope) 140, 140n
Skippon, Philip 247n
Slomp, Jan 307n
Smith, Malcom C. 220n, 222n, 223n
Smith, Thomas 318, 319
Sobczyk, Malgorzata 284n
Soen, Violet 235n
Solé, Jacques 296n
Spaans, Jo 217, 217n, 233n, 234n
Spada, Fabrizio 244n
Spilletta, Giovanni Simone 258n
Stanwood, Owen 297n
Stapfer, Philipp Albert 326
Staphyleus, Joannes 117n
St. Clair Segurado, Eva María 285n
Stefanutti, Antonio Ugo 92n
Steuco, Agostino 151
Stinger, Charles L. 139n
Stoppani, Giovanni Francesco 244n
Strayer, Brian 317n
Stupperich, Robert 150n
Suárez, Francisco 270, 272, 275–277, 277n
Superville, Daniel de 299

Tagliaferri, Filomena Viviana 196n
Talavera, Hernando de 188
Tapie, Matthew A. 256n
Tartabini, Veronica 3n, 4, 59, 85
Tateo, Francesco 175n
Teodoro (monk) 96

Terentius Afer, Publius 4
Teresa of Ávila 65, 67
Terrasson, Jeanne 297, 297n
Testa, Carmel 252n
Tetzel, John 150n
Themistius 72
Theodosius (Emperor) 146, 146n
Theophrastus 72
Thompson, Patrice 327n
Thouard, Denis 327, 331n
Timoneda, Juan de 191n
Todorov, Tzvetan 326, 326n
Tognon, Giuseppe 68, 175n
Tomas, Natalie R. 93n
Torquemada, Tomás de 70
Torsini, Roberto 135n
Tournier, Gaston 302, 302n, 316n
Toyoshima, Masayuki 285n
Tracy, James D. 134n, 136n, 218n, 229n
Tramon Castillo, Jaime 286n
Tramontano, Beatrice 1, 5, 5n, 12, 33
Trigo, Tomás 278n
Trivisani-Moreau, Isabelle 319n
Troeltsch, Ernst 335
Tuppan (slave of *Gran Visconte*) 251
Turchetti, Mario 216, 216n, 218n, 221n, 222n, 224n, 225n, 228n
Turró, Salvio 74n

Utt, Walter 317n

Valensi, Lucette 244n
Valignano, Alessandro 286–287
Valkenberg, Pim 54n
Valla, Lorenzo 63, 63n, 69, 151
Van der Borcht, Pieter 272
Van der Lem, Anton 217n, 235n
Van der Linden, David 297n, 298n
Van der Lugt, Mara 296n
Van der Meer, Matthieu H. 50n
Van de Schoor, Rob 219n
Van Nierop, Henk 229n, 235n

Van Oldenbarnevelt, Johan 230
Van Rooden, Peter 235*n*
Varchi, Benedetto 104, 104*n*, 115*n*
Vasoli, Cesare 92*n*, 93*n*, 95*n*
Vassallo, Giovanni 7, 255
Vaughan, Dorothy 241, 241*n*
Vega, Maria José 69*n*
Vella, Martino 260
Vella Gauci, Joe 252*n*
Verde, Armando F. 94*n*
Vergerio, Pier Paolo 151
Vettori, Francesco 91
Vigié, Marc 298*n*
Vilhena, António Manoel de 244
Vincent, Bernard 191*n*, 192*n*, 195*n*, 199*n*, 202*n*, 301*n*, 310, 310*n*
Violi, Carlo 325*n*
Viret, Pierre 307
Vives, Juan Luis 59, 60, 63, 71, 71*n*, 73, 74, 78–84, 86, 154, 154*n*
Voltaire (François-Marie Arouet) 296, 300
Von Martels, Zweder 42*n*

Walter, Peter 147*n*
Wanegffelen, Thierry 220*n*, 227*n*, 228*n*
Watanabe, Morimichi 44, 44*n*, 46*n*, 47*n*, 48*n*, 49*n*
Watt, Jeffrey R. 251*n*

Weber, Benjamin 36, 36*n*
Weinstein, Donald 93, 93*n*, 97*n*, 114*n*, 118*n*, 120, 120*n*
Weißenhorn, Alexander 155
Wenck, Johann 30
Wettinger, Godfrey 246*n*, 248*n*, 252*n*, 253*n*, 258*n*, 259*n*
Whelan, Ruth 298*n*
William (Prince of Orange) 218, 223, 226, 236
Witzel, Georg 150
Woelki, Thomas 44*n*, 47*n*
Woltjer, Juliaan 222*n*, 223*n*, 235*n*
Wtenbogaert, Johannes 230

Xambo, Jean-Baptiste 302, 302*n*
Xavier, Francis 284–286, 291

Zagorin, Pérez 224*n*
Zambrano, María 71*n*
Zammit, William 255*n*
Zammit-Ciantar, Joe 242*n*
Zancarini, Jean-Claude 121, 121*n*
Zarandieta Arenas, Francisco 197*n*
Zijlstra, Samme 223*n*, 235*n*
Zondadari, Marc'Antonio 253
Zunihyga, Diego Lópes (or Jacobus Lopis Stunica) 151
Zysberg, André 298*n*, 305*n*

www.ingramcontent.com/pod-product-compliance
Lightning Source LLC
Chambersburg PA
CBHW050835230426
43667CB00012B/2008